Launching a Business on the Web

NCSA Mosaic - IQuest

File Edit Options Navigate Annotate Starting Points Help

http://www.iquest.net

N C S A

MOSAIC

X Window Syst

Windows • Macin

jon@flying.high.com

Folder: Inbox

View Go Bookmarks Options Directory

11 GALLERY

NCSA Mosaic - Worldwide WWW Information

Navigate Annotate Starting Points Help

ggestions, corrections or additions.

Network Services of Indianapolis for ac

Number of Internet Hosts

see inset

Resources Available
▽ Resource Map
▣ Resource List
● Country Info

ompu
India
ed her

01/95

10/94

07/94

01/94
10/94

07/93
04/93
01/93
10/92
07/92
04/92
01/92
01/91

5000

4000

3000

Hosts (x1000)

2000

1000

ing at our Indianapolis Gallery January 21

PLUG YOURSELF INTO...

MACMILLAN INFORMATION SUPERLIBRARY™

que
SAMS PUBLISHING
Hayden Books
que COLLEGE

NRP
alpha books
Brady
ADOBE PRESS

THE MACMILLAN INFORMATION SUPERLIBRARY™

Free information and vast computer resources from the world's leading computer book publisher—online!

FIND THE BOOKS THAT ARE RIGHT FOR YOU!

A complete online catalog, plus sample chapters and tables of contents give you an in-depth look at *all* of our books, including hard-to-find titles. It's the best way to find the books you need!

- **STAY INFORMED** with the latest computer industry news through our online newsletter, press releases, and customized Information SuperLibrary Reports.

- **GET FAST ANSWERS** to your questions about MCP books and software.

- **VISIT** our online bookstore for the latest information and editions!

- **COMMUNICATE** with our expert authors through e-mail and conferences.

- **DOWNLOAD SOFTWARE** from the immense MCP library:
    - Source code and files from MCP books
    - The best shareware, freeware, and demos

- **DISCOVER HOT SPOTS** on other parts of the Internet.

- **WIN BOOKS** in ongoing contests and giveaways!

TO PLUG INTO MCP: ➜   WORLD WIDE WEB: **http://www.mcp.com**

GOPHER: gopher.mcp.com

FTP: ftp.mcp.com

Home Page   What's New   Bookstore   Reference Desk   Software Library   Macmillan Overview   Talk to Us

Launching a Business on the Web

David Cook
Deborah Sellers

Launching a Business on the Web

Copyright© 1995 by Que® Corporation.

All rights reserved. Printed in the United States of America. No part of this book may be used or reproduced in any form or by any means, or stored in a database or retrieval system, without prior written permission of the publisher except in the case of brief quotations embodied in critical articles and reviews. Making copies of any part of this book for any purpose other than your own personal use is a violation of United States copyright laws. For information, address Que Corporation, 201 W. 103rd Street, Indianapolis, IN 46290. You may reach Que's direct sales line by calling 1-800-428-5331.

Library of Congress Catalog Number: 95-69233

ISBN: 0-7897-0188-x

This book is sold *as is*, without warranty of any kind, either express or implied, respecting the contents of this book, including but not limited to implied warranties for the book's quality, performance, merchantability, or fitness for any particular purpose. Neither Que Corporation nor its dealers or distributors shall be liable to the purchaser or any other person or entity with respect to any liability, loss, or damage caused or alleged to have been caused directly or indirectly by this book.

97 96 95   4 3 2 1

Interpretation of the printing code: the rightmost double-digit number is the year of the book's printing; the rightmost single-digit number, the number of the book's printing. For example, a printing code of 95-1 shows that the first printing of the book occurred in 1995.

Screen reproductions in this book were created with Collage Complete from Inner Media, Inc., Hollis, NH.

Publisher: Roland Elgey

Vice President and Publisher: Marie Butler-Knight

Associate Publisher: Don Roche, Jr.

Director of Product Series: Charles O. Stewart III

Editorial Services Director: Elizabeth Keaffaber

Director of Marketing: Lynn E. Zingraf

Credits

Publishing Manager
Brad R. Koch

Managing Editor
Michael Cunningham

Acquisitions Editor
Cheryl D. Willoughby

Product Directors
Kathie-Jo Arnoff
Jim Minatel

Technical Editors
Jeff Bankston
Lori Leonardo

Production Editor
Lisa M. Gebken

Editors
Charles K. Bowles II
Geneil Breeze
Susan Shaw Dunn
Thomas F. Hayes
Julie A. McNamee
Nicole Rodandello
Andy Saff

Assistant Product Marketing Manager
Kim Margolius

Technical Specialist
Cari Skaggs

Acquisitions Assistant
Ruth Slates

Operations Coordinator
Patricia J. Brooks

Editorial Assistant
Andrea Duvall

Book Designer
Sandra Stevenson Schroeder

Cover Designer
Dan Armstrong

Production Team
Claudia Bell
Anne Dickerson
Daryl Kessler
Bob LaRoche
Beth Lewis
G. Alan Palmore
Kaylene Riemen
Clair Schweinler
Kris Simmons
Scott Tullis

Indexer
Carol Sheehan

Composed in *Stone* and *MCPdigital* by Que Corporation

About the Authors

David Cook was born in Gaza in 1958. He graduated from Grand Valley State Colleges in 1980 with a BS in computer science. He has over 20 years of experience in the computer field and has worked for companies as diverse as NASA, Computer Design, Inc., and TrueVision. Since he became an independent contractor, his clients have spanned the globe, from the U.S. to Japan, including the U.S. Postal Service and America Online. His company, Cookware, currently webmasters the Midwest's largest Internet provider, IQuest. Cookware, located near Indianapolis, Ind., specializes in complete World Wide Web services.

Deborah Sellers was born in Detroit, Mich., in 1958. She graduated from Grand Valley State Colleges in 1980 with a BPh in communications. She has worked in many fields, including journalism, research, marketing, computers, and radio. Ms. Sellers' poetry appears in various small-press publications, and she maintains a poetry site on the World Wide Web. She is also co-owner of Cookware.

As Net-heads, they are infinitely reachable. David and Deborah maintain e-mail at **iceman@iquest.net**, and can also be contacted via their home pages on IQuest (try **http://www.iquest.net/** or **http://www.iquest.net/cw/**). Additionally, they can often be found in IRC (Internet Relay Chat) in the **#www** group under the name **MrIcee**.

Acknowledgments

Well, here we are, writing the acknowledgments at 10:52 a.m. on the day the final manuscript is due. We are exhausted but happy, and it will feel extra good to finally be able to sleep. Writing a book while running a full-time Web business definitely makes one desire for either cloning technology or about 36 more hours in the day.

This book discusses the World Wide Web and the Internet from the aspect of someone who wants to use it to gain commercial benefits. The majority of the information that we present in this book comes from our many years of experience in the computer graphics and networking industry, as well as our learnings from our own Web business. In other words, it is based almost entirely on our experiences in this industry (with a bit of help from our friends).

There's no end to the books that tell you how to write HTML, and what the Web is. However, there are relatively few books that give you all the material necessary to put together a business plan. We hope that this book fills that niche by acting as an idea book, giving you everything you need to make a well-informed decision.

While we do cover the history of the Internet and Web, Web basics, and even include an Appendix on writing HTML, the main thrust of this book is to expose you to *how* to use the Web to your advantage. We try to keep the discussions as non-technical as possible.

When you are finished reading this book, you should have a very good idea of exactly how to use the Web to your advantage. We will cover all the facets of use, from basic home pages to placing interactive shopping systems on the Web. We also discuss in-depth how to find the proper technical help if you do not have the capability to design the elements yourself.

Before we let you get started, we should mention some of the people who helped us with this project.

First, our thanks to the folks at Que who were patient with us while we were learning the ins and outs of publishing a book of this size, especially Cheryl Willoughby and Ruth Slates. Thanks also to our primary editor Lisa Gebken, who had to edit our early-morning fuzzy thinking.

Secondly, our major and outstanding thanks to the great folks at IQuest, our network provider, who often answered questions at 2:30 in the morning. Special thanks there go to Bob Hoquim and Tom Neville.

Also on our list are Walter Wright and Mary Ann Kearns of 911 Gallery in Indianapolis, Ind., who have provided a wonderful platform for experimenting with art on the Web.

Thanks also to Bob Zigon for his insights into the Web, Web marketing, and Web database design.

And we should not forget the great folks at Shelley's Eatery (where we consumed much food and drink while writing this book), and our friends and family who have been most understanding (we're back!).

Finally, we would like to thank our clients who also put up with us being slightly less chipper than usual, in those early-morning and late-night conference calls.

We hope that this book will help your business succeed on the Web. See you on the Internet.

David Cook, Deborah Sellers

Cookware / Indianapolis, Indiana

March 31, 1995

Trademarks

All terms mentioned in this book that are known to be trademarks or service marks have been appropriately capitalized. Que cannot attest to the accuracy of this information. Use of a term in this book should not be regarded as affecting the validity of any trademark or service mark.

Contents at a Glance

An Introduction

The Basics

Products and Services

Marketing and the Web

Contents

3 Why the Net is Good for Business   55

V Security   383

17 Security and the Net   385

18 Security and Cash Transactions   403

19 What To Do When Security Has Been Breached   423

VI The Edge of the Web 445

20 Kiosks Made Easy 447

21 Non-Traditional Groups That Can Benefit from the Web 467

VII Appendix   519

Introduction

Across the nation and across the world, a silent revolution is occurring. It affects the way people shop for products and services, conduct business, gather information for personal and business use, meet people, study for school, and spend their leisure time. It's called the Internet, also known as the Information Superhighway.

Recently, the Internet has been repaved with a new, slick, easy-to-navigate surface named the World Wide Web (WWW or Web). With user-friendly WWW browsers such as Mosaic and Netscape, businesses are now finding that the advertising, marketing, and sales opportunities available on the World Wide Web are rivaling more traditional forms like print ads, catalogs, and television.

The reason for this revolution is due in part to the wonderful graphic capabilities of the World Wide Web. Company logos can be shown. Full-color photos of products or personnel can be featured. Enhanced features like audio and video make the commercial uses of the WWW even more exciting.

Another reason for all the excitement over the Internet and World Wide Web is its amazing low cost. Now it's possible to reach more people for less money than ever before. Furthermore, this new medium has also brought along with it new paradigms for advertising, marketing, and information dispensing. These new mediums, coupled with traditional marketing methods, allow even the smallest business to reach a worldwide audience.

The WWW revolution has been compared to those of television and personal computers. As with all new technology, some will take advantage of the opportunities and others will miss the boat. When the television revolution started to spread, some large companies in the entertainment industry missed a golden opportunity because they lacked the imagination to see the potential for television. It wasn't until the 1960s and 1970s when they saw the errors of their ways and started investing in television production.

Because the Web is in its infancy, there is still plenty of time to take a good idea and turn it into a gold mine via the WWW. This book gives you all the information you need to put your business or organization on the Internet. It shows you how to put an existing company on the Web. It also provides ideas for exciting new business possibilities. Wherever you want to take your business on the Information Superhighway, this book guides you along the way.

Who Should Read This Book and Why?

Anyone who has a business. Anyone who is planning a business. Anyone who is employed in advertising, sales, marketing, relations, communications, government, or education. Anyone who wants to make money.

But seeing how the Internet is the biggest event since cellular phones, many users might want to read this book just to acquaint themselves with this emerging technology. This new form of multimedia communication will certainly touch the lives—eventually—of most people in the United States and around the world.

Even if you have a working knowledge of the Internet and the WWW, this book provides you with fascinating facts and new ideas. You also learn information about emerging topics on the Web, such as security and the handling of cash transactions. There may even be a few interesting URLs that you have missed.

Throughout this book you will see terms that may be new to you. Refer to Chapter 2, "Net Components and Terminology," to become familiar with the Internet language.

Who is This Book Suited For?

This book will be very useful for the person who needs to get aquatinted with the issues of creating a successful Internet business. Likewise, users who are planning on designing, programming, and managing their own World Wide Web home page will find this book a warehouse of information and tips.

Portions of this book assume some basic computer knowledge, such as how to use a word processor and how to manage files.

For those planning a business on the WWW, this book covers key topics such as the following:

■ Informal rules of the Internet and World Wide Web

■ How to best reach your target audience

■ Design concepts

■ Methods for taking orders and collecting cash

■ Keeping your data and systems secure

■ Cutting-edge technologies such as virtual shopping carts, form remailers, databases, sticky pages, and more

■ HTML basics for creating home pages

For the reader who has a job that is impacted by the World Wide Web, this book will serve as a useful tool for obtaining all the necessary information you'll need, and includes such information as

■ A history of the Internet and World Wide Web

■ Complete descriptions of acronyms and terms

■ Advantages of doing business on the WWW

■ Demographics and growth projections

Even the casual reader can gain important information about this new technology that can change the way business is done all around the world.

Why is This Book Important?

As you will see in Chapter 2, the growth of the Internet and the World Wide Web continues to be tremendous. Small companies, large corporations, towns, states, the federal government, and foreign countries all exist on the Internet.

Currently you can do everything from ordering chocolates to sending a message to the president on the Internet. You can order a pizza from Pizza Hut™ (**http://www.pizzahut.com/**), listen to a song from the Rolling Stones and order a CD (**http://www.stones.com/**), get information about Sea World and Busch theme parks (**http://www.bev.net/education/ SeaWorld/homepage.html**), find out stock quotes (**http:// www.secapl.com/cgi-bin/qsx**), or buy a house (**http:// www.gems.com/realestate/index.html**).

If you haven't heard of the Internet in your area, you soon will. Newspapers in every town are carrying articles on how the Internet is impacting different segments of society. From the art world to senior-citizen groups, the Internet is changing how people interact.

For those who don't have computers at home, Internet access is available at some public libraries. The U.S. government has proposed access to federal, state, and local government information be made available via kiosks located in public places such as libraries, post offices, and malls.

Forward-thinking nations around the world are taking similar steps to ensure that their citizens have all the benefits of the new information-based society. Policy makers on every level have realized the importance of access to the information and services available on the Internet. Access to the Internet is so important to people that in some areas that don't have an adequate telecommunication structure, Internet access is made through packet communications and short-wave radios.

Because of the speed at which this worldwide phenomena is moving, this book is extremely important. The crucial time frame during which you can make a name and a place for yourself on the Internet will quickly narrow, allowing you to stand apart from the hordes of others that are rushing full-speed toward it. This book can help you take the lead and keep it.

Taking Advantage of the Internet

There are also many ways to use the Internet to your advantage, but they may not be immediately apparent. The rest of this section looks at ways you can take advantage of the Internet. You will see more uses throughout the book.

If you are a small restaurant or a beauty parlor in a town where there are like-minded companies, you could form your own virtual mall, similar to what was done in the town of Blacksburg, Va. (**http://crusher.bev.net/mall/index.html**). Their mall provides a convenient, one-stop location for the residents of that area to access information from a variety of geographically distant businesses. It also provides visitors to the area up-to-date information about restaurants, stores, and services.

In the Blacksburg Mall, you can use either the electronic white pages to scan an alphabetical listing of companies, or the electronic yellow pages to search for a company by category. The following is a partial list of the types of companies that are accessible:

- Hotels
- Engineering firms
- Accountants
- Chambers of commerce
- Transit Services
- Restaurants
- Carpenters
- Laundromats

- Grocery stores
- Bookstores
- Banks
- Attorneys
- Hospitals
- Radio stations
- Video production
- Computer services

Restaurants provide menus, hours of operation, and their locations. The Blacksburg Marriott provides information about its restaurants, recreational services, entertainment, and special events. Blacksburg Transit provides schedules, route maps, fare information, and a lost and found department.

Because Blacksburg is the home of Virginia Polytechnical Institute, there are plenty of students and faculty to see the Internet advertising. The town also attracts tourists who check out the town's advertising here. You may not think that this sort of venture would be commonplace, but locations as diverse as Tucson, Ariz. (**http://arizonaweb.rtd.com/index.html**) and the state of Utah (**http://www.netpub.com/utah/**) have implemented similar virtual business centers for companies and corporations to use.

One might think that some fields may not lend themselves to advertising or marketing on the Web. For example, a nurse wouldn't find it useful to advertise on the Internet. But a nurse might consider offering his or her services to sick travelers in need of medical assistance. A nurse's home page might contain a resume, references, and rates. This would also be a good way for traveling fitness trainers, masseuses, nannies, cooks, and nutrition counselors to advertise their services.

When it comes right down to it, the uses for the World Wide Web are really only limited by the imagination.

How To Use This Book

This book is set up to be used by many levels of readers. Experienced users may decide to skip certain introductory sections. A glossary exists to help new Internet users become acquainted with terms and concepts that are used throughout this book.

This book is divided into several sections. Part I, "An Introduction To the Internet and the World Wide Web," provides an overview of the Internet and World Wide Web and is good reading if you are unfamiliar with computer basics, networking jargon, or the concepts that surround the World Wide Web. This section also covers in detail why the WWW is useful for businesses and gives background information about the different ways it can be used to help your business.

Part II, "Your Business and the WWW—The Basics," discusses the basics of placing your business on the World Wide Web. This chapter helps you find the correct Internet provider, hardware, and software. You see several tips and pointers that will help make you a smart Internet shopper. This chapter also discusses Internet etiquette and the types of information that can be found on the World Wide Web.

Part III, "Selling Products and Services," discusses in-depth how to market, advertise, and sell products on the Internet and World Wide Web. Details are provided on order taking, collecting cash, order fulfillment, and order tracking. Special consideration is given to online shopping malls and pay services.

Part IV, "Marketing and the Web," discusses how to market yourself and your product effectively on the World Wide Web. This section also shows you how to collect demographics on your users and measure your success rate.

Part V, "Security," deals with issues of security and the World Wide Web, including how to detect a breach of security and what to do if your security is broken. It also covers the international laws and restrictions that concern the WWW.

Part VI, "The Edge of the Web," outlines the latest and greatest in World Wide Web technology. It includes the use of kiosks, examples of innovative Web uses, and predictions of where the Web is heading.

The Appendix is a primer on HTML, giving you all you'll need to know to get your home page on the Web.

This book is intended to reach a broad spectrum of readers. To achieve this end, it has been designed so that the reader can jump from section to section as needed.

Throughout this book the World Wide Web will also be referred to as *WWW*, *W3*, and *Web*. All three terms should be considered the same.

You should also consider the terms *Net, Internet,* and *network* to all mean the Internet.

Finally, unless it is specifically mentioned in the text, uses of the words *server, client,* and *browser* will refer specifically to World Wide Web servers, clients, and browsers.

After reading this book, there will be many options available to you. You may decide to set up your own multimedia HTML home page with links, ordering systems, cash transactions, and interactive forms. You could invest in a computer system to be your own server.

If you decide that would be too much to handle, you can have someone else do all or part of it for you. Whatever your skill level, you can do as much as you want and have a professional do the rest.

After reading this book, you may become so excited about the Web that you learn everything there is to know about the Internet and WWW and become the Webmaster of your own site!

A whole new world is waiting to be explored on the Internet and a whole new client base to be used. Good luck Web surfers!

Conventions Used in This Book

Messages that appear on-screen are printed in a special font: Document 1. New terms and variables are introduced in *italic* type. Text that you are to type appears in **boldface**. Real Internet addresses also appear in boldface:

iceman@iquest.net

You also find four other visual aids that help you cruise the Internet: **Notes**, **Tips**, **Cautions**, and **Troubleshooting**.

Note

This paragraph format indicates additional information that may help you avoid problems or that should be considered in using the described features.

Caution

This paragraph format warns the reader of hazardous procedures (for example, activities that delete files).

Tip
This paragraph format suggests easier or alternative methods of executing a procedure.

Launching a Business on the Web uses margin cross-references to help you access related information in other parts of the book. Right-facing triangles point you to related information in later chapters. Left-facing triangles point you to information in previous chapters.

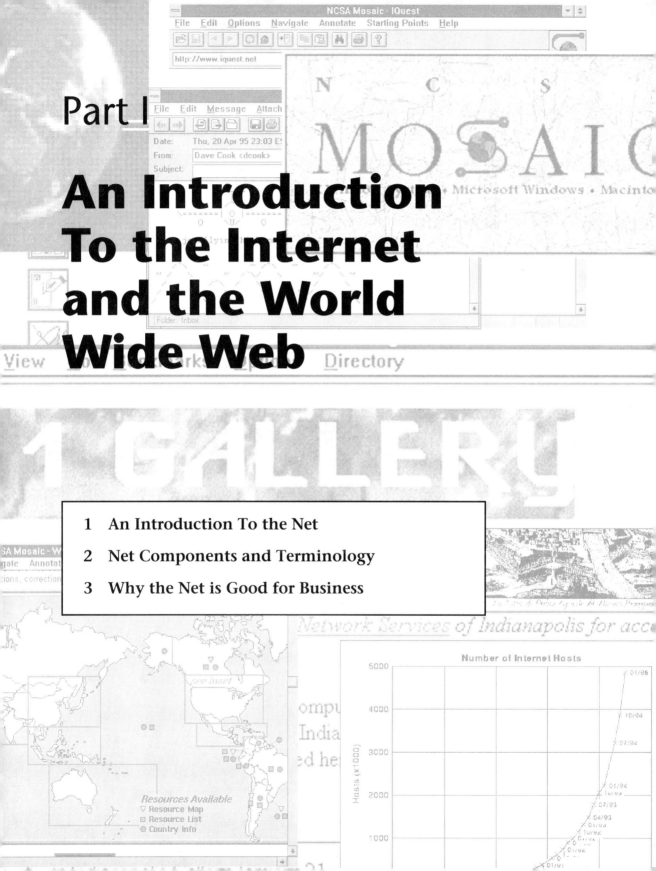

Part I

An Introduction To the Internet and the World Wide Web

Chapter 1

An Introduction To the Net

The Internet, also called the Net or the Information Superhighway, consists of a group of computers around the world that share data. Developed in the late 1970s as an experiment in computer networking, the Internet has grown into a worldwide phenomenon.

The development of e-mail introduced an easy-to-use electronic mail feature. With the concurrent growth in personal computers, a whole new group of computer users was developing that would love to use the Internet. However, these new users were intimidated by the complexity of the Internet, and therefore kept the early Internet from becoming universally accepted.

In the early 1990s, the World Wide Web was conceived as a way to share visual information in a workgroup situation. However, it soon became apparent that the same mechanism would allow the average user to easily use the Internet. With the Web, novice users could have tremendous power in finding and accessing the wealth of information located on individual computer systems around the world.

This single fact lead to a tremendous rush to the Internet—a rush so large that in 1993, the World Wide Web grew an astonishing 341,000 percent. Today because of the Web, Internet users can access information in computers from Los Angeles to Paris to Singapore with one easy user interface.

In this chapter you learn

- The history of the Internet and World Wide Web

- Who pays for the Internet and WWW

- An introduction to commercial uses

- A discussion of BBSes and how they relate to the Internet and WWW

The Internet

As noted in the Introduction, the business potential for the World Wide Web is enormous. Before you see how to put your business on the Web, you learn some historical data concerning the Internet.

Throughout this book you will become familiar with the metaphor *Information Superhighway*. To begin on this note, the Internet can be thought of as the road you will be traveling on. This road will take you to places you want to go, provided you have the proper directions. Your destinations will be computer systems around the world that are also on the Internet and store data you want to access.

You will use many different vehicles on this road, as well as encounter service stations, potholes, and other drivers. With this in mind, you can begin to think of this book as a driver's training manual to the Internet.

Just like a real highway, the Information Superhighway can be a confusing place with lots of rules, road maps, heavy traffic, and distracting landmarks. Just as you learned to turn the steering wheel, push the gas pedal, use the turn signal, understand traffic laws, avoid construction and slow-moving vehicles, listen to your friend talking, and locate the Thai restaurant all at the same time, you soon will learn to navigate the Internet with the same ease.

> **Note**
>
> Some people don't like the analogy of the Internet to a superhighway. One such person is Bill Gates, the CEO of Microsoft. His objection (which others share) is that a highway implies distance in a technology that is actually bringing people closer together. An alternative term that has been suggested is *Global Information Organization*. Regardless of what the most powerful people in America want to call the Internet, what they say is nothing compared to that of the 35 million people who use it. Anyone who spends any amount of time on it will clearly see the similarities to an actual highway.

The Beginning of the Internet

The Internet didn't start out as the great conduit of information that it is today. It began as an experiment in networking funded by the United States government. The beginnings of the Internet were first conceived by Bob Taylor while he was the director of computer research at the Department of Defense's Advance Research Project Agency (ARPA).

The Internet was designed to address the need for computer systems of different manufacturers and in different locations to be able to share data. The resulting network that emerged was called ARPANET.

> **Note**
>
> Besides Bob Taylor, other people who greatly influenced the early Internet include Charlie Herzfeld, Larry Roberts, Vinton Cerf, Jon Postel, Steve Crocker, Bill Naylor, Doug Englebart, and Roland Bryan. These people were at ARPA and the early node sites: Stanford, SRI International, and University of California at Santa Barbara.

Initially, the original networked sites were military bases, universities, and companies with defense department contracts.

As the size of this experimental network grew, so did concerns for security. The same networks used by companies and universities for military contracts were becoming more and more accessible to the public.

As a result, in 1984, ARPANET split into two separate but interconnected networks. The military side was named MILNET. The education side was still technically called ARPANET, but became increasingly known as the Internet.

The Internet Today

The basic services now offered by the Internet are e-mail, network news, access to remote computers and data acquisition systems, and the ability to transfer information between remote computers.

Currently between 35 to 45 million people use the Internet, and this number is growing at an estimated 10 to 15 percent per month. That's an incredible 3.5 million new users each month!

Because the beginnings of the Internet stem from education, many users' first experience came in college where campus e-mail and other services are available. What for many people was an interesting part of their college experience has continued, even after college, to be an integral part of their everyday lives.

The developing nations of the world are most concerned about being among the have-nots; those countries who missed out on the industrial revolution of the early 1900s cannot afford to be left out of the information revolution.

Many nations are rushing to implement the infrastructure that is needed to support the Internet. Modern telephone lines and switches are necessary to support the high bandwidth of the Internet. However, with the advent of low cost and high availability computing and networking technology, many developing countries are seeing that they can shoot right into the 21st century without having to go through an industrialization period. Many people are quickly realizing that information technology is a commodity that can be produced anywhere.

Worldwide, some nations are already emerging as regional leaders for Internet services and technology: Costa Rica in Central America, Israel in the Middle East, and Singapore in the Pacific Rim.

Here in the United States, certain states have taken the lead in the telecommunications support technology that is necessary to allow the Internet to work successfully.

> **Note**
>
> Likewise, the United States federal government has also taken advantage of the mass appeal of the Internet. Many federal agencies are available for anyone on the Internet and WWW to access. The Social Security Administration, Veterans Administration, National Institute of Health, Environmental Protection Agency, and the U.S. Postal Service are just a few examples of government agencies with publicly accessible Internet resources.

The bottom line is that what began as a government and educational research project has now blossomed into one of the most important communications mediums of today. Never before has access to so many people of such varied cultures and backgrounds been possible. The social impact of the Internet will be long and lasting, with many political and cultural dilemmas. As you will begin to appreciate, the creation of the Internet was a good investment, and now is the time to reap the reward.

Who Pays for the Internet?

Many people first experience the Internet at a university or large corporation that provides Internet access for free. Because of this, when they investigate personal Internet access, they are surprised that it costs anything at all.

Welcome to the real world. The Internet is cooperative, but it is not free.

University, Corporate, and Government Support

Here's how it works. Universities already run huge networked computer systems. Since many universities are involved in government grants, much of their Internet access is subsidized by government and/or corporations. Therefore, it's easy to provide no-cost Internet access to their students.

Similarly, large corporations who use networks for efficient internal communications often use the Internet to extend communications around the world.

Both universities and corporations have computers that they place on the Internet. Many of the computers contain information that is available from the inside and outside. The universities and companies benefit because they get connectivity with clients and users around the world.

Service Providers

With each connection to the Internet, the Internet grew slightly. As it began to grow, the need for more Internet providers occurred. This happened first in large companies needing to bring the Internet to a city for their use. Often splinter companies formed that started out as Internet-only service companies. These companies purchased high-speed lines and major Internet feeds and offered it to their clients.

As this occurred, many of the new Internet service companies found that they had extra bandwidth. They also found that because of exposure to the Internet in universities, people were beginning to ask for Internet access. The Internet service companies thus began to provide their extra bandwidth to the general public.

As public demand increased, providers began to add more lines and better access to meet the new need. Initially, cost for Internet access was quite expensive, with prices in the upper 80s and lower 90s often being more than $1,000 per month for casual commercial access. However, with more and more people needing the Internet services, a few major carriers sprang up.

One such carrier, NETCOM in San Jose, Calif., began to offer unlimited Internet access for the amazingly low price of $17.50 per month. This price was so fantastically inexpensive that people were calling from outside the United States; the long distance telephone charge was less than their local Internet access charge.

Since many of its users were in large cities outside of its local San Jose calling area, NETCOM soon began to open locations in major metropolitan areas throughout the nation. This allowed many of its current users to enjoy the $17.50 price without the long distance phone call. This also greatly increased NETCOM's user base.

NETCOM and the other similar carriers set low prices for Internet access. This has ensured very competitive rates, and in some locations, the price just seems to keep decreasing. In order to keep these large carriers out of some communities, local Internet providers have undercut their prices. Prices as low as $8.60 per month for unlimited Internet connectivity have been noted in some cities. This means that in some areas, the Internet is available for less money than cable television.

Many local governments are helping to encourage and subsidize the Internet because of the social, educational, and commercial benefits they feel will result.

But these price wars mean only one thing. The Internet is getting cheaper by the day. If it is not in your area now, it will be soon. And it is most likely nearer than you think.

You can see how the Internet began to spread around the world like wildfire. With each major provider, hundreds of minor providers pop up. Each minor provider supports thousands of users, and each user is a potential business on the Internet.

What You Get for Your Money

▶ See "Internet Terminology," p. 33

Besides your basic Internet connection, which may include a long distance phone call (if you do not have local Internet access), you will also need a computer and modem adequate for effective access of the Internet.

Once you are on the Internet, there is no additional cost for basic services. This means that if you are paying $15 per month for unlimited Internet access, it costs you no more to talk with people and computers in Japan than it does to talk to people and computers in your own community. You can basically talk to the entire world for that monthly fee.

With the advent of true commercialization of the Internet via the World Wide Web, additional charges are becoming commonplace. However, these additional charges are for specialized services; unique products or services are provided by companies who are just using the Internet as the forum for communication. These special pay services should not be confused with the basic Internet services which you should get as part of your monthly fee.

Many of the items you see on the Internet are cooperative efforts and cost nothing to access. The people who maintain this information do so because they believe in the freedom of the Internet. At first glance, this would seem to be contradicting for-pay services, but actually it is not. Some items on the Web are free; some are not. Among the free services you will probably be using include the following:

- *Searchers*. Help locate items on the Net.

- *Hotlists*. Tell you what's hot and what's not.

■ *Magazines.* Keep you up-to-date on world issues.

■ *Art galleries.* Cultural events.

■ *Comics.* Entertainment events.

■ *Software archives.* Latest freeware/shareware.

■ *Dictionaries.* Also thesaurus and fact books.

■ *Weather.* Latest forecasts and satellite pictures.

■ *Government services.* Information on services.

In the end, for the value received, the cost of the Internet is fairly small. Furthermore, the price is dropping faster than the press can keep up. When you do direct comparisons with marketing on the Internet with marketing in a magazine, you will see that for a readership of 35 million, the Internet offers far more for your advertising dollar than traditional media. Many companies will advertise themselves for less than $1,000 per year. These Internet advertisements will be full-color and reach a huge audience. Similar advertisements in magazines with two million readers will often cost more than $5,000 per month.

Stability of the Internet

The incredible interconnectivity and size of the Internet is both a curse and a blessing. Its size means that navigating it can often be cumbersome, but the size and interconnectivity means that it is hard to shut the entire Internet down. While occasionally certain locations may be inaccessible due to maintenance or technical problems, the system is designed to automatically re-route itself to avoid problem areas.

In fact, much of the Internet automatically changes its connections based on which connections are more loaded than others. This means that the path you take to get from your computer to another computer elsewhere in the world changes, often from moment to moment. All of this happens without you needing to know about it.

The greatest threat to the security of the Internet happened in 1988 when Robert T. Morris, a university student, developed a program which was supposed to travel from machine to machine on the Internet to determine its size. Such a program is called a *worm.*

▶ See "Using Robots and Worms," p. 217

Unfortunately, Morris's worm went out of control and bogged down the Internet to the point that many systems throughout the world were affected, and major portions were shut down by researchers while they attempted to isolate the problem. However, this type of activity is extremely rare, since the Internet is extremely stable. It would have to be stable for the military to use it to the degree that they do.

▶ See "Locating the Net in Your Area," p. 131

The best course of action you can take to ensure the stability of your service is to pick an adequate and reliable provider. It will be their job to ensure that your Internet feed is fast and reliable.

Commercial Uses and the Internet

For many years, commercial use of the Internet was prohibited. Much of the Internet was government subsidized, and thus people could not make money at taxpayers' expense.

After the split of the original ARPANET, commercialization became possible, due to the growth of the number of splinter groups setting up non-research oriented Internet feeds. As you learned earlier in this chapter, as time went on, the cost of the Internet decreased and the commercial growth of the Internet increased.

However, many people remain convinced that you cannot do business on the Internet. In the summer of 1994, one entrepreneur investigating the commercial uses of the Internet was told emphatically by an industry consultant that if he were to pursue commercial use of the Internet, he would be shot by the military.

This is just not true. If it were, many people would have been dead months ago. This myth is maintained by people who simply don't know any better and those who should know better but who can't understand that electricity costs money.

Some may not want to rush into this new technology, but there is no good reason to wait. In some areas, those businesses that create an early favorable market presence will have a dominant position well into the next century.

The Internet is certainly no fad or craze. While there is certainly a scramble to get on the Internet, its obvious benefits far outweigh any "fad" potential it might have. Far from being a fad however, the Internet is sure to spawn many a fad.

The Internet offers businesses e-mail, Net news, advanced communications, and remote information acquisition. With its millions of interconnections, the Internet can help you talk with industry experts around the world. Productivity can be boosted while costs are slashed by offering worldwide access to your products and services. Furthermore, with the availability of the Internet in homes throughout the world, many people can now work from home and other remote locations without any loss of productivity or communication.

The World Wide Web

What is the World Wide Web? Is it another network like the Internet? Or is it a piece of the Internet? The World Wide Web is merely a way of looking at the Internet. Instead of being a portion of the Internet, it is the whole package, just from a different perspective.

Tip
The World Wide Web is also known as W3, WWW, or the Web.

Essentially, the Web is an organization of files on the Internet. That means when you are on the WWW, you are always on the Internet. But the reverse is not true. You can be on the Internet and not the WWW. Internet users who are using e-mail or newsgroups are not on the WWW unless they do it via a WWW browser.

The WWW is a way to view information on the Internet in an easy-to-learn and use format. As you have learned, the early Internet was not popular because many people were intimidated by the complexity of navigating by typing commands. The WWW was an attempt to incorporate all the capabilities of the Internet into an easy-to-use interface.

Hypertext

Besides handling the normal capabilities of the Internet, the WWW also adds several new capabilities. The first and foremost is the ability to have hypertext documents. A *hypertext document* is one which incorporates pictures, text, animation, and sound. Such a document may appear as a magazine page, with color pictures and text. Beyond the page metaphor, however, is the fact that any word or picture can be *linked* to any other document. Selecting a linked word or picture will access the associated document, sound, movie, or picture.

Browsers

The WWW is accessed by programs called *browsers* or *clients*. There are many browsers. Most are graphic browsers which allow the pictures and text of a document to be viewed. Mosaic, Netscape, and Cello are three such popular graphic browsers. Most graphic WWW browsers are sophisticated enough to allow the access of sound, digitized movies, and interactive forms.

Note

For more information on these and other browsers, refer to Que's Special Edition *Using the Internet*.

Other browsers, called *text WWW browsers*, only view the text (ASCII) portion of documents. Text browsers such as Lynx ignore pictures and have only limited forms of support. However, these browsers allow the WWW to be accessed from even the most primitive computer system or terminal. These are also the types of browsers most often encountered in university computer labs, since these areas tend to have more text-only terminals than graphics-capable terminals.

The Beginning of the World Wide Web

In the 1990s a group at CERN, the European Particle Physics Laboratory in Geneva, Switzerland, developed the World Wide Web, which they described in an article in the Association of Computing Machinery's publication *Communications of the ACM*:

> [It] was developed to be a pool of human knowledge, which would allow collaborators in remote sites to share their ideas and all aspect of a common project. (11/94 p76)

The CERN home page (**http://www.cern.ch/**) describes it as

> A seamless world in which all information, from any source, can be accessed in a consistent and simple way.

Note

Timothy Berners-Lee was the originator of the WWW. Others that were influential in the development were Nicola Pellow, Bernd Pollerman, Carl Baker, Frederick G.M. Roeber, and Jean-Francois Groff.

The National Center for Supercomputing Applications (NCSA) in Urbana-Champaign, Ill., was pivotal in developing Mosaic, a powerful hypertext browser for the Web. Marc Andreessen and Eric Bina were among the developers of Mosaic. Marc Andreessen recently left NCSA to help lead the effort at Netscape Communications, the largest commercial WWW player.

Note

For more information on the World Wide Web and Mosaic, refer to Que's Special Edition *Using the World Wide Web and Mosaic.*

The following is the sequence of events documenting the growth of the WWW:

Date	Event
March 1989	The WWW project is first proposed by Timothy Berners-Lee at CERN.
October 1990	The proposal is redesigned.
November 1990	The prototype is developed on NeXT by the CERN team.
March 1991	The WWW is released to a limited number of groups.
January 1993	More than 50 known HTTP servers exist.
February 1993	NCSA releases its first alpha version of Marc Andreessen's Mosaic for X.
September 1993	NCSA releases a working version of Mosaic for all common platforms.
October 1993	More than 500 known HTTP servers exist.
October 1994	The W3 Consortium is created to establish international standards for client and server protocols. More than 10,000 known HTTP servers exist.

The name *World Wide Web* comes from the fact that the information (sound, text, pictures, animation) that comprises a document may come from all over the world. For example, a single document housed in New York may incorporate a picture housed in London and a sound selection housed in Tokyo, and may provide links to documents stored in India, Costa Rica, and Michigan. In this way, a single document can seem to stretch—weblike—throughout the world. When the user accesses the document in New York, all other components are instantly pulled from their locations and integrated in the document displayed to the user.

Another reason for the name *Web* is due to the interconnected nature of the Internet. When you access any given location on the Internet and Web, your request is passed from computer to computer until it reaches the destination. Here is how it works. The first computer that receives your information looks at the destination that you have specified and says, "Do I know where this is?" If not, it hands the request to one of the computers it knows that it thinks can best handle it. This transfer continues until one of the computers in the line says, "I know someone who knows this site." Your information then is passed towards your destination.

Most destinations are reached by *hopping* through no more than 30 connections, with an average number of hops between 12 to 15. Since connections and loads change, the route you take one moment may not be the one you take the next to get to the same place. In this respect, the Net is very weblike.

This interconnected nature of the Internet is exactly what the physicists at CERN were looking for. What began as a project to share information in an easy and integrated form to remote locations turned into a tremendous collaborative effort to share data without restrictions.

The effort is still continuing. The next section explores new features and options that are in development as you read this and that promise to make the WWW faster and more interactive. As the WWW matures, the true cyber-communities described in current science fiction novels will become a reality.

The WWW Today

Hundreds of thousands of businesses already exist on the Internet. They come from every state in the country, a majority of European nations, and many nations elsewhere in the world. In fact, more than 145 countries currently have some form of Internet service.

As previously stated, the World Wide Web grew more than 341,000 percent in 1993. However, the "newness" of the Web, coupled with its tremendous growth, meant that many companies found it difficult to create their own presence on the Web. The field is moving so quickly that the companies are hardpressed to stay current.

Furthermore, many companies cannot invest employees' time into researching how to put their own presence on the Web. This demand caused a need for webmastering and WWW providers. This industry quickly came together in early 1994 and now provides complete WWW services to the commercial sector. Because of the increasing number of Web sites, the people who run them—known as *webmasters*—often create businesses to help other companies make effective use of the Web.

For more information about CERN's historical and current involvement with the World Wide Web, check out the project's home page at

http://info.cern.ch/hypertext/WWW/TheProject.html

where you will find information concerning software for clients and servers, tools, gateways, and mail robots, as well as a common code library. The developers are even available for questions. Their Web page is shown in figure 1.1.

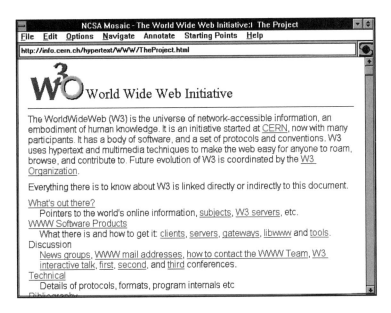

Fig. 1.1
The home page for the World Wide Web project at CERN provides all the information you need to know about WWW.

NCSA also offers a great wealth of information about the formation of the Internet and the creation of Mosaic (see fig. 1.2). This site can be found at

**http://www.ncsa.uiuc.edu/SDG/Software/Mosaic/
NCSAMosaicHome.html**

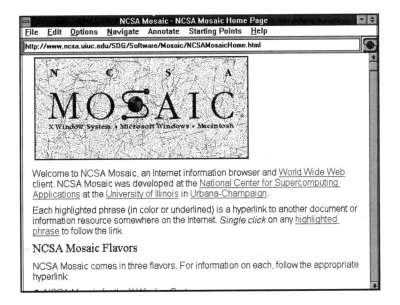

Fig. 1.2
The Mosaic home page is operated by its developers at NCSA.

Who Pays for the WWW?

Tip

JPEG and MPEG
are methods of
compressing still
and moving image
data to make it as
small as possible.

The beautiful graphics that are integral to many Web pages take a lot of space
to store and bandwidth to transmit. The files that hold the data for enhanced
features like audio selections and JPEG images or MPEG movies are even
larger in size. This means that the hardware must be faster, the disk storage
must be larger, and the connection to the Internet must be wider to accommodate the increases in loads. Because of this investment, most WWW servers and sites are run by commercial providers.

Tip

Even if you are
purchasing a large
Internet feed into
your business, you
will need to pay
for the bandwidth
you consume.

When you put a business on the World Wide Web, you can expect your provider to charge you an extra fee. After all, your pages will cause people to
come into the provider's site and use up the bandwidth. Since the provider
does not collect any compensation from the people coming in, you are
charged for the service. Popular sites can have thousands of people a day
coming through them, which can take large pieces of the average provider's
Internet lines. Also, that bandwidth cannot be used by the other paying subscribers.

Most charges are based on two factors: storage and throughput. *Storage* is the
amount of disk space your WWW pages take on your provider's machine.
You are typically charged per megabyte per month. Since most pages are
relatively small with simple use of graphics, this charge usually only amounts
to pennies a month. People storing large audio files, many images, or animations can expect to pay more because of the larger storage requirements of
these mediums.

The *throughput* charge is the amount of data that the people who come to
your site access. Throughput is measured in megabytes. The more throughput
you have, the more expensive your bill will be. Throughput is usually charged
around a dollar or two per megabyte.

▶ See "Basic
HTML," p. 521

A standard HTML home page with a modest amount of inline graphics will
not be very big. When it is accessed, even by several users, your throughput
will stay relatively low. However, large complicated graphics, audio, and
video take a lot of room. If your home page contains these, you could have a
very high throughput. This doesn't mean that you shouldn't consider these
enhanced features of the World Wide Web; it just means that you should
make sure that you use them in a cost-effective manner.

There are ways to get cheaper or free WWW service. FTP sites can be used to
store image, sounds, animations, and documents. While you can't handle
selectable image or interactive forms without a WWW server, all other functions, including hyperlinks, may be performed without a server. Since many

Internet providers and universities maintain anonymous FTP sites, you can often use these to store your pages. Because documents on the Web can point to components anywhere else on the Web, you may still use forms by pointing them to the many form handling services. These services charge you a nominal monthly fee to handle your forms and send them back to you as e-mail. Such services abound on the Internet, and the wise shopper can make use of them to lighten the already inexpensive load considerably.

One caveat with FTP service should be noted. Since this is a popular way of storing WWW pages, many FTP sites are clogged. This means that users often are turned away because there are simply too many of them accessing the site at the same time. This "traffic jam" will appear to be an error to the user accessing your page. Because of this, "free" FTP access is not always the best route.

Stability of the WWW

The Web, like the Internet, was created so it could expand infinitely. To achieve this, no central facility was designed for the World Wide Web— merely a collection of computers that allow other computers access via the *HyperText Transfer Protocol* (*HTTP*). Because it resides everywhere and nowhere at the same time, there is no way for it by itself to ever "go down." Furthermore, because the World Wide Web is based on the Internet, its stability is as good as the Internet's stability, which is very good. While there may be construction, traffic jams, and morning rush hours, in general, the Internet and Web perform as desired.

The Internet is designed to be infinitely extendible. IP addresses are not, but the Internet is. Sub-masking will undoubtedly help the low address problem.

The question of reliability does come up with browsers and servers. Because much of the WWW technology is new, some browsers—available but still in development—can be buggy and do not provide reliable access. Sticking to the most popular free browsers such as NCSA, or commercial browsers such as Netscape, will alleviate this problem. The same holds true for servers, with NCSA and CERN being the most popular free servers. Netscape and other companies also provide commercial servers.

▶ See "Servers," p. 36

Your WWW access can also be hampered if your provider or the provider of the remote location doesn't have the proper equipment to give you reliable service. Inadequate phone lines and computers that aren't powerful enough will impact the service you get while accessing the sometimes large inline graphics in many HTML pages.

An Introduction

Commercial Uses and the WWW

By now you've learned about the commercial uses of the WWW. In case you're not convinced, here are a few more facts about the WWW.

A recent Web cruise revealed the following results for information requests on the various commercial topics (Lycos search results for the following words):

- Pizza—225 entries, ranging from kosher pizza restaurants in New York City to Pizza Hut.

- Real Estate—3,076 entries.

- Accountant—61 entries.

- Lawyer—224 entries.

- Shop—1,251 entries.

- Massage—28 entries.

- Dentist—2,307 entries.

- Doctor—386 entries.

> ### Note
>
> Realize that these are not 61 accountants and 224 lawyers who have individually hung out their shingles on the Internet. It is the number or references this robot found that could include information about accountants and lawyers.

Governments as well are helping spread the Web. Many governments are helping subsidize the Web to both universities and businesses. Furthermore, a surprisingly large number of government agencies are available on the World Wide Web, including the Social Security Administration, Veterans Administration, White House, National Institute of Health, and NASA.

Various departments of the U.S. government are actively investigating public kiosks with Internet connectivity. Such projects will help bring Internet accessibility to all citizens, decreasing the gap between those with Internet access and those without. You can begin to look for both commercial and government sponsored kiosks in malls, post offices, and libraries soon.

Many U.S. states and cities, as well as foreign countries and cities, have Web pages. Some of these are just comprised of government information and statistics. Some have extensive information concerning shopping and hotel accommodations, and actively try to encourage tourism for their local businesses.

Web pages in foreign countries offer companies in those countries unprecedented access to a worldwide market, often for the first time. This allows both large and small companies to take advantage of global marketing without investing a fortune in market research and advertising costs.

▶ See "Using the Net as an Advertising Resource," p. 70

In Staunton, Va. (**http://www.elpress.com/staunton/**), you can obtain information from more than 20 of the area's antique stores. You can also receive interior and exterior pictures of historic inns as well as descriptions and rates. Information is included for the area's larger hotels and motels including Best Western, Comfort Inn, Econo Lodge, Holiday Inn, and Super 8.

Colleges and universities around the world also have pages. Similar to city and state pages, the pages for the colleges and universities range from very simple to complex, giving access to the entire teaching staff and complete program descriptions.

Taking Advantage of the World Wide Web

Whether or not you're aware of it, the Internet—and increasingly, the WWW—is all around you. In every level of commerce, government, and education, there has been a need for a low-cost, high-impact medium for the exchange of data. The WWW has proven that it is the proper medium to fulfill that need.

If as a business person you do not take advantage of the information technology, as well as the sales and marketing potential of the Web, the marketplace could take advantage of you.

When you advertise your products or services on the Web, you are on equal footing with larger companies. The casual shopper cruising the Internet will have the same opportunity to enter your storefront as the storefronts of Cartier or Chanel, which can be accessed through the Paris home page. The beauty of the WWW is that you can afford to have your business right alongside those other big-name companies.

▶ "What are Virtual Shopping Systems?" p. 328

Exactly how you use the WWW will depend on the products and services you are offering and how far you want to go. At the very least, you will want a home page that offers your products and services and provides information on contacting you via traditional methods such as the telephone or mail.

▶ See "Demographics through E-Mail and Forms," p. 354

You may decide that you want to take advantage of some of the commercial potentials of the Web like order taking, handling cash transactions, collecting demographics, and providing customer support.

▶ See "Effective Order Filling Systems," p. 293

▶ See "Alternative Methods for Collecting Cash," p. 289

How far you go on the Web depends only on how far you want to go. No matter what your business is or how much money you have to spend, you will at least want to hang a sign so that it can be seen by the increasing number of people who cruise the Information Superhighway.

The Net versus BBS and Pay Services

Many times people are confused about the differences between BBS and pay services:

■ *Bulletin Board Systems* (BBSes) are often free or low-cost computer systems which allow local people to share information. Often, BBSes will have simple interfaces to the Internet which will allow its users to employ some of the services, such as e-mail and NetNews.

■ *Pay services* have become common household names, with Prodigy, America Online, Britannica Online, GEnie, and CompuServe among the popular pay services. Pay services are similar to huge nationwide or worldwide BBSes that offer millions of users popular telecommunications capabilities.

As the following two sections discover, BBS and pay services each have their own strengths and weaknesses.

Bulletin Boards and the Net

BBS systems consist of computers sitting in people's homes or small businesses that are hooked to the phone line. You may call this computer from your computer and transfer information. Because many BBSes are local to you, they offer access to information and people in your community.

BBS systems are often free for users. By calling a BBS with your computer, you can find computer software, information, news, weather, and special interest topics.

Many BBSes allow you to have basic e-mail and NetNews services by providing intermittent Internet access. For example, as you send e-mail, the BBS will probably just compile it all. Then, once or twice a day, the BBS will connect with the Internet and send all the outgoing mail and receive all the incoming mail. In this manner, small-time BBS owners can offer the Internet to all of their users without spending a large amount of money.

Unfortunately, people who access the Internet in this manner often have the perception that the Internet is of limited value, because they cannot use the real power of the Internet from the limited BBS systems. However, for many users where local Internet access is simply unavailable, BBS access can provide a viable alternative.

> **Note**
>
> In the future, BBSes will certainly disappear (I predict within five years). The Internet allows anyone to operate a site for very little money, once connected. BBS operators will be able to operate larger sites for less money than they do now. It will soon cease to be advantageous to run a BBS the "old fashioned way."

Since the Internet connects more than two million computers and 25 million people, nothing that is on any BBS in the world cannot also be found on the Internet. Because of this, the Internet has been referred to as "the Mother of all BBSes." Instead of calling hundreds of BBSes trying to find a certain program, a simple search on the Internet will reveal hundreds of sites with the program which you can access within seconds. This fact, along with the huge community for you to access, spells the death of BBSes.

There are two types of BBSes:

- *Free*. The majority of BBSes are free. As long as you contribute software and information and are not abusive, you can use the BBS at no cost. You will be granted an account and a set amount of time per day that you can use the system. BBS operators can afford to do this because they are not accruing a tremendous cost, and the information coming in is useful to them.

- *Subscription*. Other BBSes charge for access. These systems fall under two categories. First, there are systems which have become so popular that the owner has undertaken costs such as additional phone lines, more and better computer hardware devices, more and better storage, and so on. These types of systems are usually pay systems because the commitment to keep the system current and meet the users' needs has demanded it. The second type of pay system is one that offers added services, which could include stock quotes, Internet access, or other non-standard capabilities.

The bottom line is that you really don't want to use BBS systems for anything other than learning telecommunication basics. The Internet provides everything a BBS does and much more.

▶ See "Locating the Net in Your Area," p. 131

> **Note**
>
> If you are just starting out in computers, you may want to first start with your local BBS, because it gets your feet wet for understanding your computer, using a modem to phone dial through your computer, uploading and downloading files, and talking with people. You should try this with several BBSes in your local area to get a flavor for different interfaces, rules, and content.
>
> To find out where BBSes are in your area, consult local computer papers, computer store cork boards, and the magazine *Computer Shopper*. *Computer Shopper* is available in many supermarkets and contains listings of BBSes by area code. Your area might also have a computer users' group that can help.

Figuring Out Pay Services

The major disadvantage of pay services such as America Online, CompuServe, GEnie, and Prodigy is that they cost money—lots of money. However, many of the pay services offer services that are very popular. Weekly meetings that are attended by various famous people have great crowd-drawing potential, as do the online shopping and news services.

If the early Internet had a WWW-style interface from the start, pay services would never have originated. Pay services were created for two reasons:

- They allow people to use network-type services without requiring a degree in rocket science. They usually embody special software that you load on your computer, which knows how to make the phone connection for you.

- The majority of these services have an attractive point-and-click interface.

These two factors initially made pay systems extremely popular. Some of the most popular pay services have more than a million users spanning the entire globe.

> **Caution**
>
> Do not be confused by names such as America Online, which is not restricted in any way to users in America only.

Pay services are much like the Internet. They offer their users the ability to access software and information. They also have special interest groups (thousands of them) which are often well-managed. They allow interactive, real-time talking (similar to the Internet's IRC).

▶ See "IRC," p. 46

Here is how the majority of pay services work. You subscribe to a pay service at an hourly fee, which covers basic access to the service. The fee will probably include features such as news, interactive talking, and e-mail. To get special features such as stock quotes, live discussions with famous people, or downloadable books, you can pay an extra monthly or hourly charge.

The big catch of these services is that they are costly. Whereas the Internet can have fixed prices for unlimited access, pay services often have basic prices that are several dollars per hour. If you use the system even a modest number of hours a day, your monthly bill will be large. Even in situations where the Internet is charged hourly, costs are still modest, such as 75 cents an hour; many of the pay services have hourly fees at or exceeding $4 an hour (especially when you include the phone access charge, which may be a local number but still billed at an hourly rate).

Also, some of the pay services have fairly closed systems. Most limit e-mail to other subscribers on their network; however, a few allow e-mail to come and go out to the Internet. Even these systems often have slow e-mail, unlike the instantaneous e-mail of the Internet.

People on pay services are now beginning to demand access to the Internet. Currently, people are scrambling among all the big pay services to receive both Internet and WWW access. There are 25 million users on the Internet; the few million users on the pay services want access to the rest of the world.

Pay services do currently offer other options which are hard to get on the Internet. For example, it is difficult to get a live news feed (TV-style news) on the Internet for free. Likewise, all "free" stock quotes on the Internet are currently delayed at least 15 minutes unless you subscribe to the service.

Another difference between pay services and the Internet is the cost of placing a business on the medium. Businesses can be placed on the Internet for very little cost per month, whereas pay services often pay large amounts of money. You can use the Internet to create your own pay service for much less than you could ever dream to do it via a commercial pay service.

▶ See "Subscription Services," p. 313

The bottom line is that the Internet offers everything that the pay services do, and a lot more of it. You may need to pay a little extra for similar services on the Internet, but you should never need to pay as much as the pay services are demanding. Your access to information and people will be much greater on the Internet. Additionally, as time goes on, the differences between

▶ See "Locating the Net in Your Area," p. 131

pay services and the Internet will continue to narrow. If you are going to use the special features that pay services have to offer, go ahead and subscribe. But if you are using a pay service just to get Internet and WWW access, you can probably get it cheaper from a commercial Internet provider.

From Here...

This chapter gave you a brief overview of the Internet and the World Wide Web with a particular emphasis on how this new information technology is affecting business and commerce worldwide.

A great amount of information exists about both the Internet and the World Wide Web. If you are interested in learning more, you can access numerous sources of information on the Net and the Web. Two sources (CERN and NCSA) were already given earlier in this chapter. Others will be listed throughout the book, and still others can be easily found as you learn to navigate the Web and use its various search capabilities.

For more information, refer to the following chapters:

- Chapter 2, "Net Components and Terminology," helps define many of the concepts and terms you will encounter in this book and on the Internet.

- Chapter 3, "Why the Net is Good for Business," puts many of the concepts presented in this chapter into perspective as to how they help businesses.

- Chapter 8, "Etiquette and the Net," helps explore many issues of jargon and how to deal with people you meet on the Net.

- Chapter 9, "Information on the Net," explores in more detail how to find information in the huge sea of available data.

- Chapter 14, "Subscription Services, Virtual Malls, and Instant Products," looks at how you can start your own pay services.

Chapter 2

Net Components and Terminology

Like many areas of computers, the Internet and the WWW have many new terms and acronyms. HTTP, browsers, e-mail, and URL are a few that you've already been introduced to in the previous chapter.

If you are a new user, these terms often can appear intimidating. However, with use, they'll soon become new additions to your vocabulary that will allow you to understand the Internet and WWW.

In this chapter, you learn

- The various components of the Internet

- The meaning of TCP/IP, SLIP, and PPP

- The relationship of browsers to servers

- Standard Internet protocols such as Telnet, NetNews, and e-mail

Internet Terminology

Don't worry if these terms seem confusing at first. You can always refer back to this section when needed. More helpful terms can be found in the Glossary.

Provider

Your *provider* is the organization from where you get your Internet service. Using the superhighway analogy, the provider could be compared to a filling station on an entrance ramp to a highway. In order to drive on a highway,

Tip

Don't use a word or acronym if you don't know what it means. Your mis-use of words and terms will be an-noying at best. In certain situations, it could cause real problems.

you must have fuel to help you get there. The provider gives you this "fuel" by providing you an entrance ramp to the Internet. The money you pay the provider is used to constantly upgrade the entrance ramp (in terms of new computers and faster Internet access) to match the growing needs of your community.

▶ See "Locating the Net in Your Area," p. 131

The provider purchases its Internet feed at great cost from a major Internet source. The provider also purchases many telephone lines from the local phone company. By placing computers and other hardware at the site that interface the phone lines with the Internet, the provider can sell commercial access.

The incoming Internet feed needs to be as fast as possible. The faster the feed, the more data can be accommodated simultaneously. More data means more users.

Big feeds cost the provider big bucks. The computers the provider uses must be able to handle many simultaneous online users. Often these machines take quite a beating and need to be constantly maintained and upgraded to meet the user's demands. The provider must also purchase and maintain banks of modems to allow the hundreds of simultaneous users to access the computer. All of this—along with professional fees, overhead, and support staff—can amount to a fairly hefty bill for the provider.

The provider is able to recoup the investment, while still being able to provide inexpensive service, by providing service to many people simultaneously. Providers also recoup their investment by selling major Internet hookups to big corporations in their area. Finally, many providers recoup their investment by also selling World Wide Web services.

When you purchase Internet access from a provider, you are actually purchasing many options:

- You receive an account on the provider's system. The account is a place you can store files and do your Internet work.

- You also receive a NetNews feed which allows you to access thousands of interest groups on practically any topic imaginable (see the section "NetNews" later in this chapter).

- You also receive an e-mail address, which people worldwide can use to send messages to you (see "E-Mail" later in this chapter).

- You receive full access to the entire Internet, which is what this book will help you implement.

> **Note**
>
> Not all Internet providers are "full service." They may not provide you with all the capabilities mentioned here. Be sure to ask your provider if they are full-service and that your account includes at least FTP, Telnet, e-mail, NetNews, and WWW access.

Clients and Browsers

A *client* is a software program that allows you to read information stored on the Internet. It is also often referred to as a *browser*, particularly when referencing the World Wide Web.

To continue the superhighway analogy, a client is the vehicle you use to drive or navigate on the Internet, whether it be a sports car or a pickup truck. Just as you wouldn't haul dirt in a convertible, various clients are used for different tasks on the Internet:

- *Gopher clients* handle surfing Gopher data.

- *Telnet clients* allow you to log into remote computers interactively.

- *World Wide Web clients* allow you to access information via the WWW.

- *FTP clients* allow you to get and put files via the Internet.

Client software always runs on your end of the Internet connection. It is the portions of the Internet that you interact with directly. It takes your instructions and converts them into information which can be sent to a remote site to be fulfilled.

A client always talks to a server. That is, for every type of client (WWW, FTP, Telnet, NetNews, Gopher, and so on), there is a corresponding server. (See "Servers" later in this chapter.)

> **Note**
>
> Much of this book is devoted to the World Wide Web. In general, clients or browsers are discussed in terms of how they relate to the WWW. When a chapter refers to Gopher clients or FTP clients, only the terms "Gopher" and "FTP" will be used.

Servers

A *server* is a program that allows data to be accessed from the WWW.

On the Information Superhighway, the server is your destination. Depending on the client (vehicle) you choose (such as Gopher, WWW, or FTP), the particular server you go to at the destination will vary (see "Clients and Browsers" later in this chapter). For example, if you drive up in a WWW browser, you will be directed to the WWW server. Most destinations offer all the types of servers (just as a mall would offer more than one store).

For each type of Internet service, a server must be run which will respond to requests for that service. For example, in order to use a Telnet client to access a remote site, the remote site must be running a Telnet server. These servers are, quite frequently, a single hardware machine running multiple software programs to provide the services. For instance, a single UNIX server can run Telnet, WWW, and FTP services at the same time.

> **Note**
>
> Since much of this book is devoted to the World Wide Web, the word "server" refers to WWW servers. When other types of servers are mentioned, the word "server" will follow the service type (for example, Gopher server).

Servers which deal with the World Wide Web are known as *HTTP servers*. HTTP stands for *Hyper Text Transfer Protocol.*

Tip
You can also refer to them as *HTTPD servers*. The extra "D" which is occasionally added stands for "daemon" and is computer lingo for a special type of program which is always running.

Two effective public domain WWW servers are available: the CERN server and the NCSA server. Since CERN is the creator of the World Wide Web and NCSA is the creator of Mosaic (the first hypertext WWW browser), these two servers have become the standard. Most WWW sites currently available will be running one of these two popular servers.

Additionally, several corporations have produced commercial servers, which in general are compatible with NCSA and CERN servers and offer some additional features. NCSA and CERN are 100 percent compatible with each other, and differ only in methods of handling requests, configuration, and debugging options.

Gateways and Routers

Gateways are generic terms that refer to computers which *route* information or merge two dissimilar services together.

Often, gateways are computers which allow you entrance into a service such as the Internet from another non-Internet type service. For example, many bulletin boards have e-mail capability with the Internet; they do this by using a gateway to the Internet. This is basically a computer somewhere which is connected to the Internet and hands the BBS a feed of all or a portion of the services.

TCP/IP, SLIP, and PPP

TCP/IP is the protocol that governs the Internet. In other words, it's the set of rules by which the Internet works. TCP/IP stands for *Transmission Control Protocol/Internet Protocol* and is a standard which allows computers from different manufacturers to talk together using a common means of expression.

The TCP/IP standard has been refined over the years from a basic set of requirements set by the U.S. government's Defense Advanced Research Projects Agency (DARPA), with which it remains backwardly compatible.

Basically, TCP/IP is the mechanism by which the Internet works. You cannot access the Internet without using the TCP/IP protocol at some point during the interaction. Luckily, the client and server software you use will automatically know how to deal with TCP/IP and will make this interaction completely invisible to you.

In the best of all worlds, TCP/IP is run on a high-speed network, which could include some form of copper or fiber-optic networking line or phone line via a modem. TCP/IP works best over high-speed networks such as Ethernet; the bandwidth of the network is sufficient to enable quick access to remote data.

Because of the recent advent of fast and inexpensive modem technology, SLIP and PPP protocols have been developed to allow modems to interface with TCP/IP systems. SLIP stands for *Serial Line Interface Protocol* and PPP stands for *Point-to-Point Protocol*. Both mechanisms are similar in that they understand how to handle TCP/IP over a modem.

> **Note**
>
> SL/IP and SLIP are interchangeable, but in the context of this book, Serial Line Internet Protocol is referred to as "SLIP."

By running SLIP or PPP software on your end of a connection and having similar software running at your provider's site, you can "slip into" your provider, which gives you the best possible access to the Internet.

Tip
The more modern term for gateway is *router*, which means the same thing but has become more common in usage.

An Introduction

If you do not run SLIP or PPP software, you will log into your provider's site and access the Internet from there. Accessing the Internet from the provider's site has two disadvantages. First, when you retrieve information, you retrieve it into your account at your provider's site and then transfer it from there to your computer. Because the SLIP or PPP line brings the Internet right into your computer, you only need to transfer the data once, which makes it much faster and allows you to be more productive.

> **Note**
>
> SLIP and PPP differ by how they transfer data internally. You may only use one or the other. If you pick SLIP, you should try to use a flavor named *CSLIP* where the "C" represents "compressed." CSLIP and PPP are comparable in speed. PPP is somewhat faster than non-compressed SLIP.

Your provider will help you make the proper determination of the best type of service you can get for the right price. It's important to keep in mind that SLIP and PPP service often costs slightly more than just straight Internet service.

E-Mail

E-mail is the most basic and important of Internet services. Anybody who has any Internet service at all will have e-mail capability.

E-mail consists of the ability to send an electronic message over the Internet to any of its 25 million users. E-mail may even be sent to non-Internet users by making use of one of the many online fax servers which converts an e-mail message into a fax and sends it (usually for a price).

> **Note**
>
> If you have an e-mail account, remember to check it for messages. It may be hard to remember at first, but soon you'll do it automatically just as you check the mailbox at home.

Tip
Leaving your e-mail unread and unanswered is not a good business habit.

In many scientific and technology-related fields, an e-mail address is as important as a mailing address.

When you obtain Internet access from your provider, you will be given an account name. For example, if your name is Bob Smith, your account name might be bsmith. Some providers allow you to choose a name (provided that it isn't already in use), but some assign you one that isn't changeable.

The provider itself will have a name, called a *domain name*. For example, your provider's domain name might be somewhere.com. The *.com* indicates it is a commercial provider; *somewhere* is usually the provider's name.

Putting both your account name and the provider's name together, you get an e-mail address like this:

bsmith@*somewhere*.com

This address is read as "bsmith at somewhere dot com". The "@" is used to separate the login from the provider's name. More information on how to refer to special characters frequently used in computers and the Internet is provided in the section "Jargon" later in this chapter.

This address allows the computers of the world to find you. They examine the provider's name portion of the e-mail address to determine how to find your provider. Next, your provider looks at the login name portion of the address to figure out how to find you and puts it in a special file for you to read.

To read your e-mail, you use one of the many popular e-mail readers. These programs present your e-mail to you in a simple-to-read format and usually allows you to save messages and search messages. E-mail readers also provide convenient ways to respond to people who have sent you messages.

The World Wide Web itself allows you to send and read e-mail messages by interfacing you to WWW programs which send and retrieve e-mail.

NetNews

Like e-mail, *NetNews* is another standard Internet service which all Internet users receive. NetNews posts messages from special interest groups. NetNews can be thought of as a form of public e-mail. People who share common interests can talk about their favorite topics in an open forum. NetNews is extremely popular because it can provide access to information from experts around the world who are usually more than happy to lend you their opinion.

Users interact with NetNews by selecting special interest groups to which they want to belong. Selecting a newsgroup is also referred to as *subscribing* to a group. Since there are more than 10,000 special interest groups, most people will have no problem finding several groups to subscribe to.

NetNews topics range from cats to Macintosh computers, from Hawaii to automobiles. Television programs are well-represented, especially the science

Tip
Consider adding your e-mail address to your business cards and stationery next time you have them printed.

I

An Introduction

fiction ones. Some people even form splinter groups that branch into topics dealing with specific characters or plots.

> **Note**
>
> Because the quantity of data is so large, many providers do not receive the entire NetNews daily feed. If your provider does not obtain a group you are interested in, ask to have it added. Most providers are more than happy to accommodate such requests.
>
> Some providers censor certain groups which they feel have questionable content. Depending on local laws and user pressure, certain groups may simply not appear because they are considered inappropriate for that locale.

Once inside a special interest group, users see messages which have been added by other users. Messages appear in the order received with the subject listed at the top. Most news readers let you review just the subject lines and allow you to pick ones which interest you, only then displaying the entire message.

You may respond to messages by either replying to the originator of the message privately or by sending a response to the NetNews group for everybody to read.

Because NetNews is composed of many people all expressing their opinions, arguments can ensue. When this happens, it is termed *flaming* and can often lead to *flame wars* in which more and more heated dialogs occur. You can minimize your contact with flaming and flame wars by avoiding the few groups that have unusually antagonistic participants. You can pinpoint these groups by reading a smattering of their messages.

Tip
If you receive a flame from someone on the Net, the best strategy is to simply ignore it. If you cannot ignore it, responding in a professional and polite manner—no matter how rude the flamer—will help resolve the situation faster.

People who try to quell flame wars are called *firefighters*. However, it's well-known on the Net that firefighters sometimes get drawn into the conflict.

Overall, NetNews provides an extremely useful and productive environment where people can share ideas and concepts. Questions from, "What computer should I buy?" to "Where is a good place to go for my vacation?" can be answered by any of the millions of experts on the Internet.

The protocol for reading newsgroups from the Web is *Network News Transfer Protocol* (*NNTP*). NNTP sites allow you to read NetNews from most of the popular WWW browsers.

Telnet

Telnet is a basic Internet service which allows you to physically access remote computers as if they were local to you. To use Telnet, you must have the Internet address of the remote computer (for example, *somewhere*.com). Upon telnetting to the remote computer, you are presented with a login message. Entering a valid user name and password logs you into the remote computer as if it were your local machine. Anything you enter at that point is entered into, read by, and acted up by the remote computer.

Since you must have a login in order to use a remote computer, most users do not telnet very often. However, if you ever access the Internet from out of town, you would use Telnet to access your own account from the remote location.

Note

Some sites offer the ability for anybody to telnet into their system. Usually, such systems will offer an automatic menu upon logging in. These systems often tell you how to log in when they greet you after you telnet to them.

Other sites post their instructions in NetNews groups. Such systems offer BBS-type capabilities by which you can access specialized services.

In general, if a site does not publish or offer a public service, try logging in as **guest** or **demo**. If this is not successful, the site probably does not want you telnetting in.

Most World Wide Web browsers have a handy, built-in Telnet capability which allows you to access remote computers right from the browser.

FTP

File Transfer Protocol, or *FTP* for short, is the standard protocol for copying files from computer to computer on the Internet.

Similar to Telnet, FTP allows you to access remote machines. However, where Telnet allows you free access to the power of the remote machine, FTP limits you to operations such as sending and retrieving information.

FTP allows much more freedom of access. In Telnet, you had to have an account to access a remote machine. In contrast, FTP allows what is known as *anonymous access*. When you FTP to a remote computer, you receive a login. Logging in as **anonymous** often allows you to proceed by entering your e-mail address as the password. You are then allowed to see a directory of files which you may download. Many remote systems also allow you to upload files which you want to add to the collective information.

Tip
On some comput-
ers, the "anony-
mous" login is
replaced by the
word "FTP." If
anonymous fails
for a login, try
using **FTP** instead.

The most productive use of FTP is to first use Archie to locate a host which has a file on it that you are interested in (see "Archie" later in this chapter). Once Archie has returned a list of hosts that contain the file you are inter-ested in, use FTP to go to that site and retrieve the desired file.

Note

FTP allows files to be transmitted in either ASCII or binary mode. Binary should be used on all files which are not plaintext ASCII documents. However, since ASCII mode translates the ends of lines correctly between different types of computers, there will be times when you want to use ASCII mode over binary mode.

If you are unsure about which mode to use, choose binary mode. Using ASCII mode to access a non-plaintext file causes the contents of the file to be incorrectly saved, and the information will be a mess when it ends up in your machine. Binary always retrieves the document exactly as it is stored. The mechanism for switching between binary and ASCII modes depends on your particular FTP browser.

The World Wide Web makes heavy use of FTP protocol. WWW documents may be stored on HTTP servers, but may also be stored at FTP sites. Most WWW browsers know how to access a WWW document from an FTP site. This capability allows you to store WWW home pages at inexpensive FTP anonymous sites around the world. This is one of the ways that many people initially come to the World Wide Web.

Archie

One of the primary difficulties on the Internet is finding the information you want in the mountains of information that already exist. One of the more useful tools in this constant battle is the Archie client and server.

Archie is an Internet searching mechanism. Sites which run Archie servers periodically poll major sections of the Internet and record what files are avail-able on what sites. These huge databases are then made accessible to you for searching.

To use Archie, you simply provide the name of an Archie server site and a single word you want to find. Archie returns to you a complete list with the host name, directory name, and file name for each occurrence of your word.

You can then use FTP to access the host, go to the directory, and retrieve the desired file.

Because each Archie server site only polls a portion of the Internet, different server sites return different results from a search operation. Also, because the databases are periodically updated (usually weekly or monthly), what you find one week may differ from what you find the next week.

The World Wide Web has its own searching mechanisms and thus does not need the Archie capability. However, many Archie WWW sites do exist to provide Archie access to WWW users.

Gopher

Gopher is an attempt to make transferring files from remote computers much easier than standard FTP. Gopher sites run Gopher servers, which may be accessed to deliver documents and search databases.

Unlike FTP, which shows you raw directories with often cryptic file names, Gopher displays directories with full text descriptions so you can access information easily. Furthermore, Gopher allows you to access databases for searching. This makes it a popular solution for job hunting and similar services.

Gopher falls short of other browsers such as WWW browsers in that it doesn't integrate images and sound nearly as well as WWW browsers do. However, Gopher+ (a Gopher extension run by many sites) does have support for basic WWW pages and can handle some of the formatting commands of HTML. This makes Gopher a very rudimentary WWW browser mechanism.

On the same note, WWW browsers have built-in Gopher handling mechanisms that allow them to cruise Gopher sites. Because WWW is far more visual than Gopher, many people prefer to access Gopher sites via WWW than via Gopher clients.

URL

Universal Resource Locator (URL) is a special address used by WWW browsers to access information on the Internet. In general, the World Wide Web is accessible in a point-and-click manner, which means that you do not normally need to use URLs. However, many times you will encounter a URL in print, such as in an e-mail or NetNews message or in a magazine article. In this case, you will be required to enter the URL by hand. Because of this, it's often useful to have a good understanding of exactly what a URL is.

A URL has three basic components:

- A service

- A domain name with optional port

- A path with optional file name

The first component, the service, tells the browser how to retrieve the file. The service may be one of the following types:

- **file://** or **ftp://** are identical and tell the browser to use FTP to retrieve the file. If no account information is available in the URL, the browser uses an anonymous login to access the file.

- **http://** indicates that the request is going to an HTTP server (WWW server) and will be honored by that server.

- **gopher://** indicates that the request is going to a Gopher server.

- **telnet://** allows you to open a Telnet session within your WWW browsers.

- **news:** allows you to access any NNTP NetNews reader on the Internet, and read NetNews from your WWW browser.

> **Note**
>
> **news:** does not have the **//** separators that the rest of the types do. This is how the service operates.

The second component of the URL is the name of the machine you are accessing the document from. This is usually a domain name in the form of *somewhere*.com. Occasionally, the domain name will have a number after it, separated by a colon (this sometimes is done when more than one HTTP server is running on one computer).

The final component of the URL is the path name and file name of the item you want to retrieve. The path and file name may be missing, and if it is, the default document for that machine is loaded.

Some examples of legitimate URLs include the following:

> **http://www.iquest.net/cw/**
>
> **gopher://gopher.iquest.net/**
>
> **http://www.iquest.net/iq/galaxymall.html**

> **Note**
>
> If you receive an error trying to access a URL, try again. If the location is busy, the request may have been refused because of too many users. If you continue to receive errors after repeated attempts, try other variations of the URL. For example, if the URL is
>
> http://*somewhere*.com/pub/files/my.html
>
> You could also try any of the following:
>
> http://*somewhere*.com/pub/files/
>
> http://*somewhere*.com/pub/
>
> http://*somewhere*.com/
>
> One of those may work where the others failed.

HTML

Hypertext Markup Language (*HTML*) is the language of the World Wide Web. HTML was developed at CERN, the creator of the WWW.

HTML allows a single document to contain text, color images, sounds, and movies. Any item (for example, a sound) can be *hyperlinked* to any other document, image, or sound. As the user views a document, portions of the document may be picked by the user to cause other related documents or items to be retrieved. This capability makes HTML a perfect candidate for moving around the huge, densely-packed structures of the Internet.

> **Note**
>
> Hyperlinks are also called *links* for short.

Simple HTML documents are easy to create and can be developed using any of the popular word processors like Word for Windows or Word. They may also be entered with text editors like *vi* (a popular editor on UNIX platforms).

HTML documents are always text documents that have special commands in them which indicate pictures, sounds, movies, links, and formatting. These special commands allow HTML to display colorful pictures, play music or a message from the vice president, and allow you to hop from computer to computer just by pointing and clicking.

Just as on real highways, the ability to move easily and quickly as well as having something nice to look at along the way (in the form of attractive graphics) has made the WWW one of the more popular roads.

Referring to the superhighway concept, some HTML documents can be considered the signposts and billboards along the roadside. Other HTML documents serve as your end destination, providing you with opportunities to shop, access data, meet people, or just relax.

> ### Note
>
> A brief guide to HTML programming is found in the Appendix, "An Introduction to HTML."

IRC

Internet Relay Chat (*IRC*) is a NetNews-type forum. It differs from normal NetNews in that messages posted to IRC are displayed instantaneously (or as near to it as the Internet load will allow). IRC allows its users to talk, in real time, to many people simultaneously around the world.

IRC is composed of groups or channels. Just as NetNews has thousands of special interest groups, the thousands of channels on IRC are similarly organized. Many NetNews channels have corresponding IRC channels. Where IRC differs from NetNews is that IRC is strictly real time. If you have a question, you can simply hop on a related IRC group and ask any of the members of that group the question. Anyone who knows the answer will give it to you immediately, in real time.

Because of IRC's real-time nature, it is extremely addictive. People seem to enjoy spending hours talking back and forth with other people around the world. Many deep friendships are created on IRC channels, and IRC has even spawned many romantic love affairs (where both parties rarely have met face-to-face).

> ### Caution
>
> Remember not to use words and terms whose meanings you're not exactly sure of. While it may be tempting to throw a few well-placed words around, improper use of words and terms will not gain you any friends in IRC.

IRC keeps people's identities private by allowing you to pick a nickname. This is the name that other users will know you by when you enter a group.

> **Caution**
>
> A person's IRC nickname may not reflect the user's gender. Sometimes men masquerade as women for the entertainment value that can sometimes be had by watching men try to pick up women on IRC. Women play similar pranks.
>
> In general, any obvious attempt to pick up a member of the opposite sex will mark you for a *newbie* (a new IRC user).

Tip
People often have alter-egos on IRC using names that reflect their interests or personalities.

The IRC channel **#www** is often a good place to get help in using the World Wide Web and Internet. Many webmasters and Web gurus are always available to answer questions about the Web.

WAIS

Wide Area Information Servers (*WAIS*) is a text-only database developed by Thinking Machines Corp. and made available for public use by its placement in the public domain. Although a powerful search tool, its lack of graphic capabilities has limited its growth and popularity.

In WAIS, all searches are done as part of an index. All data is returned as a text document back to the user.

WAIS would probably have been much more popular if the World Wide Web had not been invented. However, the advent of the Web meant that a much more compelling mechanism for database retrieval was available, and thus WAIS never really caught on.

WAIS database searching is not recommended because of the number of other attractive alternatives (such as custom cgi-bin WWW database searchers and WWW indexed searching).

▶ See "Databases and Virtual Shopping Systems," p. 330

Jargon

The Net has spawned a great amount of jargon over the years. This section explores some of the more colorful terms. Reviewing these terms will help you to relate both on the Net and also with some of concepts presented in the rest of this book.

Among some of the common terms you will see are words with an "e" prefix attached to it, such as *e-mail*. Some other examples include: *e-zines* for electronic magazines, *e-cash* for electronic cash, and *e-shop* or *e-store* for electronic retailers.

Taking cues from the words "hardware" and "software," pages could be filled with all the variants that people have coined. Among the more popular ones you'll see include: *freeware*, *shareware*, *payware*, *dreamware*, *vaporware*, and *crudware*.

Terms taken from the Internet and networking are *netiquette*, *net warriors*, and *net wars*.

The Net has often been related to an ocean or highway. Because of this, colorful terms such as *surfing* or *cruising the Net* can be seen. These terms simply mean to use the Internet or Web. Among traffic-related terms are *pothole* and *dirt road*, both implying routes that are bumpy or take a long time.

In the same vein, popular science fiction, especially *cyberpunk* (science fiction dealing with the Net and virtual reality), has created a whole vocabulary of jargon words. An example of this is Neil Stevenson's (author of the science-fiction book, *Snow Crash*) compelling words for the Internet, such as the *I-Way*, which plays off the Internet and information highway. Another colorful term is his use of *spew* for the Internet, referring to the sheer amount of information that is available, such as in *"surfing the spew."*

In some cases, there are many ways to say the same thing. *Crash, crash and burn, die,* and *go flatline* all refer to critical hardware or software failure.

Wizard, guru, and *netgod* are all ways of identifying Internet experts. Running in *wizard mode* means having special privileges that let you have a lot of power on a computer.

The following symbols will help you to verbalize computer addresses:

Symbol	Pronounced as
!	"bang"
.	"dot"
@	"at"
-	"dash"
^	"caret"
/	"slash"
\	"backslash"
~	"tilde" (pronounced till-dah)
_	"underscore"

The following are the more commonly used acronyms that you should acquaint yourself with:

Acronym	Pronounced as
24/7	24 hours a day, seven days a week
BTW	By The Way
FAQ	Frequently Asked Questions or FAQ lists (FAQL are lists that are maintained so that users can access answers to common, standard inquiries.)
GIGO	Garbage In, Garbage Out
HHOK	Ha Ha Only Kidding
HHOS	Ha Ha Only Serious
IANAL	I Am Not A Lawyer
IMHO	In My Humble Opinion
IMNSHO	In My Not So Humble Opinion
IWBNI	It Would Be Nice If (see WIBNI)
IYFEG	Insert Your Favorite Ethnic Group (a way to tell a whole class of jokes without offending anyone).
KISS	Keep It Simple Stupid
NRN	No Response Necessary
OTOH	On The Other Hand
RTM	Read The Manual (a frequently used variation of RTFAQ, Read The Frequently Asked Questions).
TANSTAAFL	There Ain't No Such Thing As A Free Lunch
UTSL	Use The Source, Luke. (This term refers to Luke Skywalker from the Star Wars movies. It is a gentle reminder that the information you are seeking is in the source code.)
WIBNI	Wouldn't It Be Nice If (see IWBNI)
WYSIWYG	What You See Is What You Get (pronounced "whizzy wig")

And there is still more jargon:

- *Flavor* denotes type or variety. If the flavor is *vanilla*, it means the ordinary or the standard variety of something. This term is used especially in referring to browsers and software capabilities in general.

- A *mail bomb* is an e-mail message, usually very long, which is sent to thousands of users at once. This is considered very bad, because it is both destructive to the server load and rude to the users, and usually results in losing your access.

- A *hot list* contains the addresses of a user's favorite Internet sites.

- *Mouse potato* is the computer version of a couch potato.

- *Flooding* is to send lots of repetitive messages on an IRC channel and is considered very irritating.

- *Finger* is a special program that will give you information about a particular user on IRC or can give you information about all the users within a group on IRC.

- In some circles, *hacker* denotes a person who accesses information illegally. To others, it merely means someone who is a good programmer. Because of this wide discrepancy, cautious use of the term is suggested.

Often in IRC, e-mail, and NetNews, abbreviations appear which have meaning. For example, BRB and BBL in IRC stand for "Be Right Back" and "Be Back Later." Likewise, many people abbreviate text because of the large amount of typing they do. This helps to save space and time as well as adding personality to the text, for example,

```
How r u today? I'm fine sanks. When r u going 2 lunch?
```

This sentence is fairly understandable. When you sound it out it becomes

```
How are you today? I'm fine thanks. When are you going to lunch?
```

Likewise, many people type **l8r** as "later," or replace the number zero for the letter "o", or the number 3 for the letter "e" to make text appear unusual or to add flair. Words written in this style often look like this:

```
I've h3ard gr8 things ab0ut y0u.
```

Likewise, many times text can be unusually capitalized, again to offer personalization to the wording, such as this:

```
IvE HeaRD GrEaT thingS ab0ut y0u.
```

Additionally, unusual spellings, often centered around pronunciation, appear. This is not necessarily the sign of a bad speller, but instead indicates someone who is trying to turn the normally mundane into something a little different. For example,

```
Congratulations dewd!! Bob sez ur very coolz!
```

translates to

```
Congratulations dude!! Bob says you are very cool!
```

These dialects should be taken for what they are—personalization.

Stereotyping is rampant on the Internet, and one of the most popular stereotypes falls upon new users. There are three terms which are used to refer to a new user. The first, *newbie*, is fairly explanatory. A newbie is anyone who is obviously new to a particular service. Newbies are often obvious by the questions they ask.

> ### Note
>
> Don't be concerned about a newbie status. Everyone had to start somewhere. When you are an experienced user, you should treat the newbies you encounter with tolerance.

There is nothing wrong with being a newbie, but in some circles, all newbies have the reputation for being "lame" or "wannabees."

Being *lame* or being a *lamer* is simply being lazy or not thinking something through. You could be called lame if you ask a question with an obvious answer or if you make an obvious error.

Lamers are often people who ask a lot of questions, most of which could have been answered by themselves. Most of the people answering questions on the Net are busy people, but are willing to share their knowledge and love of the Internet to newcomers. However, they don't like having their time wasted. Usually someone will let you know by typing **RTM** or one of its more colorful variants.

Wannabees are those who want to achieve a certain stage or status without going through the steps or work of getting there. Quite often these people throw around words that they have no clue of what they mean.

An Introduction

▶ See "Etiquette in Live Discussions," p. 183

> **Note**
>
> In general, you should not worry about being insulted on the Net. Although in many groups you'll see a great deal of good-natured ribbing going back and forth, it's all in fun.

There is one last type of jargon that you will encounter on the Internet— *emoticons*. These are symbols made up of colons, semicolons, parentheses, and the like. Emoticons are used to express emotions. They should be viewed by tilting your head to the left:

Emoticon	Meaning
:) or :-)	Smile
;) or ;-)	Wink
:(or :-(	Frown
:p or :-p	Tongue sticking out, raspberries
:@ or :-@	Scream

Some people have created ones that describe physical attributes, like the following:

Emoticon	Meaning
8-) B-)	Wears glasses
:-)>	Has a beard
:-()	Has a mustache

You usually see them tagged onto a statement that could be interpreted in different ways to let the reader know how he or she should take the message.

From Here...

Because the Internet and WWW were unstructured collaborative efforts in their early years—as one might say, an organic side-shoot of computer and information technology—some of its components are not neatly definable and compartmentalized.

For more information, refer to the following chapters:

- Chapter 1, "An Introduction To the Net," gives you some idea on how all these terms, concepts, and jargon fit together.

- Chapter 3, "Why the Net is Good for Business," helps put many of the concepts presented in this chapter in perspective as to how the Net helps businesses.

- Chapter 8, "Etiquette and the Net," helps explore many jargon issues and how to deal with people you meet on the Net.

- Chapter 9, "Information on the Net," explores in more detail how to find information in the huge sea of available data.

I

An Introduction

Chapter 3

Why the Net is Good for Business

In previous chapters you learned the reasons why the Internet, and specifically the WWW, is such a powerful tool for businesses.

In examining Web pages using your browser, you will see some pages that you think are really exciting, while others are boring. Remember what you like and dislike in these pages when you design your own HTML documents.

This chapter gives an overview of why the Web is good for business. You learn how it can be used for the following tasks:

- Demographics gathering
- Obtaining information
- Advertising
- Sales
- Customer support

Why Use the Net?

Businesses use the Net to do the following tasks:

1. *Reduce phones and staff.* You can allow the public to access information such as addresses, correct spelling of names, directions, and the like from a Web page.

2. *Save on printing costs.* The Internet will never completely wipe out paper, but instead of blanketing a market with flyers, brochures, or catalogs, businesses target serious clients.

3. *Save on advertising costs.* You never again have to pay a rush charge because you have to make a last-minute change before a publication deadline. Electronic media is much easier to update than paper.

4. *Save on marketing expenditures.* Don't pay expensive marketing firms to gather the information that is right at your fingertips. Do it yourself. The access logs of users who have accessed your Web pages can provide you with the time of day, location, and in some cases their e-mail address.

5. *Keep the planet green by cutting back on the amount of paper and inks used.* Some companies send their customers five and six full-color catalogs every year because they update with new products and customers lose or throw out catalogs. Companies no longer have to endure mass mailings because the latest, most up-to-date catalog is always right at their customers' fingertips via the Web. Later in this chapter you will see a list of companies that are already doing this.

Demographics and the Net

Tip
For a good source of URLs listed by category, check out Que's *Using The World Wide Web and Mosaic.*

Note
The URLs in this book are given in the hopes that you will check them out to see what is available on the Web. This allows you to acquaint yourself with the look and feel of Web documents. Keep notes on pages you like, or drop them in your hotlist.

One of the more important questions many businesses ask is, "How many people will see my page?" and "Who are these people?" Demographics and the Net is big business, but it is also difficult business.

While researchers at major universities do know exactly how much data has traversed on the Net, they do not know nearly as much about who sent the data. There is virtually no way to tell how many people are accessing the Net.

You can tell how many computers are hooked to the top level of the Internet, commonly called the *backbone*, but there is no good way to tell how many computers are hooked in at a second level. There may also be computers that are hooked into the computers, that are hooked into the computers, that are hooked into the backbone. Confusing, isn't it? And there are even fewer ways to determine how many users are on each of those machines. It is also hard to determine the exact identity of who is logged into a machine because the machine may not request the information, or an individual could be logged into another person's account.

One way to determine growth is to analyze unique e-mail addresses. Since e-mail is a fairly basic service, most users have it. E-mail addresses can be analyzed through server traffic logs and by analyzing NetNews postings. But even the e-mail analysis falls short in determining actual Net usage because many systems have multiple users per e-mail address (as do BBSes with Internet feeds, or global Telnet and anonymous sites).

Despite all the difficulties in determining demographics, many researchers on the Net are capturing statistics. The demographics do get collected, and a pattern of Net usage and growth begins to emerge. The following sections explore some of this data.

The Growth of the Net

As mentioned in previous sections, the growth on the Internet and the Web has been tremendous. Here are some charts and graphs to give you a visual idea of the growth rate.

Figure 3.1 shows the number of host computers on the Internet. This is an important statistic, because each host computer usually houses many people. The more hosts on the Net, the more people and data are on the Net.

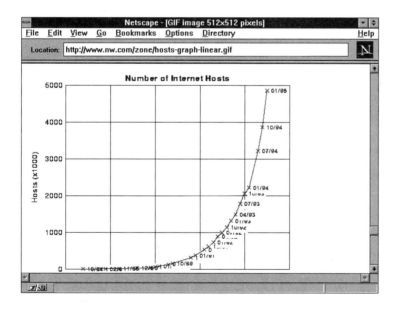

Fig. 3.1
A graph showing the number of new hosts (servers) that have appeared on the Internet can be useful in determining growth of the Net (**http://www.nw.com/zone/hosts-graph-linear.gif**).

Figure 3.2 shows the differences between Gopher and the WWW in terms of recent growth. It's a dramatic indication of just how popular the WWW really is. Before the WWW, Gopher was the most popular browser. While Gopher use remains popular, its use is not climbing nearly as quickly as that of the WWW.

Fig. 3.2

The traffic on Gopher is compared to traffic on the WWW over the past two years (**http://www.cc. gatech.edu/ gvu/stats/NSF/ Packet_3_Col.GIF**).

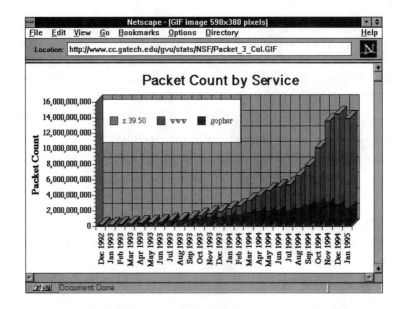

Figure 3.3 shows the current makeup of the Internet population. While educational users used to make up the primary population on the Internet, you can now see that professional users are in the majority. This reflects the sudden surge of new professional users.

Fig. 3.3

Users of the Net have been divided up by careers (**http://www. mroy.fi/ dec94.htm**).

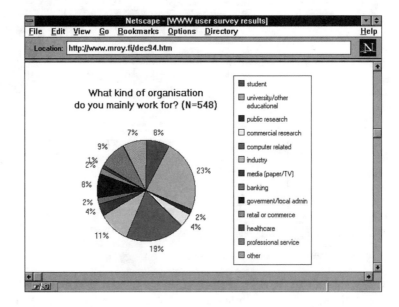

Figure 3.4 is important because it helps you plan your use of graphics in your Web pages. This chart shows the number of users of the different types of browsers. You can easily see that text browser usage such as Lynx amounts to only a small fraction of the total usage audience, while new commercial browsers such as Netscape maintain a large market hold.

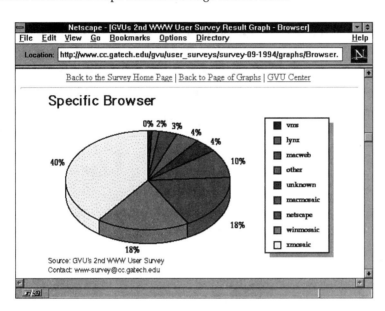

Fig. 3.4
The top 10 WWW browsers currently used by the Internet popula-tion shows that Mosaic and Netscape are the two most popular (**http:// www.cc.g atech.edu/gvu/ user_surveys/ survey-09-1994/ graphs/ Browser.html**).

People on the Net

When you go cruising on the Internet, you see a lot of business and organiza-tional names that are familiar to you. With a few notable exceptions, this isn't really the case with individuals on the Web.

Usually, businesses or organizations put up pages that provide information about board members, founders, or employees. For instance, information about the winner of the Nobel Prize for Literature 1994, Kenzaburo Oe, is provided by the Swedish Academy that presents the Nobel prizes:

http://logos.svenska.gu.se/academy.html

Rock stars have fans that spend an extremely large chunk of time creating WWW sites promoting singers' music in "unofficial" home pages, while other famous people (such as movie stars and sports celebrities) are noticeably ab-sent. These sites tend to be created by students who have the time to do a lot of programming they don't get paid for. While it is only speculation, people think this has to do with the personal tastes of the programmers who are creating these pages—they would rather spend their time creating these virtual shrines for musicians and rock bands rather than movie stars or sports celebrities.

Of course, this doesn't really hold true in the computer field. Computer experts from Jaron Lanier

http://www.well.com/Community/Jaron.Lanier/index.html

to Mitch Kapor

http://www.kei.com/homepages/mkapor/

have WWW pages that give information ranging from philosophy to their favorite sites on the Internet.

Whether you love 'em or hate 'em, you'll want to check out the home pages for Hillary Rodham Clinton

http://www.whitehouse.gov/White_House/EOP/First_Lady/ html/HILLARY_Home.html

and Tipper Gore

http://www.whitehouse.gov/White_House/EOP/VP_Wife/ html/TIPPER_Home.html

provided by the White House.

Fig. 3.5
Hillary Rodham
Clinton's home
page is provided
by the White
House.

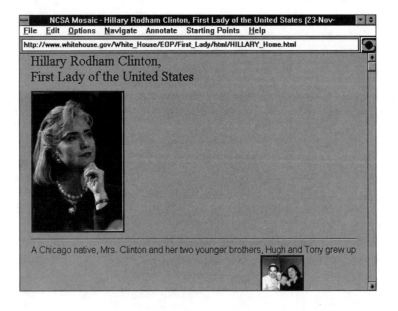

Senator Ted Kennedy (D-MA) even has a home page:

> **http://www.ai.mit.edu/projects/iiip/Kennedy/**
> **homepage.html**

Note

Notice how the address relates to the name of the company or person at that address. You can remember addresses easily when you don't have your own personal hotlist available.

Initials or part of a name might be in the address. Colleges often end the server name with .edu. Businesses often have .com or .net. Government offices usually end with .gov.

URLs are usually easier to remember than telephone numbers. Often you can guess at a company's URL and be correct.

▶ See "Domain Names," p. 159

Businesses on the Net

Commercial sites are currently the fastest-growing group on the Web. You can find them in individual storefronts or malls, selling everything from pecans to modems and offering professional services from architecture to legal.

Federal Express (**http://fedex.com/**) and Bank of America (**http://www.bankamerica.com/**) both have Web pages.

Of course, computer companies have a big presence on the Web. Here is a list of just a few:

Sun Microsystems	**http://www.sun.com/**
Digital Equipment Corp.	**http://www.dec.com/info.html**
Hewlett Packard	**http://www.hp.com/home.html**
Apple Computers	**http://www.apple.com/**
IBM	**http://www.ibm.com/**
Silicon Graphics Inc.	**http://www.sgi.com/**

Telecommunications companies are also well-represented on the Net. They provide such things as product and service information, executive profiles, corporate reports, and promotional information.

AT&T (**http://att.net/800/index.html.2**) has obviously found the Net to be a cost-effective way to disseminate information because it provides an HTML document containing a search index to its 800 numbers by category or alphabetically.

Other telecommunications companies represented on the Web include the following:

Ameritech	**http://www.aads.net/**
Bell Atlantic	**http://www.ba.com/**
Pacific Bell	**http://www.pacbell.com/**
Sprint	**http://www.sprintlink.net/**

And it's not only American companies. Overseas, the companies (and in some places, government agencies) that handle telecommunication services also have Web pages to handle customer support and service:

Swiss PTT Telcom	**http://gdv015.vptt.ch/**
Telecom Finland	**http://www.tele.fi/**
Telecom Australia Network Systems	**http://www.tansu.com.au/**

Other forms of communications such as newspapers, radio, television, and magazines all are represented on the Web. Some publications are Internet-only, and some are special versions (usually condensed) for the Net. *The News & Observer* from North Carolina has a special version of its publication called *The Nando Times* (**http://www.nando.net/newsroom/nt/ nando.html**).

In Wyoming, *The Casper Star-Tribune* has an Internet newspaper called *trib.com* (**http://www.trib.com/trib_home.html**). *The San Francisco Examiner*'s Internet publication is called *Electric Examiner* (**http://sfgate. com/examiner**). There are also foreign online newspapers like Russia's *St. Petersburg Press* (**http://www.spb.su/sppress/index.html**).

Publishers like Macmillian (**http://www.mcp.com/**) use the Web to promote and sell their books. The ABC affliate in Indianapolis, WRTV (**http:// www.iquest.net/wrtv6/**), uses the Web to provide services and information about its newscasters.

Magazines from *Mother Jones* (**http://mojones.com/motherjones.html**) to a humor magazine put out by the Evanston Township High School in Illinois called *Your MoM* (**http://www.cc.columbia.edu/~emj5/your mom/ymhome.html**) are also online.

Companies known for their catalog sales like JC Penney (**http://www. shopping2000.com/shopping2000/jcp/**) and Marshall Fields (**http:// www.shopping2000.com/shopping2000/fields/**) have Web pages that allow catalog shopping online.

Even the Home Shopping Network has its own Internet Shopping Network, ISN (**http://shop.internet.net/**), although at this time they are only selling computer-related products.

Real estate is advertised through the following sites:

Bay Net Real Estate	**http://www.baynet.com/re.html**
The Real Estate Alternative	**http://quiknet.com/alcarr.html**
The Real Estate Network	**http://www.csi.nb.ca/celerity/**

Maybe you think it's only big companies that are on the Web, but that's not the case. Small companies all around the world are finding the Internet to be a way that they can be on a more equal footing when advertising their products and services. Companies like The Sandal Dude (**http:// mmink.cts.com/mmink/kiosks/sandals/ropesandals.html** and EARRINGS, by Lisa! (**http://mmink.ct.com/mmink/kiosks/earrings/ earrings.html**) are among the many small businesses attracted to the low-cost advertising possibilities offered on the Web. Using comparable traditional advertising methods, these businesses would have to spend tens of thousands of dollars to reach the same size advertising audience that the Web provides.

Some companies decide to have their WWW site stand alone; others want to place their companies in virtual or cybermalls. If the mall is well-maintained with lots of people coming into it, then a mall can be a good place to put a storefront. Malls on the World Wide Web include the following:

Shopping IN	**http://www.onramp.net/ shopping_in/**
PICnet	**http://www.pic.net/**
Milwaukee Marketplace	**http://www.mixcom.com/**
Commerce Net	**http://www.commerce.net/**

An Introduction

Finally, if you get hungry while cruising on the Web, check out the following sites:

Smithfield Farms of Virginia	**http://www.shopkeeper.com/ shops/Smithfield_Farms/**
Peterbrooke Chocolatiers	**http://www.jkcg.com/ Webmaster/Peterbrooke/ index.html**
Tastes Unlimited	**http://ip.net/shops/ Taste_Unlimited-Savory_Sauces/**
McArthur's American Cornucopia	**http:catalog.florida.com/ mcarthur.htm**
The Fine Food Emporium	**http://www.food.emporium.com/ ~finefood/prd4.html**

Institutions on the Net

Institutions are finding that the Internet is a great way to disseminate and collect information. Everyone from technical societies, such as the Association of Computing Machinery and the Internet Society, to colleges and universities, to civic groups such as Amnesty International and Greenpeace, have Web pages and other forms of Internet communications to better serve their members and the public.

Museums provide a wide range of projects and services on the Web, including online art shows. Art galleries of all sizes are finding that the Web is a good way to promote themselves.

Art galleries and museums on the Web include the following:

The WebMuseum	**http://www.oirucf.edu/louvre/**
The Andy Warhol Museum	**http://fridge.antaire.com/ warhol/**
911 Gallery	**http://www.iquest.net/911/ iq_911.html**
Holmes Fine Art Gallery	**http://art.net/TheGallery/ Holmes/AEA/Holmes.html**

| Shelburne Museum (Vermont) | **http://cybermalls.com/cymont/ shelmus/** |
| Yale University Art Gallery | **http://www.cis.yale.edu/ yuag.yuag.html** |

Federal governments all over the world have mandated that key government information be made available to its citizens over the Internet. Among them are Costa Rica (**http://www.ucr.ac.cr/ns.cr**) and Canada (**http://www. cs.ubc.ca/opengov/**). Figure 3.6 shows the Canadian home page.

Fig. 3.6
This WWW page shows the Canadian Open Gov site (**http:// www.cs.ubc.ca/ opengov**).

The European Economic Community (EEC) provides information about its member countries concerning the European electronic information market (**http://s700.uminho.pt/ec.html**).

At least one government agency, NASA's Marshall Space Flight Center (**http://procure.msfc.nasa.gov**), provides information concerning procurement requests over the Web.

Various cities and states are beating the federal government to the punch:

| Texas | **http://info.texas.gov/tih.html** |
| North Carolina | **http://www.sips.state.nc.us/ nchome.html** |

Cambridge, Mass.	**http://www.ai.mit.edu/projects/iiip/ Cambridge/hompage.html**
Staunton, Va.	**http://www.elpress.com/Staunton**
Palo Alto, Calif.	**http://www.city.palo-alto.ca.us/ home.html**

◀ See "IRC," p. 46 Universities are well-connected to the Internet and the Web. The administrative departments use it in the same capacities that businesses do. Other departments use it to promote specific programs and to provide information. Students can use a special chat network like IRC to contact new friends. At many colleges, students have personal home pages that contain their artwork or writing, resumes and job requests, photographs, and their favorite recipes.

▶ See "Looking for Existing Information," p. 206 Here is a partial list of the many colleges and universities around the world that are on the Web:

Houston Community College	**http://www.hccs.cc.tx.us/**
Rice University	**http://www.rice..edu/**
University of Costa Rica	**http://www.ucr.ac.cr/**
Howard University	**http://www.howard.edu/**
University of Nevada at Las Vegas	**http://www.unlv.edu/**
Chinese University of Hong Kong	**http://www.cuhk.hk/**
Boston University	**http://www.bu.edu/**

The extremely large presence of the Web at institutions of higher learning should be especially significant to those businesses targeting college-educated persons for their customer base.

Students who have become accustomed to using the Web in their everyday lives at school will come home and dust off those PCs and Macintoshes that were used only for games and use it to cruise the Web.

This growing home use of the Internet and WWW is important for businesses that rely heavily on television advertising. The time spent on the Web comes from a limited pool of free time. If a person is on the Web, he or she is not doing something else, and that something else is most likely watching television. The Web will not impact how much time a person spends engaged in sporting activities or other recreational activities outside the house as much as it is going to impact television.

Now instead of clicking through an endless maze of channels, you can go hang out on the Internet.

Where the Users Are

Users are found all around the world. Figure 3.7 shows where Internet sites are concentrated throughout the world. Of course, because of the rapid growth of the Internet, by the time this book is printed and in your hands, this chart may look quite different. The biggest changes will be found in Europe and developing nations as they race to give their citizens the benefits afforded by the Internet.

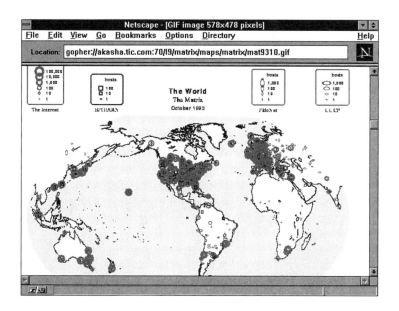

Fig. 3.7
This chart shows the geographical density of Internet users and sites (**gopher://akasha.tic.com:70/I9/matrix/maps/matrix/mat9310.gif**).

More than 91 countries have Internet access. While some of these countries only have simple e-mail feeds, a surprising number of them are getting full Internet capabilities.

> **Note**
>
> It is not surprising, however, that the United States leads the pack for Internet accessibility. Not only was the Internet developed here, but from early on, the telecommunication system needed to handle the Internet was in place and accessible by U.S. citizens. Canada, Australia, Japan, France, Germany, and England are among the nations with well-developed Internet access (although not U.S. standards).
>
> Many countries are developing their access quickly and already have many sites online. These countries include Austria, Belgium, Brazil, Costa Rica, the Czech Republic, Finland, Ireland, Israel, Italy, South Korea, the Netherlands, New Zealand, Norway, Poland, Russia, Singapore, South Africa, Spain, Sweden, Switzerland, and Taiwan.

Using the Net as an Information Resource

Some companies limit interaction with the Net to just that—information gathering. For this reason, it is a valuable tool. This section explores some of these uses.

Research and the Net

As you may have figured out from the wide variety of WWW sites already mentioned, there is a plethora of information on the Internet. No matter what your topic is, you can find information on it somewhere on the Web. If you can't find it at the Library of Congress's WWW site (**http://lcweb.loc.gov/homepage/lchp.html**), maybe you can find it at the U.S. Government's Consumer Information Center (**http://www.gsa.gov/staff/pa/cic/cic.html**) in Pueblo, Colo.

Maybe the information you want is available in the latest World Fact Book issued by the CIA; you can access it at their WWW site (**http://www.ic.gov/**).

Nearly every department of the federal government churns out reams of information each day. Some of the information can be accessed as WWW pages; the rest of it is still accessible throughout the Web, but as FTP or Gopher documents. These other forms of Internet documentation contain valuable information you need, but not with all the nice pictures of WWW.

As mentioned in the Introduction, you can get updates from the stock market through a site that offers quotes (although they are on a 15-minute delay) on a variety of stocks (**http://www.secapl.com/cgi-bin/qsx/**). It's not exactly like having a ticker tape in your office, but it is better than waiting for the evening paper.

The voting records of U.S. Congress members are recorded and evaluated by the League of Conservation Voters (**http://www.econet.apc.org/lcv/scorecard.html**).

If you are an antique dealer or owner of a doll store, you might need to check out the Barbie Web page (**http://deeptht.armory.com/~zenugirl/barbie.html**) to find out the latest prices for this collectible doll.

As you can see, there's all sorts of information on the World Wide Web. You may be wondering how to find all these URLs if you're not reading them from a book like this one. Mechanisms exist for searching the vast—and sometimes unmapped—highways of the Internet. The CUSI searcher and keyword searches are very powerful. Most of these searchers are free, and you can download them over the Internet.

Also, you will find the most up-to-date URLs on the Web. With new sites being added so quickly, there is always new data.

▶ See "Looking for Existing Information on the Net," p. 206

Sometimes the information you want is so new or so esoteric that it only exists in the head of an expert. The Internet is brimming with authorities on nearly every topic. Hopping into an IRC or NetNews group puts you in touch with specialists from every area of society.

The Internet is one of the best research tools around. This one source is a conduit to the world's storehouse of knowledge. If your business is in the information research arena, the Internet is a must for you.

▶ See "Asking the Experts," p. 220

Providing Information on the Net

The primary reason the Internet was created was to provide information. If you have a need to get information out to the general public or to specific people or groups, the Internet is your medium.

The information you currently give out about your company in such places as the Yellow Pages can easily be given out in Web pages. You can also provide information that wouldn't fit into an ad—for example, a speech that you gave to the Lion's Club about the civic obligations of small businesses. Information like this increases the public's awareness of you and your company in a positive way.

An Introduction

Tip
In a similar fashion, you can support your users by providing hints and frequently asked questions. Some companies host forums online for their users.

Most companies, from restaurants to legal firms, could benefit in freeing up personnel from the tedious task of giving out standard information on the telephone. Along with this, written directions and/or a map are much more likely than a voice message conversation (which both must be transcribed or remembered by users) to lead your potential client to your doorstep. Likewise, providing your product information and online price guides can make comparison shopping easy for your customers.

If you are in the information business itself, you can often sell the content on a per-access basis. For example, credit card processing, credit checks, research reports, Dun & Bradstreet reports, and stock reports are all types of information which users do not expect for free. These are perfect mechanisms for making money off the Internet. Because the delivery of the data can be automated, you are making money with little overhead.

Not only can you guarantee the accuracy of the information presented, but you can also control the tone. Users accessing your information will never be greeted by a harried employee who really doesn't have the time to explain how to get to your business. Also, your users will never be greeted by a receptionist who greets them with, "Will you hold please?"

All in all, providing information on the Internet is an extremely good way to save money and increase your user base.

Using the Net as an Advertising Resource

▶ See "How To Advertise on the Net," p. 227

Advertising has one goal—reaching the most people for the least amount of money. The Internet makes a great advertising resource, because it allows you to reach an increasingly large market group for a relatively low cost. And not only that, the advertising can be as exciting and innovative as anything you see on television today. It can even go one step further by providing a level of interaction with the user that television does not provide.

Using the Net To Advertise Your Product

You can use the Internet to advertise your product by offering pictures and descriptions of your product for users to see.

Since space on the Internet is inexpensive, you can offer lots of information that may be impossible to offer using any other method—testimonials, suggestions of use, other related products, discussions, future direction, company backgrounds, and more. Your possibilities are limitless.

Since most provider sites also offer statistics of your page's access, you have ample listings of who is accessing your page and from where. Listings usually consist of the domain name, time of day, and where the user visited. The listing may also include the user's e-mail address.

Using the Net To Advertise Other Products

The previous section suggested advertising your own products. However, there is and will continue to be a demand for companies providing unique solutions on the WWW.

Many companies have already been set up to do nothing more than help other companies advertise their products. These service bureaus may provide home page authoring, or may even run storefronts for companies to advertise in.

This is a perfect opportunity if you are already in or looking to be in the promotions or advertising industry. Many advertising agencies are already finding that clients are coming to them for WWW solutions, alongside of their traditional advertising. Many advertising companies may want to align with WWW service bureaus or develop in-house bureaus to address this growing market.

Advertising other people's products for them can even be automated, so that people can update it themselves. These types of systems make money with little effort, once they are put into place.

▶ See "Instant Products," p. 319

Using the Net To Sell and Provide Services

Besides the obvious use of services on the Net, such as Internet access, WWW page authoring, and WWW advertising and marketing, you can put many other services on the Net.

Traditional services, like customer support, can benefit from the Internet, because they allow users to access them interactively and online. This can be a great benefit to order entry and tracking, just to name two areas.

Also, new services that address the many capabilities the Internet has introduced are being created on a daily basis. Services of this type exist only because the Internet exists and has created the need.

These sections explore different types of indirectly related WWW services.

What Type of Services Work Well on the Net

You can advertise any service on the Web, but not all are provided on the Web. You cannot give a massage or cut hair over the Web. However, you can certainly use the Internet to help schedule a massage or haircut appointment. Local users in your town could access your site and view a calendar which shows your availability. They would be allowed to block out their desired time. Since it's all electronic, your schedule is updated instantaneously. Any service that needs or dispenses information in any form can benefit from the Internet.

Market research firms are a natural for the Net. So are research firms. Credit bureaus, lawyers, accountants, private detectives, missing persons, state agencies, insurance companies, babysitters and teachers are all examples of service providers who can use the Internet for scheduling, dispensing, or advertising their services.

Combining Traditional Services with Net Services

If you are currently a service provider, you can augment your service with the Net.

By providing your users with online order tracking and online order entry, you can alleviate many of your phone interruptions. Likewise, the Net offers great advantages for dispensing your service, provided you are information-oriented.

You also can use the Net to provide new capabilities that you didn't have before. Special databases that allow users to search your information by topic, date, or other criteria can make your catalogs and other company information much more accessible to potential customers.

All of this can be offered to your users for free or for a cost, depending on how you want to design and build your online service.

Using the Net To Sell Your Products

Not only can you advertise your products over the WWW, but you can take orders and handle cash transactions all over the World Wide Web. You can handle the actual sales transaction the way you always have by providing a phone number or mailing address for Web surfers to call or write to place their orders.

A slightly more sophisticated method is to allow ordering by e-mail. This can be cumbersome, however, because the shopper has to access the e-mail account to order.

The real power in the Web is through the use of interactive forms, enabling shoppers to purchase items immediately. No sales are lost to shoppers who forget to write or call in later, or who just simply lose interest. All needed information (from the mailing addresses to credit card numbers) can be entered by the user interactively. It can then be processed immediately or compiled in a list to be processed by you when you want. A message can even be sent back to shoppers letting them know the order was received and when to expect it.

▶ See "Taking Orders by Interactive Forms," p. 258

▶ See "Credit Card Transactions," p. 275

▶ See "Fully Integrated WWW Systems," p. 298

Selling Your Product on the Net

There are basically three different ways you can go about selling your products on the Net:

■ You can sell from your own storefront.

■ You can join a commercial mall.

■ You can do both.

> **Note**
>
> Because malls are run by WWW providers and consultants, many of them offer services that handle some of the more technical details of selling your product.

Photographs of your products can be scanned into pictures and integrated with text descriptions. Stores with thousands of products have searchable databases, allowing users to browse items by description. Order tracking information can be provided interactively and lets users know the status of their orders at any moment.

Demographics about users and their purchasing patterns can be collected by analyzing the usage logs for your pages and asking the users questions with online polls.

Selling Other Products on the Net

Maybe you are a salesperson with no products to sell. You could provide a service to sell other companies products on the Web. Do this by setting up a virtual mall or storefront.

This requires you to get your own Internet access and then sell your space to other people who want to advertise. You would set them up in your own storefront and charge them for your services.

▶ See "Consultants versus Net Service Bureaus," p. 139

If you do not want to do all the work yourself, many WWW service bureaus actually do the work involved in posting and hosting the page, allowing you to be an independent salesperson for commission.

Another way to work with a service bureau is to serve as the middle man. You are charged a flat fee for services from the bureau that you pass on to your client, but you receive payment for the projects you manage. This arrangement allows you to be independent of the bureaus and can help you recoup your investment when providing advice and direction to your client.

Using the Net as a Support Resource

Many companies currently offer telephone support lines. If their product is popular, so is their support line. The efforts that some companies go through to placate their customers who have to wait on hold are quite amusing, not to mention expensive.

> **Note**
>
> For example, Microsoft currently employs a deejay that plays music and gives information concerning the number of people waiting for service and how long they've been waiting.

Support personnel have discovered an interesting phenomenon: as customers verbalize their problems, they often end up solving their problems themselves. The same thing happens quite often when customers type their questions: they answer their questions as they lay them out on-screen and end up not having to send their questions at all. In this way, customer support handled via e-mail can cut down the time that customer support has to waste with clients who haven't thoroughly thought out their question.

Also, using e-mail to handle customer support allows your personnel to better budget their time and frees them from being tied to a ringing telephone.

◀ See "Jargon," p. 47

A common support resource is the FAQ (Frequently Asked Questions) list. You can put the answers to those questions that the receptionist or whoever has to repeatedly answer (and you know for every business there are these types of questions) in a simple and attractive format for users to peruse at their leisure.

Combining Traditional Support Service with the Net

Traditional support services can be easily integrated with the Net. Because support departments tend to have to have good internal communications, having internal Internet resources which mimic external ones can offer significant efficiency boosts.

For example, if users can access a FAQ page online, they may find their solution without bothering your department. However, if a new question is asked, your personnel handles the question and then adds it to the list. The result is less support over time, with an answer list that grows dynamically and requires no printing resources.

Because WWW sessions can be customized for each user, users can easily open multiple support sessions with your staff and use interactive dialogs via the computer to trade information. For example, a session could be opened where the user asks a basic question. After an hour, the user checks back and sees a reply asking for some additional specific information. The user provides the information in a new message and submits it. After the next meeting, the user again checks the queue and sees the answer.

> **Note**
>
> This instantaneous/non-instantaneous nature of the Internet makes it a perfect solution for support. This can greatly reduce 1-800 costs and other support costs in general.

Remote Diagnostics and the Net

The Net can be used in a rather novel way for support. Keeping in mind that any computer on the Internet can be talked to by your computer, you can actually log onto a remote computer that may be having a problem. This allows you to look at files and solve these problems without ever having to go to the client's home or place of business (or wherever the computer is housed).

You might even carry this one step further by designing some remote diagnostics capabilities into any software you might market. This would allow your users to show you problems visually, by transmitting screen snapshots as files over the Internet in real time.

Likewise, kiosks and other remote terminals can benefit from remote hookup to the Internet. Such devices can be serviced and updated remotely at any time day or night. This greatly reduces the downtime and support requirements of remote devices.

Using the Net for Market Research

You already know that you can collect demographics on the Internet. But you also can use the Net for the sole purpose of conducting market research. Opinion polls and demographics can be collected from just about anybody from anywhere.

Gathering Opinion via the Net

Opinions can be gathered from just about anything. You can use an interactive form to gather information about market awareness and degree of satisfaction. You could even make a whole business out of gathering opinion data for other companies, and collecting and collating the results.

Many online opinion polls provide real-time statistics to the user. These systems are tied to programs which analyze the user's submission in real time, integrating it with a database of user responses and statistics. These systems provide results to users as soon as they submit their entry.

Demographics examine regional interest. By looking at the logs of access, you can determine which parts of the Internet community were most interested in your poll. This information is very useful in targeting audiences.

Trying Out New Ideas on the Net

The Web is a great place to try out new ideas, because you can implement your ideas for a relatively low cost. It's also good because you can get feedback right away. Through the use of interactive forms, you can gather how well people like your idea.

On the Web, you can design a product or service, gather information on customers' preferences, and perform any necessary redesigns in a much shorter time period than with traditional marketing methods. It will allow you to deliver a better product or service to the public faster than your competition. While they're still going through phone or mail surveys, you're selling the products and services the public wants. This high-speed prototyping allows people to be daring and try out new ideas frequently; it also makes the Internet an interesting place to be.

Using the Net Inside Your Business

For the smart company or business, using the Internet will also change the way the company interacts within itself. Businesses can use the Web to improve communications, decrease office expenditures, and reduce employee expenses by improving efficiency and cutting overhead.

Systems can be kept internal, so that there is no access from outside the business. Systems also can be externalized with portions of the system accessible from the outside. These types of systems, when coupled with support and sales departments, can greatly enhance a company's productivity.

Improving Communications

Telephones are a great way for your employees to communicate with one another, that is, until it comes time for them to discuss visual information, such as an ad layout or a blueprint. Then the lines of communication break down. Using the Web to provide virtual work groups for employees can increase productivity and decrease employee stress.

Conference rooms and other work group systems can provide the ability for your employees to share ideas, pictures, and sound. Projects can be coordinated and meetings can be planned without employees having to be rounded up. Users can join conferences from remote locations around the world.

▶ See "The Unbelievable World of Instant Products," p. 319

Interactive approval sessions can also allow mark-up and critique of projects and plans. Days are often shaved off schedules since users can interact when it is convenient for them.

Paper-Free Environments

In addition to cutting down the amount of paper you use for catalogs and brochures, you also can reduce the amount of paper you use inside your business. Memos, drafts of reports, and employee handbooks all can be created on your computer and distributed to your employees through the Web. Since you probably won't be making this kind of information public, you can create these on limited access work groups.

Memos can be designed on your computer and then sent to the appropriate personnel. If you have the occasion to send sensitive or secret information, electronic memos can cut down on information being accessed by someone else who just happens to read a memo laying on someone's desk. It will also reduce the amount of shredding your company does.

Report drafts can be circulated virtually via electronic mediums, instead of on paper. This cuts down on paper and personnel costs associated with photocopying and distribution.

◀ See "Jargon,"
p. 47

Likewise, employee manuals and company policies can be stored online for authorized employees to access. Never again will employees tell you they didn't know a company policy because they lost their employee handbook. With an online handbook in place, all you have to tell a new employee is, "RTM."

Remote Employees

Many companies are finding thatit saves money for employees to work off-site. It is already common for computer programmers to work at home and "tele-commute" through their modems. The business can save on overhead costs on such items as electricity and toilet paper. Usually the employee is required to show up at the office for weekly meetings, although the meetings could be held over the Internet.

The remote employee can accomplish the following:

- Receive instructions

- Turn in assignments

- Give reports

- File paperwork

Some positions that could easily be performed remotely include the following:

- Technical writers

- Some sales positions

- Graphic artists

- Telemarketing

- Collections

- Data entry

▶ See "How the
Future Net Will
Look," p. 499

To ensure productivity while the employee is at home, you may want to set up some kind of quota to ensure that the employee is really working. Many workers find that they can get a lot more work done at home away from ringing phones and water cooler politics.

> **Note**
>
> Employees who work well at home are those who are self-motivated, work well alone, and follow instructions.
>
> Don't let any employees who are obviously having problems working at home continue in the hope that they will hit their stride. Either they are self-disciplined enough to do it or not. Allowing the situation to continue will only mean that you will lose money.

Another type of remote employee is a consultant or contractor. Instead of hiring a new employee, you can hire consultants for whom you don't have to pay social security and related employment taxes. If the person supplies his or her own equipment and sets a personal work schedule, then that employee meets the basic guidelines for contract employment. Check with your accountant for complete details on hiring contract employees.

Benefits Common To All Businesses on the Net

While each industry can find its own specific uses and capabilities on the Net, the Net offers many capabilities to all users. There are certain advantages like creating market awareness and generating leads that everyone on the Net will want to make use of.

Generating Leads and Mailing Lists

Everyone who accesses your WWW site is a potential lead and can be added to your mailing list. The problem is getting contact information, such as addresses, telephone numbers, and e-mail addresses from these users. Currently, there's no approach to glean this information about the user off the Internet.

Basically you need to get the user to fill out a form that lists all the information you want. Name, mailing address, and/or e-mail address are the pieces of information you might need. You can do a regular mailing or an e-mailing.

> **Caution**
>
> Do not do a mass e-mailing to a "cold" audience, that is, an audience that hasn't requested information or contact from you. Such behavior will get you kicked off the Internet—no ifs, ands, or buts.

You may want to collect other demographic information to coordinate your marketing and advertising efforts. Again, you have to request this information from the user, and he or she has to voluntarily fill in the information.

One way to do this is to offer a service that people want to access. However, to access this service, a user would have to provide you with information. Any service you think people would want enough to spend a few minutes filling out a form can be offered. Depending on your business, you might try anything from gardening tips or travel hints to stock market quotes. Another good draw might be a contest that is open to anyone who fills out your form.

An example is a volunteer registration form. The user doesn't have to fill out the form, but you call upon the user to be a good Internet citizen and fill it out so you can better serve that person.

A volunteer registration form is a good way to get the information you need, because quite often users skip the registration on the way into your site and then access your pages. But if they liked your site, they might reconsider and fill out your form before they leave. It's a good way to get information from people who like your product or service. However, if you want information from people who didn't like what they saw, you should offer a simple comment form that allows users offer their comments while maintaining their anonymity if they want.

Try to stick to questions that you yourself would want to answer. If you wouldn't want to answer the question, chances are neither will your users.

Using the Net To Save Money

The cost for memos, catalogs, and brochures can really add up, but when you talk about these paper items, you're also talking about inks that can be hazardous to the environment.

You may hear talk of the added electricity costs to run the computers, but it is really minimal when compared to the electricity it takes to produce the paper, manufacture the inks, and print the actual catalog, magazine, or other material. And besides, at the very least, you'd have to run a few computers for the typesetting, if not the graphics as well.

Additionally, traditional brochures often involve expensive layout costs. Your computer will most likely have the desktop publishing capabilities to do the graphics you need for your WWW site. And any capabilities that you might be lacking in are available, usually free, via the Internet.

If you still feel more comfortable with a professional, go ahead and spend your money. But really anyone with a few tips can come up with an eye-catching graphic and layout that accomplishes the feel you want.

If you have doubts about your artistic abilities, you can still save money by using one of the many companies that provide stock images. Although a single image can cost more than $200 with these companies, they are still cheaper than advertising firms (you should keep in mind, however, that your image will not be unique). You also can use images from one of the many non-copyrighted and public domain clip-art files that are available. You can usually find ads for these products in magazines targeting computer graphics, desktop publishing, and occasionally, Internet magazines.

Traveling costs can be cut by having meetings over the Internet. No need to travel three hours for a one-hour meeting. Do it over the Internet with special work groups.

You can save in-town traveling costs if you have staff that frequently uses the library. Currently the Internet won't replace a library, but acquiring references can be done at the office or at the home office and then accessed at the library.

Of course, there are the personnel savings, too. Use of the Internet should make your sales and marketing staff more productive so fewer people can do more work. The Internet can also cut down on your research staff. If used correctly for scheduling, meetings and the like, the Net can cut down on middle management by improving overall office communications and performance.

The Internet can also save your company money in the areas of order filling and shipping. If you process orders manually, you can have the ordered products printed up on a fill list and have mailing labels generated. More sophisticated systems exist that can cut cost and increase productivity even further.

▶ See "Taking Orders by Interactive Forms," p. 258

Note

How much of the Internet you decide to integrate into your business is entirely up to you. Just because you can do something, like customer support via e-mail or online ordering, doesn't mean you have to use it, especially if it doesn't fit your needs or style.

For instance, a chocolate company who has always focused on its "homemade goodness" may not want to replace its hand-addressed packages with computer printed labels.

Enhancing Market Awareness

You'll be surprised by the feedback you get on your WWW site. In some ways, navigating the Web is like using a TV remote control. People go to sites, glean the interesting bits, and move on. People surfing the Internet are constantly looking for something new. Even unnamed files are accessed just to see what's in them.

▶ See "Etiquette in Informational Postings," p. 178

You want to make sure that market awareness is positive. No reputation is better than a bad reputation, at least on the Web. If you have no reputation at all, the naturally curious Internet community will at least check you out. If you have a bad reputation, you will be shunned. And to be shunned by 35 million people is to be shunned indeed.

Of course, the key to good market awareness is the same as it would be in more traditional markets—live up to what you promise.

From Here...

If you are interested in other people, companies, or institutions that are on the Web, do a Web search on the terms "business" or "commercial." It should provide you with enough material for several days of Net cruising.

The next chapters give more detail on some of the topics touched on in this chapter:

- Chapter 6, "Placing a Business on the Web," shows you how to begin to place your business.

- Chapter 10, "Advertising on the Net," gives detailed descriptions of how to go about using the Net to advertise.

- Chapter 11, "Order Taking and the Net," teaches you the basics of taking orders over the WWW.

- Chapter 12, "Methods for Collecting Cash," presents the options available for accepting money.

- Chapter 13, "Order Filling and Tracking," helps you understand how to implement an order fulfillment system.

- Chapter 14, "Subscription Services, Virtual Malls, and Instant Products," shows you how to create self-maintaining pay systems.

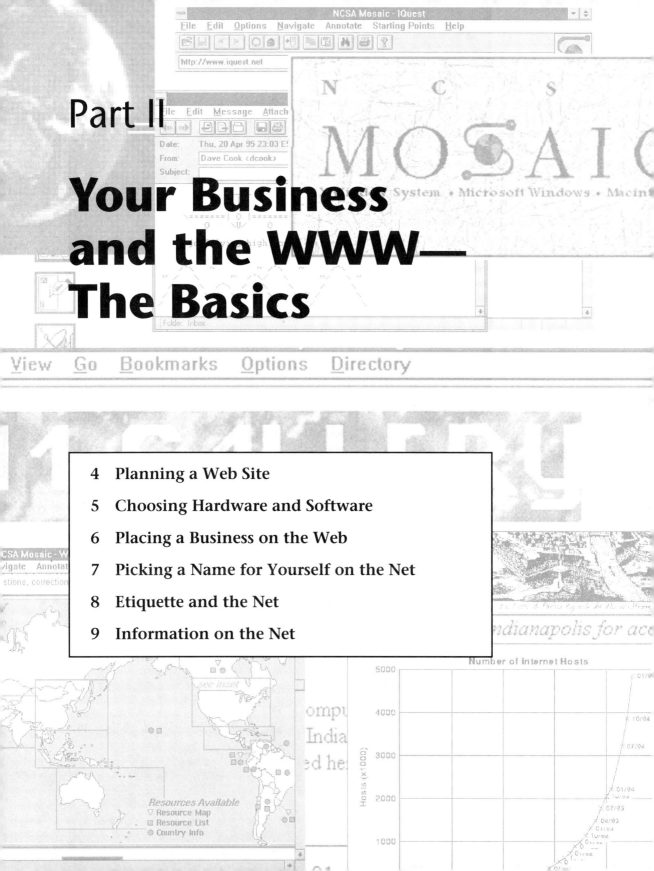

Part II

Your Business and the WWW— The Basics

NCSA Mosaic - IQuest

File Edit Options Navigate Annotate Starting Points Help

http://www.iquest.net

File Edit Message Attach

Date: Thu, 20 Apr 95 23:03 E
From: Dave Cook <dcook>
Subject:

jon@flying.high.com

Folder: Inbox

N C S
MOSAIC
X Window System • Microsoft Windows • Macir

View   Go   Bookmarks   Options   Directory

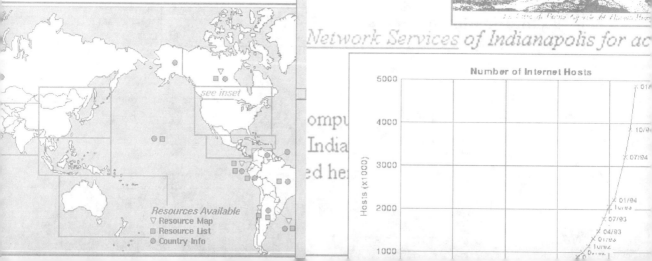

1 GALLERY

NCSA Mosaic - Worldwide WWW Information

avigate Annotate Starting Points Help

estions, corrections or additions.

see inset

Resources Available
▽ Resource Map
■ Resource List
● Country Info

Network Services of Indianapolis for ac

ompu
India
d he

Number of Internet Hosts

5000

4000

3000

2000

1000

Hosts (x1000)

Chapter 4

Planning a Web Site

Before actually designing your WWW site, you should consider how much of the technology you want to use and in what areas of your company. Who will your site be geared to? You can use it to service current customers and draw in new customers. Or, you can use it in-house to help with management tasks, scheduling, and productions. What will work best for your business?

You also need to determine who will do the work of creating the HTML programs for your WWW site. If you are adding computers to your business, you will need a system administrator who will manage the computer(s), handle security, and update software and/or hardware. Can this be accomplished with your current staff, or will you need to hire someone? And if you do decide to hire someone, where do you find them and how do you make sure you get a good employee?

Answering these questions and the others presented in this chapter—before you start making decisions and spending money—will help ensure that you get the best possible WWW site.

In this chapter, you learn

- How to make the decision to use the WWW

- How to deal with new technologies

- How much you can do yourself

- How to plan your WWW business

Making the Decision

If you are scared about getting on the Web because you think you'll find your company alone in uncharted territory, don't worry. You'll find lots of company and support along the way.

If you are excited about this decision, you should be, because you'll be joining an international society that is the future for commerce, education, and recreation.

Waiting for Better Technology

Many people might tell you to wait, because later on the Internet and its related technologies will be cheaper, easier, and faster. And they are right; in the future it will be cheaper, easier, and faster. But how long should you wait?

If Henry Ford had waited to sell his cars until airbags and anti-lock brakes had been developed, his competitors would have passed him by. Someone else would be known as "the father of the automobile."

The pitfall in waiting for the new technology to be cheaper is dangerous indeed. What invariably ends up happening is that by the time the desired technology falls at the price you want, something else has come along. Now all you are doing is waiting for yet another technology to become cheaper. This endless cycle has only one outcome—you don't get hooked up.

To be fair, the reason for this problem is the tremendous rate at which high technology is moving. Any computer equipment you purchase these days is pretty much out-of-date by the time you receive it.

So, the time to launch your business on the Web is right now. Currently, the hardware and software exists to meet nearly every commercial aspect at a price that is cost-effective.

If you just make the decision to get on the Internet and Web, you will find that you can manage quite well with the current technology. Don't be bothered when, next month, the price of the machine you just bought drops 25 percent (and it will).

One of the biggest advantages to getting involved now is the jump you will have on your competitors. Right now in your particular industry, there may not be many people on the Internet. If this is the case, now is the time for you to make your move. By establishing yourself in your field now on the Internet, your competitors are at a disadvantage when they finally decide later on to use the Internet.

Imagine your competitor's dismay when they discover the Web, take a moment to scope out the competition, and they come up with your page.

> **Note**
>
> What you don't want to be is like the gentleman who called our business, rather breathlessly, and said, "I don't really understand the Web, but my competitors are already on it and all I know is that I've got to be on it too, immediately."
>
> This is a prime example where putting off until tomorrow can cost you money. It is far better to be one of the pioneers and help mold the medium than be a lamb and follow the herd.

This is not to say that you should blindly purchase whatever the salesperson is pushing this week. You should wait before purchasing any new technology. New technology requires a payback period where the investment of research and development is paid off. Once the company recoups its research cost and competition springs up for the technology, you can begin to examine the pricing and make your decision then. That will be the point where the price begins to fall. In computers, prices tend to fall within two to four months after initial announcement. If you purchase at this time, you can still get fairly up-to-date technology at a more reasonable price.

> **Note**
>
> It also allows for any kinks to be worked out. A good example of this involved the new release of a brand new printer offered by a leading manufacturer. It received good reviews from all the magazines. After noticing the store shelves were empty, the salesman said they wouldn't be stocked anymore because of technical problems and the company would be sending out the next in the series.

Researching Your Options

As you begin to explore the Internet and World Wide Web, it is important for you to learn as much as you can from as many sources as you find. It's also crucial for you to stay current with the latest technology. Because the technology and capabilities of the computer industry move very quickly, it is easy to be left behind if you do not make an effort to stay with the technological changes as they happen.

II

The Basics

Magazines

Magazines represent a good way to stay knowledgeable. Their lead time is generally fairly short, so information is relatively current.

The best magazine to find out about hardware is *Computer Shopper* for PC-based machines and *MacWEEK* for Macintosh-based machines. In these magazines, you find all the latest machines for a range of prices. If you don't like the price quoted by one manufacturer, turn a few pages and you'll find it again cheaper. In general, the prices for mail-order machines are lower than the prices you find around town.

These magazines are available in most supermarket chains and good bookstores. The online versions of both magazines can be found at **http:// www.shopper.ziff.com/**. However, the online versions of these magazines do not have the advertisements paper versions have, so if you want to look at the ads to purchase equipment, you have to buy the magazine itself.

> **Note**
>
> When considering your purchase from a magazine ad, check out several back issues of the magazine and see whether the company has been around for awhile. This way, you can minimize your chance of encountering an unreliable company.

While many of the general computer magazines feature articles about the Web, these are not good sources to turn to because it's not their primary concern.

There are currently a few magazines which are devoted to the Internet and World Wide Web—*Wired*, *Mondo 2000*, and *Internet World*. These magazines are devoted to the Internet, World Wide Web and the entire cyberculture revolution in general.

Wired is the industry's hottest new magazine. It's *the* magazine to read to find out what's happening on the Internet and WWW. Each month features interesting and informative articles on the latest happenings and "who's who" on the Internet. Much space is devoted to new places to go and new things to do on the Web.

Wired also explores both the hard issues as well as the future of the Internet. One of the attractions to *Wired* is its modern format, which uses lots of imagery and color. Information is packed onto every page and often mixed in with the graphics, making this magazine both an enjoyable and informative read. Another benefit is that the magazine is also available online (without so much of the graphics), which is good because it shows they "walk their talk." You can find it at **http://hard.wired.com/cgi_bin/newuser**.

Mondo 2000 is a good companion to *Wired*. *Mondo 2000* was one of the first cybermagazines available. It has a similar format to *Wired*, with an integrated imagery and informational content. *Mondo 2000* is published bimonthly, which means that it is sometimes not as current as *Wired*. It also takes a more "social" stance, often spending much time investigating the cyberculture itself, rather than providing nitty-gritty how-to information. *Mondo 2000* makes a good companion to *Wired* for a total picture of what is going on in the cyberworld.

On the other end of the spectrum is *Internet World*. This magazine presents a much more traditional and conservative view of the Internet. While *Internet World* does contain lots of new information about things to do on the Internet, its more conservative nature means that the publication tends to stick to business issues and more "established" topics. *Internet World* should not be the only magazine you read on the Internet. This is primarily due to its conservative tone about a medium which is anything but conservative. However, *Internet World* is a good magazine to keep track of business issues on the Internet. You can find it at **http://www.mecklerweb.com/mags/ iw/iwhome.htm**.

Make sure you always spend time each month reading your magazines. You will find the information in them to be very valuable in navigating, understanding, and predicting the Internet and World Wide Web.

Local Clubs and Colleges

A surprisingly large number of cities and towns now have local computer clubs. These clubs are often free to join and meet monthly to discuss new topics of interest to the local members.

You can make good use of the clubs' members. Many of them tend to be younger (high school age) and very eager to help you set up and learn about your system.

To find out about the clubs in your area, check out *Computer Shopper*. This is also *the* magazine to consult if you need to find a BBS or user group in your area. Each month *Computer Shopper* lists BBS and user groups for most area codes around the U.S. and Canada. Included in the listing is meeting information, contact names, pricing information, and any special notes about what the group specializes in.

II

The Basics

Many cities have their own local computer newspaper, which is usually free and often available at supermarkets. This is a good alternative to *Computer Shopper* because it highlights meetings strictly in your area.

Another good place to browse for meetings and groups is at local computer stores or the local university or college. Both these places have corkboards with local events and information. Scan these periodically to see what's new in your area.

Tip

You may also want to talk to the store owners and university faculty. They can often point you to people, courses, and other resources to help you learn.

Many computer stores and colleges offer adult education classes in learning how to use computers and the Internet. These courses are often scheduled in the evenings and only one or two days a week. This makes them convenient to fit into work and home schedules. You should also find these courses to be affordable.

Seminars and Videos

Because of the sudden popularity of the Internet and Web, many companies are offering traveling seminars on bringing your business, and yourself, to the Internet and WWW. Likewise, videos are beginning to appear which help explain how to use the Internet and WWW.

Seminars can be valuable if they actually give you something for your money. Too many seminars promote their own products and actually offer very little information. Often people leave these seminars more confused than when they arrived.

Tip

Only go to seminars where hands-on training is a part of the seminar.

One way to ensure that you are getting your money's worth in a seminar is to contact the people who are planning the seminar and ask them a few simple questions. Find out whether you will have the ability to "try what you learn" during the seminar (in other words, will they have machines hooked up to the Internet so you can try what they are discussing?). Find out how many machines they have as compared to the number of expected attendees. If there are more than five to six people per machine, your chance of using the machines constructively is greatly diminished.

Also, find out about the people who are giving the seminar. What experience do they have? If the instructors are talking about putting a business on the Web or Internet, find out how many businesses they have personally put up. Also find out how long their lectures are and what their expertise is.

Caution

Obviously, do not go to any seminar where the lecturers have little to no practical experience. Surprisingly, this even extends to lecturers who come from university and college settings. Because of the fact that colleges and universities give free access to staff on machines with direct T1 lines and lots of storage, these type of lecturers are often out of touch with the issues that face business users. Issues such as getting a good deal on provider fees, speed of connections, storage, and throughput limitations are all very important to the business user. Universities also usually limit certain things that can be performed on their machines, like direct graphical Web access; therefore, lecturers who come from academia may not be knowledgeable about these types of features.

The same warning applies to picking video instruction. Stay away from videos that are created by providers of Internet connectivity. They are only selling their services. It's best to go with a video by a firm who has experience in placing companies on the Internet or WWW, and who is not married to any particular provider.

Resources on the Internet

Of course, the best resources are those which are physically on the Internet and WWW. Incredible amounts of information exist on the Information Superhighway concerning how to access and use the medium itself.

For information on finding WWW browsers and servers, good sites to go to, how to use the WWW, or how to write your own HTML, you should probably go into IRC (Internet Relay Chat) and join the group **#www**. This group has webmasters from around the world who are willing to help you with your questions.

▶ See "Using IRC for Instant Answers," p. 222

Note

Once you are inside IRC, join the **#www** group by typing

   _/join #www

Once you are in the **#www** group, simply ask your question. Most of the people in this group are busy writing software and designing new WWW systems, so their time is valuable. Asking, "Can I ask a question?" merely wastes time and makes them mad. Just ask the question. If nobody answers within a minute or two, wait an hour and try again. Often people are busy in another screen and do not immediately see your message.

▶ See "Etiquette in Live Discussions," p. 183

II

The Basics

▶ See "Using NetNews To Find New Information," p. 221

The second major resource on the Internet is NetNews. Using your favorite news browser, view the following groups:

comp.infosystem

comp.infosystems.www

comp.infosystems.www.providers

comp.infosystems.www.users

comp.infosystems.www.misc

These newsgroups are designed to discuss the latest in the WWW and WWW-related issues and are a good place to ask questions and find information. Very often, these groups post Frequently Asked Question lists (updated about once a week) which answer most of the popular questions.

◀ See "Archie," p. 42

The final major resource on the Internet is using Archie and other searching services to find topics of interest. Searching for "web," "www," "http," or "html" can often turn up text files and papers available for downloading.

Doing It Yourself or Having It Done for You

As you experiment and learn about the WWW and Internet, you may become unsure whether or not you have bitten off more than you can chew. Rest assured that many consultants and services bureaus are more than happy to help you with your decisions, planning, and implementation.

▶ See "Consult-ants versus Net Service Bureaus," p. 139

This section should help you understand some of the issues in making the decision of just how much work to do yourself and how much to let others do for you.

Placing a business on the Web is very much like starting your own advertising campaign. When it comes time to advertise a product, most companies do not build the billboards, publish their own magazines, create their own in-house art departments and camera departments, create their own advertising lingo, and advertise it themselves. Instead, they often rely on outside service to do this work.

Outside WWW service bureaus and consultants can help you with the following areas of your WWW business:

- Determining your audience

- Finding a provider

- Setting up your system

- Setting up a server (if you need one)

- Designing your WWW pages

- Posting your WWW pages

- Advertising your WWW pages

- Providing custom WWW and Internet solutions

You can use WWW service bureaus to cover any or all of the items in this list for you. A good service bureau is also willing (for a price) to transfer the enabling technology to you, so as time goes on you require less and less outside help.

Many people have an interest in learning HTML and creating their own pages. However, even in these cases people may need help proofing their pages or finding somewhere to host them, or trying to make their page look good with all the different browsers. They may even need advanced capabilities which are beyond their ability.

The amount of work you do to put your own business on the Web will be in direct proportion to how much time you have. To whatever degree you can provide any of the components of your pages, you will save money. Provide what you can and let the experts do the rest.

The important thing to remember is that even if you do not have the time or patience to do it all yourself, stepping to an outside bureau should not cost you an arm and a leg. Because of plummeting costs on the Internet, full-color advertising can be accomplished for a fraction of the price of doing it using traditional mediums. In other words, your cost for having a magazine ad created for you should be far more than your costs for having a set of WWW pages prepared for you.

Planning Your Net Business

Now that you have made the decision to begin your Net business, you need to plan it. Before you can even begin to consider implementing details, you should answer a few basic questions to help guide your development.

In particular, it's necessary to figure out who is your target audience. You need to determine what services you want to implement on the Net. After that, you need to determine where on the Net to get the best services for your business. And finally, you should figure out how you are going to implement this plan.

Who?

The first question you should answer when planning your WWW page is, to whom are you targeting this page?

Your WWW site may be used only internally—that is, by employees and/or existing clients. It may also be used only externally—for example, the Internet community-at-large. It could be used by a combination of both.

If you plan to use the WWW site internally, you need to consider who within your company or organization is going to have access to it. This topic is covered later in this chapter in the section, "Using the Net Inside Your Business."

Likewise, if it's to be used externally, you must decide on your target audience. This decision impacts the look and feel of your site. It also determines which hot lists you advertise on. If the site is going to be used internally and externally, you must consider all these factors.

Internal

Sales could have access to the WWW server for advertising purposes. Marketing could get user demographics via fill-in forms and access logs. Support could set up a customer service and tracking system. Technical groups can use the internal WWW for project planning.

> **Caution**
>
> Each of these groups of users have different needs and different expectations of their WWW system. Likewise, some of these groups may not be able to coexist on the same system. For example, if your technical group is doing project planning via the Web, you may not want that same system used by sales for general advertising. The use of the system by sales implies users from the outside coming in, and this may be a security risk with the technical group.

In a similar fashion, if your site is used both internally and externally and is a particularly popular site externally, you may find that there are so many users coming in from the outside that it is no longer efficient for the people inside your organization to use. This can result in a loss of productivity for your internal use of the WWW or a loss of users externally. Therefore, if your user base is large enough, you may want to have multiple WWW systems, one for each significant group of users.

External

When designing a system for external users, it is a good idea to think about the age group you are trying to attract most. You can then plan the proper look and feel for your group. If your pages are meant for a general audience, you probably want to keep the overall look (for example, graphics and text) on the simple and conservative side. This technique works best for all age groups.

If you are targeting children, you need to pay attention to the reading level indicated by the text (see fig. 4.1).

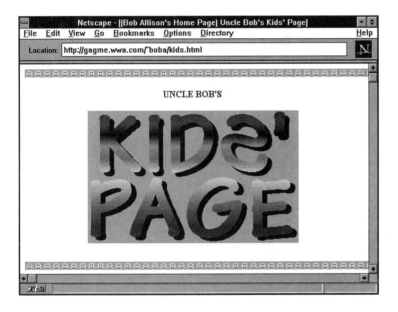

Fig. 4.1
This site aimed at children is full of links to sites for kids (**http:// gagme.wwa. com/~boba/ kids.html**).

If you are targeting teenagers—an age group heavily influenced by video games and music videos—your look and feel should appeal to their expectations (see fig. 4.2).

People on the Internet are always looking for the latest convenience. Remember this when you are planning your page. They tend to want pages which let them do the most in the simplest manner. This means using links, forms, animations, and interactive technology. Any page which offers the user conveniences that they used to find in multiple pages will be a popular page.

The Basics

Fig. 4.2
This site aimed at teenagers has an eye-catching format using loud colors that grab the viewers' attention (**http://hisurf.aloha.com/TDT/TDT.html**).

> **Note**
>
> We said, "Do the most in the simplest manner." This point should not be overlooked. Offering hundreds of links on a single page is simply not effective and will not be popular by users. However, offering lists broken into convenient categories or search engines to help the user quickly locate desired information can be a benefit to the user.

This is especially true for business users. If you are planning on offering business services, you want to make sure to offer lots of free "goodies" along with your pay services. By gearing your pages toward the business-type user and offering a wealth of things to do and information to glean, you can hook the user into needing your service on a daily basis. Once you have the user coming into your system daily or weekly, you can establish a captive audience on which to try new ideas and products.

Similarly, if the purpose of your WWW pages is to show off products for sale, you want to gear your pages for the audience you intend to reach by implementing proper graphics and text for reaching your users. Older audiences might want to see larger-sized text. Younger audiences might want to see interesting graphics and simple text.

Every audience will want an easy way to shop for your products and services. Providing just e-mail, fax, or postal mailing addresses is probably not enough. You should make it both easy and convenient for the user to order from you. Interactive forms should be used to lure the user into "buying now." You may permit the potential buyer to use e-cash or enter in a credit card number so he or she can complete the sales transaction right then and there. If you only provide telephone or mail ordering, you run the risk that potential customers will forget about the product or change their minds.

> **Note**
>
> The bottom line is that your intended audience is the single most driving force in influencing your WWW design. By examining your users' style and needs, you can tailor your pages to provide the audience members with something they want, ensuring that they find your service or product valuable. Remember, getting them to come in the door is fairly easy on the Web. However, if they step through that door and don't see anything of interest, getting them to come back could be very difficult.

What?

Now that you are beginning to think about who you are going to present services or products to, it is a good idea to think about what services you would like to offer.

Home Page

At the very least, your pages should have a main document (called the *home page*). The home page is the main entry point for users into your system. It's the first part users see and it creates that all-important first impression. It determines whether they continue in your document or decide to surf to someplace more interesting. Regardless of your service, this is the most important page in your entire design.

You want the user to get an idea of your entire service by looking at your home page, but you need to keep it simple. If your services are straightforward or you are offering only a few products, you can do this with one home page. However, you probably want to use your first page to direct the user to information contained on your other pages.

Beyond that, the components of your pages depends pretty much on what your service or product is. However, the components can be easily grouped based on functionality. This section explores some of this grouped functionality.

At the simplest level, you have *pages*, which consist only of text, graphics, audio, and links to other pages. This kind of page offers only the most modest abilities for polling the user for information and responding to the user in inventive ways. Pages of this style require no additional server support and can be stored on both FTP and HTTP systems.

Forms

The next level of complexity and functionality gives users the ability to input information into the system. This is usually done with the *WWW forms capability*. You can create a page that has text areas into which the user can type information and buttons that the user can turn on and off. You can create any type of statistical or informational questionnaire.

At the very least, you will want to use this form capability to place a small questionnaire on your page that allows the user to get a message to you. This message can be as simple as, "Please send me more information," to more complex actions such as ordering products or reporting customer information.

In order to use forms, you must have a server somewhere that is going to receive the content of the form and process it. Usually this means formatting the filled-in form and sending it to you. Because this is a popular use of forms, many systems offer form remailing capability. Using these servers is a wonderful alternative to having to create one yourself. The prices are very reasonable and usually allow you to handle all types of forms (users don't need to know what the form looks like).

Searchable Databases

The next level of functionality and complexity is to add *searchable databases*. Oftentimes you will have situations where you want to allow the user to have access to huge quantities of data.

For example, if you were selling videotapes, you might have 50,000 titles. It would be nice if the user could browse those titles by actor, title, topic, director, or genre.

While this obviously calls for a form, with nifty buttons to allow the user to select what they are polling, it cannot be handled by simply sending the users a completed form to you via e-mail. You would not want to be personally responding to thousands of requests for movies. Instead, you would want this automated.

Just as server sites offer the ability to mail you a form, many sites also offer searchable databases. The mechanism changes from site to site, but the capabilities remain the same. When a form is submitted by the user, it is received by the server, and a special program is called which knows how to interpret the form. This program takes care of adding items to the database, reading items from the database, and sending the results back to the user.

Note

This aspect of HTML programming is complicated, so unless you are going to become an expert, you probably need a searchable database created for you.

Membership-Only Systems

Next in functionality you have the ability to handle *member-only systems*. These systems are useful in situations where you have a regular paying clientele or are offering services only to specific groups. These pages require a user to sign in. *Signing in* could be as simple as providing an e-mail address for proof of identity, or as complex as requiring full mailing and phone information and credit card numbers for billing.

For an example of a free membership-only WWW site, check out the *Wired* magazine site (**http://wired.com/**). The information gathered at this type of site is used internally and provides underwriters with demographic information.

Caution

When registering with *Wired* or any other subscription service, do not answer any questions that you do not feel comfortable with.

Just because they ask the question doesn't mean you have to answer it. If your subscription form is rejected because of empty fields, type in a polite message such as

This information is private.

> **Tip**
> As you plan your own WWW site, avoid questions others may find troublesome. If you feel uncomfortable giving your home address in a questionnaire that also asks for your income, don't expect others to answer it.

Membership systems are very useful because they allow you to offer advanced services to users who pay extra for them. After registering with you (via a form such as the one shown in fig. 4.3), the user may access the services by logging or signing in with some form of name and password. The various ways to log in are infinite, but they all require one thing—a server running a membership system.

In almost all cases, membership systems must be custom-designed, since they are all different in one way or another. However, like most features on the WWW, membership systems can be created for a modest cost. Since

II

The Basics

membership systems have tremendous money-making potential, the payback can be very quick for a popular service.

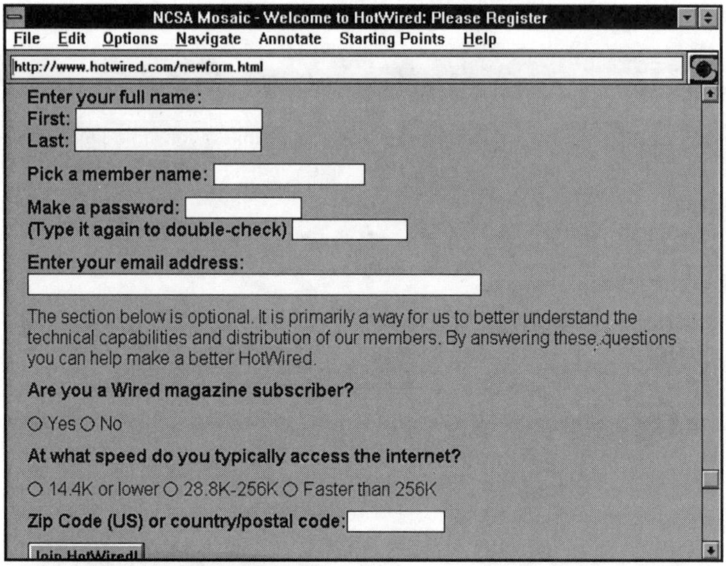

Fig. 4.3
The membership form for *Wired* is an example of a registration form (**http://www. hotwired.com/ newform.html**).

Custom-Designed Systems

At the extreme of functionality, you have totally custom-designed WWW systems. They are the most attractive and the most costly. When custom-designing a WWW system, you almost always have lots of the other various mechanisms already discussed. WWW data may even be shared via other Internet methods, such as Gopher and NetNews, so that you have parallel systems (for example, a user could interact with you via Gopher or the Web).

Custom systems offer the user many advantages and usually prove to be cost-effective. Because custom systems are handcrafted by Web experts, they can be molded to be very unique, which means they can offer services and capabilities that are not found elsewhere on the Web. All it requires is coming up with the novel idea and having it implemented.

A custom system may embody a product distribution system with tracking shipment, order entry, fulfillment, and advertising all integrated into a seamless environment. Systems of this nature can be set up to respond to individual users by creating the HTML documents on the fly from databases of information about the user and the situation. This allows the pages to be ever-changing and ever-changeable.

In many systems, the user has control over the look and feel of the environment, allowing a more pleasing interaction for the user. The amount of WWW pages physically in your system is also at a minimum. Because the software creates many of the pages in real time (based on the user's current status and request), these pages do not need to actually exist. This allows for a trade-off in some of the cost of a custom Web system.

> **Note**
>
> Remember, though, that these sophisticated WWW capabilities require expert attention. Unless you are going to become that expert or are going to select one in-house, you need to find someone to implement your custom-designed system. To find custom WWW solutions, go to any WWW service provider and discuss your needs. Most providers are happy to implement solutions for you and will work with you to find a reliable contractor.

Where?

Now that you have begun to think about the who and what of your WWW pages, the next question that comes to mind is, "Where do I store the pages?"

Housing the Server

You should begin with comparing internal versus external systems. In an internal design, as you have discovered, you have your own employees on your WWW system. If security is an issue, you definitely want to house the server at your physical location; this puts the data under your supervision and control. This also allows you to control the access to your site and its related data with more accuracy.

If an internal server is housed at some provider site, the provider and its employees have total access to the system and its data. In most situations, this is not a problem. The provider wants you to succeed, because in turn the provider will succeed.

However, sensitive data being what it is, you can house the machine at your location. If you do this, a provider can still give you the Internet connection. The provider simply arranges for the special phone and/or data lines to be dropped into your physical location. Then you give the provider access-only to those areas you want. However, having your own server at your location almost always means having at least one individual whose full-time job is the maintenance of that machine and its data.

▶ See "Crime and the Net," p. 385

Housing External WWW Systems

So what about housing external WWW systems? The answer to this is pretty much wherever you want to. Just as there are issues for picking a good provider, which is covered in detail in Chapter 6, "Placing a Business on the Web," there are also some issues for picking a good geographic location.

Despite the "great bargain" you get from a provider, you probably do not want to house your pages on the provider's system if it's in a foreign country. First, by doing so, your page's content may be in some unusual violation of that country's laws (especially as they relate to commerce). Secondly, depending on the nation, access to your pages may be less than what you expect.

A foreign nation may have its Internet access via a transatlantic cable or satellite link. In some cases, a country may only have a single 56K line or T1 servicing all its Internet users. Because of this, traffic to that country may be particularly slow.

This speed issue may work two ways:

- The Internet is worldwide, but it may work faster in some parts of the world than others. For example, you might do a large part of your business in Africa. Where do you house your pages? If most of your work is performed in Africa, it would make sense to house most of your pages in Africa. That way, your African clients would have fast access because they wouldn't need to take the transatlantic link, which can get very clogged.

- If you are servicing the entire world, you should house your pages in the country with the best demographics for you that also has the fastest and best access. Currently, the United States leads the pack with the fastest and most servers. Other countries with fairly good access include Canada, France, Germany, Great Britain, Japan, and Australia. The rest of the more than 91 countries who enjoy Internet access have far fewer servers.

To continue the example, you could decide to place your pages on a server in the United States. Does it matter geographically where you place them? Again, surprisingly it does. Just as some portions of the world are faster in accessing the Internet than others, so it is with the United States.

In the U.S., not all the states are equally connected. While every state is hooked up, states which lead in the number of servers include California, New York, Virginia, Massachusetts, Ohio, Texas, Maryland, and Colorado.

What does this statistic mean for you? If your business is such that you have a market in any of those states, you would stand a good chance of improving your business by hosting your pages on servers in those states. Because local servers get local traffic, placing yourself on those servers gets you noticed by their users.

The Internet Backbone

In all cases, you want to be as close to the Internet backbone as you possibly can. In other words, you should limit the number of computers that stand between you and the fast-moving Information Superhighway.

The backbone of the Internet is like a river. There are several backbones, but in general they are the lines that carry all the data from one location to another. All the other Internet feeds flow into them like tributaries into a river. The closer you are to the river, the faster the current carries you and the less chance you have of a log jam. The same goes for the Internet. If you are 10 computers away from a backbone, there are 10 systems and connections that can be bogged down. If you are two systems from the backbone, you have a much less chance of being delayed.

A site provider should be able to tell you how close you are to the Internet. Another mechanism for determining how close you are is the UNIX TRACEROUTE command. TRACEROUTE allows you see all the computers between you and a destination site. You can look at the output of TRACEROUTE and figure out where your backbone is and how many hops (or how many different computer systems you are routed through) it takes. This command also tells you how long it takes the information to reach the destination site. TRACEROUTE may or may not be available to you depending on your site's administrators.

Another mechanism is the UNIX PING command. PING, when issued with a destination domain name, tells you how long it takes messages to get to that machine. You won't know how many machines there are between you and the destination, but you can see the overall performance.

Normal times for each machine response ranges between 100 and 400ms, with occasional bursts as long as 1,600ms. Sustained running above 500ms is the sign of a slow or clogged link. These times are what you should see for both PING and TRACEROUTE results.

II

The Basics

> **Note**
>
> If you find that learning to use these tools is taking too much time, you can simply use the system and see if it feels comfortable. A system which is always sluggish is exhibiting too much of a load and should be avoided.

How?

This section explores how to implement your plan in a controlled manner that will produce the proper results.

Specifications Document

In order to travel on any road to a destination, you need a map. The same goes for your work on the Internet. In this case, your destination is your own WWW presence. The roadmap in this case is a specifications document.

A *specifications document* is a very detailed description of what you want your system to act like and look like. It is the blueprint that you or someone else will follow to create your system.

You should be the craftsman of the specifications document. This document is vitally important, whether you are doing the pages yourself or having them done for you.

Working with a Contractor

The specifications document is even more important if you are hiring others to complete the work. It is useful in several ways:

- It lets the contractor know how much work is going to be involved in the project. This allows the contractor to make an accurate bid on your project.

- It gives you something to judge the results by. If the results do not match the specifications document, something is wrong. It is the contractor's job to make sure that the specification can be implemented in the first place and to make the necessary changes if it is not, even before accepting the contract.

- It allows the contractor to lay out a timeline in which the project will be completed.

You can begin to appreciate the importance of a specifications document. Without one, implementation is both blind and open-ended. In situations without clear specifications documents, often both parties feel they have been abused. The clients feel slighted because they did not get the results of what they were hoping for. Likewise, the contractors feel slighted because they were not told upfront of all the work that was involved.

Avoiding Rampant Featurism

The contractor's worst fear, which should be your fear as well if you design your own system, is rampant featurism.

Rampant featurism is what happens when you don't have a good specifications document. Two things usually occur. First, you run into unforeseen roadblocks. Things that you didn't think about in enough detail result in factors that impact the design, the completion schedule, and the cost of the project. Secondly, you realize that necessary features might not have been included.

There are many responses associated with not having completed a good specifications document:

II

The Basics

- *"The system is useless without this new feature."* This is the worst phrase you can hear. It can be repeated over and over again each time you think up something new that just has to be in the project. Every time you say that phrase to a contractor, that person will shudder. Why? Each overlooked feature you add after the completed design will tend to cause at least two times the impact on the system than it would have caused if it were present in the original specification. It is even possible that due to the projects design methodology, features added later will adversely affect the whole system. This may mean that the new features cannot be smoothly integrated without a significant restructuring of the rest of the software, usually at great expense.

  > **Note**
  >
  > Plan for the growth as well as the initial design of your project. Not every feature you think of has to be implemented immediately. If you have a good specification, stick to it. Save the new ideas for future developments. They can be part of a planned growth design which allows you to re-post your site to newsgroups and hotlists with the announcement of new features.

- *"Well, I was always thinking of that."* This phrase is wonderful to utter when you ask your contractor for a feature that was never discussed but that you were thinking about. Because some projects take time to do, sometimes it's possible to forget what was originally discussed and what was just thought about. Clients are convinced they told the contractor what they wanted, while contractors are certain that they "never heard that one before." If you want it in your project, make sure it's in the specifications document.

▶ See "Your Home Page," p. 364

The specifications document is a lifeline that can make or break a design. A good specifications document leaves nothing to question. The overall look and feel should be spelled out in detail, including operations that are allowed and format of data. Literally every facet that can be imagined should be covered.

Features To Cover

A good specifications document covers the following features:

- *Hardware and software.* The document should specify what hardware and software is needed for the project, who will pay for any hardware or software purchases, and who will own them at the end of the project.

- *Look and feel.* Your specifications may say something like "hi-tech look with lots of chrome effects and computer graphics on every page," or you may specify a "down-home look achieved through the use of neutral colors and rustic graphics." If you are really picky about how things look, include an example in the specifications.

- *How the user will access data.* Do you want to limit how much data the user can access and how many users you have a day? Do you want the user to access the data with a searchable database? If so, searchable how—alphabetically, by location, or by category?

- *Timelines.* The project should be broken down into segments with deadlines for each, so you and your contractor can be sure that the project is proceeding in a timely manner.

> **Note**
>
> Specify that payments to the contractor will be made upon completion of work according to an agreed-upon time schedule. This should ensure that the work is completed in a timely fashion.
>
> Usually contractors are paid a part of their sum in the beginning when work is started, another part in the middle when some of the work has been delivered, and the remainder upon delivery of the project.
>
> No project should require you to pay all your money upfront. If your contract requests this, you might want to consider a new contractor.

Consider All the Nooks and Crannies

You can begin to appreciate what will happen when you sit down to write a specifications document. At first it seems easy. You have a simple idea, so it should be simple to put down on paper. But soon you realize all the nooks and crannies involved with planning a project. Issues like ease of use, effective layout of information, and efficiency/throughput concerns are just a few important factors that are sometimes overlooked. As you work in one portion of your specifications document, you will begin to think about other areas that are missing. These are thoughts you would probably have had too late if you didn't spend the time to write a good specifications document.

Provide the First Draft

It is your responsibility to provide the first draft of the document. If you rely on a contractor to do the first draft with your input, you can miss several items because the contractor cannot read your mind. You should write down everything you can about your project and turn that over to the contractor. The contractor then reviews it and helps you format it into a workable design that addresses all your issues.

Tip

In your design work, do not worry if the idea sounds too big to handle; the contractor is supposed to help guide you through a practical implementation of your specification.

If you are doing the work yourself, this document is just as important for all the reasons listed. The specifications document helps you make sure you have a concrete design that will hold up to the abuse of potentially millions of users.

Generating a Timeline

Once a good specifications document is in place, a timeline should be easy to generate. A specifications document will let you get an idea of implementation cycles and set timelines if you are using a contractor. Additionally, a good timeline helps you plan announcements and other marketing strategies with the release of your WWW system.

> **Note**
>
> A good timeline leaves a little extra space for unforeseen delays. Some people call this the *fudge factor*. Depending on the complexity of the project, a fudge factor of anywhere from an extra day to an extra week for a week-long project can be expected.

Beginning the Work

After the specification and timelines are finished, it's time to begin work. The work should be done, if at all possible, on the system it is actually going to be

II

The Basics

placed on. By doing this, you can avoid many problems—such as mismatches in system resources or server types when bringing up your system.

Testing

Tip
Test the links
and make sure
the links work.
Nothing is worse
than links or
pages which
don't come up.

As the pages begin to come online, it is important that you test them. If access by all WWW users is important, you need to make sure your pages work in text and graphic mode (because some of the browsers such as Lynx are text-only). You should test your pages in more than one browser. Often a page looks drastically different in another browser, and just a few subtle changes will fix the problem so that it looks consistent across all the browsers.

Announce Your Pages

Once the pages are tested, it's time to announce your pages and open for business. Pages are announced by posting or listing information about your site in the various searchers and "what's new" lists. Consider the following points when announcing your pages:

- Choose keywords that best describe your site, so that they can be listed with the searchers.

- Provide a brief description of your site. Some sites want only one sentence; others allow small paragraphs.

▶ See "How To
Advertise on
the Net,"
p. 227

- Assign a contact person for your WWW site. If you had a contractor do your work, they sometimes serve as your contact person.

Some sites you post to will immediately add you to their database. Others may take up to a month. You should see some business immediately, but the fullest impact for your business will be seen in four to six weeks. This will be important when evaluating the effectiveness of the site and in any redesign work you do.

From Here...

By now you should be well aware of the myriad of factors impacting the good design and implementation of a WWW business site. The steps covered in this chapter act as the cornerstone for the creation of a successful WWW site. The rest of this book is devoted to helping you implement all these factors correctly.

For related information, consult the following chapters:

■ Chapter 5, "Choosing Hardware and Software," shows you how to select equipment and software.

■ Chapter 6, "Placing a Business on the Web," helps you to locate Internet and WWW providers, as well as provide more information on selecting and managing contractors.

■ Chapter 16, "Your Presence on the Net," provides more discussion on image and the Internet.

■ Chapter 17, "Security and the Net," introduces issues dealing with where to store your data and how to ensure its security.

II

The Basics

Chapter 5

Choosing Hardware and Software

Salespeople are going to try to sell you whatever they can to make the highest possible commission or to get rid of what's in stock. Some will try to intimidate or bedazzle you with terms and jargon you're not sure of and even worse, talk you into buying last year's model at this year's price. This chapter shows you how to sidestep these obstacles and make a smart purchasing decision. You also learn what type of equipment you need and what to do if anything goes wrong.

This chapter gives you all the information you need to make smart choices in your purchases. Specifically, you learn

- The best places to make your purchases

- The hardware specifications you need to cruise the Web

- Pitfalls to beware of when you make your purchases

- How to make sure you get all the latest information and upgrades on your purchases

- How to save money on repairs

Hardware

Computer hardware continues to get faster and smaller at an increasing rate. Some industries' manufacturing chips are retooling every 18 months, which is obviously a great financial strain on the manufacturer. Even though there has been some talk among manufacturers about slowing down how quickly new technology appears, whether or not this happens remains to be seen.

Others in the industry think a development plateau in computer speed is approaching. If this happens, maybe the computer you purchase won't become obsolete so quickly. However, this statement has been heard many times in the past, but the limits keep getting broken.

But there is one indisputable fact about computers—if you want to surf the Web, you need one.

> ### Note
>
> You don't need a computer to simply put your business's presence on the Web. WWW service centers as well as WWW consultants can place your business on the Web without your needing a computer. However, most people will want to see how others are using the Web, and for this you will require a computer that is capable of accessing the Internet and Web.

When purchasing or upgrading your computer for the Internet, you need to answer the following questions:

- Where is the best place to buy a computer?
- How fast should it be?
- What about the screen?
- What type of modems?
- What brands?

Before you lay out your cold hard cash or credit card, you need to shop around for your hardware and decide where you are going to get the best sales and service for your money.

Where To Purchase Hardware

There are many choices for buying new hardware. Local computer stores are numerous; you can find them in even the smallest of communities. Large cities are even boasting new computer superstores, with warehouse-type layouts and huge savings. Magazines as well offer an abundance of computer hardware ads to peruse.

With all these choices, where do you go to purchase?

Magazines versus Stores

Magazines such as *Computer Shopper* offer the primary advantage of both choice and price. Even the computer superstores cannot compete with the sheer numbers of companies in a single magazine. Price is kept to a minimum because many of the companies are mail-order only. Because they do not need a well-staffed storefront, their overall costs can be kept down.

◀ See "Researching Your Options," p. 87

Magazines can also offer advantages in better technology faster. Because computer stores tend to enter agreements with certain manufacturers, they are tied to the release schedules and update times of those companies. Magazines have no such limits, with new companies offering new technologies appearing in every issue.

The primary advantage to computer stores is that they are useful in emergencies. A computer store is essential when you do not have the time to wait for a shipment, even if it's the next day.

Computer superstores also often offer prices which are sometimes close to the prices of magazine ads. If you purchase wisely from a superstore, you can often walk away with a purchase at or near a magazine's price, especially when considering shipping charges.

The final advantage of the store over the magazine is the security in knowing what you are buying and where you are buying it. With a magazine, you are purchasing on faith, but in a store you can look at, feel, and examine your purchase.

Tip

Call the Better Business Bureau to find out if there have been complaints lodged against the store you are considering buying from.

> **Note**
>
> Our recommendation is to buy from a magazine as much as possible because the savings and choices outweigh the advantages to buying locally. You may want to go to a local store to get an idea of price and features and to play around with how different systems feel to get an idea of what works for you. But then turn to the magazine ads to make the purchase.

Big Companies versus Small Companies

People often wonder if it's safer purchasing from a big-name company as opposed to a no-name company. The answer depends on whether you are buying the computer itself or some add-on peripheral device. These sections explore this topic.

II

The Basics

Computers. When perusing a magazine such as *Computer Shopper*, how can you tell when a price is a good deal or not?

As you thumb through the magazine you will probably be astonished to see the wide spread in prices. One page can show a system for $1,500; the next page can show the same configuration for $2,300. What is the difference between these systems?

One of the first things you must realize about the basic computer system itself is that each of the components that make up this system are made by only a small number of companies. For example, there are a handful of companies who make disk drives, and they are well-known with established reputations. Any disk drive you encounter will come from one of these companies. While there are differences between reliability, durability, design, and speed, all the components, regardless of the manufacturer, should work well.

> ### Note
>
> What this means is that if you bought a PC from 100 different PC clone manufacturers and dismantled each major component into its own manufacturer's pile, you would have far less than 100 piles when you were done.

This extends even to PCs manufactured by famous names such as IBM, Compaq, and Apple. Even though Apple is the only manufacturer of their computers (unlike IBM PC clones), most of the important components are not made by Apple. The disks and CPU are not made by Apple, nor is the memory. In fact, most of the components are still manufactured by third parties.

All of this comes down to a translation into quality. Because all the components are basically the same, the individual pieces are all of a known quality. The question then becomes how the components are put together.

Most of the companies merely purchase the correct components. They put them together, purchase or design and install the proper software, and test the units. These companies also often offer support/repair departments and solutions departments.

Most problems that occur with the actual computer come not from the components themselves, but how the components are interfaced to each other.

However, the majority of systems that you can purchase will be reliably crafted. Because the industry is standardized, most manufacturers' components fit well together. The computer hardware industry is highly competitive, and companies only survive by offering a superior product for less cost.

Note

Sometimes good deals can be found on used equipment. Check local newspapers and trader-type publications. However, make sure you know what you are buying. Just because the person you are buying it from bought it a year ago for $4,000 and now is selling it for $2,000, the technology might have progressed so that you can buy a brand new machine with the latest technology for less.

Caution

When purchasing this way, beware of buying hot computers. If caught with stolen hardware, you could end up without your money and without a computer. The seller should provide you with a copy of the sales receipt. This will come in handy if you ever need to have the computer worked on by the company that manufactured the machine. A great number of stolen computers come brand new in their original manufacturer's box, usually stolen from superstore shipments.

The fact that there are only a few manufacturers for each of the major components in a computer means that the prices for these components can be kept low because each manufacturer can mass-produce its component. Also, because each manufacturer specializes in just a few components, a company can concentrate its research on smaller, more efficient, and cheaper designs. Likewise, each component manufacturer can address market needs quickly, allowing new technology to be available soon after a need arises.

Price gouging is relatively unknown between the component manufacturers because of the industry's high pace. User expectations and demands mean that product lifetimes are short with aggressive development cycles. New products appear very quickly and spawn instant and aggressive competition.

So, as you are looking at the ads, make sure to compare features as well as prices. Prices may deviate because one system offers slightly different features from the other. Pick the system that most closely matches your needs at the lowest price.

The quality of the equipment from big and old companies probably won't be any better than if the company were small and new. Big companies tend to produce lots of machines at once. Many times flawed designs must be lived with until current stocks have been sold. Small companies with smaller runs can afford to make functional and ergonomic changes more quickly. Service is also not really an issue, as you learn in the section, "Hardware Support and Maintenance," later in this chapter.

Caution

When looking at an ad, do not limit yourself to slick and glossy ads by big-name companies. Large companies are almost always more expensive and often are very slow in offering new technologies. Because of their size, their overhead is bigger. New technology often has to flow through many committees and project planning sessions, not to mention expensive and carefully planned ad campaigns.

We have used both big-name systems and no-name systems for our own company and projects for years. Except for a rare instance, we have experienced no differences in overall quality between machines purchased from big companies and small companies.

The major advantage of going with the big-name companies is that they are established. They most likely will exist for a long time and you can be assured that you will get your product, as well as parts and service after you make your purchase.

Tip

The warranty should last for at least a year, allowing you to return the machine for replacement should anything go wrong during that period.

The important thing to remember when purchasing a machine from either a big or small company is to make sure the company offers a good return policy and a good warranty. If there is anything missing or damaged or if you simply do not like the quality, you want the ability to ship the machine back and either have them replace it or refund your money.

Peripherals. Buying a computer from a big-name company isn't necessarily better than purchasing from a small company. The opposite advice goes to anyone buying a peripheral such as a modem, tape drive, CD-ROM drive, networking hardware, disk drive, or more memory.

Remember the point that computers are made up of components from different manufacturers? I also suggested that these manufacturers are the ones who count, not the company who actually sells the computer. Well, the word *peripheral* is another word for "component." When you buy a peripheral, you are buying and adding a component to your computer. That component should come from a brand-name company known for producing that component. They specialize in the design of the product (hopefully) and thus can bring a better product to you for the price.

To choose the correct company, read product comparison reviews in popular magazines. *Computer Shopper* and *Byte* contain good product comparison reviews. Since the reviews cover many manufacturers, they let you compare features and prices. Most comparison reviews also spend time teaching you the technology and terms associated with the technology, and make excellent introductions to understanding your peripheral. Finally, reviews of this nature are almost always limited to the big, serious players only. Small off-brand new companies are not usually reviewed. This ensures that you are only looking at the "big names" in that area.

What Hardware To Buy

You cannot use the Information Superhighway without the proper tools. Just like a real highway, to cruise in style costs more. Because this kind of hardware is the latest, with the ability to integrate sound, visuals, and documents, it requires a much bigger engine. To meet this goal, you will either be upgrading your existing hardware or purchasing a new system.

Anyone can travel the Internet with any old clunker. Slow machines of yesteryear, using 300 baud modems, allow access to the Internet over even the greenest of monochrome computer screens.

However, using Mosaic, Netscape, or any of the Mosaic-like browsers requires machines with something more under the hood. They need more memory, a powerful CPU, and a faster link.

> **Note**
>
> For more information on how to use Mosaic and other types of browsers, refer to Que's Special Edition *Using the World Wide Web and Mosaic.*

Mosaic, Netscape, and the other popular browsers are available for many different platforms. Whether you are using IBM-compatible PCs, Apple Macintosh, or X11 workstations (such as Sun, SGI, and HP), you will be able to find a browser for your computer.

On PCs, Mosaic requires Windows 3.1 running in 32-bit extended mode. NT systems are available for some of the browsers. Hardware specifications for IBM PCs and compatibles are summarized in table 6.1.

II

The Basics

Table 6.1 Hardware Needs for IBM PCs and Compatibles		
Component	**Minimum**	**Better**
Hard Disk	20M free	60M free
Memory (RAM)	4 to 8M	8 to 32M
CPU speed	33 MHz 486	100 MHz 486

Disk Space

On all platforms, WWW browsers require lots of free disk space. The browsers like to cache images. This ability speeds up the apparent access to the pages. It works like this. As the browser accesses a page, it stores the images in a temporary directory on your local disk. If it encounters a request for the same image, the browser takes it from your local disk instead of requesting it from the network again. This capability speeds up page requests because images are often reused. The browser clears its cache of images when you exit or when an internal time factor for the image expires.

Note

Make use of your browser's caching ability in your document design by reusing graphics throughout your pages. Use fancy image bullets and text separators to increase the apparent richness and texture of your design without taxing the user's download time or adding to your own throughput.

To handle sufficient caching space, you should always make sure you have at least 20 to 60M free on your hard drive. This should be sufficient if you use anywhere between 100 and 1,600 images. Of course you can get by with less, but you will pay for it in slower access.

Processor Speed

Another factor important in surfing the Web efficiently is the speed of the processor. For PCs you will want at least a 486. The faster the 486 the better, with the minimum acceptable being around a 33 MHz 486. A 66 MHz 486 is even better, and a 100 MHz 486DX4 is better yet. Of course, if you really want to cruise the Web in style, you should use a Pentium.

> **Note**
>
> Your 386 computer will run most browsers, but will be so slow that it will waste your time. Upgrading to a 486 is also a possibility, if you have the time and inclination. In the long run, though, the 486 is cheaper.

Likewise, on an Apple you want one of the faster Macintoshes or a Power PC.

For workstations, almost anything will do because of the inherent power in workstations. Both Sun and Silicon Graphics offer inexpensive and powerful machines even at the lowest (in other words, the least expensive) end of their product lines.

The reason you need all the extra power is because your computer is going to be moving around huge amounts of data in real time. It needs to be able to play animations and sound, and integrate pictures into documents, all very quickly. This takes a powerful processor.

RAM Memory

Just as you required lots of disk space for caching, you also require lots of RAM memory for both the WWW browser program and the space the current document pictures take. For PCs, this means at least 8M. It is possible to run Mosaic on 4M, but it will be sluggish and might crash. The minimum you want to consider is 8M, with the more the better.

Eight megabytes is also the minimum required on the Macintosh, with more being highly recommend because of the Mac's operating system size.

UNIX workstations require much more RAM, with at least 16 or 32M minimum to support the multitasking requirements. However, any basic UNIX workstation configuration should handle Mosaic well. If you intend on running a WWW server, you should have at least a Pentium, Power PC, or UNIX workstation to handle the load.

Power Supply

You want to ensure that your computer's power supply can handle the power requirements of your PC. If your PC has more than one hard disk drive and more than four slots are used in its option bay, you need at least a 200 or 250 watt power supply in the machine. Power supplies below this rating could be prone to overload and shutdown—something you really don't want to happen.

Monitor

Your monitor is important. You will be spending a lot of time looking at pictures and text. First, color is a basic requirement—not that you can't surf the Web in black and white, but you're really missing a major component if you do. Consider color a requirement.

Look for a monitor with clean and crisp color. Turn on the monitor and notice what the screen looks like with just a black screen. Also check out what the monitor looks like with just a white screen.

Monitors in which the front of the glass screen is flat have better visual properties than ones with curved screens. They also cost more.

The monitor controls should be easily accessible through a recessed or covered panel on the front of the monitor. It should include controls for color or tint, brightness, contrast, horizontal centering, vertical centering, horizontal width, and vertical width. The monitor should swivel and tilt for ease of viewing.

For PCs, you want at least a VGA-compatible monitor, with Super VGA being even better. While GIF images placed inside a WWW document are limited to 256 colors, JPEG images and images which may be popped up in an external viewer may have up to 16.2 million colors. VGA handles 256 colors of the inline images but approximates the 16.2 million colors of the pop-up images. It does this quite well and should be acceptable to a majority of users. Super VGA should handle all 16.2 million colors for a stunning full-color display of any pop-up graphics, inline JPEG images, and movies.

Pointing Device

A pointing device such as a mouse is critical to using the Web because Mosaic and its related browsers are all point-and-click. A mouse is ridiculously inexpensive and can be purchased for less than $20. However, you might opt for a slightly more expensive and ergonomically designed mouse. Pick a mouse which looks and feels comfortable. If you really like the Web, you could be spending hours each day on it. It's important that you are comfortable.

> **Note**
>
> Certain repetitive motion injuries such as carpal tunnel syndrome are common in the computer field. Making sure that your mouse and keyboard don't put undue stress on your wrists is an important factor in protecting yourself.
>
> Ergonomic keyboards, chairs, and computer tables are available that help reduce the strains of using a computer. Coupled with a good swivel tilt monitor, these products can help reduce the risk of injury.

Modem

Your modem is the final important factor. To surf the Web in style, you need a fast modem. You need at least a 9,600 baud modem, with 14.4 baud being standard and 28.8 baud being (currently) top of the line. At the time of this writing, 28.8 baud modems can be purchased for around $150, with top of the line 28.8 baud selling for around $400.

You need to check with your provider to make sure that they support 28.8 baud modems. Since the standard for 28.8 baud modems is still not finished, make sure you pick a modem that is compatible with the equipment of your Internet provider.

If you have heavy usage requirements, you may want an ISDN modem. These can be purchased for a little more than regular modems, but require special ISDN phone lines. ISDN phone lines are available in many large cities. The line charge rates vary, but seem to average around $30 per month. ISDN gives you multiple 56K lines and enables you to transfer data and voice simultaneously. Of course your provider's fees are higher for the ISDN connection on their end as well.

> **Note**
>
> Whatever modem you get, it should be Hayes-compatible. Hayes is a company who pioneered much of modern commercial modem technology. They set the industry standard on modem communications. Almost 100 percent of all modems conform to the Hayes standard. Because all communications software knows about Hayes, you should try to stick to only modems that are Hayes-compatible. All Hayes-compatible modems proudly announce this fact on the packaging, so confirming it should not be difficult.

You can choose from one of two kinds of modems:

- Internal modems
- External modems

Internal modems are a few dollars cheaper because they do not require a power supply. However, it's recommended that you purchase external modems for several reasons:

- Since these modems are external, they save a slot in your computer. This may be important if you are a power user.

Tip

Your provider should be happy to suggest a good modem or at least tell you what type of modem to look for.

II

The Basics

- If you ever change your computer or temporarily use another computer, being able to move your modem easily may prove beneficial.

- If you ever change your platform—say from a PC to an Apple—you find your external modem still useful but your internal modem useless.

For people who need laptop portability and still want an external modem, PCMCIA modems are an alternative. These credit-card sized modems offer full baud rates and provide the ultimate in portability. However, to use one you need to equip your computer with a PCMCIA slot (which most laptops have). PCMCIA adapters are also available for desktop PCs, allowing you to share your modem between your laptop and PC.

Laptops

If you need access to the Web on the road and are considering a portable, think seriously about an active matrix color LCD screen. While these screens place about $1,000 price increase on your hardware costs, they provide normal monitor quality graphics.

Indeed, 486DX4 laptops with 300M drives, 8M of RAM, and full-color LCD screens are available for around $3,000. Most of this price is the screen (about 1/3 the cost), but it is well worth it. Having this type of machine as a portable means you can travel with performance that is equivalent to a desktop computer's.

This type of system, coupled with a credit-card thin PCMCIA 14.4K baud modem and a cellular phone link, can allow you to access the World Wide Web even from the slopes of a volcano in Hawaii. Because you can get Pentium-powered laptops (if price is not a problem), you should seriously consider purchasing your machine as a laptop. The savings in a dual office/portable device are quite attractive, and the LCD flat screen is a joy to use.

Learning About Your Hardware

The first step after purchasing new equipment is to read your documentation. Many problems can be avoided if you read the documentation first.

Tip

Place your manuals along with receipt of purchase in a safe place so you can refer to them if needed.

Besides having special installation and setup instructions, the documentation often points out special features that greatly increase your enjoyment of the machine.

After reading the documentation, locate the owner registration/warrantee cards, fill them out, and send them in. Your warranty period begins when the company receives your information. In some cases, you can't ask for technical support if you have not sent in your registration card (though this happens mostly with software, not hardware).

> **Note**
>
> If you are traveling to a foreign country with a portable, you should bring a photocopy of your receipt to prove the purchase was not made within that country.
>
> Some underdeveloped countries place limits on the speed that telephone lines can be accessed. Violation can mean forfeiture of your machines or worse—fines or prison time.
>
> Questions about restrictions can usually be answered by the embassy of the country in question. Another source of information is the U.S. State Department.

Online help manuals are prevalent for most platforms and should be referenced for information that may be more current than the printed manuals.

You also should set aside a few hours to back up any software that came with your machine. Keep the backups in a safe, known place away from metal, magnets, and other electronics, which may have magnetic properties. Instructions on how to back up the software are found with your computer.

Businesses can hire consultants to come in for a half or whole day and give company-wide lectures on using computers. This can help get everybody involved in talking about and integrating computing technology. Private tutors also are available, but can be rather expensive.

Tip
Do not overlook computer magazines for up-to-date articles on how to get the most out of your computer.

Software

Computer software is available from many companies and institutions. Some software is free. Some software is shareware. And some software costs serious bucks. What constitutes good software and bad software? Can good software be free?

Where To Get Your Software

There are three ways to acquire software:

- You can get it for free.

- You can acquire the shareware.

- You can purchase the software.

The Basics

Freeware

Freeware has been around as long as there have been programmers. The concept of freeware is that a programmer, or group of programmers, sees a need and spends the time and energy to fulfill the need. They are then so enamored with their results that they give the program away for others to use. In many cases the programs become very popular, and support then becomes a labor of love for the creators. In some cases, like PKZIP, Doom, and Mosaic, free programs have spawned entire companies.

Acquiring freeware is simple—simply call a BBS or surf the Internet. Many files can be found for downloading.

> **Caution**
>
> Make sure to read the documentation that accompanies the files to make sure that it is free and not shareware. Often it is difficult to tell shareware and freeware apart without looking at the documentation.

Many places on the Internet have huge CD-ROM archives of software online for your searching. Entire archives are devoted to DOS, Windows, Macs, and UNIX machines.

Tip
Regardless of where you found the software, always run a virus checker on it before you begin to use it. This keeps your system safer and less vulnerable to attacks.

◀ See "The Beginning of the World Wide Web," p. 20

When downloading freeware, it's best to get it from the creator's own system. This ensures that you have the latest, cleanest (not modified by someone else), and virus-free version.

Much of the software you need to cruise the Internet can be found on the Internet itself. Both the NCSA and CERN sites offer libraries of browsers, servers, tools, and documentation. Tools include hypertext browsers, hypertext authoring tools, SLIP, FTP, e-mail, NetNews, and Telnet software. It's all free for the taking and usable under the terms of their license agreements.

These sites are often so popular that they are nearly impossible to get into. In those occasions, you might want to try one of the mirror sites. A *mirror site* is another computer with an identical file system. Computers with heavy throughput loads can have alternative sites which you can visit to download the same software. Use Archie to help you determine where mirror sites are located.

Shareware

A second way to acquire software is to get it as shareware. Everything mentioned for acquiring freeware holds for shareware. Read the documentation to find out how much it costs and what rights you have to use it without payment.

Shareware generally costs between $5 and $50 per program. The payment mechanism relies on the honor system. You are usually allowed to use the program for an unlimited time and are trusted to send in your money.

> **Note**
>
> While many people do not pay for their shareware, a surprising number of people do, making shareware a good mechanism for distribution.
>
> The author of a shareware program will often send printed manuals as well as current upgrades to registered users. This gives even more reason to send in the shareware fee.

Another form of shareware allows you to try the product for a certain number of days or times and then purchase it. After the day or time expires, the product no longer runs. These programs are nice because they allow the user to try the product first, but still ensures that the revenue goes to the creator.

Purchased Software

The final method for acquiring software is to purchase it from a professional software company. Software acquired this way is usually top dollar. However, you will also receive the most support and professional documentation.

Cost versus Quality

As discovered in the previous section, one of the differences between purchased software and freeware or shareware is that the purchased software generally has better support and documentation. However, how does the rest of the quality compare? Do you get better software for your money if you pay or if you get it free?

While there is plenty of shareware and freeware which does not work properly, the same thing can be said for professional software.

Good programmers are hard to find and keep. Commercial software tends to be written to fit corporate deadlines and are often sloppily revised after the fact to fulfill user demands.

> **Note**
>
> If you have software that doesn't run or crashes, make sure you notify the company or site you received the software from. Some places have a number or e-mail address to report bugs.
>
> Popular Internet programs often have lists of reported problems for you to refer to.

II

The Basics

Sometimes freeware is better than commercial software because it was an "act of love" from the creator and thus hand-crafted. However, commercial software that has survived the test of time is usually very solid and packed with features.

In general, the higher the version number, the better and more robust the software. This is true for freeware, shareware, and commercial software. This means that version 6.0 should be better than version 5.0.

Commercial software often has more full-bodied capabilities and can conform to standards better than freeware. The investment required to research, develop, and implement many new standards is often easier for a large company to handle than a single creative individual.

The bottom line is, if it's free and it works, use it. If not, try shareware. If that doesn't work, go commercial. If that doesn't work, hire a contractor to custom design your dreams.

Caution

Look at a software product's documentation to see what the minimum requirements are for a computer to run it. This ensures you do not purchase software that you can't run on your machine.

Software is available to fit nearly every need. A little searching should come up with whatever you need.

What's in a Name?

While it does not matter who made the software you are running, there are other names that are very important.

Software is often written to standards. The Internet and WWW are full of standards. These standards regulate everything from network protocols to image file formats.

When purchasing software, you want to make sure that it is compatible with the places and data you will encounter and need on the Net. For example, if you are purchasing a paint package to help you make nice graphics and icons for your home page, make sure to get one which outputs .GIF files. This is the CompuServe file format and is used exclusively by WWW browsers for saving inline images. If the paint package you want to use does not support GIF images, look for conversion programs (filters) that convert from your format into GIF and back again. Likewise, you should choose audio programs that are compatible with the .AU Sun audio file format.

And of course, your network software must be TCP/IP compatible, and your communications software must be Hayes compatible.

These names are the important names in software—not so much the manufacturer, but the protocols.

What Software To Buy

You will need the following items to successfully interact with the Internet and World Wide Web. Many of these are described in Chapter 2, "Net Components and Terminology."

- *FTP.* File transfer protocol is a program that lets you transfer files to and from remote computers. This is the primary way that you send and receive data when not using the World Wide Web.

- *Telnet.* This program allows you to log onto a remote computer as if it were attached to your computer. This is necessary to access your remote accounts on your provider's machine.

- *Archie.* An Archie program finds files on the Net that fit a search word that you provide. Once you locate a file, use FTP to get it.

- *NetNews.* A NetNews newsreader allows you to peruse any of the thousands of special interest newsgroups on the Net.

- *E-mail.* An e-mail reader allows you to receive and send personal electronic mail to anyone on the Internet.

- *SLIP.* A Serial Line Interface Protocol program or a PPP (Point to Point Protocol) program is mandatory to talk to the Internet in the first place. This program takes care of interfacing your modem to the Internet.

- *WWW browser.* A browser such as Mosaic or Netscape allows you to surf the WWW with all its capabilities.

These programs are the minimum needed to be well-equipped on the Internet.

Learning About Your Software

Once you have your software in place, it is time to learn how it works. Begin by reading any online README documentation. This alerts you to any last-minute important changes which might not have made it into the printed documentation.

Next, take the documentation and begin to read it. Hopefully, it is well-written and provides tutorials and examples for you to follow.

II

The Basics

As you begin to experiment with the software, keep the manual handy to refer to for quick tips and hints. Also explore the online documentation. Many software packages have significantly better online help than their paper documentation provides.

> **Note**
>
> Do not be concerned with learning every feature. Get a basic understanding of how to make the software perform for you, adding to your expertise as time goes on.

Many popular software programs are discussed in magazines and books. These resources are good for learning more about your software. Oftentimes you can learn hints from the books that even the creators don't use. Remember, the developers are probably too busy to use their software for more than just testing purposes, thus they are not the best people to write about its effective use. Many times actual users of the software write the best books about the software.

Classes and seminars also can be useful for learning complex programs such as word processing or some Internet software. These courses give you practical hands-on experience and get you using your software effectively in a short period of time. Look to computer stores and universities in your area for classes on using popular computer programs.

Software Support and Maintenance

When installing and running software, you can often experience problems. Some software may be incomplete or may generate errors upon startup. Other software may work fine for awhile, but then cease to work. What do you do when this happens?

If you encounter problems while installing software or upon initial startup, check the documentation carefully for anything you might have missed. Follow the steps again and note everything that happens. Oftentimes a simple typo or missed step is the culprit.

Tip
Do not expect too much from freeware authors, because they really have no obligation to assist you.

If you cannot get the software installed and the manual is no help, ask the manufacturer. While freeware and shareware is generally harder to do anything about, it is not impossible. Many authors of freeware post their e-mail addresses along with their software. Be polite but firm in asking about your problem.

If your program was working fine but suddenly stopped working, check your manual, as well as your hardware and disk drive (this method differs for different platforms), and make sure there are no errors. You might want to run one of the many inexpensive diagnostic programs to try to isolate the problem. Often a corrupted drive mangles a file or program, rendering it unusable.

If you cannot get the program to restart, back up your data to new floppies and reinstall the original software over the old system. Run it and see if the problem is fixed. If it is and all your old data is intact, you are fine. If the program works but your old data is gone, reinstall your backup and call the manufacturer.

> **Note**
>
> Performing proper maintenance on your computer helps prevent most of your problems. Check your disk drive frequently, especially if you run out of disk space or generate any other rare type of error (as rare errors tend to be the least well-tested in software). Refer to the user's manual to diagnose any problems and then call the manufacturer. You also may want to try NetNews, IRC, and BBS groups where you can often find lively discussions about popular software packages. Increasingly, many companies also have WWW sites to provide customer support services.

From Here...

In this chapter, you learned where and how to acquire your hardware and software. You also determined what hardware and software components you need.

You cannot always tell good hardware and software by its cover. Good values exist around every corner, and the smart shopper can be poised to take advantage of it. Keep in mind that the smart shopper is the well-informed shopper. You need to arm yourself with the latest information from resources such as magazines and books.

For more information, refer to the following chapters:

- Chapter 4, "Planning a Web Site," offers suggestions on where to research the latest technology and how to plan your Net business.

- Chapter 6, "Placing a Business on the Web," shows you how to design your WWW presence.

- Chapter 17, "Security and the Net," explores issues in security, viruses, and hacking.

- Chapter 20, "Kiosks Made Easy," explores other novel uses of the WWW and the hardware and software that make it work.

II

The Basics

Chapter 6

Placing a Business on the Web

Your Web site can be housed either at your provider or at your business location, but either way, you still need an Internet provider. You want to make sure that you get the best one you can.

When placing your business on the Web, you may decide to seek professional help. Knowing if, when, and how to use outside professionals may be the key to getting your business launched in a cost-effective and timely manner.

Also, you may be hiring new employees or training existing ones. Many factors will govern your decisions in this area, including the type, size, and configuration of your Web business. Making the right decisions will be important.

In this chapter, you learn

- How to find Internet and WWW providers

- How to find the best and most cost-effective provider for your geographic location

- When to use outside help and how to make sure the help is effective

- Methods to help the training process and in dealing with computer-phobic employees

Locating the Net in Your Area

While most everybody has heard of the Information Superhighway and may even have a vague idea of what it is, they probably have no idea how to get on it. Actually, it's fairly simple. All you need is a computer, a modem, some software, and a provider. It's not hard to find stores that sell computers, modems, and software, even in small towns. But for the uninitiated, finding a provider, determining a good provider from a bad provider, and knowing what is a fair price for services can be a real hassle.

How To Find the Net

The Internet is unfortunately not as evenly spread out as it should be. Some cities have so many Internet providers that some are beginning to go out of business due to the stiff competition. Other cities have only one or two providers, and the majority of smaller cities have no access.

While the Internet is certainly spreading like wildfire across the globe, there is still much territory to cover, and it will take time for it to penetrate certain areas. Your ease of finding inexpensive access will depend on where you live.

If you are fortunate to live in a major metropolitan area, you most likely have multiple Internet providers in your area. Almost all state capitals and other large cities have commercial Internet access (see fig. 6.1).

Fig. 6.1
Internet access can be found in almost every state capital and major city in North America.

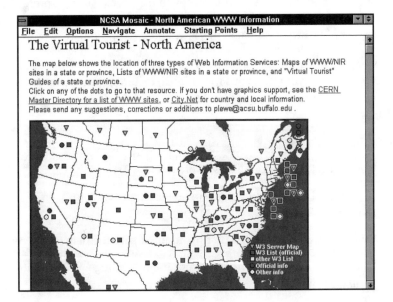

However, the majority of Internet providers do not advertise aggressively. Their hands are usually so full between dealing with system load, upgrades, new users, and maintenance that they have little time to promote themselves. Finding them takes a little more work on your part.

Some methods of finding Internet providers in your area have been discussed in previous chapters. But it will benefit you to review them and add some new methods to your list.

User Groups and BBSes

Begin by picking up a copy of *Computer Shopper* and paging toward the back to the "User Group" and "BBS" sections. Look in your region for any user groups and local BBSes.

If you can find a local user group, go to a meeting and ask the local experts. Even most small cities have computer clubs.

To get in touch with a local BBS, dial their phone number using your computer and modem. Read the message areas for any information about local Internet access. You may find that some of the BBSes offer limited Internet access. If you still have difficulty, ask questions from users in the various conferences and groups and from the system operators.

Universities

Universities almost always have Internet access, and it is often available for free to local citizens. Terminals can usually be found in libraries and other public access areas. You cannot use these for commercial profit, but they do provide access onto the Internet to perform research and offer help in finding a provider. While you are at the university, be sure to stop by the computer department to see if they sell commercial time (as many universities do) or if they know of anyone who does.

Server Finders

The InterNIC maintains a list of providers around the nation, which is available via its Internet Starter Kit. While the list is not up-to-date in accuracy, it will benefit you to consult it.

Likewise, many sites exist on the Internet which list providers around the world. The Virtual Tourist site, for example, allows you to point at a map to find servers for that location (see fig. 6.2). This is just one of the many server finders available on the Internet.

Pay Systems

If you still cannot find access in your area, it's time to succumb to some of the nationwide pay systems such as America Online or CompuServe. While these services may give you somewhat restricted Internet access, they allow you to do ample research and begin to use some of the WWW's

◄ See "Research-
ing Your Op-
tions," p. 87

► See "Maga-
zines," p. 148

Tip

A good place to look for user groups is in local computer stores, as well as your local high schools and junior colleges where the Internet is almost certain to be a hot topic.

◄ See "Local
Clubs and
Colleges," p. 89

Tip

The InterNIC is the organization which distributes domain names. They may be reached at 1-800-444-4345 or by e-mail at **info@is. internic.net**.

► See "How To
Register a Do-
main Name,"
p. 164

II

The Basics

money-making capabilities. However, you may want to weigh the added cost of using a nationwide pay service against a local long distance call to a nearby provider.

Fig. 6.2
The Virtual Tourist at URL **http:// wings.buffalo. edu/world/** lists many server sites around the world.

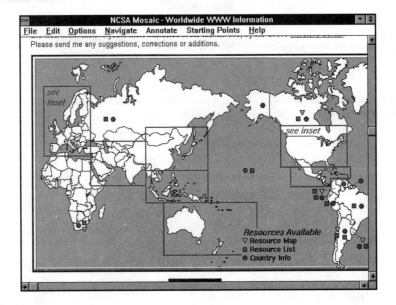

Becoming a Provider

If you are particularly wealthy and ambitious and still cannot find Internet access, you should consider bringing the Internet into your area yourself. Becoming a provider can be a lucrative venture. However, this is a topic for at least a small library of books, and way beyond the scope of this book.

How To Price the Net

As you will find, the Net and the Web both contain many different prices and pricing structures. You may end up with several bills at the end of each month, each for different types of Internet and WWW services. However, nowhere does it say that you must get all your services from one provider.

Your Internet provider should be close to your location so that the phone call is local to you. Your WWW provider can be pretty much anywhere you want. Once you are on the Internet, you can go wherever you want to.

You could portion out all the services to the cheapest bidders, making a patchwork-quilt (so to speak) of Internet access. For example, you might decide to pick a form remailing service from one provider, a conferencing system from another, your shopping system from still someone else, while putting your HTML documents on a fourth system. Doing this type of integration would allow you to pick the cheapest services.

> **Note**
>
> A *form remailing service* forwards a form from the WWW page to the recipient via e-mail. This service, along with shopping carts, conference rooms, and so on are examples of how you can distribute your services from various companies.

> **Caution**
>
> While this method will certainly work, it is not recommended. The more you fracture your service, the more the user has to traverse the Internet to get your information. Even though the software does this automatically, the mere fact that you are distributed over more routes and more computers means that there is a better chance of clogging a route. If this happens, the user determines that a particular service within your page is unavailable. Your loss of business probably won't be worth the pennies you save in fracturing the services.

The best way to price the Net is to find one or two providers who offer all the features you need. Some of the features may be a little more expensive, and others may be cheaper, but the overall combination should be something that works for you. The end result will be pages which are much more integrated and have a higher stability factor.

As with any purchase, you should shop around for your WWW services. Contacting several providers lets you compare costs, quality, and methodology. You also want to examine the "look and feel" of the services offered. This may impact your decision on who you choose and for what price. Again, picking the cheapest may not always be the best choice for attracting clients into your business. Likewise, going with the most expensive may look foolish to the Net-savvy crowd, as well as waste money.

Good Deals versus Bad Providers

The worst thing that can happen to you is getting a provider who is full of great promises but cannot deliver. The Internet represents an incredible gold mine of opportunity and money-making possibilities. Many people are deciding to cash in on the service of providing Internet access to others.

Most people who desire to become a provider have no idea what is in store for them. The following gives you just a sampling of the types of things that providers have to expect:

- Hardware failure

- Incompatible software

- Problems with phone lines

- Naive users calling for support 24 hours a day

- Security breaches by crackers

- Upgrading to meet customer demand

Little do most amateur providers realize, you need a full education in UNIX systems administration, networking, routing, setting up gateways, servers, user accounts, gophers, WWW systems, firewalls, and thousands of other maintenance programs.

To compound the problem, most providers do not understand how much a byte costs them to transmit. It's hard to determine a byte's cost. If sent at peak time, a byte costs much more than one sent during a lull, and the difference is difficult to calculate.

Most early providers underestimate their start-up capital and are underfunded. As they begin to grow quickly (and they will), these providers invariably meet with bottlenecks where demand outweighs supply.

Often the best deals come from the newest providers. They simply do not understand the ins and outs of the business. Be wary of ridiculously low prices—a major indicator that the provider may not have a grasp on the high bandwidth generated by people surfing the Net and their future growth patterns.

Likewise, be wary of the extremely expensive. These people have not taken a good look at the market and are just trying to capitalize on naive users. One of the largest Internet WWW providers—who would not even begin to talk to companies for less than several thousand dollars—has already pulled their WWW project. The advent of reasonably priced pages made such expensive services seem outlandish.

Bartering Your Way To Cheaper Access

The previous section probably made you want to totally avoid all newcomers in the provider market. However, new providers do offer you some advantages.

If you find a new provider who appears to have a plan for incremental growth and is willing to work with you, suggest that they work with you as an experiment to place your business on the Net. Chances are, they are just starting their WWW business and would welcome the ability to try the server on a real project.

Additionally, and perhaps more importantly, small and new provider services are often in need of businesses to make their storefronts look full. This attracts more people into the storefront, whereas a storefront with one or two stores attracts very few customers. Often these providers can be convinced to trade your presence for reduced Internet and WWW service fees.

> **Note**
>
> You should always keep in mind, however, when bartering for your access, that the terms of the agreement may change as the growth of the system changes. When the provider's storefront becomes populated with paying customers, they may decide to stop offering a reduced service fee.

The bottom line, however, is that alignment with new providers can be beneficial, if you are willing to do a little extra work and travel a little rougher road.

Working with Your Provider

Whether your provider is new or seasoned, it is important to build a rapport with them. There will be times when you will need favors or advice, and having the provider on your side will definitely help.

> **Caution**
>
> The old adage, "Don't bite the hand that feeds you," holds very well here. If you are caught harassing other users—either by mass mailings, improper solicitations, or other untolerated methods—your provider has eminent say over your fate. Also, if your company becomes too much of a drain on system resources because of size or failure to observe system regulations, your provider may decide to drop you as a client.

As you begin to place your business on the Web, you may start to use advanced capabilities such as databases, Gopher tie-ins, and other services. These systems may take more and more resources from the provider's machine. Be sure to listen to your provider if they say that resource drain is becoming a problem. Often providers want you to perform heavy processing, such as large mailings, rebuilding databases, and other Internet-taxing tasks during non-prime time so that the impact to other users is minimized.

Tip

Try to respond to
your provider's
needs.

By making an effort to keep the load on the provider to a minimum, you
help the provider keep other users happy. This in turn makes the provider
much more willing to help you when you need new features or advice.

The Evils of Changing Providers

Changing providers can often cause problems. However, there are mechanisms that can be employed if you do decide to change providers.

For many people, changing Internet providers is not an option because there
simply is not that many choices in the immediate area. However, it is easy to
find multitudes of WWW servers, because having a WWW site does not require it to be in close proximity to you.

The title of this section implies that there is some "horror" associated with
changing Internet providers. Let us give you an example of just how horrible
it can be.

We began advertising our own business on the Web by placing our pages in a
nationwide carrier via **ftp://** access. In a matter of days, we had up to 100
people a day visiting our site. Of these visitors we would generate leads at a
rate of between 5 and 10 percent.

After the first month, our provider made a decision to change the address for
FTP access. This amounted to pretty much the same result as if we had
changed providers. At the moment this change happened, our daily walk-ins
fell from more than 100 to zero.

Here's what happened. In order to advertise our business, we had placed links
to our pages in popular lists throughout the Internet. When our provider
changed the FTP address, all the links suddenly failed. People using those
links started receiving errors. Many of those people probably assumed that we
were no longer in business, and didn't know how to look for us elsewhere.

▶ See "How To
Correct Your
Advertising,"
p. 247

Obviously, we then changed primary Internet providers and found a provider
who cared about its users.

The moral to this story is that changing Internet providers—or even changing
addresses—can cause some loss of business. Chapter 10, "Advertising on the
Net," provides you with hints on how to handle changing addresses, but first
you should learn what types of changes cause the most problems.

The previous example indicated that changing the IP address of a machine—
and in fact changing the entire domain name of the machine—caused the
main problem. One could also imagine that if we had changed e-mail addresses, or providers in general, we would have a similar problem.

> **Note**
>
> Changing providers, e-mail addresses, IP addresses, and domain names is much like moving to a new house. If you have ever moved, you know how difficult it is to get all the mail changed over to the new address.
>
> The idea on the Internet is to move as little as possible. However, the primary reason that people move on the Internet is that the provider they are using is not providing adequate service. The best way to avoid having to change providers due to poor service is to pick a stable and wise provider.

To continue the example, when we changed our provider to our new, stable, and friendly provider, about four months after changing they announced that Internet addresses would change for them as well. You can imagine our disappointment because we had just begun to build our business up again.

However, as we said, our provider was indeed wise and cared about its users. They engineered an upgrade path to the new names and IP numbers that happened over many months. The new numbers and names were activated, and the old ones were kept. After several months, people had changed to the new information, and the old numbers were then deleted. This innovative process caused us no noticeable loss of business.

The obvious difference here is that one provider cared and one did not. The biggest indicator of a provider who cares is whether or not they are willing to work with you to help you understand their issues and care about the issues that affect you. Even if they don't recognize a situation at first, one would hope that when pointed out, they would do more than just "study it" (which is what our original provider said they would do).

Obtaining Outside Help—Consultants versus Net Service Bureaus

In previous chapters of this book, you learned that under certain conditions, you want to use outside help in creating and/or promoting your Web business. How much you want to do yourself will, of course, be an individual choice. It depends on your skill levels, personnel resources, and how much time you have.

Chapter 4, "Planning a Web Site," discussed briefly how to write a specification. You want to draw one up before you enter into any work agreements with outside help. You don't have to create a contract, but you should know what you want, when it will be completed, and how much it will cost. Nothing is more disheartening to both a client and contractor when a project is finished and the client says, "Well, that isn't exactly what I wanted."

Tip
Write down any information concerning what you expect from the project.

However, you should examine in more detail when and how to use outside help. The following sections should help you identify situations where going outside will benefit you, and how to go about finding outside help.

Why Use Outside Help?

The majority of people's pages consist of only one or two HTML documents and a sprinkling of links and pictures. For the most part, anyone with even the most rudimentary computer background should be capable of creating his or her own simple HTML pages.

The only software tools you need are the following:

- A word processor that can save straight ASCII files (in other words, any word processor).

- A paint program or other similar graphic design program. This can be as easy as a clip art library with a simple coloring program. A more complete system would include a color scanner and professional paint and tiling package.

- A WWW browser such as Mosaic, and the proper Internet hookup software (such as SLIP).

The low end for these software tools costs you less than $100 and gives you everything you need to compose simple pages.

However, most businesses need much more than simple pages. They may need sophisticated forms capability in order to enable users with feedback or input. They may require tie-ins to in-house databases or special databases designed for their application. They may require a login system to restrict access to paying customers or a billing system to allow them to track and charge users. They may have huge quantities of text which need to be scanned and converted into a computer-readable form. They may want high resolution photographic quality artwork. All of these features require special knowledge and capabilities beyond the casual computer user.

Many people start creating their own pages, but as the project becomes too much to handle (either in sophistication or time), they hand it off to a WWW agency to complete it for them.

Composing your own pages can be useful because it helps increase your background in HTML and your understanding of what creating effective HTML pages entails. Creating your own pages also saves you money with the consultant because service centers have a different price for fixing and proofing pages than they do for creating a page.

> **Note**
>
> Simple changes that you make can keep information and prices in your pages current and up-to-date. Doing these small changes yourself will save a lot of money as compared to having a professional do them for you.

> **Note**
>
> If you write your own pages, you may want to see whether there are any interactive HTML checkers on the Net. From time to time, various webmasters in the IRC group **#www** create systems that check your URLs for consistency. With these programs, you simply type in your URL. They fetch and examine your page and tell you if anything is missing or wrong. The best way to find HTML checkers is to hop on IRC, type **html checkers**, **/join #www**, and ask whether anyone knows of a current WWW Lint site (as these are often called).

However, the majority of large business projects require either your own well-trained staff or the use of a professional agency.

Anyone with a modern word processor has all the tools to create his or her own book. Likewise, you can think up snappy advertising slogans in your head. However, just because you can do this does not mean that when it comes time for creating a new company brochure that you obtain reams of paper, design the art, take the pictures, lay it out, design the ad copy, get the inks, run the press, bind it, and distribute it.

Instead, most of us opt to do portions of the work, such as writing the basic ad copy and supplying some of the pictures, and let a professional put it all together. This is done not only because it saves time, but also you tend to trust the professional to do a better job.

The Web business is even more complex. Some of the things you may want to do requires a staff with advanced levels of UNIX, Internet, C programming, and systems management experience. Designing secure and robust databases and virtual HTML systems requires both expertise and a very sound education in many areas of computing. Unless you have a small staff of computer experts just sitting idle waiting for a project, you will probably save money by using the professional.

Finding Good Help

The Internet is the place to go when looking for someone to help you. Hop on a WWW browser and cruise the lists and links looking for WWW service centers.

Most WWW service centers try to align themselves with one or more providers, so going into a WWW server site will most likely get you access to the people who designed the various companies who are on that site.

This is not to say that if you go with that company, you would also be tied to that particular WWW provider. Most WWW service centers work with you to help you find the proper provider, or work with your existing provider to get your pages installed. Many times these centers design and test your pages on their own provider's server, and when finished, move them to your server. This allows the center to compose your pages without having to bother you for access to your system until the pages are complete.

WWW professionals do not yet advertise in magazines and newspapers very much. While this trend may change, the best place to find WWW pros is still the Internet. There are so many people rushing to the Net that aggressive non-Internet advertising is simply not required. As more professionals enter the picture and as competition stiffens, you can expect to see more traditional advertisements.

Another way to find a WWW professional is to go to your favorite Web sites. Most pages have the name of the designer at the bottom of the page with either an e-mail address or a hyperlink to their home pages. However, you should be careful to see whether the person who designed the page you are looking at is simply a private individual on a "labor of love" or is associated with a professional WWW company.

Avoiding Disappointment

You now have some items to remember when working with professionals. Chapter 4, "Planning a Web Site," discussed how to plan your site, and included detailed information concerning designing a specification.

◀ See "Planning Your Net Business," p. 93

If you are seeking professional help with a relatively small project and are providing some information for them to work with, no specification may be needed. In many cases, the service center mocks up the system for you to look at, provide one level of changes, and be off and running. These situations are very simple and straightforward.

However, when embarking on a large project, more effort is required. In this case, a detailed specification is the number one major factor you need to establish. This "contract" should make the goal clear to both parties to avoid any hidden surprises.

Another factor which helps is to make sure the professional you picked has good references. In this situation, you may want to look over some of their pages. When asking for references, try to get ones that are not all on the same server. In other words, ask for ones from different domain names. Many times the "look" of a professional is based on the client he or she is working for and the site in which the pages are housed. Looking at only one site for a professional may not give you a good idea of the scope of that person's work.

Tip

All WWW professionals should be able to provide you with various projects that they have worked on.

Caution

You might want to be wary of a WWW professional who does not have pages at sites other than his or her own provider's site. These consultants may be unwilling or unable to work with other servers. This factor can be important if you don't like the appearance of the site they work with. If hosting on a specific site is important to you, ask the WWW professional if they can work on that site.

You should expect that a WWW service center might prefer a certain WWW server over others. The center seeks to align itself with stable and good providers. However, the service center staff should be more than happy to recommend alternative solutions and should be able to tell you the pros and cons of any given site you may select.

The final factor in avoiding disappointment in a WWW professional is to make sure to have good communication. Tell the person up front what you have seen that you like and what you want for your pages. If you have a direction in mind, state it. If you see the professional take a direction you don't like, tell him or her right away. Think of it as the same as getting a new haircut. If you are not part of the process, you might not like what you get.

What is a Good Price?

It is important to keep in mind that you are getting a service, not a product. Because of the dynamic and changing nature of the Internet, you want to keep your pages current and fresh. WWW professionals will help you plan the best way to do this. They can periodically freshen your graphics or update your information. Systems can even be designed that change on their own, either matching an internal plan or conforming to their users' needs.

II

The Basics

However, all of these options cost money, and knowing what is a good price and what isn't can be difficult. Why? The industry is so new and prices are still fluctuating wildly because people are trying out the medium and getting a fix on how much it costs to use. As the technology grows, new, cheaper, and better methods are coming out, all of which impacts both what is available to use and how much it costs.

WWW service centers charge as little as $10 per page or as much as $5,000 per page. Neither of these choices in pricing are the proper solution.

An average text-only page should cost between $30 and $100 and be limited in length (usually about a few screen's worth). You are charged for each physical "page" in your system, where a page is a file which is accessed and displayed as HTML. The charge for text should reflect whether you provide ASCII text (the cheapest) or if the material has to be typed or scanned (which usually costs more).

Graphics added to pages usually cost extra, ranging from a few dollars for incorporating simple things like custom bullets and borders, to hundreds of dollars for custom-designed backgrounds and logos. The general range for pictures falls between $20 and $200 per picture depending on whether it needs to be scanned, formatted, cropped, color-reduced, resized, or converted to the proper WWW format (usually GIF or JPG).

Links can be billed either per page or per link. The charge for links should be less than $20 per link and should cover testing of *all* the links in *all* the pages. This testing can get complicated, especially for virtual systems (where the links are created on the fly) and for systems with many interconnected links.

Tip

If there is a link to the company who created your home pages, they should not charge you for that link.

Forms are usually input at a standard price, but managing the output of the form may involve a monthly charge. The form itself is separate from the software which handles transmitting the form data to you. The form itself would incur a one-time charge, usually around $100, with the form handling software usually a monthly fee based on usage.

Other items such as audio, movies, databases, login systems, tracking systems, and all the other wonderful but custom-designed options are usually quoted based on the project itself.

Some WWW professionals offer promotional services. This involves advertising your pages to all the robots and lists on the WWW. These services typically incur a one-time fee and can be good to use. The WWW professionals keep up on the lists and knows when new ones come and old ones go. They know the best places to place your advertisements to bring in your target audience.

They also know how the list managers want information. This one service alone can be worth your while to obtain because getting your name out to the public is the major factor for drawing people into your pages.

Almost all ad broadcasting services cost money, with different amounts being paid depending on the number and type of lists. Prices for this type of advertising can range from $25 to several hundred dollars.

▶ See "How To Advertise on the Net," p. 227

For example, you could have five simple pages with two pictures on each page and four links on each page. Your pricing might look like this:

5 pages @ $100	$500
10 pictures @ $50	$500
20 links @ $10	$200
Total:	$1,200

You can decrease the price of your pages by providing as much information in digital form as possible. Providing your text as ASCII files helps. Your images should be already in GIF format at the size you want them to be on the page. These types of things can cut your page costs in half by reducing the work for the professional.

> **Note**
>
> Keep in mind that some services are monthly; for example, recurring fees are usually based on your usage of a special feature such as e-mailing forms as users fill them out. You should expect to pay a setup charge, as well as the monthly usage charge for such services.

Educating Your Employees

Unless you are currently a high-tech company or have no employees, you probably need to train your existing personnel in how to use the Internet and maybe even how to use a computer.

In an information age, technologically knowledgeable employees and staff become increasingly important. So far, the trend has been for more computers to be used in more and more companies, regardless of the company's size. More and more of these computers are networked either privately or

II

The Basics

through the Internet. Employees with technological knowledge in even non-technological businesses are a valuable resource.

You may encounter the Internet even if you're just opening a burger franchise. The larger franchises all use computerized cash registers that are networked to national or regional headquarters which track sales and inventory. Bookstores not only have computers to keep track of their own inventory, but are networked to stores at other locations. Book orders to some publishers can even be made over the Internet.

Some people can learn about computers with just a manual. They read, they experiment, they learn. Others become lost, frustrated, and confused. You need to know how your employees best operate. If your employees can learn on their own, give them the material they need and let them go at it. However, if your employees are like most, they need help with the ins and outs of computers in general, and with the Internet and WWW in particular.

When training your employees, various options are open to you as an employer. You probably want to use a combination of the following:

- Classes
- Seminars
- Consultants
- Magazines
- Subsidies

> **Caution**
>
> An untrained employee will very rarely wander into an area of your computer where he or she can do real harm. However, an employee with a false sense of personal level of knowledge and training could attempt things that can be very costly in terms of both time and money.

Classes

Classes may be offered through your local school system; a nearby college, university, or technical school; a computer store; or a local computer club. Such classes generally cover a range of topics, from computer basics to using the Internet to UNIX operating systems.

Large corporations usually encourage employees to broaden their education, sometimes paying for part or all of the tuition. If you operate a small company, classes might be a good route if you only have a few employees to train or if you have several employees to train but in different areas.

Classes offer a paced learning schedule that, in general, is the best way for someone to learn something most effectively.

> **Caution**
>
> Classes can run up to 12 or 15 weeks. If time is a factor, you may want to consider other alternatives.
>
> Also, depending on the institution, the costs for classes may mean a sizable monetary investment for your employee or your company.

Seminars

Seminars are more intensive than classes. They often cover the same material as a class but in a shorter period of time. Seminars are advertised in computer-related periodicals. Ads for seminars covering hot topics like the Internet and WWW are found in more general publications like the newspaper and local business magazines.

> **Caution**
>
> Seminars can be costly. Only those employees who can handle the learning curve should attend. Also beware of seminars who promise to teach you everything in a day. If a seminar boasts that it will give all the information needed to put a company on the Internet in just one day, your employees will come back with a glut of information that they can't remember or use.

Tip
Short seminars are best when relaying an overview of a topic or delving into a specific aspect of a topic.

When using seminars, you should make sure the seminar offers hands-on training. Ask how many computers will be there and how many participants. Seminars with a low computer-to-participant ratio can be less than effective.

Consultants

If you have a large number of employees to be trained, you probably want to consider hiring outside consultants. Companies exist that provide in-house seminars as well as more in-depth, one-on-one training.

Training in-house can be more convenient than classes and seminars because it can be achieved according to your own schedule.

II

The Basics

Your outside consultant doesn't have to be a big company, either. Computer professors sometimes offer their services outside of the university. You might even find a college or high school student that can do the job.

Magazines

Magazines and other periodicals are a great way to educate employees and keep them current. Large companies may have subscriptions for individuals, while small companies probably have one copy that is passed around.

Also, you may want to suggest certain articles to read. For example, if you come across a story about advertising and the Web, you can tell your advertising department to read it before their next meeting. If the magazine wasn't available to everyone, photocopies should be made and distributed or posted on company cork boards.

Subsidies

Depending on your field, you may want to encourage your employees to have home computers by offering subsidies. Employees who use computers at home are generally more comfortable with them. The skills they acquire and sharpen at home should benefit their performance at work. Providing machines at home also decreases the likelihood that the user will "play" with the machines at work.

Tip
Power down equipment during a thunderstorm. Make sure to unplug printers, modems, and phone lines. Lightning hitting just one connected wire can travel to all attached equipment, whether they are plugged in or not.

You may find that you need to train certain personnel who don't even use the computer. If you run a small company where sometimes the only staff member is a receptionist (even if it's only during lunch), you should teach that person the basics, or at least how to bring down your computer in case of emergency.

> **Note**
>
> One such situation would be a thunderstorm. If lightning hits your building and your computer is hooked into the wiring of your building (in other words, plugged into a wall socket or the phone system), the lightning travels through your computer and almost always fries it. Those surge protectors you bought can't protect you from the millions of volts of electricity generated by a lightning strike, no matter what the guy who sold it to you said. (Remember, if it makes it from the sky to the ground, two inches of plastic won't do a thing.)

Contacting the System Administrator

One task you need to show your employees is when to contact the system administrator. Basically, the *system administrator* or *SYSOP* is the person responsible for making sure the computer is running and operating correctly.

The system administrator could be you, some kid that comes in after school, or a highly paid professional. This person is the one contacted in the event of severe problems.

You want to educate your employees on which problems they can solve themselves and which need to handled by the administrator.

System administrators are also responsible for assigning login names and managing the overall systems.

Teaching Old Dogs New Tricks

In the following sections, you learn more about training employees in-house by outside consultants, another employee, or yourself. You learn techniques for training a non-computer user in basic computer usage, WWW browsing, and HTML creation. Some of this you'll want to keep in mind even if your training is being done elsewhere.

Tip

If an employee is computer illiterate, the first thing to teach them is locating the on/off switch.

If Computers are Foreign Territory

If computers are foreign territory for your employees, don't expect your employees to learn too much too fast. Don't expect them to remember everything the first time they hear it. Anything learned well is learned from doing it over and over again.

Novice users tend to be afraid that they are going to break the machine. When new users receive their first error message, they think the worst. If a program takes awhile to load, they assume they've crashed the machine. One of the goals up front is to comfort new users and assure them that mistakes just require correction, not panic.

Areas that new users sometimes have trouble with include the following:

Tip

If you are training your employees, remember what you had trouble with or were confused by when you learned about computers and the Internet. Make sure to cover these areas with your employees.

- Remembering to move the cursor to where they want to type. If they are looking at one page, the cursor could actually be somewhere else.

- Pressing Enter to send instructions to the computer.

- Knowing where on-screen to look for information. A screen full of icons and data can be confusing.

- Responding to error messages or requests for input. Employees need to know that some error messages can be ignored, others they can handle themselves, and still others require them to contact the SYSOP. Input requests are quite often self-explanatory if the new user reads the screen carefully.

II

The Basics

A final area that new users have trouble with is understanding how information is stored on the computer and how to find it. If you need to explain this to an employee, a good analogy for you to use is a real filing system. Here, a document is stored in a file folder which contains other documents. The file folder itself may be placed in a bigger folder that holds file folders which is in a filing cabinet. The filing cabinet is in a room which, in turn, is in a building. It is a branching structure that is similar to how data is managed on a computer.

If an employee needs access to a document named SMITH.DOC in subdirectory LEADS of the directory CLIENTS on disk drive C, the employee should know that when he or she uses the computer, it may not be in that directory, subdirectory, or disk drive. Similarly, if an employee saves a document under SMITH.DOC but doesn't remember to note which subdirectory and/or directory it is saved in, that person wastes time looking for it later.

Another valuable training method is to make the employee explain to you or another employee what he or she has learned. Verbalizing information actually makes you learn it faster. Once employees have the basics down, have them teach someone else. As they explain the materials to others, it can reinforce their own learning and lead to a deeper understanding of the material. It can also improve their confidence with computers.

> **Note**
>
> It is important, however, to ensure that the information being reiterated is done so accurately. Teaching incorrect information is rarely an effective means of training.

Employees Using the Web

While using the World Wide Web itself is very easy, the steps your employee has to go through to get there may not be that simple. The procedure for putting information on the WWW involves more than just pointing and clicking.

If employees are just using the Web, they need to know the following:

■ How to get to the program they will use to access the Web. This may involve changing directories on the computer, opening programming, and initiating a Telnet session.

▶ See "How To Search for Existing Information," p. 213

■ How to use the program. The program will be a WWW browser, such as Mosaic or a Mosaic-type browser.

Employees Creating HTML Documents

If employees will be creating portions or an entire HTML document, they need to know the following:

■ Information on how to use an editor so they can enter the HTML document and formatting instructions

■ HyperText Markup Language (HTML) Launching to create the hypertext document

■ Graphics applications to create graphics, icons, and buttons for your WWW site

▶ See "Your Home Page," p. 364

▶ See "Basic HTML," p. 521

What the System Administrator Needs To Know

Of course one person doesn't have to do it all. The information to be contained in the document could be keyed in by a typist or secretary with the editor currently used. Your SYSOP WWW staff could add the HTML instructions and integrate the graphics that were created by your in-house artist or by a commercial graphics house.

Your system administrator needs to know the following:

■ How to handle security

■ The operating system of your computer, plus the UNIX operating system and TCP/IP protocols

■ Some hardware knowledge

> **Note**
>
> Your customers don't want to hear, "Oh, we just got this new computer system and I'm still trying to get the hang of it," while waiting for your flustered employees to figure out why the computer isn't working the way they expect.
>
> Don't put your employees in front of the public until they are ready. It's irritating for the customer and can affect employee confidence and productivity.

Dealing with Computerphobic Employees

Generally, employees who are computerphobic are not just lazy or unmotivated to learn something new. They may be afraid of breaking a machine which would cost you money or their job. They could have been conditioned to think that they aren't smart enough to use computers. Executives and upper management could even be afraid of appearing inept or could think that anything related to a keyboard is for secretaries.

If some of your employees are afraid of computers and you need them on the machine, you should try the following strategy.

Tip
Realize that this takes time. If you can't or don't want to make that investment in your employee, hire someone else.

First, introduce your employee gradually and make sure that person's first experiences are non-threatening. For example, have the employee sit down at a computer that already has a Solitaire game loaded and ready to play. Almost everyone knows how to play the game (if not, it's easy to learn), so the employee can concentrate on things like using a mouse or keyboard and knowing where on-screen to look for information.

> **Note**
>
> Be patient and considerate. If you bring in outside help to train your employee, be aware of the instructor's interpersonal skills. For example, a college student who is such a whiz at running your computer system may speak too quickly and assume too much to train a non-technical or older employee.

After the employee is comfortable with the game (which probably won't be after just the first time), have that person load the game on his or her own.

If the employee has to log in to the system, take it step-by-step backward through the procedures this person needs to go through from login to loading the Solitaire game. If the employee has to turn the computer off and on, this should be the last task learned.

Determining Who Gets What Access

When bringing the Internet into your business, you should give careful consideration to whom you give access. Often a full Internet feed into you company can mean that information can flow out as well as in.

▶ See "Crime and the Net," p. 385

Placing terminals in or near areas dealing with sensitive information only invites people to share that information over the Internet. Likewise, placing sensitive information physically on the same system that handles the Internet is probably not a wise decision.

In general, it's a good idea to restrict your Internet access to only those who have direct need for it. Having open Internet access for e-mail and news is great for all employees, but you should limit the full access to after hours or only to those who need it. Doing this decreases the amount of "playing" that goes on.

Where To Find the Right Employee

The right employee may be closer than you think. If you have an employee with a home computer and who uses it a lot, that person may have skills you can use. Maybe the teenager of an employee is a computer whiz. If that person is mature and responsible, you could have him or her manage a system or train employees. Ask around—it seems like everyone knows someone who is good with computers.

> **Note**
>
> If your company is planning on integrating computers and/or the Internet into some aspect of your business, you may want to begin hiring employees now with at least some computer experience.
>
> For example, if you own a pizza parlor in a college town, you could consider a WWW ordering system. You could start hiring delivery drivers and staff who can deal with computers. Just a class or two in high school is better than nothing. Even if you decide against the new ordering system, you haven't lost anything by hiring the delivery person who had the computer training over the person who didn't.

As previously mentioned, contact high schools, universities, and the like. Call the head of the math or computer department and explain what you need. They should be able to put you in contact with a student, a recent graduate, or perhaps even a faculty member who can fill your needs.

> **Note**
>
> High schools and universities can also be a source for interns. If your project is interesting, the school might even be interested in helping you out as a project for a class.

Head hunters and recruiting agencies also help find professionals for you. While many of these are expensive, the Internet offers quite a few which are reasonably priced.

If you need someone to input a finite amount of text and you don't have the staff in-house, a temporary agency can provide you with typists who are familiar with just about any computer word processor.

From Here...

This chapter discussed the nuts and bolts of putting your business on the Web. You learned how to find the best provider for your Web site and ways to work with your provider that can be beneficial to you both.

This chapter also showed you how to manage staffing considerations, the benefits and pitfalls of using outside help, and what your employees need to know, as well as techniques to use in training employees about computers and the Internet.

For more information, refer to the following chapters:

- Chapter 10, "Advertising on the Net," provides specific details on placing your advertisements on the Web.

- Chapter 11, "Order Taking and the Net," shows you how to sell products and services on the Web.

- Chapter 14, "Subscription Services, Virtual Malls, and Instant Products," discusses more ways your company can make money on the Web.

- Chapter 20, "Kiosks Made Easy," shows you how to implement yet another money-maker using the Internet and WWW.

Chapter 7

Picking a Name for Yourself on the Net

In reality, you will probably choose more than one name. As you start your business on the Web, you will begin to put names to yourself and your business. Depending on your level of interaction with the Web, the names you choose will range from simple login and e-mail names to actual domain names.

For the most part, names are important on the Web. Everybody likes a catchy name. A good business or site name should inform and yet entice. Several names tend to be high tech. However, if your company or organization wouldn't be enhanced by that kind of image, don't do it. A cookie company selling "homemade cookies like grandma used to make" doesn't want to name itself "Cybercookies."

Some businesses just use the corporate name and that's that. Other companies come up with a hybrid to denote the Internet aspect of their company. For example, the Web version of the *San Francisco Examiner* is known as the *Electric Examiner*.

If you already have a business name and don't want to change it, perhaps a slogan for your Internet business would achieve the effect you want. Names used in e-mail and NetNews can reflect hobbies, areas of interest, self-perceptions, or simply your real name.

For domain names, it can be very important to have the right one, and also to make sure that others don't beat you to using your company or corporate name as their domain name.

In this chapter, you learn

- How to choose names for login and e-mail purposes

- How to pick passwords that offer more security

- What domain names are and why they are important

- How to register domain names

- How and when to create multiple presences

- How to select a business or site name that can help bring you business

Picking Login and E-Mail Names

Usually in big companies or universities, your login and e-mail name is assigned to you. Bob Smith at Acme Corp. may be bob@acme, or at a larger company, bsmith@acme. If you don't like a name given to you, ask the appropriate authorities—your server or the system administrator—if you can change.

Oftentimes you can tell how important people are at a company by looking at their e-mail or login name. In a company with five Bobs, usually the highest-ranked person will get the easy login of just bob (this applies only to corporate accounts).

At almost all services, you need a login name. If the group is large, your first choice may already be taken. When one of us registered with the online version of *WIRED* magazine, we had to go through five names before finding one that wasn't already given out.

> **Note**
>
> When choosing login names, make sure to choose one you'll remember. The other alternative is to write it down.
>
> Security is not an issue with your login name, because this is the same name that will appear in your e-mail. Your password, on the other hand, should never be written down.

Identity and Recognition

As mentioned in the previous section, login and e-mail names can reflect personal interests or an image that a person wants to project.

Business users tend to select names appropriate to their field. It can be hard to put your trust in someone with a silly or offensive nickname. For example, a law firm probably doesn't want e-mail received at their place of business for "studly." On the other hand, it could be a perfectly appropriate e-mail name for the owner/operator of a motorcycle repair shop.

If you can get an e-mail name that is descriptive of your business or service, by all means take it. You will only be able to use the name if someone else on your server doesn't already have it. E-mail names like "acepilot," "flowerman," or "golfpro" can lead to greater market recognition and increased revenues.

Selecting Passwords

Passwords are used to protect data from unauthorized users, to bill for pay systems, and to track data for free systems. If there's a password, it's probably used for a good reason.

> ### Caution
>
> You shouldn't choose passwords that are easily decipherable. Never pick a password that is the name of your spouse, pet, or child. Do not pick your birthday or wedding anniversary, or portions of your address, Social Security number, or phone number. If someone is going to steal your password, at least make them work for it.

The reason why people choose personal words for passwords is that they're easy to remember. What you need to do instead is come up with something else that is easy for you to remember. Keep the following pointers in mind:

- You should use a combination of letters, numbers, and special characters.

- Instead of using names, you could resort to short phrases arranged in an interesting style. Since most passwords need to be eight characters or less, you need to be inventive. Here are some ideas:

    iam4u

    2bornt2b

    me2(u2)

Tip

If you are worried that your friends and associates who know you as Bob Smith or Jane Jones won't be able to find you, get another e-mail account with your name attached to it.

II

The Basics

Each of these passwords are easy to remember. The first, iam4u, is "I am for you." The second is the famous phrase, "To be or not to be," and the third says, "Me too (you too)." These names are nonpersonal, use letters and numbers or symbols in combination, are certainly cryptic, and are easy to remember. Endless combinations and variations can be created allowing you to change the password frequently.

These examples are much better than naming your password "david1" or "pass5," which are very easy to break by determined hackers.

■ If you have various sites and systems that all require passwords, you might consider using the same password at all sites. That way you don't have to remember which password goes with which system. This is a good tactic for users whose security need lies in discouraging casual, prying eyes. People who have access to sensitive data would not want to do this because of the potential security ramifications.

> **Note**
>
> Keep in mind, though, that if someone has enough time and computing power, he or she can break any password. If this is a risk in your industry, you may want to change passwords from time to time.

▶ See "Encryption," p. 406

■ Sometimes passwords need to be chosen for a group of people. You can give each user his or her own password, or you can issue a group password. Group passwords, by nature, are less secure and should be changed more frequently.

> **Caution**
>
> In general, you do not want to write down passwords. You may not be able to find where you wrote it down, or worse, someone else who shouldn't have that information could find it.

How you treat passwords depends on what you are trying to protect. If you are registering for a free online service, you're really not protecting anything. However, if your company has online work groups in a highly competitive industry, poor password selection or writing them down can mean that the cleaning crew at night could be emptying more than just your wastebaskets.

Likewise, keep in mind that not all password systems are created equal. On UNIX systems, even the system administrators don't know your password. But many BBS systems do allow their administrators to know passwords.

Using the same password in a BBS and on a UNIX system may release your password to the BBS operator.

In general, it's a good idea to have a "frivolous" password that you use when trying out a service, later changing it to a more "serious" password when actually using a service. This also works if you need to give someone temporary access to an account. Just change your password to something like "temp" and give it out with your login name (which doesn't change). When the person is finished with your account, change your password back.

▶ See "Crime and the Net," p. 385

Domain Names

Domain names are used by companies or organizations who have SLIP or PPP connections to allow users on the Internet to come into their site.

Picking a good domain name follows the same common sense as picking an e-mail name. However, domain names have much more importance than a simple e-mail address.

When choosing a domain name, getting the right one can be very important. Look at some of the domain names listed in the URLs of computer companies here and in Chapter 3, "Why the Net is Good for Business":

- sun.com for Sun Microsystems

- apple.com for Apple Computers

- sgi.com for Silicon Graphics Inc.

You can see that each of these names are fairly descriptive of the company who owns them. The following sections explain the ins and outs of domain names.

What Are Domain Names?

Just as you use street addresses to find another person's home, computers on the Internet use IP numbers as addresses to find each other. *IP*, or *Internet Protocol*, is basically a super-detailed zip code.

Imagine that someone could locate your house by zip code alone. As it stands, the four-digit extension added recently by the U.S. Postal Service is similar to this concept. But, instead of having two components as expanded zip codes do, IP numbers are composed of a series of four numbers put together. Each number is separated from the previous one by a period and can't be larger than 255 (0 being a valid number).

The Basics

For example, **192.203.155.99** is an IP number. This is the number that was assigned to one of our computers. Our other computers that are SLIPped into the Internet have different IP numbers. IP numbers are given out in blocks, where the smallest block contains 256 numbers. These blocks are called *classes*, and the smallest block, of 256 numbers, is called a Class-C block. Most Internet providers will assign you a single number from their block of numbers, but in situations where you have your own internal network, your own block of addresses can be beneficial. Your provider will help you determine your needs.

> **Note**
>
> Whenever you transmit any data over the Internet—whether it be e-mail, NetNews, or simply chatting to a friend—an IP address must always be specified. The IP number accompanying your data tells all the computers between you and your final destination where your destination is. This allows the computers that handle routing to accurately deliver your request.

If you do not have your own SLIP or PPP account, the IP number associated with your Internet transactions is the IP number of the computer at your server which is currently serving you.

IP addresses are allocated to you instead of you simply picking your own address. To illustrate why, return to the zip code example. What would happen if everybody could randomly pick their own zip code? It would obviously be extremely difficult to deliver the mail. The major problem would occur if more than one person picked the same number.

The same goes for the Internet. Because IP numbers are used for any TCP/IP network (even if it is not on the Internet), many people have networks which are only used in-house and never make it onto the Information Superhighway. What often occurs is that when they set up their in-house network, they simply pick IP numbers randomly. This serves them okay because their network is internal only.

However, at some point, when you decide to hook up to the Internet, this number must be changed. You may find, after hooking up, that you are using someone else's number. When this happens, the computer with the established number wins out; all the computers on the Internet that handle routing know that this IP number is for the other computer, not yours. In other words, your e-mail will be directed to them.

Imagine that the only item you had to identify each other's houses were IP numbers. You would soon be overcome with digits. Remembering more than just a few houses would be difficult. It would be nice to use a name to reference a given computer instead of just a number.

That's what a domain name is. The *domain* is your computer system or systems (think of it being the "ruler of your domain"). The *name* is a title you use to label your network. It is also the name that Internet routing computers use to look up your IP number.

For example, cookware's Internet provider is a company named IQuest. Their domain name is iquest.net. Likewise, our company name is cookware, and one of our registered domain names is cookware.com.

If you have ever sent e-mail, you are already familiar with domain names. Sending e-mail to us, for example, would consist of sending to **iceman@iquest.net**. Here you can see the two components: iceman is our user name on IQuest, and following that, separated by @, is the domain name.

When sending information over the Internet, you can use either IP numbers or domain names. If you use the domain name, the computer first consults a master list of names to determine the proper IP number. It then substitutes the number for the name and continues the transmission. This small capability makes it exceedingly easier for all of us to get around on the Internet.

Looking at our e-mail address of **iceman@iquest.net**, you can understand what happens. The mailer program sees iquest.net and looks up the appropriate IP number. The request is then routed from machine to machine until it reaches our Internet provider, IQuest. At that point, IQuest looks up in its user list to find the user iceman; the mail is then placed in our mail file. Later in the day, when we check our mail, we can find the message from you.

Deciphering Domain Names

An experienced Internet user is able to glean much information from a domain name. In fact, a domain name acts like a map, telling you about the site you are going into.

There are few restrictions as to what a domain name can be, but the Internet has adopted a fairly standard method of naming. Because of this standard, which is followed in almost 100 percent of the cases, reading a domain name is easy.

Tip
If you think about it, you see that this is almost identical to what goes on when the post office delivers a letter to you.

The Basics

A domain name consists of three basic components, each separated by a period:

machine_name.site_name.domain_type

The *machine_name* may be missing, or there may be more than one machine. These are separated by a period.

The *domain_type* is the most important thing to look at. This is always present in a domain name and follows a fairly fixed set of rules. The *domain_type* specifies what kind of domain this is. The most frequently used domain types include the following:

domain_type	Description
.com	Commercial users
.net	Network providers
.edu	Educational
.org	Non-profit organizations
.gov	United States government (non-military)
.mil	United States military

Besides these, there are domain types which signify foreign countries. These are extensions specific to a country. For example, domain names ending in .jp are in Japan, while ones ending in .fr are in France, .ca in Canada, and .au in Australia.

> **Note**
>
> I've seen occasional use of .us for the United States, but it is very rare indeed, since the U.S. led the way for Internet usage. I also know of no place that lists all the domain extensions, because new ones are being created daily. In general, most people figure it out by usage.

You can begin to appreciate how this final code in all domain names is useful. It tells you something about the site. If it is .mil, you are dealing with the military or a military user. A .com is always some commercial venture.

Domains ending in .net are a little trickier. Because .net indicates an Internet service provider, they may have many users. Some of these users run businesses. Therefore, a .net ending for a commercial site occurs when the business doesn't have its own domain name and operates from the provider's name, or is itself providing net access services.

The portion of the domain name to the left of the domain type is the *site_name*. The *site_name* is the part which actually identifies the owner of the domain name. For example, in the domain name iquest.net, the site name iquest identifies our provider IQuest as the owner. If you read the two components together, it says, "a business named IQuest (iquest) that is an Internet provider (.net)."

The domain name usually refers to an actual machine. The domain name maps to an IP address which is assigned to a physical machine. However, users who have SLIP accounts appear as a unique machine and often have their own IP numbers. Therefore, you can have a domain name even if you are using a commercial Internet provider.

Tip
Any other name to the left of the site name indicates a particular machine at that site.

For example, if your company was Bob's Ice Cream Parlor and you were at IQuest, you might have a domain name of icecream.iquest.net. This would map to your SLIP connection.

Because the name can actually be anything, your Internet provider can have your domain name changed such that it is any name. For example, you might prefer that your name be icecream.com instead of icecream.iquest.net.

By looking at the domain names you encounter as you cruise the Internet, you should now be able to easily tell information about the users.

Why You Should Register a Domain Name

If you only have terminal access to the Internet and are not SLIPped or PPPed into the Net, you cannot make use of a domain name. However, since almost all users of the Web have SLIP or PPP access, most of them can use a domain name.

The domain name makes it easy for a user to reach you. Many times people can simply guess a domain name to see whether that company is on the Web.

Suppose you are a high-profile company named Skids. A person trying to find you on the Internet may look for skids.com or skids.net. A surprising number of companies can be found this way. Use Ping to try the name (**ping skids.net**) or the WHOIS database (**whois skids**) to let the user know that you are on the Internet.

II

The Basics

> **Note**
>
> The UNIX commands PING, WHOIS, FINGER, and NSLOOKUP can all be useful for determining if a domain name is valid. Often non-UNIX platforms have versions of these commands as well. For more information, turn to the UNIX manual pages for these commands, or the SLIP software for non-UNIX platforms.

By creating your domain name from your business name, you help establish market awareness. It also ensures that your precious name is not taken by someone else.

Many companies place their domain name such that each entrance into their company has a different machine name. For example, when ftping to skids.com, the address might be ftp.skids.com. But when accessing their WWW pages, you might get them from www.skids.com. Likewise, their Gopher information might be at gopher.skids.com. In reality, all these names are probably (but not necessarily) the same machine. The different leading names just make it convenient for the user.

Armed with this information, you could then begin to guess at names. If you needed the domain name of the White House, you would probably say whitehouse.gov and you'd be correct!

Let's try another one. If you wanted to know the name of the Rolling Stones WWW home page, what would you say? Well, the answer is www.stones. com. You might have said www.rolling.net or www.rolling.stones.com. Any of these would have been good guesses, but in this case, would not have been correct. However, most Internet users are bright enough to try different combinations when looking for you.

> **Note**
>
> There is an advantage to using skids.com. If you change Internet providers, you merely change the mapping of the IP address to your name, but the name stays the same. This means that users can still access you by skids.com. Your new Internet provider should help you make the change.

How To Register a Domain Name

There are two methods you can choose to register your domain name. The first method is free and simply requires your time and energy. The second method costs money, but is usually worth the hassle.

Before you learn how to register your name, you should know where you register your name.

The companies of General Atomics, AT&T, and Network Solutions Inc. have the contracts to handle the domain name and IP databases. They take care of handing out IP addresses and domain names. They also ensure that names conform to standards and are unique. This whole structure falls under the name InterNIC, which is overseen by the National Science Foundation.

You can get information about domain names from the InterNIC Services Reference Desk run by General Atomics. The access information for this is as follows:

InterNIC Services Reference Desk / General Atomics	
Toll-free:	800-444-4345
Phone:	619-455-4600
Fax:	619-455-4640
E-mail:	**info@internic.net**
Postal address:	InterNIC Information Services General Atomics P.O. Box 85608 San Diego, CA 92186-9784

When you want to register your name, contact Network Solutions. They handle the actual assignment of the domain names and IP numbers.

InterNIC Registration Services / Network Solutions Inc.	
Phone:	703-742-4777
E-mail:	**hostmaster@rs.internic.net**
Postal address:	Network Solutions Attn: InterNIC Registration Services 505 Huntmar Park Dr. Herndon, VA 22070

Both companies have support staff to help you get your names. Likewise, complete online information, including the ability to see if a name is already registered, is available on the World Wide Web at **http:// www.internic.net/**. Here you find links to all these companies as well as registration forms and answers to all the most frequently asked questions.

The InterNIC forms require information that your provider can help you with. The forms are very clear as to what is needed, and ample help is available from both the support staff and online documents.

If this seems a little complex, use the second method of obtaining your domain name. Talk to your Internet service provider, who should offer the ability to make, move, or change your domain name. Fees usually range from $25 to $100 and are generally worth the money.

Once the forms have been submitted, it will take awhile for your name to be registered because of the incredible number of domain name requests that are received each day. Domain names are usually granted, assuming no problems, within about eight weeks or so. Be patient.

> **Note**
>
> InterNIC is beginning to frown on companies who register more than one domain name. Because of the overload experienced in the rush for domain names, many companies are being refused second and third names.

Tip
When you make the request, have two or three other names available as alternates in case your first choice doesn't fly.

You should not experience a problem unless the forms were incorrectly filled out or the name you requested is already in use. Your request will not be honored if it flagrantly violates the naming scheme (for example, if you try to get .mil and you are not military). If any problem occurs, correct your information and resubmit the form. If you have questions, ask your Internet provider or call any of the access numbers listed earlier.

Domain Names and the Competition

You would think that most companies would pick a domain name similar to their own business name. However, you might be surprised to learn that some companies have actually picked domain names that contain all or part of their competitor's name.

There you are, working late at night on the Internet. You are thinking about getting your company, Skids, a domain name. You access the InterNIC to see whether your name is available and see that someone is already using skids.com. Upon further investigation, you discover that skids.com has been taken by your arch rival, Skads.

What do you say? This can't happen? Wrong! It has happened and does happen. The laws on the Internet simply do not exist yet. While the InterNIC takes pains to make sure duplicate and obvious entries are not given out, there is no way they can ensure that someone doesn't take your company business name.

Here is another example. As a perhaps unethical but yet enterprising individual, I go out and register the domain names of all the leading worldwide companies who do not yet have them. I then go knocking on their doors and offer to sell them the domain name for a large sum. Or I don't even need to make the effort of contacting them because eventually they will track me down when they create their domain name. They of course will pay me that money because they want and need that name.

The problems are compounded by the restrictions of the domain name. For example, a company named Woodmill Lumber of Virginia makes skids. They may want the domain name of skids.com. This has no competitive value against a company named Skids, who has nothing to do with the wooden variety. There could even be two companies named Skids.

> **Note**
>
> Domain names are always in lowercase. Therefore, the name Skids.com is not acceptable, but skids.com is acceptable. No special characters should be in the name, either. For example, $skids$.com is not usable. Underscore characters are also not valid within domain names.

Now take this problem to a worldwide market and see how difficult enforcement becomes. Suing an American company in American courts for taking your company name may or may not be successful. But how would suing a company in Japan for taking your American company name work? And Korea? And the Soviet Union? And India?

The laws have definitely not been written on this one.

If Your Name is Used

If, horrors of horrors, you discover that your desired domain name is in use, what do you do?

First, you should determine if the name is actually active. Some names have been issued where the user, for whatever reason, never fully activates the name. In these cases, you may be able to convince the owner to relinquish the name to you by simply contacting them in writing or by e-mail.

However, chances are good that the domain is active and in use. You can try to talk to the owners into giving up the name, but chances are they will be unlikely to relinquish the identity, especially if they have users who already know about it. Domain names, once established, are valuable to the owner. If you are a high-profile company with lots of money and good lawyers and you want to try to set some precedence, you can try to sue to get possession of the name.

The best solution is to pick a different name. This is why even the InterNIC forms have a spot for more than one name, just in case the first name is already in use.

You can expect this to be a bigger problem as more and more people come onto the Internet.

> **Note**
>
> Copyrighted and trademarked names have had minor success in being upheld as ownership when it comes to domain name usage. However, because of the worldwide aspect of domain names, even copyrighted and trademarked names are hard to uphold. For example, www.coke.com could indicate anyone from a soft drink company to a coal mining establishment. Ownership over such names is hard to uphold worldwide, at least at this point.

Multiple Presences

Because the Internet is such a wide, open place where you rarely come face-to-face with the people you interact with, it can be hard to know just who you are dealing with. On one level, this can be a problem if you run across unscrupulous people.

▶ See "Misrepresentation," p. 387

Businesses and organizations can use multiple presences as a valid way to draw more people into their site. This section helps you understand how to do this and shows the benefits associated with having more than one presence.

Before you explore the benefits and uses of multiple presences, you need to understand the term. Having a *multiple presence* means that there is more than one way to get to your information and each way appears to be different to the user. In this case, the user may not realize that each of the entrances lead to the same store.

As you'll see in the following sections, having multiple presences and multiple entrances for your business is one of the most effective ways to advertise yourself.

The Benefit of Having Multiple Presences

At first glance, having multiple presences may seem to be somewhat unethical. If multiple presences are used for misrepresentation, they may indeed be unethical. However, there are many times when you can benefit from having multiple presences.

Suppose you are a well-known publisher of fine literature. However, you are beginning to experiment with the romance novel industry, but are afraid of how this might impact your current standing. In this case, you might use multiple presences to try out this new industry. You would create a new name, a new look, and a new feel with different WWW pages. In this way, you would be able to experiment with the romance field without jeopardizing your current standing.

Another example of a good use of multiple presences is to draw a wide spectrum of users into your business. You have a product which is attractive to more than one age group. In this case, you might want to market to each group separately. To older people, you might want to market the product under a more conservative corporate banner. For a younger audience, you may pick a more modern profile. Having multiple presences allows you to do this without having your marketing to one group interfere with another.

> **Note**
>
> Multiple presences used in this manner are similar to TV ads for the same product that are released in different versions to appeal to specific target audiences.

In both of the previous examples, you could even register the business under different domain names and company names. The user never needs to see a relation between the companies. This might be useful when entering new markets, or markets in which you previously had difficulties penetrating.

You could also use both names when dealing with different countries. You could rename your company to attract a specific culture, using pages written in the regional language and culturally meaningful icons. This would allow you to market more effectively to your intended audiences.

Multiple presences can be used in both a positive and negative manner. Note that this example shows a fine line between ethical and nonethical. You establish a new business and want to grow as quickly as possible. To do this, you decide to make 10 versions of your business, each with different names and pages. Each business advertises your services but under a different name. To the end user, it appears as 10 different firms, but in reality, all work is funneled to you. Is this unethical or not?

One way to view this scenario is to consider nine of the virtual firms to be "franchises" or stores opened in other locations. An entrepreneur who owns the West Side Grocery Store is under no obligation to call the next purchased grocery store the same name. There is certainly no restrictions placed on real businesses for having multiple names, and likewise none on the Internet. In this case, the use of multiple presences may be viewed as ethical.

However, take the same example but with a different intention. In this case, you create multiple presences in order to mislead your competition. The new companies are truly virtual and serve only to throw off the competition. Your advertising may elude to products which do not exist, or pricing which is fixed. These could be used to influence your competitors' plans, or at least cause them to lose some time. The alternative companies could be bidding against each other to create bidding wars. This purpose could be considered an unhealthy use of multiple presences.

The current Internet community has not seen too much yet in the way of unethical business practices. Doing business on the current Internet is not like doing business in the real world, where the motto generally is "anything's fair in love and war." The Internet community, conceived and still maintained as a sort of collaborative and open forum (even though it is going commercial), will not accept certain practices that might be accepted in the business community.

Tip

Understanding the etiquette and mindset of the Net community is very important. Breaching the rules of fair play could foil any attempt to make in-roads in the Net market.

However, as people begin to explore this new territory, you should realistically expect to see an increasing misuse of the Internet, including both traditional and novel forms of unethical behavior.

Since laws have not yet been written for the Internet, one only knows what types of libel cases will stem from a sullied reputation through IRC conversations. Damage can be done very quickly and over a large geographical area. While you are fighting it out in court, your name can still mean "mud" to over 35 million users. And a lawsuit over what was perceived (by the Internet community) as a righteous flame could further degrade your reputation on the Net.

The bottom line in multiple presences is that they can be very useful when used correctly. However, your intent in using multiple presences will be the deciding factor in how ethical it is.

And for the user, as they say in Latin, "caveat emptor" ("buyer beware"). If you are asking for competitive bids, it's up to you to investigate the company. Check domain names and ask for references.

Creating Multiple Presences

The simplest way to create multiple presences is to create multiple sets of your pages. Each page can then be tailored to fit the audience you are seeking. E-mail addresses and domain names may be left the same or changed, depending on how complete you want your new identity to be.

For example, if you are starting to market your product in Japan, you may want to add new e-mail and domain names which are meaningful to Japanese-speaking users. Remember that the car model Nova didn't do too well in Spanish-speaking countries. "*No va*" in Spanish means "no go." Try not to make a similar mistake.

For maintainability sake, you probably want all your pages at the same site. However, this is not necessary, and there are times when you may benefit from picking multiple sites.

If your current site is particularly busy or your page is particularly popular, dividing your pages between multiple sites can offer your users better access. Likewise, if some of your users are located in the U.S. and some are in Japan, you may want to host your Japanese pages in Japan to allow those users faster and more reliable access to your page.

While this may seem trivial, it can become significant. For example, one of our favorite searchers is CUSI, which is run by Nexor in England. CUSI itself ties to many of the popular WWW search engines throughout the world, including some in the United States.

We regularly access CUSI many times a day. However, consider the path our information takes from the U.S. to England, over often-clogged transatlantic data lines. We can wait several seconds for the initial response to get to CUSI. The response for the initial page must then return from CUSI to us.

Next we pick the desired searcher, enter our search string, and submit it. And back it zooms (or crawls depending on traffic conditions) over the Atlantic Ocean to England. CUSI now fulfills the order, and if the searcher we requested is in the U.S., it must send the request back to the U.S. The request is filled by the U.S. server and sent back to CUSI in England. Lastly, CUSI finally routes the information to us.

Whew! What an awful amount of work just to perform a simple search. It's like going from New York to Chicago via Timbuktu! While this does not necessarily impact Nexor—the server site for CUSI—it does impact us. What could be a few seconds has now turned into a minute or more of waiting. It also impacts bandwidth, as each of those recursive messages traveling across the Atlantic prevent others from sending and receiving messages.

Tip

You already know how to register domain names. You can have the e-mail in the new account forwarded to your existing account, making it easier to keep up on user input.

II

The Basics

Here's one way to effectively use the CUSI searcher (or any similar searcher). If you are using the Lycos robot for a request, you don't need to keep going back to CUSI to make another Lycos request. Only return to the CUSI page when you switch to another searcher like Web Crawler or the CUI W3 Catalog.

Nexor could have made this easier by providing CUSI search tie-ins at different locations around the world. In this way, responses would be faster and more reliable. Duplicate sites are called *mirrored sites*. The site in figure 7.1 offers a mirrored site. Notice the wording of their message is polite and to the point.

Fig. 7.1

A mirrored site has duplicate files to other sites, allowing them to share bandwidth load over many users. Users receiving a busy site at one location simply hop to a less busy mirrored site.

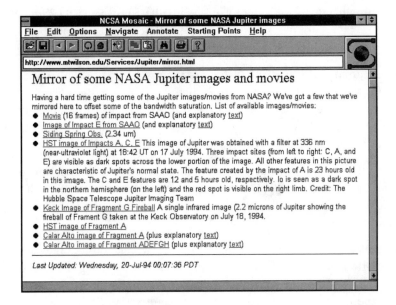

Since CUSI is a free service and does not bring money into Nexor, they do not duplicate it on other servers.

However, if your WWW site brings in business and dollars, consider adding the small overhead of maintaining a mirrored site. It can improve your accessibility, especially if your users and clients are spread throughout the world. Remember, customers can't place orders if your server site is too clogged to admit them. Net advertising can be useless if, in the time it takes to upload your site, users become bored and wander off.

The decision as to whether or not to keep your separate presences truly separate is up to you. You can have a single home page which then directs the users into the multiple presences, or you can keep them separate. The decision is yours and should be based on your needs and how you want your users to perceive you.

For example, if you are offering your pages in multiple languages, you may want a single page which greets users and directs them into the separate areas. To do this, you could greet the user with a single line in each of the languages that you support, and have that person select the desired line to go to pages completely in that language. Other, more advanced capabilities include the ability to sense the country of origin of the user or the language settings of the user's browser, and have the pages automatically configure themselves to address that user.

Tip
Multiple languages could be perceived as a benefit, because you are letting your clients know that you care enough about them to provide multiple language versions.

> **Note**
>
> All Internet users will, by necessity, know enough English to get around on the Net. However, subtle nuances may get lost in translation. If your Web page contains descriptive information or content that has cultural meaning, you may want to provide the information in the user's native language.

If you supplied separate home pages for each language, those users may be completely unaware that you are doing this for other languages. Again, it depends totally on what perception you are trying to show to the user. Figures 7.2 and 7.3 show a WWW site that maintains two pages with the same information displayed in English and Italian.

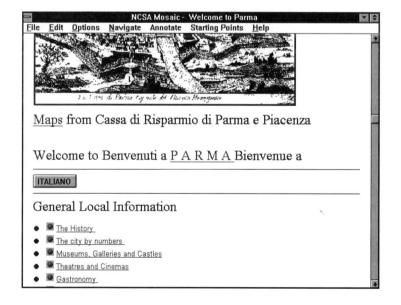

Fig. 7.2
This page is for English-speaking users.

Fig. 7.3
This page is the same as shown in fig. 7.2, but is targeted toward Italian speaking users.

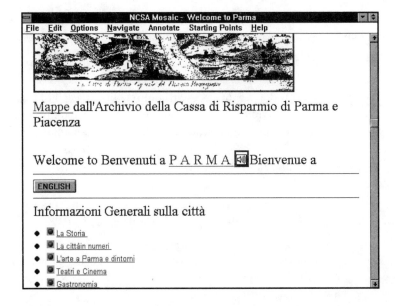

Users can choose which language the information is presented in by the push of a button.

> **Note**
>
> Users that request languages which require special characters in their alphabet (such as Japanese) need special software to display and/or read these pages.
>
> WWW modified browsers exist on many Japanese sites for public downloading and allow special WWW pages to be viewed using the traditional Japanese characters.

Creating Multiple Entrance Points

Having multiple entrance points to your pages is different from having multiple presences. To put this image in simpler terms, if you draw an analogy between rooms and your pages you could have the following:

- One room with one door

- Many rooms with one door

- Many rooms with many doors

- One room with many doors

If there is only one entrance for your room(s), all users are funneled to the same starting page. This option can be potentially useful for counting users, making users aware of all your services, and recording e-mail addresses from users.

However, if you have multiple entrances to your room(s), some of your sub-pages could be accessed by external hyperlinks. As you advertise your business on the Web, you will be placing links to your pages in lists and storefronts around the world. This allows users who encounter that link to find you. The more links you sprinkle around, the more likely you are to be found.

The question is, what links do you place in the lists? You would more than likely place a link to your home page to funnel users through your front door. But you might want some users to take side entrances. For example, imagine that you are a business consultant who specializes in product man-agement, marketing, and advertising. Some of your ads would promote you simply as a business consultant and would provide a link to your main home page that, in turn, would point to pages that cover each of your specialties. However, you could also place ads for each of your specialties with links di-rectly to those pages, bypassing the home page.

Strategies like this work very well, because they serve to act as multiple pres-ences as well as multiple entrance points simultaneously. They also grab the attention of users who might not go into your home page, because upon initial scanning they overlooked the one service area they were interested in. By having separate advertisements for each of your individual areas, you stand a better chance of being seen by an interested client.

Having the separate entrances may work to your advantage in other ways. Some users may prefer a specialist over a full-coverage type business. They may not be attracted to your home page because they may feel you are spread too thin. However, upon encountering your individual ad, they may be en-ticed into your service, giving you a chance to win them over before showing your other services.

II

The Basics

Note

When advertising your company in some of the available lists, notice that the lists are often organized by specialty. By offering separate entrances to your business, you can make the best use of these lists. You will want to place many ads in each of the cat-egories that you offer products or services. This gives you maximum presence with minimum effort. And what's the best part about this kind of advertising? It's free.

There are other uses for side entrances into your business. By planning your ads such that each list you advertise on has a unique link into your pages, you can collect demographics on how your users are finding you. By examining the access logs of your pages and looking at how many users came in which door, you can see which ads are pulling in the most clients. This information can help you to target your advertising more effectively.

This same mechanism can also be used to divide your audience into categories without their knowing it. For example, by placing unique links in pages oriented to kids, versus other links in pages oriented to adults, you have instant demographics on how much usage each age group is generating, all collected without the users' knowledge.

All in all, using multiple doors with multiple presences offers you the most effective way to attract clients into your business on the Web.

From Here...

This chapter dealt with one of the many factors that affect your image on the Web—the names associated with your business and you. Your name will create that important first impression. Make sure you use it to your best advantage.

For related information, refer to the following chapters:

- Chapter 8, "Etiquette and the Net," provides further information on Net philosophy and tips on what to do and what not to do.

- Chapter 10, "Advertising on the Net," shows you how to place advertising on the WWW.

- Chapter 16, "Your Presence on the Net," tells you about more factors that affect your company's image on the Net.

- Chapter 17, "Security and the Net," shows you how to keep your accounts and domain names secure.

- Chapter 22, "The Future of the Net," reveals trends that could affect your business.

Chapter 8

Etiquette and the Net

The Internet has spawned a whole international subculture. The most extreme form is cyberculture, which affects the way a person dresses and speaks. Underlying cyberculture is a code of ethics which, while sometimes difficult to define, is strictly adhered to. The corresponding rules are sometimes referred to as *netiquette*.

This chapter helps you understand how to talk and relate to users while in the various portions of the Internet. Because IRC, NetNews, and e-mail are all parts of the Web as well as the Internet, this section covers more than just the Web. As you discover throughout the book, these other areas are useful not only for locating resources and information, but also for enhancing the capabilities of your WWW business.

In this chapter you learn

- How to be a good Net citizen

- What to do about Net warriors and channel hackers

- How to manage private discussions

- How to deal with overseas users

- How to express emotions in an appropriate manner

> **Note**
>
> This chapter deals with etiquette in e-mail, NetNews, and IRC. As pointed out throughout the book, all three mechanisms are useful resources for any WWW pro-ject you intend to initiate. This chapter assumes that you have some basic background in using e-mail, NetNews, and IRC. If you would like more
>
> (continues)

(continued)

information, consult your local bookstore for any of the many books which are specific to the Internet, such as the following books from Que:

- Special Edition *Using the Internet*
- Special Edition *Using HTML*
- Special Edition *Using Internet E-Mail*
- *Using Internet Relay Chat*

Etiquette in Informational Postings

The majority of people and businesses on the Internet and WWW trade information via e-mail and NetNews. When people need to know answers to questions, they often hop into a NetNews group and post a question. Other people reading the question can answer either in private e-mail or publicly through NetNews.

Even though much of the Internet is unregulated, a set of Net manners has evolved which are fairly strictly adhered to. These manners enable people to talk to each other with the least amount of misunderstanding. The following sections help you understand these customs as they relate to informational postings such as e-mail and NetNews. Understanding these issues will help you in your business by making it easier for you to comprehend and respond to people whom you meet on the Internet.

Appealing To the Largest Audience

Sending e-mail is much like sending a private letter. When writing a private letter, you tailor the letter to the individual receiving the letter. However, many times on the Internet you will be providing information which is designed to appeal to a much larger audience than just a single individual.

You may be designing your information to reach a particular group of people, or you may design your information to target a mass audience.

Regardless of who your information target is, one fact is clear—you should try to be as succinct as possible. On the Net, you'll be dealing with an audience who does not appreciate a waste of its time or Internet resources.

When sending e-mail or NetNews, you should always make use of the subject capability. Place a single line into Subject which best describes the contents of the message. This enables users to easily see whether they are interested in investigating your message (see fig. 8.1).

Fig. 8.1
Messages without subjects are less likely to be read immediately. Of the message subjects shown here, which would you be most likely to read first?

Putting the most important words first in your Subject line ensures that the meaning is conveyed even if the line is cut short. For example, looking again at figure 8.1, of the messages with subjects, which are more effective—the long line or the ones with short lines?

The body of your message should also be clear and well-written. If you are asking a question, state the question immediately at the beginning so that the reader does not need to wade through the document to find what you are asking about.

Always make sure to provide all the necessary information. Do not expect users to assume anything; they may simply not respond to your message because they have too many questions about what you need. For example, if you are asking a question about software, make sure to provide complete information, such as what computer you are running on and the version of the operating system. Providing this information up front not only increases the likelihood of a response, but also cuts down on the amount of mail sent to clear up vague postings.

Tip
When posting notices to NetNews groups, it's often a good idea to read some of the existing messages. This gives you a good idea as to what is expected in that particular channel.

To best reach your NetNews and e-mail audience, follow these tips:

- Be concise.

- Use the Subject line.

- State any questions up front.

- Make sure to provide all necessary information.

Some news channels and e-mail groups are *moderated* (though the majority are not). This means that one or more people will read and censor messages that are sent by users of the group. These people are called *moderators*. Moderated groups may have their own rules of conduct. When sending messages to these groups, any attempts you make to conform to the ways of the group will enhance the chance that your questions are answered or your posts read. Again, the best way to do this is simply to read other messages to see how they are formatted.

Expressing Emotion in Informational Postings

Expressing emotion in informational postings is oftentimes necessary in order to get a concept across. Because users cannot see each other in person, it becomes important to reduce the chance of a misunderstanding.

Informational postings such as e-mail and NetNews messages have similar emotional mechanisms, as are found on IRC-type discussions. These mechanisms are known as *emoticons*, and include things like smiley faces such as

    :-)

for happiness, or

    @—>—>—

for a flower. Other types of emotions are stated with emphasis using asterisks, such as *sigh*. For more information on these types of emoticons, see the section, "Expressing Emotion in Live Discussions," later in this chapter.

However, because informational postings lack the real-time interaction of live discussions, other forms of emotion conveyance have been invented.

The most unusual of these is the flame. A *flame* is the Internet analogy to a heated argument. Flames usually result when people either misunderstand each other or understand each other all too well. When ideas or beliefs clash, sparks can fly.

Flaming is so prevalent on the Internet that special NetNews groups have been set up just for people who like to yell. However, in general, flaming is not considered good, and shows a certain lack of maturity. You do not want to be branded as someone who flames frequently, since this tends to make people appear not only narrow-minded, but angry and aggressive as well.

◀ See "NetNews," p. 39

The Pros and Cons of Using Signatures

Signatures are used to identify people. These most often appear at the end of e-mail and NetNews postings and often may appear at the bottom of pages on the Web.

Web pages tend to use signatures as links to the creators of the pages or links back to home pages or links to previous pages. These types of signatures tend to be as simple as the name of the company that created the page, for example,

```
John Smith / cookware / (the opinions expressed in this post are
not necessarily the opinions of my employers)
```

or

```
>>>— —Arrow Industries— —> Debbie Sellers
```

On the other hand, e-mail and NetNews signatures can be quite complex. Entire philosophies can be expressed in signatures. Indeed, a signature can tell quite a bit about a particular poster.

Most e-mail and NetNews signatures consist of the user's e-mail address and name. Beyond this, signatures may also contain useful information such as phone numbers, fax numbers, addresses, pertinent company information, and WWW URLs. Signatures may also convey personal information such as mottoes, beliefs, jokes, and desires.

Finally, many people use the signature area to be artistic, and often provide little pictures made out of text characters (such as the Arrow Industries example earlier or the signature shown in fig. 8.2).

The use of signatures can become old quickly. Large signatures are a waste of bandwidth (see "Etiquette in Bandwidth Use" later this chapter) and can add significant size to messages (for example, the signature in fig. 8.2 is a bit large).

The standard business signature should consist of a name, e-mail address, company information (phone, address), and any WWW URLs. If the business has a motto, this would be appropriate as well. Personal sayings should not be used in signatures that contain company content.

II

The Basics

Fig. 8.2
This e-mail message signature shows the sender's love for flying.

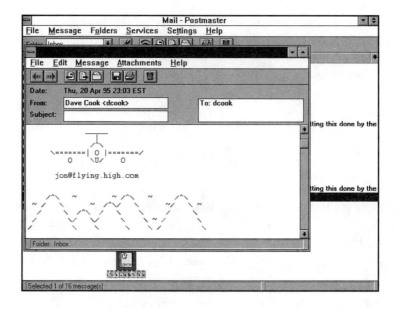

Fig. 8.3
A good business signature should reflect both the sender and the business.

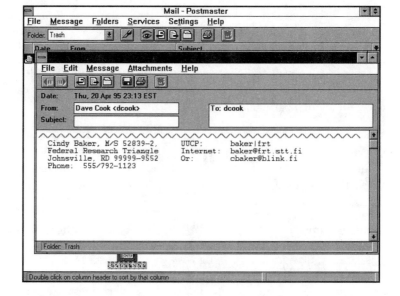

Responding To Rude People

You will invariably encounter some people who disagree or misunderstand some of your postings. These people may decide that it is their job to correct your error, and they may do this in a less-than-pleasant manner.

Most rude people respond to informational postings in private e-mail messages. The best way to deal with these types of people is to simply ignore the message. Responding to irrational people often just encourages them.

If you do decide to respond to irate users, always be polite. Never succumb to their level. Explain your point of view, correct any misconceptions, and invite those users to enter into a sane dialog with you on the topic. However, if users persist in unproductive dialog, simply ignore any future e-mail unless you are paying per message, in which case you should contact their system administrator.

▶ See "How To Search for People," p. 217

> **Note**
>
> In the rare event that a user becomes very abusive with constant rude e-mail, simply tell that person to stop or you will tell the site administrator. If it does not stop, simply send e-mail to the user root at that person's site. For example, if the rude person is jbole@run.me.com, then sending mail to root@run.me.com will access that user's site administrator. Make sure to identify who the user is (jbole in this example) and explain the problem you are having.

However, you should not encounter too many rude people in NetNews or e-mail. Most angry mail is the result of simple misconceptions and is usually easily cleared up with simple explanations. Many times people agree with each other, but simply do not realize it because of differences in semantics. Tolerance is the best advice.

Etiquette in Live Discussions

Inter Relay Chat (IRC) and other types of interactive talk systems allow you to discuss topics in real time with users and clients around the world. While these systems are currently limited to talking via typing, they do provide a much more interactive atmosphere than simple NetNews and e-mail. As the following sections demonstrate, dealing with users in live discussions often calls for different forms of patience and etiquette.

◀ See "IRC," p. 46

▶ See "Using IRC for Instant Answers," p. 222

Identifying a New User

The IRC community consists of both old-timers and new users (often referred to as newbies). While most old-timers are tolerant of new users, it pays to understand how people interface with IRC and to try to fit in as much as possible. Developing an awareness of IRC customs allows you to get along in

II

The Basics

any group and helps you get answers to your questions with the least amount of work and frustration.

There are many ways to identify an IRC newbie. Most new users have not had the opportunity to learn IRC very well and thus do not know what opportunities are possible. This usually becomes evident as soon as they enter a channel, because invariably all newbies ask the following three questions:

- Where are you?

- How old are you?

- Are you male or female?

Whatever you ask, do not ask these three questions. Those three questions label you as a newbie faster than any other questions you could ask. All three questions stem from the fact that people cannot physically see each other on IRC. Because of this, the first questions usually asked are ones which help the users visualize each other. Seasoned IRC users never do this. They understand the value of IRC as far more than idle chit-chat.

The best way to deal with IRC as a new user is to join a group and wait about 30 seconds to a minute. See whether anyone greets you. If they do, greet them back with a single line. People on IRC prefer that you not be verbose and that you get to the point quickly.

Many groups have their own internal rules, which even the most seasoned IRC user can accidentally break. These rules are set by the members of the group and outline the way they expect people to behave while in their group. In general, these rules are not posted and must be learned by trial and error.

For example, the **#www** group abhor people who ask whether or not they can ask a question. Usually, if you go in and ask, "May I ask a question?" you are ignored completely. If, on the other hand, you join and immediately state your question in an open post, you find that one or more people respond to you almost instantly.

If you are a new user, take time to understand how each channel works before you try it yourself. This is best accomplished by watching others talk and seeing what type of response they get. If you are a seasoned user and you encounter a new user, be polite and help them understand how to talk to people and get what they need.

Note

Some channels don't like people who come in and don't say anything. Unless you are well-known in a group, it is generally a good idea to give a simple one- or two-word greeting such as "Hello!" when entering a group. This breaks the tension of a new member and also offers other users an opportunity to talk to you. If you do not get an immediate response, just sit back and watch a little dialog to get an idea of what to do.

Sometimes it's not necessary to talk. In some of the more socially oriented groups, some member's input to the discussion consists of laughing from time to time: "Hehehehe" or "Hahaha," for instance.

Understanding Lag

Interactive sessions between many people scattered throughout the world suffer from problems of delayed transmission, or *lag*. Anyone who has ever made a long distance call to parts of Europe and experienced the frustration of talking with several seconds of delay while the signals cross the Atlantic will understand lag.

For example, three businessmen meet in a private IRC channel to discuss a new contract. One is in France, one in Japan, and one in the U.S. Each of these users are connected by a chain of IRC servers to each other. Typically there are around 10 or so servers routing messages from one user to another user.

As the French businessman types, his messages are delivered via a complicated route to the Japanese and American businessmen. However, each message takes a different route. Because each of the connections between the machines along the route have different speeds and loads, the messages take longer or shorter times to get to their destinations.

Suppose the link between the U.S. and Europe is particularly clogged, but the European-Japanese link is very fast. In this case, the Japanese businessman is able to read and respond to the message before his American counterpart. In fact, lag can be so bad that it is possible for the Japanese and European to be able to share an entire conversation before the American sees even the first message.

There are really three links involved in our example: the American-European link, the European-Japanese link, and the Japanese-American link. While one or more of these may run via the same route as others, it is entirely possible that they all might be independent.

How does this impact your understanding of lag? In the example, the European-Japanese link was very fast, allowing the businessmen to type quickly to each other, while the American was unable to see any messages from the European. However, suppose the American link to Japan is very good, and everything the Japanese businessman is typing is instantly relayed to the American; however, nothing is coming in from the European. The American sees only half the conversation. You can begin to appreciate what will happen. Messages begin to be misunderstood and are responded to incorrectly.

In reality, lag is not that hard to deal with. However, during especially busy times it is possible that lags of over 100 seconds are experienced. These lags are temporary and should soon clear.

If a lag becomes too serious and a connection is physically lost, a *netsplit* occurs. A netsplit causes at least one of the users to leave the group. To one user, it appears as though the other two users have left. The other two users, on the other hand, think the single user is gone. When the situation has cleared, the connection is reestablished and all three users are rejoined.

The first step in dealing with lag is to identify how long the lag actually takes. Most talk systems have a method to do this. IRC uses the /ping username command. These commands return with the number of seconds it takes typed text to travel from you to the user you specify in the command as username. This lets you gauge how long the lag is, or if a lag is non-existent and you're just being ignored.

If you decide to wait out the lag, you should immediately inform the other users that you are lagged. You can type a message such as

I'm lagged with *xx*-second response.

Remember that because of the lag it also takes time for the other users to see this message. Once they see it, the other users should begin to monitor the lag themselves and gear their conversations so that they wait for responses from you.

If lag becomes unbearable, you should change servers. For example, if the other two users are on an IRC server different from yours, you might want to change over to their IRC server. As soon as you do this, you should experience a faster response time (depending on the route between you and that server). In general, changing servers can improve your lag time immensely (in IRC, this is the /server sitename command).

Note

Another good indication of a newbie is someone who goes into a channel, types in "Hello?", waits about two seconds, and then leaves because no response was received. This person obviously does not understand lag.

When entering a new channel, always wait 30 to 60 seconds after your greeting to see if there are any responses. Likewise, when leaving a channel and saying goodbye, wait for the same period of time to let people have the chance to say any last-minute items to you. Remember, lag is different for each person.

The bottom line in lag is that when it occurs, there's almost always a moment or two of confusion while users determine what is happening and when people begin adjusting to the situation. Since lag is an always-changing event with the lag shortening or lengthening, you always need to be attuned to your response time.

Expressing Emotion in Live Discussions

While the future of the Net is quickly moving toward a fully immersive virtual reality where we see and hear each other, the current Net is rather impersonal. You cannot see someone's face or hear the inflection in his or her voice. This unfortunate condition has resulted in the creation of an entire new language for expressing humor, sorrow, and other emotions.

Because IRC-type talk systems are interactive, expression to emotion is a culture within itself. The suggestions in this section should help you read and write correctly to individuals you may encounter.

Most of the text typed in IRC is written in lowercase. People are typing as fast as possible to each other and thus do not want to be bothered by the Shift keys. Because of this, typing in all capitals tends to make your message stand out in a crowd. This is known as *yelling*. IF YOU TYPE A SENTENCE LIKE THIS IN CAPITAL LETTERS, you might be asked, "Hey! why are you yelling?" You may be told, "Please stop yelling!!!" On the other hand, if you want to make a point, you may want to YELL A LITTLE!

Likewise, many people use the bell capability (Ctrl+G) of their computer to send an audio beep to the other members. This is another form of yelling, and it causes people to look at their screen. Of all the forms of yelling, the beep is the worst. Most often you cannot tell who beeped, because nothing actually appears on-screen.

II

The Basics

This can be so annoying that some groups, such as **#www,** have no-beeping rules. Beeping in these groups causes you to instantly be kicked out of the group. Most people come right back in with a simple, "Whoops, I forgot," and there are no hard feelings. (The **#www** members created this rule because they were all busy building new pieces of the Web and the beep caused them to stop what they were doing to see if they were getting a private message.)

Other forms of emotion come as the proverbial *smiley*. Of all places using smileys, IRC has the most. These are all seen as pictures by tilting your head to the left:

> : -) smile, happy

> ; -) winking

> : - (unhappy

> : -0 surprised

> : -P sticking your tongue out

> : -@ yelling or screaming

There are other variations:

> :^)   a pointed nose

> :)   a quicker version of :-)

> 8 -)   glasses

> B -)   glasses

> :-{) mustache

Roses can be sent to someone with

> @—>—>—

and likewise "raspberries" (sticking your tongue out) can be sent with

> **:-P......**

You will see many more as you read entries on IRC. Most people use some form of smiley every few sentences, as questions are asked and information is exchanged.

Another mechanism is to replace the smiley with an emotion bracketed by asterisks. For example,

> ***sigh* I guess I've got to do it again *grrrrrrr***

These little additions add that small element of humor which helps express to the other users how you feel.

Private Discussions

One of the benefits of IRC is its ability to create private discussions. This is where IRC really shines as a business tool.

If you have clients or partners who are spread throughout the world, you can get together to discuss important items, in real time, over IRC. While not as efficient as a human voice, IRC discussions of this nature allow large numbers of remote people to talk together at once.

To create a private group, simply use the JOIN command to join a channel which does not exist. For example, if your name was Mary, you can type

> **/join #mary101**

As soon as you do this, the channel is created and you become the operator. To make the channel secret and private, lock the channel by typing

> **/mode #mary101 +inst**

Next, you are ready to invite participants. Do this by issuing an invite to each participant. For example, if one participant is named "george," you would type

> **/invite george #mary101**

Once all the members have joined, you are ready to begin your discussion.

If someone comes into your group before you have a chance to make it private and you do not want them there, politely ask them to leave. If they do not leave, kick them out. For example, if the rude user's name is "rudedog" you can kick them out by typing

> **/kick #mary101 rudedog**

When you are finished with your meeting and the last member leaves, your group automatically disappears.

II

The Basics

Tip
To remove opera-
tor status from the
user, you would
type **-o** instead
of **+o**.

Remember that if you are going to leave your group while the meeting is
going on, you need to make someone else the operator so that they can invite you back in. To make a user named "sue" the operator, you would type

/mode #mary101 +o sue

Finally, to get invited into a private channel, you should send a message to
the moderator of the channel. If you are "sue" and the moderator is "mary,"
typing

/msg mary Please invite me in

would work. Once you receive the invite message, type

/join #mary101

to join the conference.

Handling Unruly Guests

If you are engaged in a private meeting, you should ensure that your channel
is private so unexpected guests do not barge in. However, often you will be in
a public channel where anyone can join.

> **Note**
>
> For example, perhaps you have joined **#www** to ask a question about HTML, or
> perhaps you have decided to host your own public channel discussing a topic per-
> taining to your business. In these cases, anyone can join your conference.

Since you are dealing with people throughout the world, you have users of all
personalities, lifestyles, and current moods. Because of this, you will occasionally encounter unruly guests. Knowing how to spot and stop them will often
help keep nasty situations from escalating out of control.

Since many problems stem from simple misunderstandings, situations may
often be avoided by stepping in and clearing up the misinterpretation as soon
as it happens. The sooner you address the problem, the sooner it goes away.

However, some users are not so easily pacified. In certain cases, hostile atti-
tudes result in an online yelling match via pounding fingers on keyboards. In
situations like this, it is best to have the channel moderator remove the unruly guests. This can be accomplished by sending a private message to the
moderator. (On IRC, you would type **/msg "name" message**.)

Handling Channel Hackers

The ultimate unruly guest is the *channel hacker*. The channel hacker tries to take over your channel and kick everybody out. This person can then invite his or her own group of unruly friends into the channel to have a party while you and your group sit outside and fume.

Channel hackers are sophisticated enough that they can even take over private channels. They wait for extreme periods of lag to occur. During these times, a channel may split from the main group and for a brief instant its private setting may be turned off.

This is the moment a channel hacker waits for and then slips in. When you rejoin the channel after the split, the hacker maintains operator status and simply kicks you out and bans you from reentering. This happens so quickly that most users cannot respond quickly enough. Skilled channel hackers can even force a channel to split, allowing them to take a channel at any time.

> **Note**
>
> However, you do not need to worry too much. Most channel hackers like to go after established groups. The occasional private business meeting will generally be left alone. Also, with all the existing channels, an individual channel will only be bothered a couple days out of the year.

There is an interesting way to deal with channel hackers and one you may get some enjoyment out of. Obviously, kicking them out of your group or banning them will just make hackers madder. The best course is to put the fear of the Net gods in them by leaving your group and changing your IRC nickname to something like **IRCOP**, **COP**, **POLICE**, or **NETCIA**.

Next, send the hackers a private IRC message politely asking them to cease and desist. They will most likely either be rude or put up an argument. Be firm, polite, and persistent. If they don't give in within about five minutes, tell them you are reporting their actions to the immediate site administration and that they stand to lose their Internet access.

Tip
Usually a channel is vacated fairly quickly (within about 10 minutes or so), if you always appear calm, polite, but firm.

This solution works well because no one is sure who is who on the Internet. They are fearful of one thing only—losing access by being caught. The threat of telling their site administrator is especially effective, because you are not lying. If hackers become extremely obnoxious, you can report them to their Internet provider. Determine the user's name (in IRC, type **/whois "users_nick"**) and send the information to root at that address.

II

The Basics

For example, suppose that in an IRC session a user with the nickname I-RULEZ has taken over. Typing **/whois i-rulez** shows that the user is really j012gg@knights.net. Sending a *polite* e-mail message to root@knights.net accesses the administrator of that machine. Explain the problem and ask the administrator if there is anything that they can do to help. Most SYSOPs are more than happy to remove users who do not follow standard rules of conduct.

To illustrate just how rarely this occurs, we are on IRC 24 hours a day and have only had to deal with three channel takeovers in the two years we've been on. In none of those cases did we actually report the user to the site administrator. In all cases, the problem was solved within a few minutes. In two of the three cases, the perpetrator actually became a valuable member of the group. And in the end, a channel hacker on your side is the best defense in the world against having your channel taken over.

Knowing When To Quit

For some, interactive chat groups are addictive, similar to a drug. Many people get on IRC and won't leave, forgoing school, work, and friends.

The draw to IRC is the ability to meet people from all over the world and share information with them. It is interesting to talk with other people and see their different perspectives. There may also be a bit of the "pouring your heart out to the stranger next to you on the airplane" syndrome.

As you use IRC and other talk-type programs to solve your business problems or host interactive client sessions, you should keep in mind that IRC is inherently inefficient. While IRC does provide near-real-time discussions between remote parties, it does so only via typing, which, for most, is a slow means of communicating. Coupled with the time it takes to get the message to the other parties and receive their responses, this means that the IRC's efficiency decreases significantly.

As you begin to use IRC, you will be amazed to see how time flies. Knowing when to stop is just a matter of willpower and common sense.

While forgoing your favorite TV program is probably okay, having missed more than two consecutive meals is probably a good indication that you are spending too much time on IRC. Seriously though, if you simply use IRC for what it is good for—getting answers to questions and remote group discussions—you should experience little problem with IRC overuse.

If you have employees or staff that use IRC or NetNews, you may want to make sure that they are using it for business purposes. Many companies allow employees to spend some of their personal time using the Net for entertainment or R&R; however, it should not decrease an employee's productivity rate. You might want to restrict personal use to after-business hours, or limit access to certain NetNews groups. If an employee becomes really hooked, you might want to suggest that they obtain a private account and cruise at home.

Dealing with Foreign Users and Different Cultures

One of the more interesting problems in interactive talking is dealing with people in other countries. Almost all the IRC users worldwide possess good language skills and can type English very well. However, reading responses is often very different.

Talking with people from different cultures and languages requires a little more patience than talking with people from your own culture. The major problem comes in the use of expressions which are localized. Slang, analogies, metaphors, jokes, and puns are often misunderstood or completely lost in meaning. Including them can lead to confusion.

Likewise, keep in mind that laws differ from location to location. What one person can talk about in one country may have nothing to do with what you can talk about in your location. One notable example is with encryption technology, which you can use here in the U.S. but is usually illegal to make available to people overseas.

> **Tip**
>
> Not only will slang cause problems, but everyday phrases like, "Don't look a gift horse in the mouth," can be confusing for people who speak English as a second (or third) language.
>
> ▶ See "Encryption," p. 406

Note

If you are doing business in countries where English is not the primary language, you may want to offer your site in more than one language.

This is typically done by offering a button or link which then will re-direct the user to pages where the information is presented in the desired language.

Also, some social customs may differ. For instance, some cultures expect a lot of small talk before handling any business. Other cultures expect you to get right to the point and not waste time. Although technology does provide somewhat of a unifying factor, a successful international businessperson will make sure not to offend any potential clients. If your business warrants it, you may want to enroll in a class that teaches you how to conduct business overseas. Check with the community education division of your local high school or university.

II

The Basics

> **Note**
>
> If you are conducting business overseas, you should contact the commercial attaché at that country's embassy as well as the U.S. Commerce Department for any regulations you need to be aware of.

> **Caution**
>
> Be aware of national holidays that might affect your business. Your foreign business associate might assume that you know an important holiday is coming up and that businesses will be closed.

Remember that there are regional differences even in the United States. This applies to both customs and state laws.

Finally, it is important to note that people live in different time zones. Certain channels are more popular during certain times of the day. For example, at 9 a.m. (EST), typically no one is in the **#hawaii** group; with a five-hour time difference, it is 4 a.m. in Hawaii. When looking for people you have met, you should remember where they are in the world and use that as a clue to the best times to meet them again.

> **Note**
>
> The use of smiley faces and other Net jargon extends across the world. One of the first things learned by new IRC users, regardless of where they are, is the Net lingo. Where a joke or slang may fail, a smiley face is much more effective.

Another culture you will encounter is the cyberculture of the Net itself. Part of the cyberculture has derived from science fiction novels. If you are interested in this aspect of the Internet, you should read these novels. There also exists cyberculture and cyberpunk WWW sites. A search for either term provides you with plenty of sites to keep you busy.

> **Note**
>
> *Cyberculture* and *cyberpunk* are two terms popular in modern science fiction. These terms refer to the society that is beginning to surround the computer and networking industry.

In the end, you should remember that the Internet and WWW are not an exclusively American phenomena. It is definitely international in scope. The very development of the Superhighway was done in the spirit of cooperation and collaboration. Do your part to make sure that this continues in the future.

Etiquette in Mass Mailings

Mass mailings on the Net are exactly like their real-world counterpart except they don't use paper. A *mass mailing* consists of a standardized message being sent on a wide scale to people who may or may not want the information.

Of the services available for businesses on the World Wide Web, one of the more interesting ones is the ability to know who is visiting your pages. Depending on the implementation, this may even include the exact e-mail address of each visitor.

As the following sections explain, mass e-mailing is potentially very bad and at the extreme can even get you banned from the Internet. However, as you will see, there are some ways in which to handle mass e-mailing successfully.

One Word of Advice: Don't Mass E-Mail

This is the number one rule of e-mail. Don't mass e-mail! This will avoid all the problems associated with mass e-mails.

The primary problem with mass e-mailing is that it tends to bog down servers. If you send instant e-mail to thousands of people, or even just hundreds, you will probably arouse the suspicion of your system's administrator, who watches for things like that. Such a sudden, unexpected load cannot only cause problems for your provider's servers, but also servers down the road through which your e-mail is routed.

The second problem with mass e-mailing is that of a user's reaction. Just because a user has visited your page doesn't mean that this person is interested in receiving your advertising. Many people consider unsolicited e-mail advertising to be the same as breaking and entering, and tend to become very hostile. If you send a mass e-mail, you should expect some amount of harassment from the recipients.

II

The Basics

> **Caution**
>
> In situations where you send enough messages to enough people, you can have your Internet privileges suspended. This has happened several times on the Internet already. In situations where enough mail was sent that several major servers crashed, the entire provider site where the messages originated have been shut down. Your mass e-mail may even cause your provider to be put out of business, possibly even permanently.

If You Do It Anyway, Here's How To Do It

Just because we say that you shouldn't mass e-mail doesn't mean that there isn't a way to take advantage of your growing e-mail list of users. In fact, you *can* do mass e-mailings if you do them carefully.

▶ See "The HTTPD Log," p. 342

▶ See "Page Counters," p. 348

First, you should never target users who have visited your site only once. Instead, if you target users who have come into your site at least four or more times, you will most likely avoid all harassing messages from these e-mail recipients, because they are probably interested in what you have to say. Information about who is visiting your site should be available from your WWW provider as part of monthly or daily statistics.

Second, never make direct solicitations over e-mail. This simply infuriates users. Instead, state that because you have noticed them frequenting your site, you want to make them aware of new items which they may like to check out during their free time. This type of tone switches the e-mail from a solicitation to an informational type message, which is much more acceptable.

Next, how you send your e-mail is important. If you are mailing to hundreds of people all over the world, you don't need to be quite as careful as you would if you were mailing to hundreds of people at one site.

However, at the very least you will want to space out the mailings, so that the servers have a chance to dispatch the messages without getting bottlenecked with too many messages at once. You should space the mailings out over several days.

> **Caution**
>
> If you disregard this information about e-mailings, realize that not only will you personally receive complaints, but your message will be discussed all over the Internet. You can get an extremely bad reputation with an extremely large number of people in an extremely short period of time.

Finally, never e-mail one message to many users at one time. Instead, mail each user the message individually. Why? If the user does send you a response by using the Reply feature of the mailer, he or she may accidentally include all other users in the response. The original mailing causes enough problems, but if even one or two users accidentally send their reply to all the users in that original posting, the problem becomes compounded, and people become more irate.

> **Note**
>
> If you are planning some limited type of mass e-mailing, you might want to mention the fact to your provider. Let the provider know that you understand the possible problems and that you will take care to avoid them. Outline your plan and see whether your provider has any suggestions on reducing any potential harm that can result.

The keys to successful mass mailings include the following:

- Target your audience carefully.

- Be careful of how your message is phrased.

- Don't bog down the Internet. In other words, don't target a specific server site, and space out the mailings over several days.

- Send each message separately.

- Notify your server.

The final word in mass e-mailing is, if you do it, be very careful and conscientious as to the impact your mailing is going to have.

Etiquette in Bandwidth Use

One of the oldest forms of netiquette is that of conservation of the Internet itself. Many people view the Internet as a commodity which can be used up. Hogging the Internet resources is considered bad. This section explores both the myths and realities surrounding these views.

What is Bandwidth?

Bandwidth, in this context, is the amount of information that can be transmitted at a given moment in time. When used in slang, it refers to the amount of information you have placed in a posting or message. Bandwidth

II

The Basics

can also refer to just the size of the "Internet pipe" coming into your provider. Of the total bandwidth coming in, you are allocated a portion based on what you are using at that time.

For example, a high-bandwidth site might be one with lots of pictures and audio; this site requires a wide information highway to deliver the goods. Likewise, a small text-only WWW page would be considered low bandwidth.

Messages such as those found in e-mail and NetNews can also be high-bandwidth. If you are responding to someone else's message and you include that person's entire message within your message, you may be accused of being a high-bandwidth user. In this case, high bandwidth indicates someone who is wasting bytes on the Internet with meaningless information.

If you are extremely high-bandwidth, you may be accused of being an "info hog."

Is Bandwidth Conservation Important?

The idea of conserving bandwidth is as old as the Internet itself. It stems from the fact that in the "old days," the Internet was not as big as it is now. With narrower channels, smaller amounts of data went through at slower speeds. Because of this, it was important to conserve your data size since you were sharing the road with other users.

Today, the importance of bandwidth conservation is not so pertinent. While many of the "old timers" are appalled by the wanton use of the Internet, the natural changes in technology are driving us towards more and more multimedia requirements. This movement is forcing the Internet to transmit higher and higher bandwidths.

For example, typing the string **Welcome to our site** takes only 19 bytes to transmit. Hearing the sender say, "Welcome to our site," as an audio file in a WWW page says the same thing, but in about 60,000 bytes. Having a movie with audio saying, "Welcome to our site," would take up several megabytes.

So just what are the rules for bandwidth? The answer is unfortunately complex.

Commercial providers have added an interesting ingredient to the bandwidth equation. As their bandwidth demands increase, they simply pave more and bigger roads. This keeps the usage such that each individual has quite a bit of available bandwidth. Since this is all done for profit, the money is available to create new roads. Because of this, a relaxed attitude now exists towards bandwidth wasting.

To a degree, the commercial providers help to control the bandwidth drain. They accomplish this by charging for throughput on WWW access. When you are charged for the amount of bandwidth that you take, you tend to take it less for granted.

Bandwidth shouldn't be wasted, though. Indeed, being overly verbose in messages and pages simply makes other users irritated. Many times users have to pay for their access and don't want to receive lots of long messages that they have to wade through. Likewise, users will probably be turned off at WWW pages that offer an excess of information. The next section explores ways to decrease your apparent bandwidth usage.

How To Conserve Bandwidth

Knowing how to conserve your bandwidth helps keep your costs lower, while making your information content more popular to users who are paying for their access.

When responding to postings via e-mail or NetNews, it's often customary to include the previous posting for a reference as to what you are talking about. The entire previous message is probably not required to include the references you need, so it is preferable that you edit the reply and remove the unnecessary portions.

You can save a surprising amount of bandwidth this way, with several hundred bytes saved from each e-mail message. As a message is sent from machine to machine (especially in NetNews), these savings soon result in megabytes per message and even more over time.

Likewise, WWW pages can be made more efficient. Pictures can be compressed into using fewer colors. Text can be entered in HTML without extra spaces and carriage returns. This saves potentially thousands of bytes per HTML page, which again saves you money and also a significant amount of traffic a server is handing out.

Conservation of bandwidth in reading information is also important. By remembering that the more you take, the less there is for anyone else to use, you can help keep the Internet fast-moving. By accessing information smartly, you can delay the speed at which new information spigots are needed and thus keep the overall cost down.

Bandwidth savings in FTP and other information access can be helped by making those requests in off-hour times. The impact of several simultaneous users is kept to a minimum, and it's also guaranteed that you spend the least amount of time accessing the information as necessary.

Tip

Knowing how to conserve outgoing bandwidth requires common sense, not a degree in rocket science.

II

The Basics

> **Note**
>
> In WWW pages, if you are searching just for information, you should turn off image loading so that it loads the text only. Text is the smaller portion of any WWW page; therefore, not displaying the graphics is advantageous in saving both bandwidth space and your time.
>
> When you get to a page on which you want to add graphics, simply turn the graphics loading back on before accessing the page. If you are already at that page, reload the page after enabling the graphics.

Remember, because of the way the Internet is networked, saving just a single byte on your end can translate into thousands of bytes at the destination end.

Dealing with Net Dummies

You will occasionally interface with someone, either on IRC or via e-mail, who completely misunderstands not only what you are trying to say, but also just how to get around on the Internet in general.

Since the Internet is a giant community, users try to help each other as much as possible. Just as you may have relied on help from some Net guru, others may come to you for help when they get stuck.

> **Note**
>
> Remember to use the online FAQs and data sheets as a primary source for answering your questions.

While users try to be as helpful as possible, it's easy to be caught in a situation where you are simply wasting your time. These sections help you avoid and deal with those situations.

You may also want to examine this section from another perspective, since the following pages also show you how not to be a waste of time to someone else.

Identifying a Waste of Time

People who are going to simply waste your time are not as easy to identify as you would think. In general, you would expect new users to have a larger learning curve, and you should be patient when dealing with them. This, coupled with the differences in culture and languages, means that it may take wording a particular phrase several times until the correct meaning is relayed.

However, there are some fairly good guides to go by in determining a time waster:

- Is the person who he says he is?

- Is the person polite?

- After you give advice, what does this person do with your suggestion?

As you might guess, some people might not be who they appear to be. The following story is a disturbing example of this, and one where inconsistency finally made us realize what was happening.

One of us was in an IRC group when a young woman came in. She was distraught and appeared to be very depressed. She asked a few easy IRC questions and quickly zeroed in on two of us who were offering help. She began to send private messages to each of us independently, but did not realize that we were also talking between ourselves and comparing notes on the messages she was sending.

After she asked some simple IRC questions, she began to talk in an even more depressing tone. Feeling concerned, we continued to talk to her. At one point we were so concerned with her comments that we began to trace the user to be able to locate her should we need to contact authorities in her area.

However, after she had completely hooked us, the conversation took a very slight but interesting turn. She began to "recover" and in thanking us, began to extract personal information ("Thanks for your help. You sure know a lot. How old are you anyway?"). After finding out that one of us was married, she immediately ceased conversation with that person. We became suspicious and continued to watch her interact with other people. It soon became clear that this person was looking for a rich husband. Her depression was a ruse used to hook the unsuspecting.

This story, while unfortunate, helps to illustrate that not everybody has the same motives for using the Internet. While such occurrences are extremely rare, they should be expected, due to the large and diverse nature of the Internet users. Just as you have scams and misrepresentations in real life, so too will you have on the Internet.

II

The Basics

A consistent story is important in identifying a time-wasting individual. Some people use questions as a method of breaking the ice in a conversation in which they may have other motives.

The second identifier is the person's politeness. People seeking help are not generally rude. If someone demands help from you or insists that you are not being helpful enough, that person is probably a time waster.

The final indicator is what the user does when you give them a pointer. The expected action is (assuming the user understood your information) that the user would immediately say thanks and go try out what you said. However, all too often conversations go like this:

```
[user] Hello, anybody know of any good server sites?

[guru] Yes, try http://www.iquest.net/

[user] Great! What's there?

[guru] Lots of stores and WWW goodies.

[user] Wow! What kind of goodies?

[guru] Just go check it out, you won't be disappointed.

[user] Anybody else got any good sites?
```

This conversation is extremely typical. It happens many times a day in the **#www** IRC channel alone. Here the user asked a question and received a response. Instead of thanking the respondent, the user continues to ask for more information. This is a major waste of time.

The upshot of this is that once a question is answered, anything short of clearing up misunderstandings and exchanging pleasantries is simply a waste of your time.

Handling a Waste of Time

In general, once you identify an individual who is a time waster, you should get rid of this person quickly. The best way to do this is to firmly but politely ask the user to please try out what you have suggested or ask a different question. If the user becomes rude at that point, simply ignore the response.

Usually ignoring a user causes the user to try to talk to you, perhaps even through a private channel. However, if you simply ignore the questions, the

Tip
If you are given information via e-mail or NetNews that you need to reference again, write it down or cut and paste it into a notebook file on your computer. You should never have to ask the same question twice.

user should quickly tire and go away. Usually the user doesn't reappear because this person isn't interested in users who don't play according to the time waster's rules.

The ignore rule applies to time wasters in all categories. If a time waster sends you e-mail, don't bother replying. Simply delete and ignore the message. Replying only encourages that individual to keep wasting your time.

From Here...

This chapter should give you a good foundation on netiquette. With experience, you will become more knowledgeable, and others will begin turning to you for advice. While e-mail and NetNews are increasingly indispensable business tools, they also may provide you with a friend or two.

The section on foreign users and different cultures helps to make you aware of the aspects of doing business overseas and in an international forum. It isn't meant to be a substitute for educating yourself in the laws and customs of the countries where you do business.

From here, refer to the following chapters:

- Chapter 2, "Net Components and Terminology," provides information on Net jargon.

- Chapter 9, "Information on the Net," shows you more information on getting your questions answered in NetNews and IRC.

- The Appendix, "An Introduction To HTML," teaches you how to start programming your own WWW home pages.

Chapter 9

Information on the Net

There is a lot of valuable information on the Internet. In some ways, there is almost too much. Some users have referred to it as an "info glut." The problem then becomes accessing the information you need in a timely manner. Users can spend all day searching for and locating information that they could have found in 10 minutes at the library. The key is learning how to access this information efficiently. Remember that computers are supposed to save you time. If computers are not saving your time, you'll want to evaluate how the computer is being used.

Fortunately, a number of methods exist for searching the Web for information, most of which even the novice can easily use. Such programs as the Nexus CUSI Searcher, Lycos robot, and CUI W3 lists can serve as your new information gathering tools. The goal is for you and your employees to be able to gather more information in less time and not have to go to the library or elsewhere to do it.

For some of the information you want, there may be more than one way to get it. This chapter tells you the best method of obtaining information for your application.

Many methods are available to you to search the Internet. Since this book focuses on the Web, this chapter handles mainly WWW documents that are found with HTTP; however, you should realize your Web searches may also give you Gopher and FTP sites as well.

In this chapter you learn

- The methods for searching the WWW for information

- How to use each method efficiently

- Other Internet resources you may want to use

Looking for Existing Information

A great deal of the information you want already exists on the Web. It is stored as documents, graphs, and pictures on computers all over the world. In doing your searches, you are going to become an armchair world traveler. You'll be featured in computers in all the big cities around the United States, and in some cases, around the world.

Do you want to know laws concerning international trade? Hop on the federal government network and get the information from the U.S. Commerce Department. Need to know more about the Macintosh software you just bought? Cruise over to the Apple site and get installation tips and ways to use the software more effectively.

You'll be learning a new way to access information, which really mimics the way you currently seek information. You look up a topic or keyword, gather references, and then access the information—only here your card file is the whole Internet and what matters most is how you look through the card catalog. Also, now you won't have to write down a bunch of numbers and go wandering up and down the aisles looking for a book that may or may not be on the shelf.

▶ See "How To Correct Your Advertising," p. 247

On the Internet, the references are presented for you to pick and choose from. When you find one you want, you sit tight while the computer goes out and gets it for you. If the computer is able to access the information, you receive it in a matter of seconds. Otherwise, you try the resource again later or pick another resource to try. Often information changes, and the lists are somewhat slow to catch up with the move. In other situations, the information or site is so popular that the machine was simply too busy to serve the document to you.

A Brief Introduction To WWW Browsers

If you are familiar with any applications programs—for example, Word for Windows—you are acquainted with how information is presented on a computer screen. Novice users may not understand standard icons, how to use a toolbar or drop-down list, and how to input data into a field. If you are familiar with these operations and tools, skip to the next section.

When you sit down to cruise the WWW, the screen may be mostly blank, but at the top of your screen (or perhaps at the bottom, depending on your browser) is the information you need to get started (see fig. 9.1).

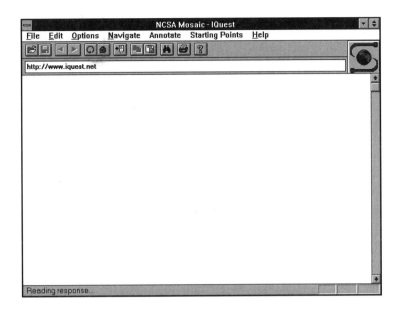

Fig. 9.1
The Mosaic browse
page appears upon
initially running.

At the top are menus such as **F**ile, **O**ptions, **N**avigate, and Annotate. Depending on the browser you use, your buttons and choices may be named slightly differently, but are still similar.

The File Menu

The **F**ile menu allows you to open multiple windows (if your computer supports them), open a URL, and print screens.

The most important of these choices is Open URL. This button may be labeled Open Location in other browsers but performs the same function.

The Open URL selection in the File menu allows you to type in the location of a page that you want to go to. Even though it is suggested that you navigate with the mouse and click items to go there, often you will encounter a URL in a magazine article or book. To get that URL into the computer, you must type it by hand. To do this, choose Open URL (or Open Location). A window pops up with a place for you to type. Move the cursor and select the area to type, and enter the URL. When you are finished, press Enter. The computer should immediately try to access the requested page.

If the computer comes back with a No such host error, simply examine what you typed for errors. Make sure the proper number of / characters are present. If the final word in the URL does not end in .html or .htm, you might try placing a single / character at the end of the URL (if it did not have one already). If it does have one, try removing it. Different browsers respond differently to the final slash, with many browsers demanding it be there if a physical .html file is not given.

The Print Command

Another important command is **P**rint. Not all browsers have Print, but you will find that standard NCSA Mosaic does, as do several commercial versions. As you would expect, the Print command prints your screen.

On Macintosh and Windows platforms, printing interfaces with your existing printer drivers. On UNIX platforms, you need to supply a driver for the printer you intend to use.

Most Mosaic browsers allow you to format the document you want to print in several ways. Your choices often include printing the source HTML, the screen as text-only, or the screen as PostScript. Printing the screen as Post-Script can give you outstanding results that match the original, especially if you are using a color printer such as an inexpensive color ink jet (available for around $300). Some browsers on certain platforms will simply print the screen using the current printer driver.

Different browsers format the printout differently. Since the size of the paper differs from the size of your screen, the browsers must reformat the text and rejustify the paragraphs. Some browsers try to fit it all on one page, and will even place information into columns to make it fit—a very unusual thing to see but interesting nonetheless. Such is the case of InternetWorks by BookLink, which even allows you to select the desired format of one- or two-column output (see fig. 9.2).

Reload Commands

In NCSA Mosaic for UNIX, the File menu also has two choices marked Reload Images and Reload Current. In the Windows version these are found in the **N**avigate menu, and in Netscape they appear in the **V**iew menu.

Reload Images is very useful. Many times when surfing the Net you abort a request that is taking too long to load. Since text is always loaded first, you will have the document minus one or more of its pictures. This capability allows you to move very quickly through places that you don't care about by simply aborting the request before the images load. If you would like to see the images for that page, simply click Reload Images to cause all the images in your page to be acquired again from the destination.

Fig. 9.2
The InternetWorks
Print Layout dialog
box allows many
interesting con-
trols for printing
your pages.

Note

Remember that each image in a page is a separate request to a computer. If a system is extremely busy, some requests may not be fulfilled in time. In these cases, you see some pictures for a page missing. Reloading the images for that page can often access the missing pictures.

Many browsers have a *cache*, which remembers documents and images. When a image is needed for a document, the browser first looks in its cache. If the image is in the cache, it reads it out of there instead of across the Internet. This means that once the browser loads an image, the image can be viewed on other pages or within the same page again, without having to load it from the Internet. This process saves you time when viewing documents with many of the same elements.

Note

When designing your own HTML documents, you should use Reload Images to see any changes you make to pictures. Remember that your machine caches your images so even if you change the picture, reloading the page may show you the old (cached) image. Reloading Images allows you to acquire the new, changed image.

Reload Current acquires the text of your document again, but not any of the cached pictures. Any pictures which were not already loaded are attempted again.

Many browsers have the Save options in their File menu. These options allow you to save the current page as HTML to your disk. Only the HTML document is saved, not the GIF pictures associated with the document. However, this is useful for capturing other users' WWW pages so you can examine them later for techniques (an interesting form of plagiarism).

The Options Menu

The **O**ptions menu allows you to set various features of your browser. Each browser displays and sets its options in a totally different way; this section outlines the basic functions that many browsers offer for your use.

Tip

Different font sizes are useful for making presentations where many people are clustered around a monitor, or late at night when the large letters help pry your eyes open.

Options in font sizes allow you to display the text of your document at various sizes and in various fonts. The Options menu usually enables you to set the display of hyperlinks, often allowing color, density, and underlining to be modified.

Many browsers also enable you to set the default home page under Options. The default home page is the first page that is shown when the browser is launched. Most browsers default this to the home page of the company who created the browser. Changing this to your favorite site saves time when launching your browser again and again.

The Options menu also usually allows for control over how the images are handled. Usually the size of the cache can be controlled, as well as the length of time that they stay active. Note that you want a cache of at least 10 to 20M to handle serious surfing.

> **Note**
>
> Remember that WWW browsers cache images while you surf the Web. Caching in this case means that browsers store the image locally on your hard drive. When accessing the image later, the browser retrieves it from your hard drive—if the image is still there—instead of over the Internet. This saves an amazing amount of time when bouncing around in documents.

The Navigate Menu

The **N**avigate menu contains controls that help you move. Here you find Back and Forward. Use the Back option to move to the page you were just on. Because the browser keeps a history of where you have been, you can usually go back many times. The number of times you can go back is determined by the amount of space available on your machine and the particular browser you use. Some browsers such as Netscape allow you to set the size of the history.

If you use the Back option to go to a previous page and want to return to where you started, use the Forward option to move forward again. You can move forward until you are at the most recent position page you accessed.

Almost all browsers have a History option in the Navigate menu. History brings up the history list and allows you to select from it. This is more convenient than Back and Forward if you need to move a great distance.

Another very important command in Navigate is the Hotlist option (see fig. 9.3). When you land on a page that you like and you want to remember it, simply add it to your hotlist. Most browsers have an Add Current to Hotlist option which automatically adds the current page to your hotlist. At any time in the future you can access your hotlist and select any of the sites you saved. The titles of each site are then displayed. Simply click the desired site and confirm the selection with GoTo or OK (as your browser displays).

> **Tip**
> This option is often called Bookmark in other browsers.

Note

Your history is forgotten when you leave your browser. However, your hotlist is remembered forever. Always put important sites in your hotlist to make sure you remember them.

The Annotate Menu

The Annotate menu allows you to add personal comments to the end of any page. When the page is retrieved in the future, your comments will be available. The comments are stored only on your machine, and thus are visible to no one but you. This seldom-used feature is nice if you want to remember something unique about a page.

Also, all or some of these options may have buttons associated with them somewhere on the display. Instead of going to the menus, you can just use the buttons. The buttons appear either beneath the menus or at the bottom of the window. Most popular buttons include Back, Forward, Home (gets the default document), and Reload. There is also often a place to type a URL to prevent from using the Open URL option in the File menu. These buttons save you lots of time and energy and are recommended over using the menus.

Fig. 9.3

A hotlist menu of favorite sites allows the user to travel to any site by selecting the name.

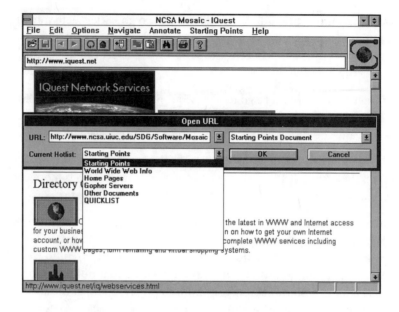

Tip

When creating links yourself, always remember to test them. That way your customers won't be greeted with an Error 404, URL not found... message that could have been avoided.

When you finally access a URL, the document appears on-screen. Somewhere on the screen should be the URL of your current location.

In most WWW browsers, links to other pages are shown in blue. As you move your cursor over the blue items, the bottom of the screen shows the URL of that particular link. Selecting the blue outlined word or picture causes the link to be activated and the associated document, picture, sound, or movie to be retrieved.

In some cases, clicking a link produces an error message. One error message you may see a lot is Error 404, URL not found.... You could get this error for any number of reasons:

■ You may have typed the URL incorrectly. If you leave off the "p" from "http" or only put in one / instead of two, you will definitely receive the Error 404 message.

Tip

You also get this message if the site for some reason was closed down for maintenance or has moved.

■ If you got this message from a link you chose, it could be that the person who created the link typed the wrong URL or simply never finished the link. The pages may also still be under construction.

■ This error may also indicate that you simply never reached the site due to some Internet clog somewhere along the Information Superhighway.

You may get a message telling you that you were denied access for some reason (see fig. 9.4), which could include any of the following:

■ There are too many users. In this case, you are asked to try again later.

■ You may be trying to access a for-pay or registered-user only system. Some of these messages tell you how to subscribe or register; others won't. Sometimes access may be limited to a specific geographic location or institution.

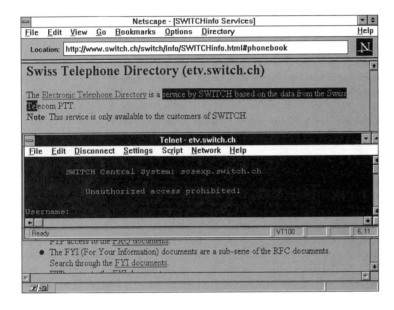

Fig. 9.4
A message from the Swiss phone book site shows you that you cannot access without permission.

The message in figure 9.4 originated from a Swiss phone book site. Even though this site is on the WWW and potentially available worldwide, the managing organization only allows users from the domain .ch (Switzerland). They probably don't want their site resources used up by those accessing the list for entertainment purposes.

How To Search for Existing Information

Three simple and basic ways to retrieve information are by URL, from a hotlist or bookmark, or via a link.

To continue the library analogy, if you already know the library number associated with that book, you just go to the shelf and pull it. Similarly, if you already had a URL (that perhaps you read in this book or found in a magazine article), you can just type the URL and access the document.

Using a hotlist or a bookmark is similar to obtaining a list of books to read for a class while you were in school. The instructor issues a list of books and also supplies you with the location of the book. Since you know the location, you proceed directly to the shelves and pull the desired book.

As you access information, some sites also provide you with their hotlists and bookmarks. If you liked the information in their site, you may be interested in their hotlist. The hotlist is linked to URLs that take you to the document when you choose a particular one.

As you explore the Web, you will also be creating your own hotlists. A good hotlist is very important and saves you lots of time. If you write down URLs, you might lose the paper or make a mistake when typing it.

Caution

Don't enter a URL string if you don't have to. Even the best navigators forget to type two // or will forget the "p" in "http." Valuable research time is wasted as the computer attempts to access an invalid address and you try to figure out whether it's just a site not currently in operation or if you typed it wrong. Hotlists help avoid this problem by remembering the URL for you.

Note

Remember, you have to be at the site to drop it in your hotlist—in other words, when you see the URL at the top of your screen. If you see the URL for the link to the site at the bottom of screen and choose to add it to your hotlist, you will be adding the site that contains the link you want to go to, not the site you wanted to add.

Also, if you get a Site too busy error message when you attempt the link, look at the top of your screen. The URL of the desired site is there. If you add the page to your hotlist and include the URL to be entered, you can check it out later when the Net isn't so busy.

The third way is through a link. The hotlist and bookmarks are also linked, but this refers to the links that are scattered within a document and not necessarily organized into a list.

You can find links in documents you have already accessed. It may be a link to another document on a related topic. Sometimes the text of a document is divided into smaller parts, and you are asked to choose what section you wish to access. You are presented with a table of contents that are linked to the appropriate section. You just pick which section you want, point and click the mouse, and you're there. Other times large documents are divided and organized in a way that you access the information sequentially. You are given a portion of a document, and when you are finished you go on to the next portion.

Note

The most useful documents allow you to access the information through a table of contents or in sequential order.

In this way, a link can be thought of as a chapter of a book or an appendix. If you want to read that material, the author has provided it for you. All you have to do is turn to the correct page number to access the information. You can do it while you're in the middle of your current reading or you can go there when you're finished.

Another way to think of links are as books you find on the shelf on your way to get the book you referenced from the card catalog. For example, as you are retrieving a book on business practices and customs in Thailand, on a nearby shelf you may also find a book covering how to transport products to Southeast Asia. If your business is considering exporting food products to Thailand, you probably want both books.

This isn't totally true of the Web. For example, you may have found a reference entitled *Wong's Guide To Doing Business In Thailand*. When you get there, you find the book contains information provided by Wong's Import/ Export that is used to generate business. Besides offering information about Thailand, they also provide a link to their main home page. Here they may provide information about other countries in the area as well as give information about their services and prices.

However if Mr. Wong is a fishing enthusiast, he may also share with you his fishing stories, locations of good fishing spots, and pictures of his prize-winning catches. At the bottom of the page you may see something like Page design by S. Wong with a link over the name S. Wong. Thinking that you could find something useful, you go to it. Instead you find the personal home page of Susie Wong, the owner's teenage computer whiz who actually created her dad's Web site. She may decide to share her ideas about school, her favorite rock stars and recipes, and a link to her favorite online sci-fi magazines.

> **Note**
>
> If you're not sure whether a link is one you want or not, make sure to look at the URL before going to it. Domain name, domain type, or file names may give you some leads.
>
> If you want official government information, pick a .gov site, not a .com site. Although if you become desperate, check it out. They may have a link to the government site you need.
>
> Also keep in mind that an .edu site could be an official site run at a university, or it could be information that a student posted for fun. For example, an address like
>
>   http://www.univ.edu/bigcorp/
>
> or
>
>   http://www.univ.edu/bigcorp/welcome.html
>
> will probably be an official site; whereas
>
>   http://www.univ.edu/~bsmith/bs/bigcorp/bigcorp.html
>
> probably won't be. The "~bsmith" indicates a personal account (~), and the fact that it is at an .edu probably means the owner is a student.

Generally, you hop into the site, see it doesn't have what you want, and continue on. The problem comes when you see something that interests you that doesn't correspond to what you are actually researching. If you allow yourself to access every link you find interesting, you will spend many hours on the Web and not get the information you need.

This is especially important if you are paying for your service by the hour or by how much data you pull down. In general, stick to the topic you are researching. If you can't resist that sci-fi magazine, link to it, drop it in your hotlist (resist the temptation to read it now), and continue with your search.

> **Note**
>
> If you have a research staff that uses the Web, you especially want to make sure that they are doing their work and not accessing information for their next vacation.
>
> To minimize this likelihood, you may want to allow each person access after business hours to do private research. That way, you're only out the money for the access and not their wages or salaries. Besides, the experience and savvy your employees gain surfing on their own time should benefit their work for you.

Also, the finding of spurious information could work to your benefit. When researchers access information about Aruba, they may find it is from the home page of a Thai student at MIT. In addition to their vacation information, they may offer information about their native country or offer translation services.

How To Search for People

If you are just looking for information about an individual, perform the search in the same way that you would for any topic. Within the CUSI Searcher there is a people searcher that can be very useful. It's the first way you attempt to locate someone. You can search by that person's name or by e-mail address or partial e-mail address.

However, searching for people is becoming increasingly difficult on the Internet. Many people don't want to be found so easily, and many institutions are making it harder to find out the names of the users on their site.

If the user you are looking for is at a university or college, accessing the college's home page may get you to a student and faculty location service. Likewise, many businesses offer their employees lists and manager profiles in their home pages.

Other methods of finding individuals is to frequent places you think the person might go. Inquire of other people in that area if they know of or have seen recently the person you are looking for. Both NetNews and IRC can find people in this way.

Using Robots and Worms

In one sense, *robots* and *worms* can be thought of as the card catalog file of a library or a periodical's index. Just as you go to the card catalog, look up a topic, and find cards referencing individual books, with robots and worms you enter the topic to search. You are then presented with the references to documents under that category.

However, in a card catalog, if you were researching the Shakespearean character Ophelia, you probably won't find a category on just her. You would have to look under the general heading of "Shakespeare."

Here you would be presented with all the books by and about Shakespeare and his works. You definitely want to look into a book covering heroines in Shakespearean tragedies and ignore a book of his sonnets. However, what about a book dealing with the life of Shakespeare? You don't know whether

II

The Basics

you need it or not. Perhaps in this book you might find a reference that Ophelia might have been based on a person that Shakespeare knew. Because of the generalized nature of the card catalog and the limits of what can be put on a card, you'll have to actually get the book to find out.

Robots and worms have an important advantage. You can enter the specific term you want. For example, if you wanted information on Ophelia, you would bring up a robot searcher page and type **Ophelia** into an area provided by the robot. Most robots and worms scan titles and document descriptions for the desired term. Others actually scan documents themselves and give back all the references they find for your search term. Remember that depending on the size of the database and the number of users currently accessing it, these type of extensive searches take longer to complete.

Tip
If you can't find the information you need, try rephrasing. Typing **business** gets you many references, but what kind of business do you want? Try to be specific. Terms like **retail** or **wholesale** might give you better results.

Robots and worms are programs which go out on the Web looking for URLs. When they find a URL, they go to that site looking for more. Each one they find they add to a database. You can search this database by calling up a WWW page for that robot or worm. These are extremely powerful tools for finding information on the Internet. The robots and worms are generally run once a month to freshen the list with new information, so are almost always up-to-date.

As you cruise the Net, you will naturally find the searchers that work best for you. Here is one to get you started:

CUSI: **http://pubweb.nexor.co.uk/public/cusi/doc/list.html**

CUSI (also called SUSI) is a wonderful searcher and is actually a compilation of many searchers into one. It has the ability to find documents, businesses, people, software, and other tidbits of information, and represents a one-stop solution for WWW searching. CUSI contains worms and robots as well as libraries and lists of all types.

When you are connected with the searcher, there is a form area for you to enter the word or term you want to search. After you have typed the word or term, click the Submit button. Depending on how many references it finds and the lag time on the Net, it could take a few seconds or a minute or two. Eventually it comes back with either an error message or a list of entries it found that corresponds in some way to your search request.

Each searcher within CUSI sends back a differently formatted list; you will find some more helpful than others.

After performing a search, you could have maybe 10 to 100 references (this is the amount you get from a standard Lycos search on heavily documented subjects) in front of you. Now, to get that information, all you have to do is click the link (the word that is highlighted, usually in blue) and click again. The browser retrieves the document for you (assuming of course that the system it's on is up and running).

> **Note**
>
> If a searcher doesn't honor your first request and gives you back an error that says the system refused to serve you, try again. Users get this error when the Internet is busy.
>
> Also, if your machine seems to be taking a long time to make the connection, try canceling your request and resubmitting it. Sometimes your first request gets stuck in a sudden traffic jam. By resubmitting your request, the searcher hopefully chooses a route that isn't as busy.

If you don't like the references you received from one searcher, it doesn't mean that what you want isn't out there. Try again with a different searcher. You may get some of the same references, but there will be others that the first one didn't show you.

The reason for this is that the results from some of the searches give you thousands of results. To best serve a large number of researchers, these systems have been restricted to only give you the 10 to 20 most significant that it accesses. Getting to these other references can be difficult and sometimes best achieved by going to a smaller searcher or rephrasing your question. Oftentimes the home page for the searcher has options that allow you to tailor the search and set the maximum number of returned entries.

As you surf around, you'll find other searchers and lists that have a lot of interesting sites. Make sure to drop these into your hotlist; that way, you'll be able to access them with ease.

If you need to access the WWW sites of businesses already on the Web, one useful place is Open Market's commercial listing, found at **http://www.directory.net/**, which contains a searchable database of businesses on the Internet and WWW.

Some programs periodically go offline for updating and servicing. The administrators of these sites try to choose an off-peak time (that is, off-peak to their target audience). So if you can't access a program, that doesn't mean they've gone away forever. Try the program again in a few hours or the next time you're on.

II

The Basics

> **Note**
>
> Some sites are down on Sunday mornings, which appears to be one of the most popular times for maintenance.

Using Lists and Libraries

For most of your searching, you want to stick to robots and worms, since these tend to bring in the most results with the least effort.

However, because the list of references returned by robots and worms are sometimes unwieldy, lists and libraries may be useful for several reasons.

Many lists are maintained by universities and run by students. Often these lists are updated less frequently during school breaks, but usually resume after the students return. In fact, the most popular list on the Internet is run this way—the NCSA What's New list. It's the number one place on the Internet to find out the latest, greatest, and newest sites on the WWW. You can find it at

> **http://www.ncsa.uiuc.edu/UDG/Software/Mosaic/Docs/ whats-new.html**

The majority of people read the What's New list by picking a day to sit down and peruse the thousands of entries for that particular month. Since the list is archived each month, users tend to wait until the end of the month so that they get the most at once. This is an advantage because you are guaranteed that people will see your description as they peruse the list. Robots require you to tell them what you want to find, but lists present you with sites that you didn't even know existed.

You should do all your searching in robots, but reserve some time each month to look at the What's New list and acquaint yourself with the latest and greatest the WWW has to offer.

Asking the Experts

If you can't find the information you need through any of these previously mentioned efforts, it doesn't mean that you can't get that information. You may have to ask in person.

The wonderful thing about the Internet is the immediacy of the medium. Questions asked are answered in hours, and sometimes even seconds.

Since it is human nature to have an opinion, they are extremely easy to come by on the Net. Keep this fact in mind as you surf for answers, and gauge the the responses you receive with what you are expecting. Never hesitate to get a second, third, or even fourth opinion. After all, there are 35 million users, each with his or her own knowledge and experience.

Using NetNews To Find New Information

NetNews is a great place to ask questions and get answers. The thousands of existing interest groups are sure to have something you want and need. Hopping into an interest group and posing a question can usually provide results for you in a matter of hours.

Since people tend to read NetNews daily, you are guaranteed that your message will get lots of attention. This helps especially when asking tough questions, because the more people you ask, the better chances you have of receiving an answer.

The beauty of NetNews is that you get to watch how others ask questions so you can learn from their mistakes. Then, when it is time for you to ask your question, you can do it the right way with a sense of confidence.

In general, you can trust the answers because you usually get more than one back. Pick the answers that tend to agree, and you most certainly have picked the right one. Likewise, because most of the answers come to you not in e-mail but in return postings to NetNews, any errors are quickly spotted by other users and the poster of the incorrect answer is immediately pounced upon by others in the group.

Remember that when posting your own questions to NetNews, use the Subject line in your mail message. By placing a short and concise explanation of what you need, you attract the most number of respondents. Many people don't bother to read the body of your text if the Subject line does not tell them what the message is about.

If you do not frequent NetNews, be sure to tell the readers in your post to respond to you via e-mail. Their responses have a much stronger chance of reaching you, so they don't end up in the NetNews group where you won't see them.

Tip

Ask your provider if they supply an NTTP server. This is a news server and may be linked by your WWW browser. You can read (but not respond to) NetNews from within the WWW.

II

The Basics

Note

If you do not receive an answer to your question after a day or so, restate your question. Remember to avoid weekends, when many users are not on the Internet.

Using IRC for Instant Answers

While NetNews can be rewarding for finding answers, it can be slow. In this day of instant everything, one common expectation is an instant answer to the posted question. IRC provides this.

> **Caution**
>
> One thing you should know about IRC is that it can be terribly addictive. Because you are going to be talking with individuals from around the world in real time, you find a new way to make friends and find out about what is happening in faraway places. Use IRC with some willpower.

◄ See "Etiquette in Live Discussions," p. 183

You should see how to get exactly what you want out of IRC. Suppose you need help designing your WWW pages. In this case, the place to go is **#www** to ask people there what to do.

The first time you step into the group, you should just watch others ask questions and see how they get their answers. Because most of the gurus in **#www** are off surfing the web, it's often difficult to get their attention. Beeping in the group instantly kicks you out, but being patient and asking your question several times tends to generate a response.

When asking your question, make sure it is clear and contains all the necessary information to ensure the fastest and most accurate response. As in NetNews, incorrect information is almost instantly corrected by the other members of the group.

Intelligent Agents

Intelligent agents are programs which go out and find information for you. These programs are very much like robots and worms with the exception of how they work.

A robot or worm bases itself in one location and probes remote locations looking for information. An intelligent agent acts like a little ferret, going from site to site and tapping each on the shoulder asking about certain information. When it's completed or after a given period of time, it reports back to you.

Intelligent agents are rather new to computing. Several devices that make use of intelligent agents are now appearing. However, the Internet has seen intelligent agents for some time, not only in the guise of robots and worms but also in listservers.

A *listserver* is a program hooked up to an e-mail address. Sending e-mail to the address activates the program, which looks at your e-mail message and fulfills some request it finds in the message. Listservers can perform several interesting functions. For example, you could inform a listserver to e-mail you product information about a company the server knows about.

There are many forms of listservers on the Internet. For the most part, WWW users do not bother with listservers because the WWW has more than enough to do. However, listservers are quite useful, and analogies to them on the WWW are beginning to appear.

More sophisticated servers can actually be programmed to watch for things you are interested in. For example, you could ask a watch server to look for anything having to do with HTML in NetNews. Any NetNews articles in the groups that you specify to watch which have HTML in their text are copied to you via e-mail.

In this manner, a program acts like a little agent, going out and doing something for you while you are busy doing other things.

Other Interactive Discussion Services

The Internet is a vast research jungle where many interactive programs have been written. Some of these programs have even made it into popular use.

One such program is CU-SeeMe. This program, available from Cornell University and many NASA sites, allows you to transmit video over the Internet in pseudo-real time. You obviously need some special equipment, but it nonetheless begins to provide you with some rudimentary video conferencing capabilities over existing Internet channels.

Another mechanism for discussions is Conference Rooms and other similar services such as WebChat. These act as NetNews-ish or IRC-ish type mechanisms but are implemented in the WWW. Conference Rooms allows users to join favorite public or private groups and participate in dialogs.

▶ See "The Unbelievable World of Instant Products," p. 319

These types of added facilities are often perfect for remote project planning and other remote conference needs.

From Here...

In this chapter, you learned how to search for information and people using the WWW. You also saw how to post information for searches and how to ask questions of the many experts you will encounter.

II

The Basics

For more information, refer to the following chapters:

- Chapter 10, "Advertising on the Net," provides information on creating effective Web ads.

- Chapter 15, "Acquiring Demographics About Your Users," shows you another way to gather information from the Web.

- Chapter 16, "Your Presence on the Net," suggests ways to make sure your best foot is always in front on the Information Superhighway.

Part III

Selling Products and Services

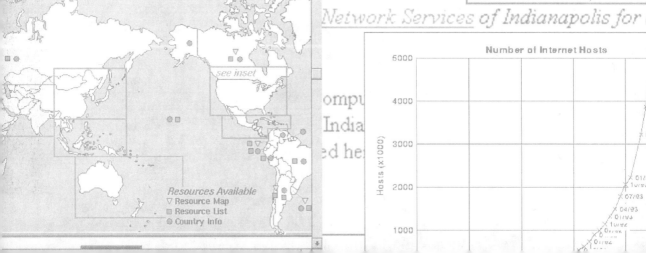

Chapter 10

Advertising on the Net

The keys to advertising on the Net are similar to tactics used in traditional advertising—the creation of exciting and effective ads and making sure your target audience sees them.

The ads themselves include many of the same concepts for traditional print ads, TV commercials, and radio spots. Of course, there are some special considerations. Making sure that your ad is seen depends not so much on the placement of the actual advertising, but on the placement of references to your company, products, or services that contain links to your advertising. In some cases you might want to consider promotional devices to entice people to the location of the advertising.

In this chapter you learn

- The best ways to let people know about your advertising

- Ways to encourage repeat visits

- How to mix traditional and WWW advertising

- The components of multimedia advertising

- What virtual storefronts, malls, and cityscapes are

- What to do if you need to change or correct your advertising

How To Advertise on the Net

When you place an ad in a magazine, newspaper, or on TV, people reading that publication or watching that station will see your ad. In order for them to not see your ad, they must make some effort, such as turning the page or leaving the room.

Tip
Check to see
whether any of
your competitors
are on the WWW.
If they are, you
might want to
take their advertis-
ing into consider-
ation as you create
your own.

On the Net, however, you must make the customer come to your advertisement. They must type the URL or choose the link. Even if another site places
a link to your pages within their site, your potential customer must reach that
site by some conscious effort.

In traditional advertising, the success of an ad depends not only on how the
ad looks, but in what magazine it appears in or during what TV program it is
shown. Likewise, the success your WWW advertising will depend on where
and how you promote your advertising as well as how it looks.

Choosing the Best Place To Advertise

The WWW is unique in that advertising does not come to users like it does in
TV and radio. Instead, users must seek out the advertising. As the advertiser,
you must find places to put your advertisements where users will run into
them.

The best place to post this information is in the various lists that are maintained around the world. These lists are managed by companies, universities,
and individuals.

You will want to promote your business on those lists and sites that are used
by the audience you want to reach. For instance, if you are interested in generating business overseas, you want to make sure you post on lists that are
seen overseas.

While many of the lists are general, providing information on many topics,
some of them target specific audiences. You can take advantage of these lists
by posting to all of them that apply to you.

For example, if you were selling toys, you might want to target children as
well as parents. In this case, you'll be promoting your WWW site on lists that
are used by both children and adults.

There are a few sites that every business will want to post on:

- NCSA What's New List

  **http://www.ncsa.uiuc.edu/SDG/Software/Mosaic/Docs/
  Whats-New.html**

- Open Market's Commercial Sites Index (see fig. 10.1)

  http://www.directory.net/

■ Stanford Universities Yahoo Server

http://www.yahoo.com/

■ Carnegie-Mellon University Lycos Robot

http://query1.lycos.cs.cmu.edu/lyco-form.html

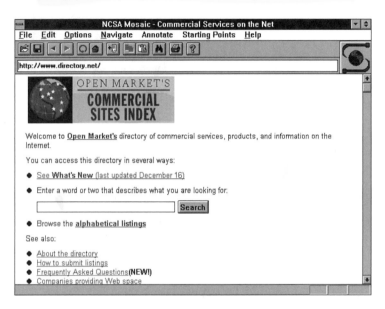

Fig. 10.1
The Open Market's Commercial Sites Index is a popular listing of businesses on the World Wide Web at URL **http://www.directory.net/**.

You may come across lists that are divided into categories. If these lists allow you to post to more than one category, make sure to post in every category that fits. If you can only post to one category, you want to make sure that it's the best one.

Some lists you post to are updated as soon as you submit the data. These lists are nice because you can submit your information and the post is there immediately. Many of these lists also allow you to modify and remove your listing, making it convenient if the address changes, products change, or even if you just make an error.

On other lists, the information you submit is reviewed by the maintainer of the list and added by them. Sometimes it takes a long time for your information to be added to these lists. Some of the larger and more popular lists are run this way, so you should post to them despite the time factor. Because a maintainer views your post, this person decides where to place it; the maintainer also decides if it's inappropriate for the list. Almost all of the maintainers send you back e-mail saying they have added your items to the list, though some do not. The best way to check is to watch the list for a week after you make the post to see if your ad appears. If it does not and no message is sent to you, resubmit it.

> **Note**
>
> You may also find that users on the Net help promote your material. Users who have their own home page and like your page may put it into their public hotlist. Other companies might have a reason to put a link from their site to yours. While surfing the Web, you may be surprised at finding a link for your site that you didn't know existed.

If you go to some of the same robots and worm sites that you learned about in Chapter 9, "Information on the Net," you can now make use of these sites to advertise yourself. Many of the robots and worms automatically find you and add you to their list, after about a month or so. However, you can speed up this process by giving the robot or worm your URL. In that case, your URL and description are instantly accessible to anyone searching the database.

To add your business to a list, simply bring up your WWW browser and go to the list where you want to be added. Look at the top or bottom of the page for information about how to submit to the list. Almost all lists allow you to submit to them in some manner. Many of the lists allow you to send e-mail to get added. Others allow you to add your information interactively via HTML pages set up to take your information.

In any case, the individual list you are looking at will have instructions, either on your page or a page some levels higher, that tell you how to post.

Each list requires you to format information in a slightly different manner. Some lists want you to submit your descriptions in HTML. Others want just plain text. Some require that you word your advertisement in third person. Look at the list to see how others have posted, read carefully what the list maintainers want you to do, and then try it yourself. You might want to pick one of the sites which allows you to add yourself, to get the hang of the mechanism in a situation where you can edit your errors.

◀ See "Consult-
ants versus
Net Service
Bureaus,"
p. 139

Remember that many WWW professionals have services they provide which post to all the popular lists for you. This may make it easier for you if you are having problems understanding how to post to lists or simply don't have the time.

Note

If you are posting to a list maintained by a university (look for .edu in the domain name) via e-mail, you should be patient with them to add it. Because universities take regular breaks, e-mail requests often pile up and take awhile to add when students come back to school. The What's New list at NCSA is one such list. This is THE most popular list on the Internet, but is often slow at posting because of its popularity and schedule. Posting to that page can take anywhere from a week to four months to appear.

There is one drawback with the ease of having links to your pages. You can't control who is putting links to your page and you can't control what they say it links to. However, trust your Internet clients to remember that you don't have control over who points to your page.

It is fairly obvious that you should advertise your Web pages on the WWW itself; however, NetNews also makes a good mechanism for advertising. Placing information about your site in the various NetNews groups which are interested in what you have is a good way to pull users into your pages. However, remember to only post to NetNews sites who have a genuine interest. Posting to groups with little interest generally creates a lot of e-mail telling you to please not do it again.

One last suggestion for a good place to put your URLs is in the bottom of all your e-mail messages. If you make them a standard part of your signature, you will be letting anyone who sees one of your messages, be it on e-mail or NetNews, that you offer a WWW site.

Remember, if you don't advertise the fact that you have WWW pages, people won't be able to find you on the Internet!

Generating Awareness for Your Advertising

Sometimes because of the new nature of commercial ventures using the Web, potential customers may not even be aware that the Web is a place to purchase your product or service. You may need to use promotional devices to entice people to your site. This involves offering something that people want to do or see.

There are all sorts of things you can offer people. The device you use depends on the audience you are trying to reach.

Tip
Make sure any promotional devices you use are keeping with your company's image.

III

Products and Services

You can use almost anything: jokes, cartoons, recipes, decorating tips, repair information, horoscopes, music, pictures or photographs, stock and investment tips, or health care advice.

Caution

Don't provide information that is illegal for you to give. For example, if you offer legal tips or health care information, make sure it doesn't pass into the realm of practicing law or medicine, unless of course you are a lawyer or doctor.

You could choose a device that relates to your area of business, such as stock tips from a broker, back care advice from a chiropractor, or travel tips from a travel agency.

You could also decide to use a device to target a particular audience. A travel agent who wanted to target business people might offer investment tips.

Pictures and information about famous people are popular, but you need to make sure that you aren't violating any copyrights. The things you offer as promotional devices should either be of your own creation or public domain material, or you must have the rights to use the material. Plagiarism is dealt with further in this chapter in the section, "A Word About Plagiarism."

Offering links to other sites can be another way to generate awareness and interest in your site. For example, if you are a stockbroker, you may have links to popular stock pages on the Web. This would make your page a popular place to go to for people who want all the stock information in one location. Maintaining your own list can be rewarding, because it brings people directly into your own organization. However, keep in mind that if your list becomes popular, you may find your investment to keep it up-to-date increasing.

Tip
Advertising blurbs are generally short, so keep your keywords to one or two that you think work the best.

You can take advantage of your list in another way. If, for example, you listed some of the better links you provide in your advertising, people doing searches on names would find your name when they searched for the name that is in your list. For example, here is an advertising blurb you might release:

```
Select <here> to come to News Clipping Industries.
Join our growing customer base who make use of our
online news gathering resources. Or cruise our
super government list with links to the White House,
United Nations, and more!
```

In this ad, people searching the URL databases for "White House" or "United Nations" would also stumble into your pages, because you have included those words in the ad and offered the user the link as a service. Words that are used to associate searches to your page are called *keywords*.

How To Keep People Coming Back

Most devices you use bring people in once, but even the funniest joke is only read once. If you want people to return to your site, you have to give them something more. This is easily done by periodically changing the information.

Your jokes, tips, or artwork can be updated daily, weekly, or monthly. How often you change the material depends on how often you want the user to come back. Make sure you let the potential client know that the information will be updated or changed and on what schedule. If they liked what they saw, they'll be back to see your new pages.

Making periodic changes to your pages also gives you a perfect excuse to rebroadcast your pages to the What's New lists. While you do not need to freshen robots (who will keep your URLs forever), reposting to a What's New list grabs the attention of those people who may have forgotten about you and new users as they glance to see what has been added to the WWW.

In lists where you can modify your information yourself, you may want to periodically change your ad copy to reflect the changed content of your pages.

All these things help in getting a customer to notice you. However, one thing shines above all else—if you offer a service which the user finds indispensable. Chapter 14, "Subscription Services, Virtual Malls, and Instant Products," describes such products in detail. Each of these are mechanisms for you to offer fantastic services to your clients. These services cannot only make you money, but they can also provide enormous attractions for getting clients into your business.

For example, suppose you are an auto parts distributor who mail-orders auto parts worldwide. You decide to offer a system by which people can diagnose their own car problem through a question-and-answer dialog. They are shown pictures of the parts in question with diagrams of what and how to fix it. Instant links to your products are provided which allows them to pick the needed part and buy it instantly.

This system requires a lot more investment than just making simple HTML pages. However, it serves as a fantastic gateway for just about anyone who wants to save some money on car repairs. Not only can they buy the product, but they can diagnose and determine the problem, all online!

▶ See "Subscription Services," p. 313

You can begin to see how such a system would be extremely popular, and you can make even more money from the service by packaging it in subscription systems or instant products!

▶ See "Instant Products," p. 319

Mixing Traditional Advertising with Net Advertising

Many companies want to combine their existing advertising with their network presence. This can be very useful for many reasons.

Any company with national or international clout will probably want to mirror their advertising onto their WWW pages. Slogans, jingles, colors, and style can all be changed to reflect new ad campaigns. Promotions and contests can be mirrored on the Internet to provide alternative methods for users to enter the drawings.

However, your WWW presence can also impact your traditional advertising. At least one major television network now lists its e-mail address after the evening news. This says a lot of things, including that it considers the Internet audience mainstream enough to provide access for.

By placing your e-mail address and URL in your advertising, you are informing your audience that an alternative source of information about you, your company, and your products or services exists. This helps to build awareness and also makes it easier for consumers to get ahold of your product or service.

Because of the initial popularity of the Internet, companies who promote their Internet presence early will benefit the most from the novelty. After a few years, when most businesses will be hooked up to e-mail and WWW pages are prevalent, it will be considered unusual not to have them listed.

Likewise, it's easy to place your e-mail address and URL information on your letterhead and business cards. This tactic again serves to remind people about your WWW presence and Internet capabilities.

If you currently advertise your product in any high-tech magazines, you will definitely benefit from listing your electronic access information. Audiences of these magazines generally access the Internet and appreciate knowing that you are there.

You should also include your e-mail and WWW addresses on any catalogs that you might produce. If you currently allow people to fax your orders,

your e-mail address and URL should be listed alongside the fax number. If
users have a fax machine, they quite possibly have Internet access as well.

Finally, choosing a name for yourself that reflects your advertising, slogan,
look, or product allows you to tie in your URL information more easily. A
travel agent with an e-mail address of henry@spock.net does not work. The
advertising looks funny with that user name next to a picture of white sandy
beaches. However, having an e-mail address of vacations@travel.com is more
effective.

◀ See "Why You
Should Register
a Domain
Name," p. 163

The World of Multimedia Advertising

The Internet will open up new doors to many companies. Many businesses
never dreamed that they could have full-color advertising with worldwide
distribution. This new multimedia capability allows companies to show
products and offer services in ways they never could before.

This section outlines the major WWW multimedia capabilities and shows
you methods for using them in your business.

Using Still and Moving Graphics

The WWW allows both still and moving graphics to be integrated into
WWW pages. Still graphics may be placed directly in the WWW document
itself so that it appears with the text of the document. This is called an *inline
image*.

Movies always pop up in a window of their own and play in that window.
Images can also be made to appear in a window by themselves.

▶ See "Adding
Images To Your
Pages," p. 534

Still Graphics

How and where you use graphics depends on what type of impact you want
to make. For obvious reasons, almost all companies want their logo at the top
of their pages. Many designs place a large logo on the first page and a smaller
logo on the secondary pages.

If throughput is an issue, however, a design often has a smaller version of the
logo on the main page, and a larger version on secondary pages (see figs. 10.2
and 10.3). By placing the smaller picture on the first page you are guarantee-
ing lower throughput for that page. Users reaching that page by accident will
leave without going further, and therefore you will have less throughput than
if you had put the larger graphic on the first page.

III

Products and Services

Fig. 10.2
The main page of this site (**http://www.iquest.net/tra/**) displays its company logo. Compare this to one of the secondary pages shown in figure 10.3.

Fig. 10.3
This is one of the secondary pages at URL **http://www.iquest.net/tra/thomp02.html**. Note how the logo was changed from figure 10.2 but is still consistent in style.

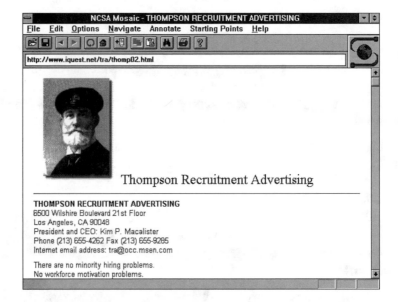

You may also decide to highlight some or all of your products with pictures. Most people design their pages so that very small pictures of a product are presented alongside text describing the product. By keeping the pictures small, you allow users to see more products at once, which lets them narrow their decision more quickly (see fig. 10.4).

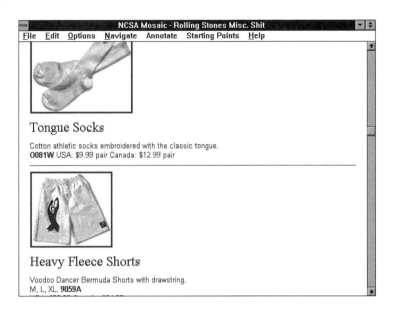

Fig. 10.4
A product page shows different small product pictures next to their descriptions, available at the Rolling Stones site (**http://www. stones.com/**).

You can incorporate the pop-up picture with the inline picture by making the small product photos bring up large pictures of the product when the user clicks the link around the picture. By linking the inline image to a larger picture stored on disk, the picture is displayed only when the user chooses that particular item. This allows users to quickly preview products and then examine desired selections in more detail before making a decision (see fig. 10.5). In some browsers such as Netscape, the pop-up pictures appear on a page by themselves instead of popping up in a separate window.

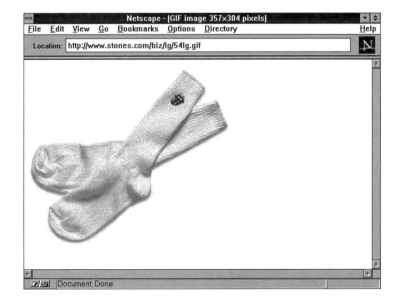

Fig. 10.5
A larger pop-up view of the product shown in figure 10.4 appears after selecting the smaller image on that page (**http://www. stones.com/**).

III

Products and Services

In some cases, you may need more than one photo, either showing the product from different sides or in different settings. In this case, photo montages could be created that describe various parts of the photo when users clicked the image. By tying into the sound capabilities (discussed in the next section), you can even give audio descriptions when they point to portions of the picture.

Moving Graphics

Moving graphics can also offer some businesses the ability to display detailed visual information about their products or services. Movies allow you to show video clips over the Internet. The movie is downloaded into the user's machine and played at full speed from there.

Tip

Because movies take a large amount of storage, place them at FTP sites and access them via **ftp://** in your pages. FTP sites often have storage charges only and no throughput charges. The user's browser gets the movie off the site without charging you for the throughput.

Currently, using movies in your pages is rare, due to the long download time involved. However, as the Internet grows in capability, more and more sites will offer movie and video clips.

Not all businesses will want to take advantage of the movie capability. However, for some businesses, movies can offer a better way to see a product. Clothing stores can use short movie clips to model latest fashions. Real estate companies could offer "short walks" through various properties. Rock bands have already used them to show portions of their music videos and concerts.

A very important use of graphics is the small borders and bullets that make up any page. While HTML comes with its own default bullets and line separators, having your own colorful bullets and borders adds life to a page.

Tip

Make use of seasonal themes. During the winter season, snowmen, snowballs, snow-flakes, and Christmas trees can adorn the borders and bullets of your pages, adding a festive feel.

Borders and bullets are very small and thus load very quickly. You can afford to have different bullets and borders on each page. For example, the bottom of each page could have a small cartoon border. People might want to go to each of your pages to check out the small cartoon at the bottom. Likewise, new products could have a small exploding "new" graphic bullet next to them. A gift store could have small wrapped presents as the bullets.

Interestingly, it is often these little things that can really improve the appearance of a page (see figs. 10.6 and 10.7).

Try not to overuse graphics on each page. An artist would say that you were not making good use of "white space;" in other words, the page is too crowded. If an over-cluttered page uses too many conflicting colors, it may be called in Net jargon "an angry fruit salad." Based on the canned variety of fruit salad, it refers to computer layouts that are poorly designed.

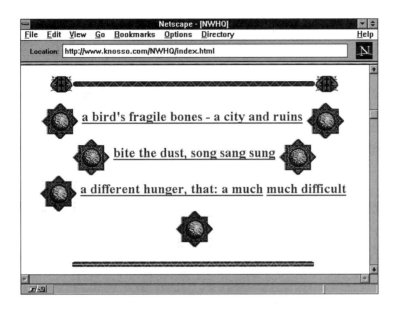

Fig. 10.6
Novel use of
bullets can serve
to draw the users
attention to the
page (**http://
www.knosso.
com/NWHQ/
index.html**).

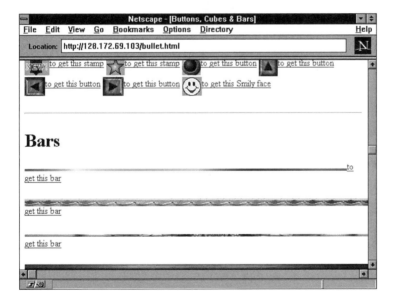

Fig. 10.7
Different types of
interesting borders
and bullets can be
used to add
interest to a home
page (**http://
128.172.69.103/
bullet.html**).

Crowded pages tend to confuse people and present a cluttered and congested
look to a site. Confused users won't know where on your page to look for
information or how to access additional information. In these cases, users
may move on to a site that is more understandable and easier to use. Pages

should "breathe" so that there is space and balance to the page. The graphics should serve to augment the text, not overpower it.

Some pages embody all the information in a graphic. While expensive to access, these pages have more possibilities in layout and design. Because the text itself is a part of the image, special fonts and layouts can be achieved which can really spice up a page (see fig. 10.8).

Fig. 10.8
The White House page contains all the controls as a part of a large image (**http://www. whitehouse. gov/**).

Using Audio

If you are selling music of any type such as CDs, a band, cassettes, or movie soundtracks, or you are a record label, producer, or promoter, you can make use of WWW's audio capability.

Likewise, politicians, speakers, educators, and scientists would all find audio capability an effective means of talking to their audience. In fact, many people and businesses can use audio, from poets to companies with memorable theme songs.

The beautiful thing about audio is that it is not forced on the user. The current capabilities of most WWW browsers do not allow audio to be played automatically upon entering a page. This means that audio selections are always activated by the user when the user desires. This means that they will only impact your throughput when used, unlike graphics which are always loaded when your pages are accessed, unless the user has chosen to disable inline graphics in the browser.

In order to allow a user to access audio, you must provide a link to the audio file in your page.

▶ See "Adding Sounds and Other External Files To Your Pages," p. 538

Usually people hyperlink a picture. The picture can show the source of the sound (for example, CD cover art or a politician giving a speech), but usually the picture is some icon which represents sound. Popular choices for icons include ears, musical notes, and hands cupped to ears. These icons universally indicate that an audio selection is available by clicking that particular button.

> **Note**
>
> Audio is often as large as 40,000 bytes for each second of speech, making it quite expensive both in terms of storage and throughput. Because of this, you may want to place them at FTP sites and access them via **ftp://** in your pages. FTP sites often have storage charges only and no throughput charges. The users browser obtains the audio off the site without charging you for the throughput.

Remember not to embody too much functionality in audio, since many users do not want to sit through the download (see fig. 10.9). Additionally, not all users have audio playback capability.

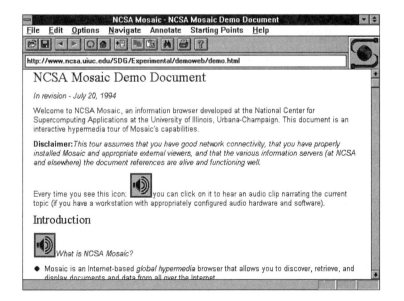

Fig. 10.9
Pages with audio links usually denote the link with some type of icon.

III

Products and Services

Using Hyperlinks and Other References

The WWW is really all about linking. If you couldn't link, you wouldn't be able to move from place to place. What a boring thing that would be!

Linking provides you with the ability to have your information organized in pieces which can more closely represent how you want to present your data.

For example, many pages start with a home page, which is the main entrance into the business. This page greets the user, gives a basic overview of the page, and then lists the main areas you can go to from there.

The "go to from there" part is the link. Any object can be linked. For example, a word or phrase on a page can be linked to another document, movie, sound bite, or picture. Likewise, a picture can be linked to any sound or other pictures, documents, and movies. By selecting the linked item with the mouse, the proper object is retrieved and displayed to the user.

Of course, each linked item can itself have links—voila, the World Wide Web is born!

Most pages have a standard set of links. These include links that leave the page and take the user back to some master page, which can either be your provider's home page or some other page of your choice. In pages after your home page, the link which leaves goes to your home page. In general, you always want this link to go to the previous page. This link often appears at the very top or bottom of a page.

Tip
The most boring page is a page with absolutely no graphics or links on it anywhere.

Likewise, most pages have the name of the creator of the page at the bottom, which often takes the form of a linked e-mail address. Activating the link usually takes you to the business' home page, or to the home page of the individual who created the page.

As mentioned before, having links to other related sites within your pages is a nice service to offer the user. These links should be checked periodically to make sure they still work and point to things you are interested in.

> **Caution**
>
> Be careful, however, not to place your favorite "other sites list" on your first page. Make the user look at your other pages before discovering other sites. The idea should be to keep users in, not get rid of them as soon as possible.

You should try to avoid having everything linked. Some pages have every third word linked—this indicates an HTML designer gone mad. Most people avoid such a page, since it offers so much to do that people just can't make a choice. A good rule is to try to limit your links to no more than one or two per paragraph, and even that is probably too much.

While you should expect product and list-type pages to have lots of links on them, non-product and non-list-oriented pages usually have between two and 10 links per page.

Using Too Much of a Good Thing

With all these creative tools to use in your home page advertising, you may be tempted to put in lots of big, full-color pictures, an audio selection with the name of your company, a snappy jingle, or maybe even a couple of video clips.

How do you know if you're using too much of a good thing? The answer boils down to time and money. You should ask yourself two questions:

- How long will it take for the average user to access your home page, and how likely are they to wait that long?

- Does the revenue created by the advertising cover the expenses you'll incur?

In general, the longer people have to wait, the less likely it is that they will make it to your site. At some point they'll move on. How long users have to wait and the length of time they're willing to wait depends on several factors.

How long the users have to wait is determined by the speed of their hookup to the Internet and the rate of speed that information leaves your home page site. If your average users are accessing the Net on a 9,600 baud modem, it takes them a long time to download pictures, audio and video.

We have already mentioned that most WWW servers charge for throughput. Even if your pictures are moderately sized and you are accessed by hundreds of users a day, your throughput charges might run $1,000 per month or more.

◀ See "How To Price the Net," p. 134

However, if you are running a highly successful subscriber dating service, pictures will be among the mainstay of your business, and you would be foolish to scrimp on them.

The answer to "What's too much of a good thing?" is highly individualized. You want to carefully weigh all the different factors in making your decision

III

Products and Services

as to what advanced features to include. The nice thing about the Net is that if you make a miscalculation, you can change it easily and quickly.

A Word About Plagiarism

Don't.

While most people would never think of stealing something belonging to someone else, it is often harder to remember this when looking for spiffy graphics to place at the top of your page.

Many sites offer clip art and images for people to download. All too often the unsuspecting page creator grabs a picture from an icon library, only to find out later that the picture is copyrighted.

When we were starting out in our WWW practice, we used to get all of our imagery off the Internet. However, after being contacted by authors of images that we were using, we soon learned that it was better to purchase imagery from companies who supply CD-ROM libraries. These libraries allow us to use them without worrying about copyright.

You should basically avoid putting in any information which you did not create yourself, which is not in the public domain, or which you do not have explicit rights to use. This includes audio, magazine articles, pictures from books and magazines, art, and trademarked slogans.

All About Storefronts and Cityscapes

Many companies on the Internet are creating virtual malls on the World Wide Web. These malls, similar to real-life malls, house many businesses under one roof. These sections examine the benefits and uses of these types of virtual malls as well as the Internet community on a whole.

The Concept of a Virtual Community

The Internet can be thought of as millions of individuals and companies each doing their own thing. However, this view would be fairly naive.

The Internet is actually a large number of overlapping and interrelating groups. Each group is actually fairly small and regionally based. The communities are virtual in that as you move about on the Internet, you move from community to community.

For example, as you dial your local provider, you join your immediate real community of users. From there you may decide to hop over to NetNews to catch up on the latest business dealings in Korea. While doing this, you are dealing with the virtual Korean community, filled with people from all over the world with an interest in Korea. Finally, onto IRC you go for some quick questions in the #www group, which is its own little community of WWW wizards and gurus, and then out onto the Web for a look at today's stock quotations, where you join the business community.

The Internet, therefore, is the realization of the new-age and often overused term "the global village."

However, many businesses are not content to leave it alone at that. In an effort to identify, group, and catalog, many businesses are creating malls and villages on the Internet. These experiments are very interesting because they allow the Internet to mimic the real world.

The Internet is unusual real estate in that there are not any "bad parts of town." Sure, there are slow access sites and these are perhaps undesirable, but in general, it doesn't really matter too much where you place your store. In other words, there are no advantages to being placed in a "high-rent" district.

Storefronts that are reasonably priced do offer some advantages. By being placed with other companies, you are guaranteed somewhat more of a stream of business than if you are simply by yourself.

Malls may come free with the WWW provider. In most sites, for example, people who have their WWW pages hosted there are automatically added to the mall or storefront running on that site. In this way, the mall serves to attract new customers into the provider.

However, there are many virtual malls where you can place your business, no matter where your pages are housed. Some allow you to exist for free, while others consider themselves premium services and charge you to belong.

The virtual communities who consider themselves premium services often do have something to offer. Many times these businesses have electronic trans-action processing, faxing, and other business services for their clients. These can many times be useful for businesses.

Caution

You should stay away from virtual communities that try to attract you based on their "big name." The price you pay for the service you get will most likely not be worth it. Remember, because there is really no bad part of town there is also no good part of town, or rather, it's all good. (This is referring to capability, not speed of access, but the big names don't always have the best access either.)

Belonging To Multiple Communities

Want to franchise your store but just don't have the money? Now you do!

There are many communities on the Internet who would love to have you onboard for free or for an affordable price. Remember, success on the Internet is based on how many people come into your pages, so having your name out there is the primary goal.

By placing your name in more than one mall, you are in effect franchising your business. However, you do not want to have your pages duplicated in each mall. This would be not only wasteful, but hard to manage.

Instead, you should host your pages in one location but have links to your pages placed in other malls. This is very similar to placing your links in lists, but instead of the link being in just a list, it's in a virtual mall or *cityscape* (another popular term for virtual communities). Again, you most likely will pay a monthly fee to be part of the cityscape, so pick one with the profile and direction that you think best enhances your company.

For example, suppose your company sells CDs. You have found an inexpensive server in your city to house your pages. However, there are many CD sites and groups on the Internet. Some are located in malls where it would be nice to have your own presence.

Simply contact the mall owners (by their home page information) and find out how much it costs to have a link to your pages placed in their mall. Any user who comes into the mall sees your entrance and can be instantly teleported into your storefront in your local server.

Remember, the more communities you belong to, the more people you have coming into your site.

The Future of Storefronts, Malls, and Cityscapes

As the Internet and WWW grow and mature, you can expect that cityscapes and malls will grow as well.

In the future, huge malls—very similar to real malls—could appear online. You should also expect to see the merging of real malls and virtual malls, so that "shop at home" and "shop in the store" become shared experiences.

Already huge mall and store presences are beginning to appear. JC Penney and Spiegel are just two large stores that currently have a presence on the Web. You can include on this list Spencer Gifts and television's own Home Shopping Network. These stores are just the beginnings of the huge mall presence that is about to emerge.

As the Internet transforms into a more virtual and graphical environment, virtual malls will begin to become meeting places and entertainment spots as well as just shopping outlets.

How To Correct Your Advertising

You just posted your new pages to over 20 groups on the Internet only to discover that the link you put in is incorrect. What do you do?

This section helps you correct postings that you have made. You should be warned that it may be physically impossible to fix all links. In some cases, you just have to wait for time to remove the error.

The Horror of an Incorrect Posting

It should be painfully obvious that once you post your link to a site or list, you should try out the link. Even if you place the information into the computer perfectly, there is nothing that says that the computer or program at the other end didn't mangle your data. Test it to make sure it works. Testing it immediately removes the possibility that you'll hear about it later.

Before you learn about the ways to correct a mistake, you should know the types of mistakes you can make:

- *Errors in e-mail.* As soon as you enter the message, you have committed yourself. This is the same as saying that as soon as you seal the envelope that you can't rewrite the letter. This can be a problem if you said the wrong thing, or if you accidentally e-mailed the wrong person.

- *Accidentally sent messages.* Some e-mail programs will send a message even if you abort the message while writing it. In these frustrating situations a message that you really did not want to send is going to be sent anyway (most likely incomplete, if you aborted the mailer before completing the message).

- *Bounced messages.* Messages that are sent to an incorrect e-mail address will bounce back to you. However, many times bounced mail recirculates in an attempt to find the destined user, only to finally bounce back to you weeks later. This is particularly inconvenient if your e-mail concerned time-sensitive information.

Think of what would happen if you accidentally sent an e-mail message to a NetNews group. Instead of blundering to just one individual, you have blundered to the entire NetNews community, involving hundreds of thousands—or even millions—of readers of the group you posted to.

The most frustrating errors in the Web are links which are wrong or missing HTML syntax. For example, a missing quote mark or HTML command terminator breaks the link to your page or causes your page to look strange.

Likewise, when adding to lists on the Web, it's often easy to misread the way lists' authors want you to submit your information. Submitting it incorrectly often leads to an inaccurate posting that's sometimes very difficult to repair.

The bottom line is to read very carefully everything you plan to submit before you commit to it. Only once you are certain that it is correct should you finish the transaction. Then immediately check to see if the page or posting was successful and if the message says what you want it to say.

Retracting Incorrect Information

Imagine the following scenario. You just posted the wrong URL to over 20 lists and 10 NetNews groups. You also sent it out to over 40 people on your e-mail list. What do you do?

After sitting and crying for at least five minutes, perhaps kicking yourself once or twice for not double-checking that entry before you sent it, and repeating a few solemn oaths to never do it again, you should be ready to try to fix the damage.

Start with those 40 e-mail messages. Unfortunately, the Internet is, if anything, very fast at delivering e-mail. Most of the e-mail sent is transmitted within one or two seconds to the resulting party. It is very unlikely that you could abort the message before it was sent.

Probably the only recourse you have for e-mail is sending another message immediately, in which you correct the first and apologize for a mistake. Some e-mail programs display mail starting with the most recent message received and ending with the oldest message received. In these e-mail programs the users see your last message first. This way, you can use the later message to inform the recipients that the previous message should be ignored. Remember, they see the second message first. However, not all e-mail programs show mail in this order. Some of the more popular programs for PC and Mac will show messages in the order they were received—the oldest message showing first. In these cases, make sure the Subject line of your e-mail helps to relay that this message is a correction.

OK, now for NetNews. Unfortunately the NetNews system uses the mail system for its messages, so it's just as fast as e-mail. Again, sending a message to counteract the first one helps but is not nearly as effective as with e-mail. The size of the audience affected is much larger. Many people respond to the first posting immediately upon seeing it, and won't wait for the second posting.

If your NetNews group is moderated, you should immediately send e-mail to the moderator asking that person to pull the messages. This action may get the messages pulled before they propagate too much, but in general there's not much else you can do for NetNews.

So far the advice has been "tough luck." Don't forget—you have to deal with the 20 errors in your URLs.

Depending on the list you posted the URL to, you can correct it. Some of the lists are interactive, and thus you can correct them at any time. Many of these lists want you to assign a password so that only you can modify your items.

Tip
Make sure you remember your password, or your information is forever locked.

If you cannot change the information yourself, find out the e-mail address of the person who maintains the list. You can find this address at the bottom or top of one of the list pages. Send a short e-mail message to that person asking politely if he or she would either remove or correct the problem. Monitor the link, and if the error is not fixed within one week, repeat the request.

If the error is still not fixed, try reposting the corrected version of the ad. If you are lucky, you can supersede your previous posting, and at the very least, let new people see the new posting, not the old one.

The important thing to remember when trying to fix URL and WWW ads is that it might take time for the fix to propagate to all the lists and sites in the world. This could take several months, so be somewhat patient.

Changing E-Mail Addresses
If, for whatever reason, you change your e-mail address, there are several steps you can take to inform the world:

1. Obviously, first change all your e-mail and NetNews signatures to reflect the new address.

2. Next, if you changed physical providers, ask your old provider to keep a forwarding file for you for at least 30 days. This will automatically forward your mail to your new address. It works just like mail forwarding in the post office.

   Tip
   Your old provider should not charge you for this service (but it would not be unheard of if they did).

   If you kept the same provider but merely changed accounts, have them place an alias to your new name. This allows mail to come to both addresses and get routed to you correctly.

III

Products and Services

3. As soon as you have your new address, check it out by sending mail to yourself.

4. Once it works correctly, send mail to your entire list of correspondents, asking them to change their lists.

5. Keep an eye on mail sent to your old addresses and retransmit to those people the change of address.

Changing Net Providers

Changing your Net provider can cause a lot of problems for your Web business. If you switch Internet providers, your URL will change. And if your URL changes, everyone who has your old address won't be able to find you. This includes all the people who dropped you into their hotlist or anyone who wrote it down elsewhere. If your URL has been distributed on business cards, stationery or posted in ads and articles in magazines or newspapers, all those people have the wrong address, too. Also, all the links you have created are incorrect. It can be a real hassle, so you'll want to consider that before you make any changes.

You want to consider changing providers if:

- You're moving and the old provider is no longer a local phone call.

- You can't get on. This means when you call their number, it's busy.

- It's unbearably slow all the time. This applies to e-mail and other Internet services besides the WWW.

- Your provider isn't full-service. Some shortcomings might include: they can't give you a SLIP connection, don't provide a full NetNews feed, or don't allow FTP.

- The money you would save on the cheaper service is greater than what it would cost you to change and update your new URL. Remember to include the cost of any possible lost business from customers who might have difficulty in finding you.

If you do change Internet providers, you need to take care of several things. Have your old provider give out a forwarding address for you. Even if you are charged a monthly fee, it will be worth it. Your old provider can re-route users automatically to your new site. This can be done by automatic forwarding or by placing a page that instructs users where to find the new page (usually with a hyperlink).

It helps if you list the fact that you are moving at least three weeks before you move. People can have an opportunity to anticipate the time when your link will change. Likewise, once you have moved, keep the announcement for at least 30 days that this is the new address. This reminds people to update their hotlists with your new information.

Make sure to visit all the lists, as explained earlier in this chapter, and correct your URLs. You might want to go to a robot such as Lycos or WebCrawler to do a search for your company and/or site name and see who has placed links for your pages. If you find any, contact the site administrator (usually there will be an e-mail address) and ask them to update the link with your new address.

If you have a registered domain name and IP numbers, you need to get the new numbers from your new provider. The new provider should also be able to change your information so that your domain name stays the same and just the numbers change. You should anticipate a small fee attached to this service, but it's well worth it.

If your domain name changes, you may need to update all of the URLs in your WWW pages. Make sure to try each and every link to ensure that all are pointing to the new provider.

Tip
When contacting a site administrator about the links they have made to your pages, you should also thank them for listing your site.

The Advantages of Multiple Providers

One recommendation is that if you change providers, do not drop the previous one. This may seem a little odd at first. Most people when they move to a new town do not keep their old phone lines turned on.

However, having multiple providers and access can be quite beneficial. First, the cost is fairly minimal. You are probably getting your Internet access anywhere between $10 and $25 per month. Having more than one provider is not going to be too expensive.

One of the major benefits of keeping a old provider when you move to a new provider is that you can keep your old name and e-mail address. This may be a real benefit if you have broadcasted the old address to enough people. By placing a forwarding file in your account on your old provider, you can have your e-mail automatically routed to your new account, meaning that you rarely need to log onto the old account.

However, having the old account also gives you other benefits. Because you can telnet to any location from any other location, you can still use the old system from your new location without the long distance phone call. In

III

other words, your old account becomes a "backup" to you. In the event that your main account is not up, you can still telnet to your old account.

Likewise, by keeping the old account, you can still make the long distance call to get into the system. If your local access phone is down due to system maintenance, bad weather, or other reasons, you still have a way to obtain your information.

From Here...

This chapter covered what you need to know to effectively advertise your company, product, or service.

For more information, refer to the following chapters:

- Chapter 11, "Order Taking and the Net," provides various ways to take orders from Internet customers.

- Chapter 14, "Subscription Services, Virtual Malls, and Instant Products," offers information about special Internet businesses.

- Chapter 15, "Acquiring Demographics About Your Users," teaches you how to gather important demographic information.

- Chapter 21, "Non-Traditional Groups That Can Benefit from the Web," provides information about how artists and civic groups can use the Internet.

Chapter 11

Order Taking and the Net

One of the reasons the Internet and WWW are so popular is that they enable businesses to take electronic orders for products. This not only saves money in printing costs for brochures, telephone time, and personnel, but it also allows you to reach a huge audience.

There are many ways to take orders over the Internet and WWW, and each method has its own pluses and minuses. This chapter helps you to understand the methods of order taking.

In this chapter you learn

- How to take orders by e-mail

- What interactive WWW forms are

- How to take orders by interactive WWW forms

- Other types of WWW Internet order taking

- How to tie Net orders into your business

- How to send back user response receipts

Taking Orders by E-Mail

E-mail offers an effective means for taking orders on the Internet. Since e-mail is the most rudimentary service the Internet has to offer, all 35 million users have it. Therefore, by offering your products for purchase via e-mail, you have the entire Internet population as potential customers.

The simplest e-mail order taking systems can be set up by you with no help from your provider or WWW professional. Simple e-mail order systems are fairly easy to run and can be very productive, while demanding very little of your time.

> **Note**
>
> To accept orders via e-mail you must, of course, have an e-mail account. This means that you need basic Internet services, including e-mail, NetNews, Archie, FTP, and Telnet.

Writing a Simple Advertisement

At the very least, all you need to do is advertise your service via either the NetNews system or by your own WWW page. The advertisement should point the users to your e-mail address and should also have instructions as to how to submit the orders. For example, such an advertisement could be formatted as follows:

```
For a copy of our book, Life Among the Hackers, please send e-mail
to hackers@mybook.com with your name, address, and phone number.
Either include your credit card number and expiration date or
postal mail a check or money order in U.S. funds to:
     Hackers Book, P.O. Box 555, Somewhere, Indiana
You will receive the book within seven days of your funds clearing.
```

As the e-mail comes in, you check it for validity, place the order, and send the user back some form of e-mail acknowledgment.

Writing a More Efficient Advertisement

For many businesses, the preceding scenario is very effective. It may not be elegant and it may not be state-of-the-art, but it works and it also services the widest audience.

One can imagine, however, that some products exceed the capabilities of a basic e-mail system. For example, if you have 20,000 CDs in your online music shop, having a free-form order entry system as described earlier could become a nightmare. Some users may submit a CD name; others may use the product number. In this case, you have required the user to create an order form themselves, which they will send to you. This may work for small orders, but for large orders this quickly becomes error-prone.

For larger systems such as this, it is often better to offer a two-tiered approach. By placing a version of your product catalog online, you can have users pull it off either by FTP or by selecting it in the WWW page. Users can then access your catalog, which can include a handy form for them to use, and send it back to you via either e-mail or postal mail. In this case, your advertisement may look something like this:

```
For a copy of our complete catalog and order form with over 20,000
CD titles, send e-mail to newmusic@cdrom.com asking for catalog #5.
```

Again, as the requests come in, you simply read them and fill the orders.

As you have seen, these mechanisms require very little initial effort to place an order. Larger companies, or companies with a tremendously popular product line, will want to automate the entire process as much as possible, enabling them to reduce the number of personnel required to answer the e-mail. Ideally, you can reduce the number of support staff to zero (other than those needed for the initial setup).

Automating the Response System

Automated e-mail response systems are known as listservers. Listservers are powerful because they allow you to do much more than accept an order. While various listservers work in different ways, most of them get their instructions from the Subject line of the e-mail message.

◄ See "Intelligent Agents," p. 222

An advertisement that makes use of a listserver may look something like this:

```
Welcome to CD Warehouse! You can now order our complete product
line from the comfort of your own home using e-mail. For informa-
tion or order forms, place one of the following lines as the
SUBJECT of your e-mail:

ROCK          Our Rock and Roll catalog
MASH          Our Alternative selections
JAZZ          Jazz and Blues selections
BACH          Classical selections
CATALOG       Our entire product list
ORDER FORM    A copy of our order form
SHIPPING      Shipping information
CONTACT       Who we are
```

You can imagine that a system such as this one would be difficult for a person to manage. Many messages might be coming in, each with different requests. In a high-volume business, the number of people to staff the requests may be quite large.

III

Products and Services

The listserver plays the role of your staff. As mail arrives, it is compiled into a file just as any normal user's mail is handled. For example, any mail sent to newmusic@cdrom.com would automatically end up in that account's mail file.

Periodically, the listserver looks at the "newmusic" mail file and reads the contents. The file contains each mail message sent to it, one after the other. As the listserver reads the messages, it looks for Subject lines containing one of the words shown earlier. When found, the proper file is retrieved, embodied into an e-mail message, and sent to the sender of the original message.

> **Note**
>
> On many systems, the mail file for a user is kept in the /usr/spool/mail directory under a file with the name of the user. For example, if the username is newmusic, the user's mail file is newmusic in the directory /usr/spool/mail. Listservers read this file to find the e-mail.
>
> Notice that some systems place the file in your directory instead of the /usr/spool/ mail directory. Files in this directory are only readable by their owners.

If the subject is missing or is incorrect, most listservers automatically e-mail the sender of the message a list of commands and how to use them.

Some listservers might go as far as to search the body of the e-mail message for the commands, just to make sure the user did not misunderstand and place them in the body instead of the subject.

As stated, listservers run periodically; response to the user is not instantaneous. While most listservers may respond in a matter of minutes, some take days or even weeks to respond.

One example of this type of listserver is the people finder available at MIT. This finder is geared to try to locate people based on their postings on the UseNet. We have used this successfully to find many people including several who had "unpublished" e-mail addresses. To use the service you need to do the following:

1. Send mail to **mail_server@rtfm.mit.com**. In the body of the message (not the subject, in this case), include a line similar to this:

   send usenet-*addresses*/*name*

2. Make *name* one or more names of the person you are looking for. For example, if you were looking for Bob Jones, your session might look like this:

$ mail server@rtfm.mit.com

send usenet-*addresses*/Bob Jones

When the message is received, it is stored at MIT. Later, it is executed along with all the other requests that have compiled, and the results are mailed back. This server takes up to a week to return any results, indicating that it runs only once a week.

Hopefully you noticed that listservers seem to be much more complex than simply handling the mail yourself. You should also have noticed that it is much more efficient, and affords many capabilities that allow you to organize your information and data as you like.

> **Note**
>
> There are many listservers available in the public domain on the Internet. If you have programming experience you can download these and experiment with them. However, if you do not have programming experience, you should talk to your provider or a WWW professional. They can help you configure an efficient system that works for you.

Pros and Cons of E-Mail Order Taking

While taking orders by e-mail is both efficient and simple to implement, it should not be your only source of order taking.

E-mail order taking is highly primitive. Because much of the WWW is designed to be easy to use, people look for solutions which save them time. E-mail ordering, while simple for you, is not simple for your users.

When a user gets an e-mail order form, they must save the message to a file. Next, they must load the message into an editor or word processor and modify it. Finally, they must again redirect the message back to you via e-mail.

This sequence of events requires not only knowledge of the e-mail system (how to save messages), but also potentially FTP (getting the mail to your machine so it can be edited) and some form of word processing that edits and saves pure ASCII files (as most word processors allow).

This is hardly as simple as just filling out an interactive form on a WWW page, as the next section, "Taking Orders by Interactive Forms," demonstrates.

However, this should not be taken as a reason not to implement e-mail ordering. Because e-mail is the most basic of services, it is available to the entire Internet population. This alone is a major reason to offer e-mail ordering in conjunction with your other ordering mechanisms.

> **Note**
>
> We should also point out our own experience with e-mail. We get about 100 messages a day via e-mail. About a third of those are from people asking about our services. These people have found us on the WWW, where we have our complete services and prices posted. However, they have sent e-mail to us to begin the dialog or ask further questions. In fact, almost 90 percent of our business starts with an e-mail message from a client. Even with all our sophisticated WWW pages and the information we have online, users still prefer to come "in person" (by e-mail).

▶ See "Credit Card Transactions," p. 275

▶ See "Can Internet Cash Transactions Ever Be Safe?" p. 403

Another negative aspect to e-mail order taking is sending credit card numbers via e-mail. Some people feel uneasy placing their credit card information in an e-mail message. As the messages are moved from machine to machine toward the destination, they are being stored briefly on each of those machines. During the process of transmission, it is possible for these messages to be intercepted. However, later chapters offer insights and solutions to this problem and alternatives to having the user place readable credit information in the form.

Taking Orders by Interactive Forms

Interactive forms provide the perfect mechanism for inputting order information. Interactive form capability is provided by HTML, and most all graphical WWW browsers support forms.

Using a Simple Input Form

▶ See "Basic HTML," p. 521

HTML provides an interactive form capability. This section provides a basic introduction on how to use HTML forms and what they can do for you. After reading this section, you should be able to specify to a contractor how you want your forms to appear. Taken together with the Appendix, you should be able to create your own forms.

First, you should learn what HTML forms are. Figure 11.1 shows you an example of a form.

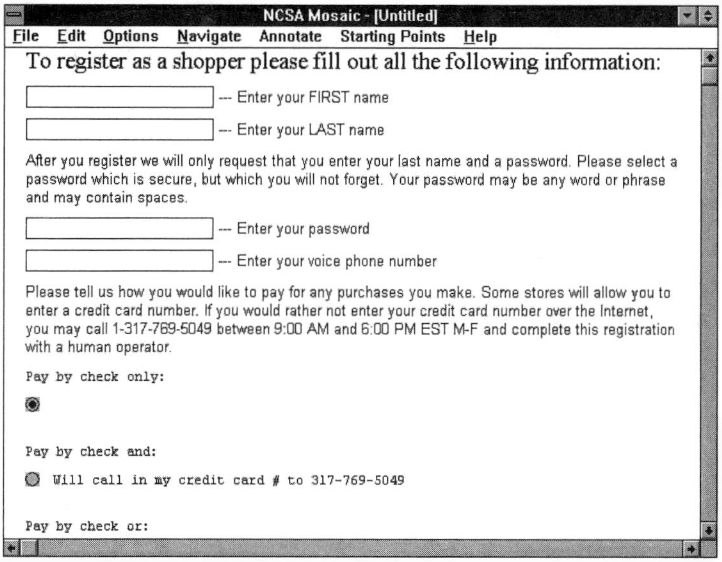

Fig. 11.1
This interactive HTML form is an example of a form that might be used for an online shopping system.

The form in figure 11.1 has several controls. First there are input windows. An *input window* allows you to type a single line of text. The line may be any length (though the document itself can specify a maximum length) but is restricted to only a single line long. Looking at figure 11.2, you see several examples of the input window.

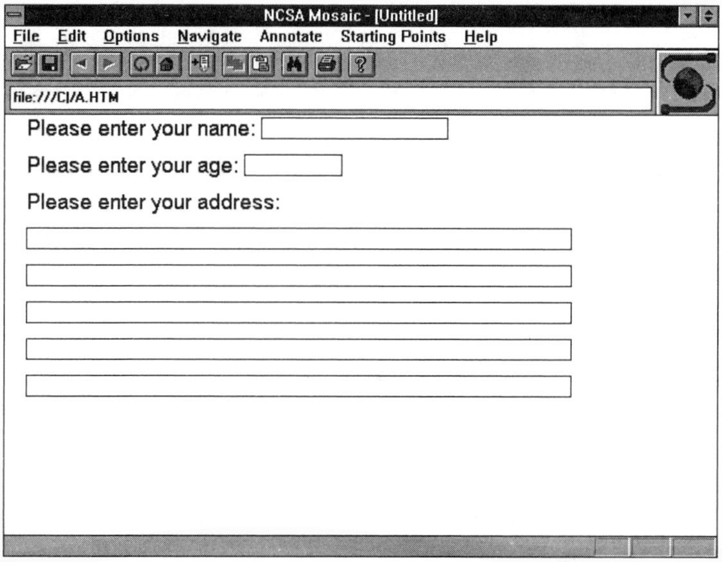

Fig. 11.2
Here, each line is a different HTML form INPUT statement.

III

Products and Services

> **Note**
>
> A form may consist of as many INPUT windows as you want. You are not restricted in any way as to the content of the information that may be typed there.

You should be able to see that this form is perfect for collecting address information and order information. In fact, an order form using INPUT windows is much nicer than the paper version. If you have ever purchased anything from a mail-order catalog, you have probably noted that the amount of room they give you to enter a description is rarely enough. In INPUT windows, even if the box width is only 20 characters wide, you can still type as much as you want.

This is accomplished as follows. As you type and your cursor moves toward the end of the window, the contents of the window automatically begin to scroll. You can type much more than you can see. You can use the keyboard arrow keys to go back and forth to edit the field, or the cursor to highlight sections to modify.

Normally, INPUT windows show you what you type as you type it, and exactly how you typed it. However, INPUT windows may be created that hide the text as it is typed. In this case, as you type, the characters you are typing all turn into a character, such as *. This is useful when you want to ask the user for something secret, such as a password, PIN number, or other personal information.

> **Note**
>
> If you use a feature such as input windows with hidden text (see the PASSWORD feature of the INPUT element in the Appendix), you may want to consider asking for the information twice. Because the information is hidden from users, it is more difficult for them to know whether they made a mistake. By entering the information twice, it can be compared to see whether they entered it accurately.

Using a Multi-Window Input Form

Many times the user wants to type information that takes up multiple lines. For example, you could ask for a billing address. While you can certainly place several INPUT windows together to make a multiline billing address, it's not as convenient for the user as a single multiline window is. The user usually needs to move the mouse to each line in order to enter that window. This requires a lot more effort for the user than simply typing several lines at once.

Convenience isn't the most important factor, though. Being able to specify a window that allows multiple lines really cleans up a form. Where you might have had five INPUT windows to collect an address, you only need one multiline window. When users brings up a form, whether or not they proceed depends largely on how complex the form looks. If there are lots of questions, users may be less inclined to fill it out.

A multi-window input area is termed a TEXTAREA (see fig. 11.3). When you specify the TEXTAREA in your document, you also tell it how many columns and rows you want the window to be. Just as in INPUT windows, users may type more if they want. Scroll bars for moving up and down and left and right are available on the window to allow users to see the portions they typed beyond the window's boundary.

▶ See "Adding Forms To Your Pages," p. 539

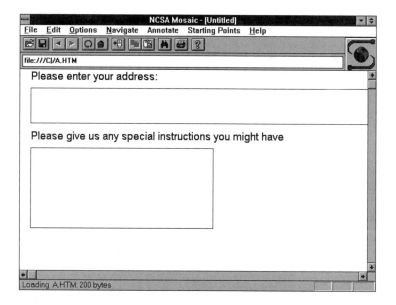

Fig. 11.3
This page consists of several form TEXTAREA elements.

Narrowing the Scope of User Responses

While typing free-form information is very useful, many times you may want information from users that is much narrower in scope. For example, you may want to know what credit card users are using, or what color they want their product in. In these cases, you may only want one of several possible replies.

If you had an INPUT or TEXTAREA here, users could type anything. Perhaps the product is only available in green, blue, or white, but the user types **puce**. It would be far more useful if you could narrow the scope of user responses.

HTML again comes to the rescue with *radio buttons*. These are unique in that of a group of these buttons, only one may be pressed at any one time. This allows you to find out a one-of-many selection from the user without giving the user free range of input.

You may have many groups of radio buttons on a form, with only one button from each group being pressed at a single time. HTML even allows you to pick a button to be clicked when the form initially comes up, allowing you to default the most popular or desired choice (see fig. 11.4).

Fig. 11.4
A page contains several groups of radio-style buttons. Note that only one button from each group is selected.

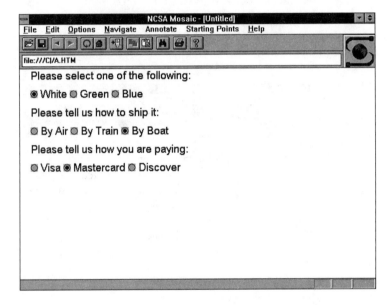

But what if you wanted users to pick several choices? For example, if you are ordering a car, you might choose Tinted Windows, Stereo Package, Sports Package, High Efficiency Engine, and Power Windows. Each of these represents a choice, and in particular, you want to allow users to pick as many as they want. Likewise, if you were picking toppings for a pizza you would want to select as many as you wish.

HTML provides this capability with a *check box* form element. The check box is almost identical to the radio button, except that you may have as many choices as you want selected at any time (see fig. 11.5).

Widening the Selection of User Responses

Suppose you have a situation where you want users to pick one or more brochures that they want. In fact, suppose that you have more than 200 brochures from which they can select.

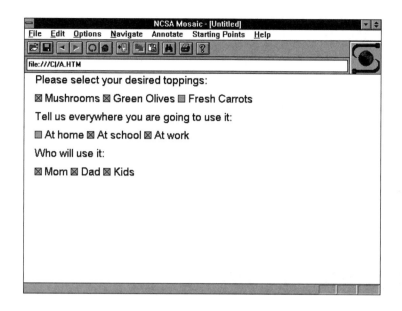

Fig. 11.5
This page contains several groups of check box style buttons. Note that several buttons from each group may be selected at one time.

Designing 200 check box lines is probably not very efficient. The user will have a huge page that quickly becomes overpowering. Instead, it would be more useful if HTML had some way to quantify hundreds of choices in a small area. In fact, HTML does have such a capability; it's called a *select box*.

Like check boxes and radio buttons, select boxes come in two styles. The first allows you to select one of many choices. The second allows you to select many of many choices.

If you want the user to select only one of the choices, your box looks like figure 11.6.

In this case, when you select the bar containing the current choice, a window appears, allowing you to change that choice by selecting one of the other choices that appear. After you select the choice, the window disappears and your new choice is shown in the bar.

If you specify that you want multiple choices for your select box, you can set the number you want displayed at one time. For example, you may specify that the window contains eight items. This means that the user can view eight of your brochures at one time in the select window. In this case, the window has sliders on the side which allow you to scroll the list up and down to view all 200 brochures. The user can select multiple items from the list by selecting in the window (some browsers want you to press the Shift or Control keys to select a range of items).

III

Products and Services

Fig. 11.6
The CUSI searcher page combines many search forms on one page. Using one-of-several select boxes allows you to pick which list you want to search.

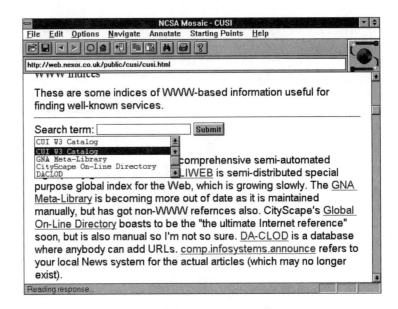

Figure 11.7 shows a very good use of multiple select windows. This figure shows one of the pages from the On-Line Career Center's WWW job search system. Note that each of the select windows allows you to pick a different aspect of the job you want to search for. The list of actual items in each window is extensive, but by limiting the display, the user is not overwhelmed with information.

Fig. 11.7
A page from a WWW job search system shows multiple select windows for organizing the information in the search.

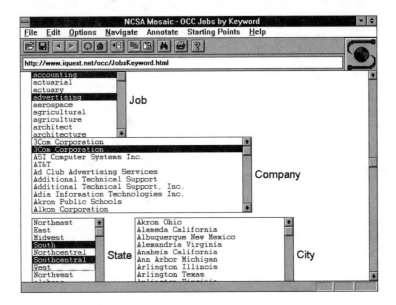

Other Input Form Tools

There are two other types of buttons that are found on most forms—RESET and SUBMIT. These are both forms of the INPUT command.

RESET appears as a button with the word RESET (or text of your choice) in it. If the user clicks the button, the contents of the form are cleared to their default values.

Most form items won't have defaults specified, so they display as either empty text windows or as buttons in the off position. However, you can set default values for both text and buttons in HTML.

The SUBMIT button is used to transmit a filled-out form to software that will handle what the user entered. SUBMIT appears as a button with the word SUBMIT (or text of your choice) in it. For example, you could have the form read, "Click here to send this form." Regardless of what it says, SUBMIT appears as a button the user can click with the mouse. This is the most important button on the page, because clicking it causes the form to be submitted.

All forms include a header. The form header instructs the SUBMIT button where to send the form when the button is selected. When the user clicks the SUBMIT button, all the fields and selections in the form are put together and sent to a computer somewhere on the WWW. The next section explores just what happens when the information reaches the destination computer.

Tip

This allows you to load text into a window, or pre-check a choice, when the user loads the page for the first time. These "defaults" can always be modified by the user.

▶ See "The FORM Element," p. 541

> **Note**
>
> A SUBMIT button should be present on all forms. Clicking this button causes the form to actually be sent.
>
> You can encounter forms without a SUBMIT button. Most browsers are smart in that if the form has only one INPUT area, pressing Return after typing in the area also submits the form. However, to be consistent and user-friendly, you should always include a SUBMIT button in all your forms.

What Happens To the User's Input?

Forms require one step in setup that simple HTML documents don't need—getting the information the user enters into the form to you.

In order to see why this is a necessary step, you need to understand how forms work. Refer to figure 11.7, which shows the job search system. In this case, the form allowed the user to perform job searches.

Now, keeping in mind the job search, suppose you have a flower seed company with an order form on the Net. Figure 11.8 shows an example of how this could appear.

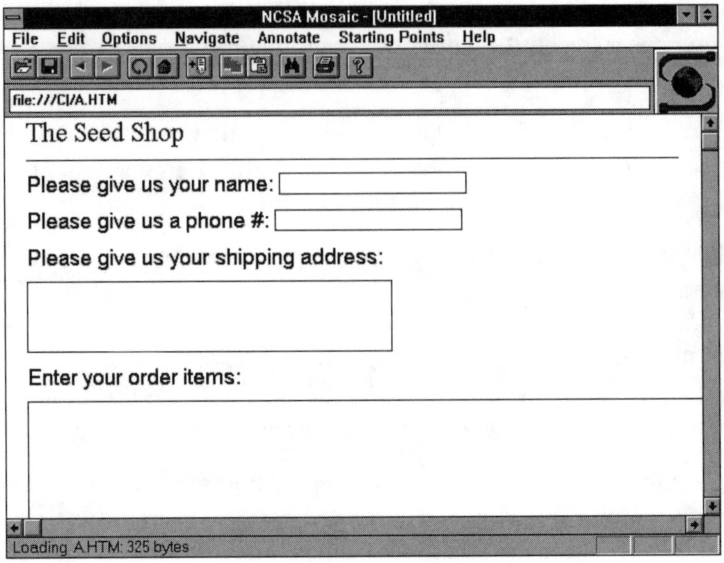

Fig. 11.8
This screen shows an example form that a flower seed company might use.

By comparing these two examples, you see immediately that they differ completely from each other. Both forms input information but in each case, the information is used for completely different reasons.

In the job search service, the information entered by the user was taken and a database search was initiated. The results were immediately returned to the user.

In the second example, the flower seed company is accepting an order form. The order form needs to be checked for consistency (perhaps) and an acknowledgment of the order sent to the user.

Examining How Forms Work

Whether you are using your forms for database searching, order entry, or something completely different, each of these uses requires totally different engines behind the form system.

To examine how the forms work, you should see what happens when the user enters information into the form, beginning with the job search system.

When the user selects from the list in the job search form and clicks the SUB-MIT button, the items that were selected are put into a message by the user's browser. The message is then transmitted to a computer somewhere on the Internet.

The computer that the message is sent to must be running an HTTP (WWW) server. Within the header of the message is information which specifics a program or script on the destination computer which knows how to handle that form.

When the message arrives at the destination computer, the server looks at the form header and sends it to the specified program. That program then examines what the user selected and searches a database for the appropriate matching entries. The results are formatted by the program into a valid HTML document and sent back to the server. The server then sends the document over the Internet back to the user where the user's browser displays the document.

Fairly complex, isn't it?

Now examine the flower seed form. The user fills out the form and clicks the SUBMIT button. The contents of the form are formatted into a message and transmitted over the Internet to the destination computer specified by the form's header. Again, the destination computer must be running an HTTP server.

The server takes the flower form, looks at it, and calls the appropriate program as specified in the header. The program, in this case, takes the contents of the form and changes it into an easier-to-read format, and e-mails the form to the flower company owner. The program then sends an HTML document back to the user verifying that the e-mail was sent.

Now, what are the differences between the flower company and the job search service? Each was identical until the server called a program to handle the form. At that point, the program took control and "did the right thing" with the data.

Aha! This means that in order for you to make a form work, you need a piece of software at some server somewhere in the world that reads, understands, executes, and responds to the contents of your form.

III

Products and Services

Using a Server To Process Input

How do you go about getting the software on the server? There are several ways.

At the very least, you can use some of the many commercial form remailing services that are running. These services, such as the one shown in figure 11.9, allow you to point at any form that you make and have the contents e-mailed back to you. These usually cost a nominal monthly fee to use and may provide just the kind of cost-effective service you are seeking.

Fig. 11.9
This form remailing service is run by the authors. This service is one of many available form handling services on the WWW.

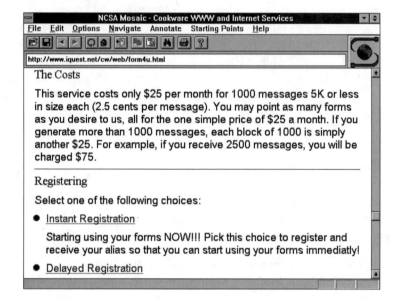

While the form remailing services work well in a large number of situations, sometimes e-mailing the form back to you is not always the solution you are seeking. For example, the job search service performed no e-mailing. It was required to interactively respond to the user. How do you enable something like that? There are three possible methods:

Tip
WWW professionals should help you choose and position your program on the best site for your money.

1. First, if you or your employees have any programming experience, you can write one yourself.

2. Second, if you lack the expertise or the time to write your own, you can hire a WWW professional to write one for you. In either case, you need a server site that is willing to run the program.

3. A third solution is also available. Many of these specialized programs are available for free on the Internet and WWW. The NCSA site has

many such programs, and other sites with them also exist. If your needs are not too specific, these programs can often be used as ready-to-implement solutions. You would then only need a WWW provider willing to run the program for you. Talk to your WWW provider (where you house your home pages) to see if they allow you to run the program, or have services to help you design the programs you need.

Pros and Cons of Interactive Forms

Order entry using forms is very valuable and should not be avoided. At the very least, there are form remailing services set up to handle e-mailing your form to you. These services allow you to use forms today, without having to wait around for anything to be designed or written—just build your desired form page and go.

Another advantage to the form remailing services is that you can change the look and feel of your form at any time, without having to notify anyone or make any changes in the form remailer itself. Most of the remailers handle sending any form back to you, regardless of the contents.

Earlier in this chapter you learned that e-mail order entry is good to have because all 35 million (or so) Internet users have e-mail capability. If you create your forms so that customers e-mail the orders to you, you can unify your approach. This saves you work because instead of having to check both your e-mail and WWW orders, all orders come in via e-mail.

You also found out more about using e-mail listservers. Again, coupled with e-mailed WWW forms, a listserver can automate both sides of the order process (both e-mail and WWW orders). Sounds like an integrated solution!

Are there negative sides to using special form programs? Besides the added expense and slight hassle of getting set up initially, not really.

Form programs provide one of the few methods for making your pages do something truly unique—something that other people have never seen before. This use of form programs makes them an extremely powerful advertising tool as well as an effective order entry system.

If there was one negative feature with forms in general, it would be this: forms don't work on all versions of all browsers. However, almost all the popular browsers today, including text-only browsers such as Lynx, support forms in all their glory. Only early versions and some beta versions of software do not support forms.

Tip
Form programs can help turn your pages into winning designs, and are usually worth the price you pay for in capability.

▶ See "Instant Products," p. 319

III

Products and Services

You will still occasionally find some browsers that treat the form elements differently. Some browsers do not allow text areas to be variably sized and do not display the scrolling sliders. The user is limited to typing into the window only, and not beyond the window.

These are small prices to pay for the use of forms. You only need to try your form in a few of the most popular browsers (such as NCSA Mosaic, Netscape, and Lynx) to make sure they are usable. Any differences in how the forms are displayed between the browsers is usually fixed within a few seconds of simple HTML editing on your part.

If you are using a WWW professional to help you design your forms and form programs, you should expect this person to handle making your forms consistent across browsers. However, do not expect the professional to fix inherent flaws in the browsers themselves. The best thing to do if you find a particular browser failing on your pages and you are unable to fix the problem, is to inform the user in your page of the specific browser that does not work well. You should also tell the users which browsers do work well. Some people even provide links to the browser sites to encourage people to change to a better class of browser.

Most often, when browsers fail on certain forms, the next version of the browser will work. Why? The browser creators are always looking to better their products. The bottom line here is that almost all the current products support full form capability, and the small errors that can remain are quickly disappearing.

Forms are very powerful, popular, and fun to use. They offer an amazingly easy method for order entry for your company.

Other Alternatives for Order Taking

The previous sections have outlined the two most popular methods for taking orders over the Internet and WWW. However, other schemes exist for dispensing information and products, and for taking orders. This section briefly looks at a few of these methods.

You have seen how listservers can respond to users who send e-mail requesting information, order forms, and product orders. However, the Internet abounds with alternative methods for taking orders.

Handling Orders with FTP

FTP (File Transfer Protocol) offers a very simple mechanism for order taking and also offers some interesting opportunities.

◀ See "FTP,"
p. 41

FTP is the second most popular service after e-mail, and the majority of all Internet users have FTP capability. By supplying FTP access to your system, you can provide order forms for people to download.

Because FTP is bidirectional (meaning that people can upload as well as download), the finished order form can be uploaded into a common directory.

FTP also allows you to protect directories. People can effectively upload order forms without seeing other people's order forms, which provides additional security for orders.

> **Note**
>
> The interesting feature about taking orders via FTP is that more than just order forms can be uploaded. While most businesses don't make use of this fact, some businesses do. For example, if you had a promotional business and allowed people to place pictures on shirts, calendars, and coffee mugs, you might let people upload their photographs to you via an FTP connection. This would be extremely efficient.

Likewise, if you accepted data from a client for some service you provided, FTP is a much more reliable mechanism than e-mail. The connection is direct and not delayed, while the intermediate machines store and pass on your information.

Simulating a BBS with Telnet

Another mechanism for online order taking is using Telnet to simulate a BBS.

Since Telnet lets you actually log into a computer, you can provide an account that runs a BBS type shell. When users log in, they get a menu of choices. Since the menu is ASCII based, you can accept any user regardless of the type of computer or Internet connection the user has.

When the users log in, they are greeted with a menu that directs them to product information. This menu provides them the ability to send messages to you and the ability to place an order. Since the connection is direct, messages are passed for the most part in real time, making the connection at least somewhat more secure than e-mail.

Another interesting advantage to this type of system is that you can mimic the design over traditional phone-in BBS lines. This gives the same order potential via a standard phone number (or 800 or 900 phone number) to users with a modem, regardless of whether or not they have Internet service.

Because your system is tied to the Internet, you can even offer Internet access to your non-Internet BBS call-in customers. This is accomplished by having choices in their menu that allow them to enter e-mail or read news. The e-mail is then sent by the BBS software over the Internet. In this way, users never actually accesses the Internet directly.

Dispensing Order Forms and Information with Gophers

Gophers also offer the opportunity to dispense order forms and product information. Because Gophers act similarly to FTP but in one direction only, you can use them as access points for people to get at your information and order forms.

> **Caution**
>
> The down side to gophers is that they are one-way only. You still need to send orders via e-mail or FTP.

Providing Alternative Ways To Respond

The final suggestion is to make sure to advertise your phone-in number, fax, and postal mail address. Even though you are providing electronic ordering, some people do not want or trust that mechanism. By providing alternative access information alongside of your ordering information, you allow users to place an order using whatever method makes them feel most comfortable.

Tying Net Orders into Your Existing Order Stream

◀ See "Mixing Traditional Advertising with Net Advertising," p. 234

In the previous chapter, you learned that you can tie your traditional advertising with your Net advertising. In this section, you find that you can do the same for your order entry.

One good way to advertise your site is to print your Internet access information on your paper order form. Include URLs, e-mail addresses, or any other access methods that you offer.

Because the WWW is so large, many of your customers may not realize you are on the Net. These customers may prefer the convenience of ordering via the Net, or at least may be interested enough to simply check it out. By combining your Internet order information on your traditional order forms, you are increasing your clients' awareness.

If you are a company with many smaller franchises, you may want to look at e-mail as a mechanism for communicating between all your stores. All order entries, whether Internet or at the physical store, can be funneled via e-mail or another mechanism to a central fulfillment facility. This type of integrated approach is cost-effective, because the same mechanisms work for both the electronic and the non-electronic side of the order process.

Providing User Receipts

In WWW order taking, users usually receive more receipts than they do in traditional sales.

▶ See "Effective Order Filling Systems," p. 293

For example, a user submits via a WWW page an order for a product. In this case, the store owner does not have Internet access, so the order is faxed automatically to the company owner for fulfillment. Because of busy phone lines or other outgoing faxes, the fax may not be dispatched immediately, meaning there is no way to verify the transaction with the user at that moment.

In situations like this, the software immediately gives a receipt to the user indicating that the transaction is on its way. Later, when the transaction is faxed, if a failure in the fax occurs the user is again sent an e-mail message telling the user about the failure and why it occurred.

Likewise, the store owner, upon finishing the transaction, may send yet another receipt to the user indicating that the transaction was successful and that the product was shipped.

This type of delayed receipt system means that transactions must be watched along their path, from the user to the fulfillment center. Any deviation along the path should be reported immediately to the user, as well as to the proper administrators. This type of receipt system ensures customer confidence that the order arrived and that the product will be shipped.

> **Note**
>
> Advanced systems may even have order tracking to aid in this process. These types of systems are discussed in more detail in Chapter 13.

III

Products and Services

From Here...

This chapter covered the different methods of order taking. You found out what interactive WWW forms are and how they can be used for effective order taking.

For more information, refer to the following chapters:

■ Chapter 12, "Methods for Collecting Cash," shows you various ways to take orders from Internet customers.

■ Chapter 13, "Order Filling and Tracking," shows you how to fill orders and handle issues involved with shipping and tracking your product.

■ Chapter 14, "Subscription Services, Virtual Malls, and Instant Products," provides information on special Internet businesses.

■ Chapter 15, "Acquiring Demographics About Your Users," teaches you how to gather important demographic information.

■ Chapter 21, "Non-Traditional Groups That Can Benefit from the Web," provides information about how artists and civic groups use the Internet.

Chapter 12

Methods for Collecting Cash

Once you have someone's order, the next step is to determine how the customer will pay for it. From credit card to purchase orders, there are many ways for business owners to collect cash from their customers.

In this chapter, you learn

- How to handle credit card transactions and issues regarding credit card security

- How to accept checks

- The ins and outs of purchase orders

Credit Card Transactions

Most people are shocked to find out that they can accept credit card orders over the Net. People do transactions by phones and by mail, so why not by the Net?

Credit card transactions via the Internet are not only possible, they are being done more and more frequently. Credit card processing represents the easiest, quickest, and surest way of collecting cash on the Internet.

When dealing with a credit card system, you need to answer several basic questions:

- How is the card information transmitted?

- Who is clearing the card?

- How is the validation handled?

How is the Card Information Transmitted?

▶ See "Crime and the Net," p. 385

The first question, how is the information transmitted, has to do with how users get the credit card number they have entered into the online form to you. The biggest issue here is security of the card information.

Most browsers in use today have no security measures in place for sending information over the Internet. When users enter their card information, it is transmitted—as-is—to the server. The nefarious data pirate has ample opportunity to copy it while it's enroute to you.

Quite a few sites now run traps and alarms which alert the system administration to attempts at penetrating their data. This means that the information is safeguarded at the storage site.

▶ See "Can Internet Cash Transactions Ever Be Safe?" p. 403

However, the actual communications channel is the next likely place for tampering. Tampering with the main Internet channels, however, is not as easy as it might seem. It requires access to data and information that is very hard for the casual data pirate to access.

Currently, there is not much of this type of illegal behavior on the Net, but we suspect that as commerce trading increases, so will the desire to scam the system.

> **Note**
>
> Accepting credit cards is just one way of taking orders through the Internet. By providing your clients with multiple methods, you can ensure that they will feel comfortable with at least one of them. As you learn later in this section, there are many things you can do to your pages and forms to keep your client's confidence high in your ordering and purchasing systems.

The easiest method for accepting credit card information is to simply have the user enter it into the order form with each order. While this is certainly easy for users to do, the repeat customer or regular user may feel uncomfortable or get tired of entering the information time after time.

One way to avoid having the user enter his or her credit card information again and again is to register the user as a member to your pages. A membership system would take the credit card information once when the user registers. Each time the customer revisits your store and makes a purchase, the customer uses his or her "account." If the user decides to pay for the order with a credit card, the user simply indicates that as the method of payment. Membership systems are outlined later in this chapter.

Membership systems have the added benefit of providing a "membership" look and feel to your pages, which can often increase their apparent value by making users feel like they "belong." While membership systems cost more to implement than simple forms, their ease of use can do quite a bit for attracting customers to your site, and can usually pay for the extra cost in increased usage.

Another mechanism for collecting credit card numbers is to allow the user to phone a human or automated system which then completes the registration. This system comforts many users who are more willing to give credit card numbers over the phone. However, we personally don't see much difference between this and giving it out over the Internet—either trust the human or trust the machine. And many users who would balk at entering their number via the Internet would easily use their cordless or cellular phone, both of which are extremely open to eavesdropping.

Tip

Not only do member systems increase transaction security, but they can also be considered as a feature to users by allowing users to feel as if they belong to a club or group.

Finally, you can also accept credit card numbers via e-mail, faxes, and Telnet login. Fax is very secure, as long as your fax machine printouts are secure. Telnet can allow users to log in and receive a menu of services, including credit card registration.

> **Caution**
>
> While Telnet entry is sometimes viewed as more secure than the WWW and e-mail, in truth it is not, because the information must flow through very similar channels and is still prone to being intercepted.

However, as time goes on, people will become more and more accustomed and willing to enter credit card and other personal information over the Internet. The Internet will become just another telephone for them to use.

This is not to say that people do not enter credit card numbers now. Many purchases are made daily using credit card information via the Internet. It's just a good idea—until commerce servers and digital signature are more prevalent in everyday society—to offer several options of payment for your users. This little effort on your part will ensure that your customers have as many ways as possible to reach you.

The pages shown in figures 12.1 and 12.2 each show different order forms and order mechanisms. Figure 12.1 shows an order form which allows the user to enter the credit card information right along with the order, while figure 12.2 shows two different types of membership systems.

III

Products and Services

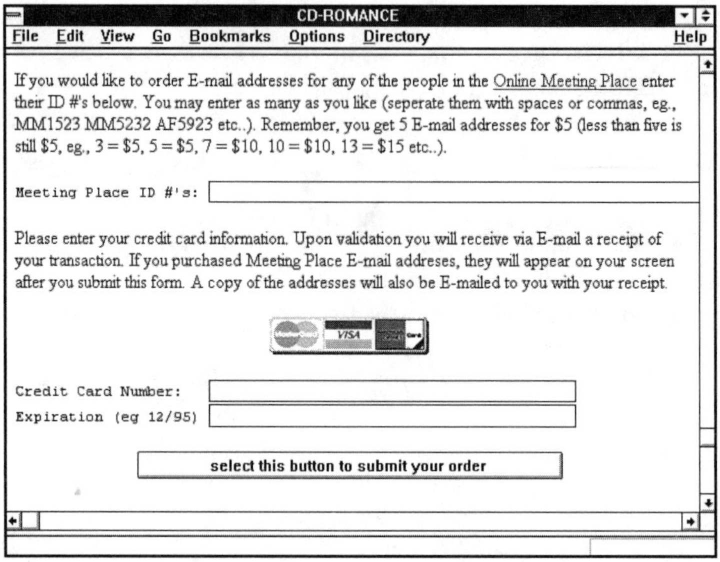

Fig. 12.1
An order form allows the user to purchase with a credit card.

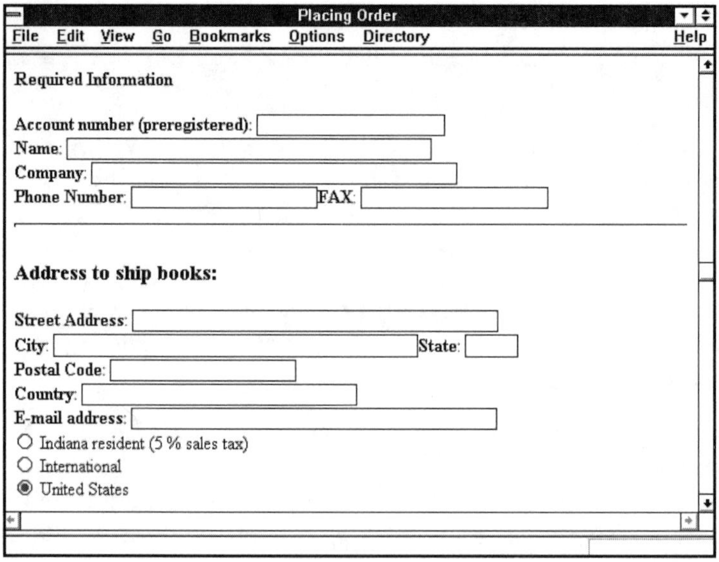

Fig. 12.2
An order form that requires the user to be a member usually asks specific questions of the user for both identity and billing purposes.

Who is Clearing the Card?

The next major issue in credit card handling is, who is handling the transaction? Just because you cannot clear (or approve) a credit card yourself doesn't mean that you cannot use credit card processing.

Many services exist which allow you to clear a credit card for a fee. Some of these services are now located on the Internet. These services will be more than happy to clear credit cards for you, for a percentage of the transaction. Often the percentage will differ depending on whether you already do or do not have a merchant's account.

> **Note**
>
> The amounts taken by these companies and services vary, from 1 percent to sometimes as much as 10 to 12 percent, depending on the service, purchase price, and credit card.

To use the credit card bureaus, you simply route the order through them; they handle the cash transaction, credit your account, and forward the order to you for fulfillment.

However, many companies already have the capability to handle a credit card transaction. If this is the case for your business, you are all set. Simply have the credit card information routed to you via the form and process the card information just as you would for a mail-in order.

▶ See "Effective Order Filling Systems," p. 293

The simplest way to handle this is via the e-mail system. Orders can be delivered to you for processing within a few seconds of the user submitting them to you, while still being fairly secure (in fact, some cash transaction systems encrypt the e-mail for an added layer of security between the server and your company).

How is Validation Handled?

Many times it is not possible to determine the status of a credit card number instantaneously. This is because credit handling is done in different manners, some requiring periodic modem transfers to clearinghouses. In these cases, the credit information may actually clear several minutes after the transaction has been completed by the user.

This may even be the case if you are clearing the credit card number yourself. In this case, you are not tied directly into the user. The user is entering a credit card number into a WWW form and submitting it. The form then is most likely being e-mailed to you. This is followed by the amount of time your own staff needs to read the e-mail and complete the transaction. By this time, the user is long gone. If there is a problem with the user's card, the user isn't notified that the order won't be sent. Or, in cases like online kiosks which sells products, the customer may have already walked away with the product.

III

Products and Services

▶ See "Kiosk
Basics," p. 448

Users must receive some form of acknowledgment or receipt at the moment they enter the transaction. In most cases, the form handler will not know the result of the transaction; it should simply send back a message stating that the transaction has been sent and that users will receive an update of its status at a later time.

▶ See "User Re-
ceipts and
Feedback,"
p. 306

If you are tied into instant credit card handling—such as a commerce server—you can respond to the user with the correct information at the time of the order. While this is certainly smoother, it's not that much more inconvenient for the user to get the delayed receipt, which often comes via the e-mail system within a few minutes of making the transaction.

> **Note**
>
> In the case of either instantaneous or delayed credit card handling, users should always receive a confirmation via e-mail anyway. This helps to ensure that they received verification and are aware of the status of the order.

Commerce Servers

In order to address the concern that many users have in entering private or secure information over a network, many WWW technology companies are scrambling to introduce a whole range of secure server and browser products. These products promise to make the Internet secure for cash and other types of private transactions.

Currently, Netscape Communications is one of the companies attempting to push the security issue through at full speed. The Netscape browsers already identify forms that do not transmit information using secure encryption and alert the user to the fact that the form is submitted through a non-secure channel. Figure 12.3 shows the screen which is displayed in Netscape when you submit a form that is not secure.

> **Note**
>
> Currently, systems such as Netscape will inform you that a form is insecure, whether or not the form needs to be secure. In other words, Netscape will tell you a form is insecure even if no personal information or cash transaction is being performed. Because of this, may people simply disregard such warnings.

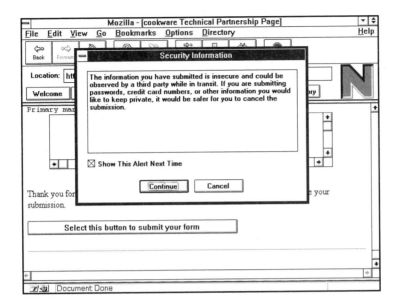

Fig. 12.3
This Netscape Communications screen warns that the current form being submitted is not going via a secure method.

The new breed of secure servers and browsers, available from Netscape Communications and other organizations, allow cash and other private transactions to occur over the Internet using encryption technology. This type of system will encrypt the data before it is transmitted. The method is so good that only the most powerful computers (such as those operated by the government) can be used to break the code.

While the world certainly needs and waits for more secure servers, there is (at the time of this writing) currently no set standard to perform a secure transaction. It's still unclear as to which company and products will win the secure server/browser battle.

Until this battle is won, you shouldn't require that such products be used to secure your cash transactions. The reason for this is simple: until a secure standard is adopted, buying into one solution might make you unusable to all other solutions. In other words, if you adopt the standard for security from Company X, only users of company X browsers will be able to handle your transactions and not the users of Company Y.

III

Products and Services

> **Note**
>
> Even when secure transactions are commonplace, you should not assume that your data is unbreakable. The old adages of "the bigger they are the harder they fall" and "rules were made to be broken" holds true. As soon as a lock is made, someone will figure out how to break it.
>
> In the world of computers, it's becoming more and more difficult to "break" the lock; however, it is not impossible. Governments and large organizations posses the money and computing capabilities to break most of the known encryption schemes if they so desire. However, encryption technology will discourage the majority of computer criminals, who would opt for easier targets.

Once a standard is adopted by the WWW community, you can be assured that all browser manufacturers will rush to include the capability in their product. At that time, secure transactions will become more and more commonplace. We estimate that secure transactions will become a standard sometime within the next year.

Acceptance of Checks

While credit card handling is certainly more convenient for many people and companies, some people refuse to use credit cards or will not enter them over an unsecured network. For these people, you need an alternative form of accepting cash.

Personal and corporate checks or money orders are almost universally accepted. The user can complete the order online and then send the payment to you via normal secure mail. You can then clear the transaction after you receive the funds.

Again, this is much like mail ordering where you have the ability to pay by cash or check. The difference in mail order is that you place your order at the time you submit the check. On the Internet you place your order instantly, and it is fulfilled when the store owner receives and clears your check.

> **Caution**
>
> Do not fulfill an online order before you receive the payment, whatever the form.

A system which accept checks in this manner consists of a normal order form with a place for the check number. When the user submits the form, the receipt returned to the user consists of an order number or purchase ID. The user is told the amount of the check, where to send it, and how to place the order number on the check. The transaction is logged to the store, either via fax, e-mail, or logging the transaction in a file in the owner's directory.

When the payment arrives to the store owner, the owner simply checks against the transaction IDs on file and completes your order. This system has the added advantage because it lets the store owners anticipate the order, allowing the owner to plan inventory.

> **Note**
>
> If you accept checks worldwide, specify on your interactive order form how the checks must be drawn. For example, if you are in America, you may want the checks drawn from an American bank and in U.S. dollars.

Purchase Orders

The traditional purchase order can work just as effectively on the Internet as it does off the Internet. Purchase orders are usually tied into membership systems because they require you to check and clear users before you accept their initial purchase order.

When taking an order via a purchase order system, users need to enter only their account number and a company password. You should design your system with the following in mind:

- Purchase orders should be submitted along with a company password.

- The clients should be given a secure, though simple, method of changing their password.

Following these requirements will ensure that your purchase order system will be both simple and secure for the following reasons:

- By forcing purchase orders to be submitted along with a company password, you help to ensure that users cannot use a PO number, either accidentally or on purpose, that does not belong to them.

- If you provide clients a mechanism by which they can change their password, you allow them to make changes should they accidentally release their own password, without having to tell you.

- By shipping only to the address specified by the account listed on the purchase order, you ensure that if a PO number and password is guessed, the package is still delivered to a known location.

Purchase order systems rarely stand by themselves. In other words, any system which handles a PO will probably also handle a credit card transaction. Because of this, setting up a PO is as easy as simply giving extra room on the order form for the user to enter the appropriate information. Since the information will most likely consist of a PO number and corporate ID or password, you are at most adding two fields to an order form.

> **Note**
>
> Keep any password fields hidden in your form by specifying the field type to be **PASSWORD** (TYPE="PASSWORD"). This ensures that casual observers will not see the password as it is typed. If added security is desired, keep both the password and the PO number hidden.

Once an order is received with a purchase order, you need to look up the PO number in your records and verify the transaction. If desired, you can create more advanced order systems that would verify automatically as part of the order processing.

Membership Systems

Many cash handlers rely on membership systems to make the handler more convenient as well as secure for the user.

There are many ways to implement a membership system. However, you must first decide whether or not users can register themselves. This is the difference between an instant and delayed registration system:

- *Instant registration system.* Users can sign up to become members and are instantly granted the membership. You have the ability to review their application in your own time, but during that time, users are allowed to place orders based on their preliminary membership. This is the most convenient mechanism for users because there is no delay in them being able to make their first order.

■ *Delayed registration system*. Users can sign up interactively but are not given access until you review the application they submitted. When you decide to accept their account (either based on your credit check of them or some other clearance method), you then activate their account and notify users of their acceptance (usually by e-mail). At this point, users can now submit orders for fulfillment.

Membership systems are very useful to the store owner. In particular, they provide the shop owner with a known client base. Because the user is a "member," the shop owner can track the user's purchasing habits and other demographic information, and can use this to orient future products, advertising, or promotions. You can even notify individual customers when products become available.

> **Note**
>
> The casual observer might argue that you can get the same benefits from a non-membership system that you can from a membership system. However, consider asking users time and time again for demographic information, billing addresses, shipping addresses, phone numbers, payment information, expiration dates, and all the other items you want users to enter. Non-membership systems often have very simple order forms and do not go to great lengths to find out about user needs, likes, and dislikes.

Because the key feature of a membership system is that users register once—and only once—you have a perfect situation in which you can ask users as many questions of any type that you want. Users are assured that this only happens once, and should be more than happy to comply (assuming that your questions are within reason).

One of the other primary advantages to the membership system is in the membership itself. Users are more likely to return instead of buying from another store, because they can avoid the hassle and insecurity of filling out forms and information.

> **Note**
>
> We have mentioned briefly the ability to collect demographics from the user in a membership system. This fact should not be overlooked because it is of immense value. Most shop owners would like to get as much information from the user as possible, such as what the user likes or dislikes, buying habits, and so forth. By asking for this information when users register, you have the perfect chance to collect this information. You can also tailor the site to your clients' needs.

III

Products and Services

▶ See "The
HTTPD Log,"
p. 342

Since membership systems track the user, you will have all the demographics you want concerning where any given user went and what the user did. This information can be used by you to change your site. If, for example, you find that certain pages are never frequented by members, you can take steps to change those pages. Likewise, if you find certain pages that seem very popular, you can modify those pages to take even more advantage of their advertising potential.

In the same way, clients who come back many times can be targeted for e-mail and snailmail press releases and product announcements. The demographics you received from the user can help you identify the needs of the client and then orient the proper product information to them.

Figures 12.4 through 12.8 show the various screens of a membership system. In this case, the site is an eye-care product distributor. Figure 12.4 shows the product selection page. The user is allowed to select products without having to be a member. This is especially important because forcing users to become members *before* they see the products you have to offer will tend to discourage them from investing the time to become members.

Fig. 12.4
An iCare Direct
WWW product
page allows the
user to purchase
items by simply
clicking the item
description.

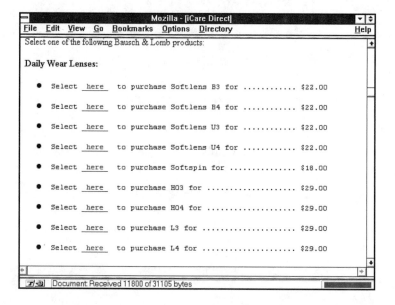

As a user selects one or more products, the products are added to the user's "shopping cart" (see fig. 12.5). Notice that the user can modify the quantity by changing the number to the left of the description or can remove an item from the shopping cart by turning off the check box to the left of the number.

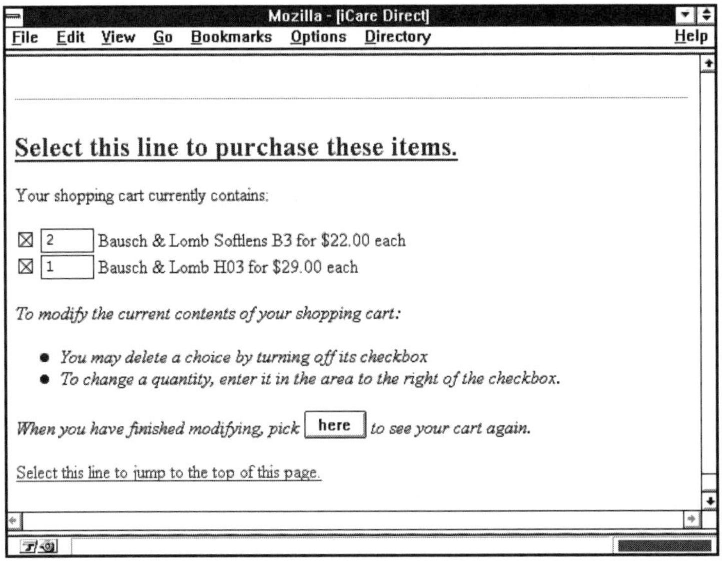

Fig. 12.5
The Virtual Shopping Cart appears at the bottom of the iCare Direct page. The user has selected several items.

Once the user has selected the products to purchase, the user then selects the `Select this line to purchase these items` choice in the shopping cart, and is greeted with output similar to figure 12.6. In this figure, an electronic receipt is shown to the user so that he or she can easily record what was purchased. The screen also allows the user to type membership information—in this example, a password and the user's last name. Towards the base of the page is a link which allows the user to become a member, if he or she is not already.

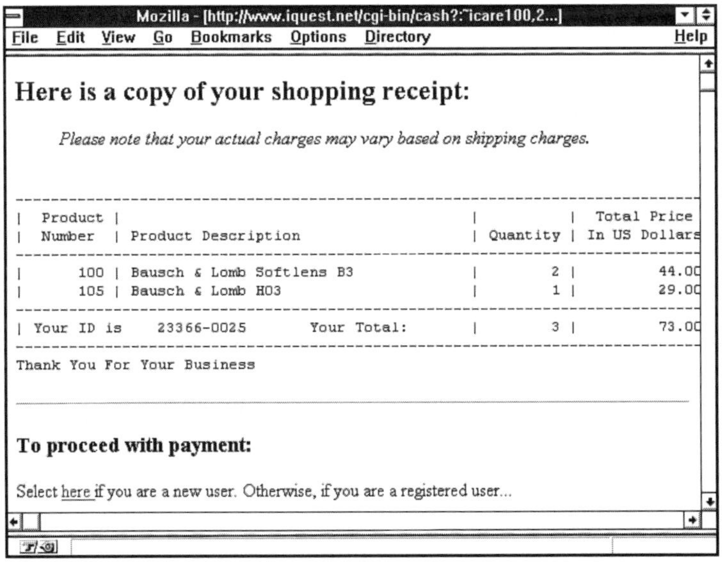

Fig. 12.6
When users are finished shopping, they are greeted by a screen which contains a receipt of the purchase they are about to make.

III

Products and Services

New users who choose the link for new members are greeted with a screen similar to figure 12.7. This screen accepts the membership information from the user including how the user wants to pay, billing address, and other contact information.

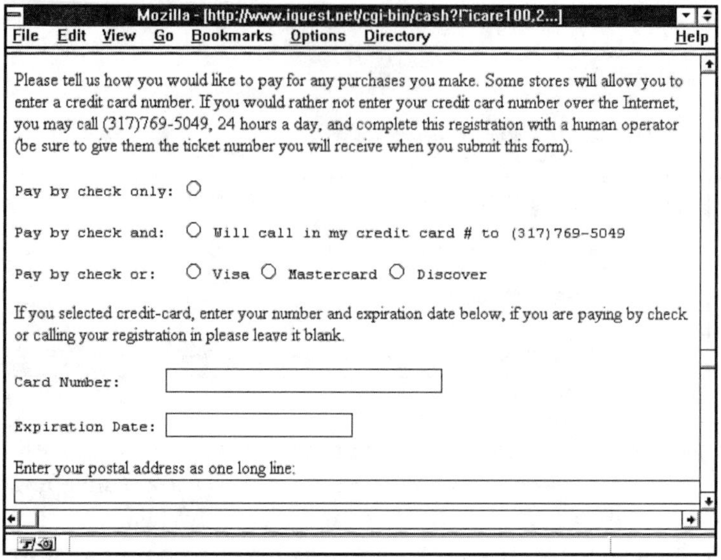

Fig. 12.7
New users see a membership page which asks for billing and address information.

Once the user registers as a new member or enters an existing membership password and user name, the purchase is completed, and a finalized receipt is generated and returned to the user via both the WWW and e-mail, as shown in figure 12.8.

Another added benefit of membership systems include those companies who are worried about high throughput on their site when it might not necessarily be accompanied by high sales. Sites which might be considered by the Internet population to have a high entertainment value could encounter this type of problem. For example, a lingerie catalog could attract users who just want to see pictures of women in lingerie and not necessarily make purchases. By making the site a membership system, you will help ensure that the throughput is for paying customers only.

However, if that site was a membership-only site, members who don't make purchases within a given time period or number of visits would be deleted from the membership roster. Companies who plan to do this should make sure to notify members and potential members of such restrictions. This policy can be considered analogous to those for paper mail-order catalogs.

Most companies can't afford to and therefore do not continue to send catalogs to people who do not make purchases.

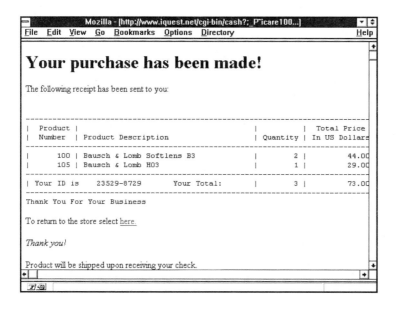

Fig. 12.8
The final receipt page is given to the user after he or she completes the purchase as a member.

Alternative Methods for Collecting Cash

Besides simple cash acceptance mechanisms such as credit card authorization and check clearing, other schemes for accepting money can be arranged.

Specialized methods include the following:

- Debit-type cards for kiosks

- Company cash

Debit cards for kiosks (also often called *smart cards*) often have a magnetic strip similar to cards used in video arcades and phone cards. Cards are purchased by users, either in set denominations or for however much the user wants to put into the card. The user must insert the card into the kiosk in order to use it or purchase from it. Money for products and services are debited from the card, which is returned to the user after the kiosk session is finished.

▶ See "Kiosk Basics," p. 448

This card has a downside, though. If it's lost, anyone can use it. You can also run into potential problems if the card is accidentally exposed to magnetic fields or is otherwise damaged. However, debit cards offer the user freedom from accounting, no interest rates, and greater security than credit cards.

Company cash is a similar concept but without a card, just an online credit account. Users deposit money into their account which is used against purchases they make.

Company cash systems would by necessity include some form of membership system. In the future, for example, it might be a good method for kiosks to offer business service in airports. A traveling salesperson, regardless of what airport he or she was in, could just enter the password and have full access to the services offered by your kiosk without the hassles of money, credit cards, or debit cards.

Various forms of company cash systems are also beginning to appear on the Internet. Company cash offers a type of secure cash transaction. By paying real cash to a company, they in turn give you digital cash which can be used to make purchases. Stores who accept the digital cash will have authentication mechanisms to ensure that it is you using your cash. These types of electronic cash systems are currently highly experimental, but do offer advantages over debit and credit systems:

- Company cash systems are secure because they can be implemented with digital signatures.

- They are as convenient as cash by offering no-interest and no-credit shopping convenience.

As time goes on, more and more digital cash systems will appear.

From Here...

The decision as to how you will collect money from your customers on your Web-based business should be based on your business and how you plan to integrate the Web into it. If you are planning a new business on the Web, make sure that your money-handling capabilities tie in to your overall design plan.

Remember that in any Web transaction, you should take all the precautions you would on non-Web transactions.

For more information, refer to the following chapters:

- Chapter 13, "Order Filling and Tracking," shows you the next step in setting up a Web-based mail order system.

- Chapter 14, "Subscription Services, Virtual Malls, and Instant Products," explains how membership systems can be used in subscription services.

- Chapter 15, "Acquiring Demographics About Your Users," teaches you the best ways to get user demographics.

- Chapter 18, "Security and Cash Transactions," provides more information about security issues and handling money over the Web.

III

Products and Services

Chapter 13

Order Filling and Tracking

Being able to quickly and efficiently send out the orders you receive online is the culmination to any online ordering system. Some businesses can get by with simple systems that more or less stand by themselves and are adjunct to existing systems. Other businesses will want more sophisticated systems that tie into a larger information system.

In this chapter you learn

- Key components in an online filling and tracking system

- How to deal with taxes

- Shipping considerations

- The intricacies of filling international orders

- How to generate electronic receipts

- Methods for efficient user feedback

- What to do with incomplete orders

- Ways your ordering system can be used in other areas of your business

Effective Order Filling Systems

Some of the earlier chapters have outlined mechanisms for taking orders and handling cash transactions. However, once you have the order, how do you fulfill it? And what customer support issues are involved? An effective order filling system will help to decrease—rather than increase—your customer support problems.

As you learned in Chapter 11, "Order Taking and the Net," users can route orders to you using one of many methods. This section examines how to take care of order fulfillment for each type of order entry system.

The two largest issues in product fulfillment over the WWW is user confidence and user satisfaction. In many cases, the product purchased by a user will not be dispensed at the point of purchase. Because of this, user confidence is critical. The user must be confident that cash transactions will be dealt with securely and confidentially and that your ordering system can fulfill the order quickly and correctly.

Imagine an order entry system that, when you submit your payment information, simply comes back with the same page or comes back with a blank page. Even just returning a page that reads "Thank You" would be inappropriate, because the user asks, "What now?"

Instead, you should attempt to give as much information to the user as possible; you might even want to include online order confirmation as well as tracking.

◀ See "Membership Systems," p. 284

For example, a user could purchase an item using a membership system such as the one described in Chapter 12, "Methods for Collecting Cash." Upon submitting the order, the user should be provided with information concerning the total dollar amount for the purchase, how the product(s) will be shipped, when to expect them, and most importantly, a purchase ID number which is unique to the transaction.

Furthermore, the user is also sent via e-mail, an electronic receipt that contains the same information. And finally, when the user wishes, he or she can access your pages, enter a purchase ID number, and instantly retrieve the stage of the order within your system.

Tip

Everything from the wording of the order form to the graphics should be chosen to instill maximum confidence of your system to your potential client.

This example shows a system which is all-inclusive and keeps both user confidence and satisfaction very high with the order process. Users don't need much faith in whether or not they will receive the product because they can check for themselves and confirm what stage the product is in, in the fulfillment process.

Not every business needs the all-inclusive order entry system. Indeed, many small companies will have the simplest and cheapest order system possible. Order entry systems can be created for as little as $100 or as much as tens of thousands of dollars. It will be up to the business to determine their needs versus what they can afford. However, even if you can only afford a rudimentary ordering system, it should work every time a client accesses it, and it must work correctly. An inexpensive system shouldn't mean a shoddy system.

Note

This system just described helped the user every step of the way. Even if your company cannot afford the capital investment, that is no reason not to take advantage of an online ordering system. Our next example will show you how to apply some of the same concepts to a rock-bottom priced system.

The very lowest level of an order entry system is one in which the user fills out a form and submits it, and the form is then e-mailed to the business. This is just a standard form system, which can be developed using a simple page, an interactive form, and form remailer service. If you create your own pages and forms, your only costs include a monthly service fee for the form remailer, which can run as low as $25 per month.

▶ See "Adding Forms To Your Pages," p. 539

With this type of system, because the form remailer is off-the-shelf, you may not be able to send back to the user anything other than a generic message like, "Thank you for your order." Figure 13.1 shows such a returned message from a generic form-handling system.

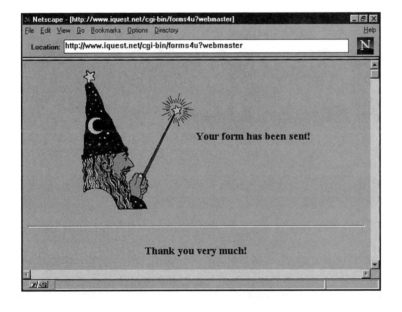

Fig. 13.1
A generic message stating that a form has been submitted is often the only answer that simple form handlers can present to the user.

In this case, user confidence will need some boosting. You can do this by including assurances to the user that the order will be filled quickly and efficiently. You could place these messages at the top of the order form page or just in front of the button that submits the order form page to you.

> **Note**
>
> We recommend that you assure users that once you received their order, you send them e-mail with a receipt and the status of their order.

Upon receiving an order (which arrives to you via e-mail), send out a simple receipt to users and then process their order. Depending on your company's size, in the receipt you might decide to include an order number as well as contact information. Users now have a means of tracking their order via the telephone—again, building user confidence and satisfaction.

> **Note**
>
> Whether or not you pick a totally automatic and integrated system or a very simple system, an effective order entry should also mean that it is easy on your company. Any user feedback and customer support should be integrated into your company such that it flows easily with your current structure.

You learn in the following sections how to organize such a system. However, you should keep your mind open to allowing the WWW to help change your existing methodologies, because the solutions provided by the Web can be applied to—and can benefit—the company as well as the user.

Accepting an Order

One of the key goals in an efficient online order system is to accept the order in such a way that it integrates into your own physical order entry system. In general, you will be bound by a few rules on the WWW, unless you are custom-designing your own order entry system.

Most WWW-based order entry systems allow you to receive your order in one or more ways. The most common method is to receive your order by e-mail. In this case, when the user submits an order, it is routed to a cgi-bin program, which formats the order and e-mails it to you. Upon reaching your designated e-mail address, the order simply enters your mail queue like all your other messages. You then must read your mail and respond to the orders.

Most of the popular e-mail programs allow you to save your e-mail messages in files. You can either save the orders in individual files, or (as some mail programs allow) save all messages in a common folder or file. You can then edit this file(s), examine the orders, and fulfill them.

> **Caution**
>
> You don't want orders going to the same e-mail address as your personal e-mail, unless you are not expecting many orders.
>
> If you have all your orders sent to an e-mail address specifically set up for orders, you will never have to worry about routing any of the messages as anything but orders.

The electronic orders can be taken right off the screen or printed and sent through your order system in hard-copy form.

Some order entry systems will fax orders to you, usually for a per-fax charge. Often the charge is inexpensive enough to consider this method of order entry as a good alternative. Faxing systems can take two forms:

■ A normal order entry system that uses e-mail can send the e-mail to a fax server. The fax server then sends the e-mail message to you as a standard fax. When it arrives at your company, you simply fill it out as you would any other faxed order.

■ The order entry system itself can be tied directly to fax software via a custom-designed interface. This option would give you more security; the order would not pass unencrypted through the mail system to the fax handler, but instead be delivered directly to the fax handler through a proprietary mechanism.

Another popular method for delivering orders is to append the orders into a file in one of your online accounts. This method is popular as an alternative to e-mail because it can be made more secure. You would interface to it in much the same way as e-mail, looking at each of the orders in the larger order file.

If your design consists of just a simple order form tied to a form remailer, no receipt is being generated by the user. The first thing you should do is create a receipt and send it to the user. Refer to the section "User Receipts and Feedback" later in this chapter to find out more on how to handle receipts.

Once you receive the order, in any of the methods listed earlier, you should enter it into your physical order stream at the very earliest point. In other words, it is to your advantage to make it look like every other order right up front. In this way, you can take advantage of all the checks, balances, and tracking mechanisms you already have in place.

III

Products and Services

Again, the most basic shop will simply integrate the order by reading and printing their e-mail and sending the order through their normal channels.

Unfortunately, this method is very dry and boring. It's not really integrated at all. What we want to do is really take advantage of the incredible potential the WWW has to offer.

Fully Integrated WWW Systems

The WWW offers so much more than just simple order entry from the outside world. To see the WWW for what it is, first consider the browser. It is really just a nice GUI with forms support. It also just happens to be network savvy. That's all it is. You can apply this type of technology to a huge area of company problems and come up winning each and every time.

◀ See "The Beginning of the World Wide Web," p. 20

Consider the following scenario. A large company decides to use the WWW as a means to facilitate communication and interaction for group projects. (After all, this is the very reason CERN invented the mechanism in the first place.) The company installs terminals in each department of the company: order entry, customer support, shipping, sales, and billing. Each terminal is tied to a local WWW, running just within the company on the company's server. The server is also tied to the Internet and the global WWW as well.

Users coming in from the outside see the company's storefront presence. They can browse and purchase, all from an extremely sophisticated shopping system. Once they make a purchase, they can track the status of their order. And once they receive their order, they can use the customer service system to report any problems or ask questions.

On the company side, employees see forms specifically designed for their tasks. For an optimal system, each terminal—besides having a keyboard—would also be touch-sensitive, allowing employees to input information directly into the screen without requiring a physical keyboard or typing ability. Fax orders are automatically converted into WWW form data by computer.

Voice orders are entered by employees directly into WWW forms and processed in the same way as orders coming in from external WWW users. As the orders come in, integrated software handles its routing where the first stop will be order fulfillment.

In order fulfillment, employees see the order on their screen as the next sequential order, process it, and indicate the status, primarily via the touch screen. As each step of the process occurs, a single simple touch relays the information via the internal WWW form to the computer. On the outside, users can access tracking and instantly see the position of the order. This includes handling out-of-stock items and other problems, which are either automatically noted by the software or simply indicated with a touch of the panel by the employees.

Not only is the status of any order instantly available for users on the outside, but e-mail can automatically be dispatched to users or snail mail printed for your non-Internet orders.

Likewise in shipping, the status of the order is kept active, and an estimated arrival date is added to the order. Also indicated is the method of shipping. If the order is shipped using an overnight courier, the courier-tracking information and phone number are also provided. On the outside, links to FedEx and other tracking WWW pages are given (if you don't think this is possible, check out **http://www.fedex.com/** as shown in fig. 13.2).

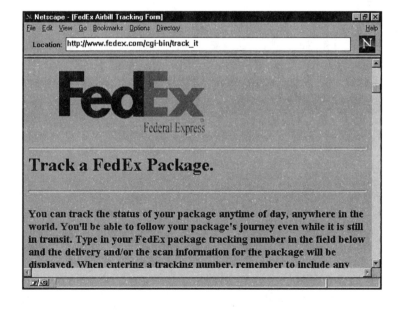

Fig. 13.2
Systems such as the Federal Express tracking system allow users to track their overnight shipments via the World Wide Web.

In customer support, support calls are logged and tracked with the online system, which accommodates both Internet and voice users. Persistent questions are added by employees to a FAQ page which is available to users on the WWW as well as to the customer support personnel. Database searching of calls leads both users as well as personnel to solutions almost instantly, allowing them to build off each other's answers in real time.

Each step along the way, the order status is entered, giving complete tracking and instant knowledge and control of the order process. Tied into automatic inventory and automatic report generation, the president and vice presidents of the company can sit back and access pages specifically designed for them to see how well the entire process is working.

You should be able to see that a scheme such as the one described here can be an extremely powerful, effective, and time-saving tool. You can also use the same mechanism to promote employee morale, offering your employees the ability to have their own personal pages as well as internal company chat areas, internal conferencing capability, work groups, intercompany e-mail, and other wonderful benefits.

> **Note**
>
> The most sophisticated, integrated business systems will allow employees to have personal Web pages that are offered to clients as a way to meet your company's staff. It will also feature internal conferencing, work groups, and interoffice e-mail.
>
> Sales representatives on the road can also tie into the system via cellular phone link to the WWW and enter orders or access tracking information, customer support, or any other area from virtually anywhere.

▶ See "Kiosk Basics," p. 448

And don't forget about point-of-sale kiosks that you can sprinkle in malls and stores. Simply provide the kiosks with a phone line, and any walk-up user can surf and order from your pages.

▶ See "Virtual Shopping Systems," p. 328

> **Note**
>
> We realize that fully integrated systems are not cheap to design, engineer, and implement. As more and more of these systems become commonplace, the prices will begin to drop and lower-priced, pre-packaged designs will begin to emerge.
>
> We also realize that such a large system is not needed by the average small business. However, small businesses can use bits and pieces of the grand design, taking only those areas that make financial sense to them.

Handling Taxes

Here in the United States, whether or not you add sales tax to a product will depend on the laws in the state where you are located, as well as the state you are shipping to. Also, in most situations, you will have to collect sales tax if you are selling a product, but not if you are selling a service.

How does all this relate to taxes? You can begin to imagine that sales tax is difficult to calculate. It is even more difficult to express it in the pricing of an item. However, adequate solutions exist for all ranges of order entry systems.

> **Note**
>
> Seek the appropriate legal and financial help for determining issues concerning your pages such as taxes, paperwork for shipping to foreign countries, and laws concerning your product itself. We are computer scientists—not lawyers or accountants; we can at best recommend. Use our advice as a guideline, but make sure to confirm your plans with your legal and financial staff since laws differ widely from state to state and country to country.

> **Caution**
>
> Choosing to ignore the sales tax issue by not collecting and paying the tax is not a good option. It is unlikely that it will go unnoticed, and big fines can be levied for avoiding taxes.

The low-end system that is just a static form cannot calculate tax interactively. In this type of system, the user sees the product information along with a price. For this type of system you have two basic options. Both methods require you to use a tax table for the various places you are selling to:

- You can raise your product by the largest amount of tax for all the areas you are shipping to. While this raises the overall price of the product, it has the advantage of having a fixed price, "sales tax included." In many cases, you end up with a slight profit because of the differing tax rates.

- You can tell the user that sales tax has not been included. This is fine for credit card orders, because you can then charge the card accordingly, but this makes check handling difficult because it's up to the user to calculate the tax.

Tip
By specifying that users send in a copy of the receipt when paying by check, you can ensure that they will write the check for the amount on the receipt, which will include the proper tax.

▶ See "Virtual Shopping Systems," p. 328

The proper solution is to bring the calculation of tax to the next level with a cgi-bin tax calculation program. This program takes a table of locations and taxes, calculates the proper tax, and either presents that in the form or in the receipt. This small addition will greatly free up the time spent calculating taxes.

Advanced design shopping systems, such as virtual shopping carts, will often have built-in tax handling software. These systems will automatically calculate the proper prices and display them where appropriate to the user. Again, these work with software that matches the user's location—usually state and country information—to a table of tax multipliers. This information is used against their purchased items to calculate the appropriate rates.

Keep in mind that in some cases, taxes vary for different products. For example, if you sell food products, alcohol and tobacco are often taxed differently than other food items. A gourmet food shop may have several tax calculations to perform. In good designs, product categories specify the tax that each product needs.

Handling Shipping Issues

Currently, the majority of stores on the Web are oriented towards worldwide sales. However, as time goes on you will begin to see more and more stores selling for their local area, as the local online customer base begins to grow. One thing you must keep in mind when placing a storefront on the Internet is that you will be advertising and selling to a worldwide audience, even if you don't want to.

If you are limited in your ability to ship your product or provide services to a worldwide audience, you must take care to explain that fact throughout your pages. Not only do you want to avoid the hassle of receiving orders from places you can't ship to, but you also want to avoid having your Internet bandwidth taken up by people who can't receive your product.

Note

We recommend placing any major restrictions you might have at the top and bottom of each page. You can do this with either a simple link or a pleasing sentence or two explaining the restriction. A small icon should be present to help draw the users' eyes to the restriction.

To whatever degree possible, you will want to have the software catch orders that can't be handled and notify users instantly that they should not have ordered. You can do this by accepting location information from the user up front and only then allowing them access.

When shipping a product overseas, laws will vary about the legality of products, and you may be restricted from shipping your particular product to certain countries. For example, many food- and liquor-oriented products cannot be shipped just anywhere. Restrictions on types of food, how it is packaged, or what type of inspections are required exist in many places.

Even shipping between the U.S. and Canada is highly restricted. You will find that even shipping between states in the U.S. itself may be restricted. For example, Hawaii does not allow certain items in or out, for fear of agricultural contamination from insects and bacteria. Similar restrictions are enforced in California and Alaska.

Caution

Keep in mind that some products may be illegal to export outside of the U.S. In some cases, not the product but the shipping itself is illegal. For example, sending or shipping encryption or decryption tools outside of the U.S. is currently illegal (because encryption is viewed as munitions), depending on where you are sending it. While you can send information as encrypted, you cannot send the tools to encrypt or decrypt (see fig. 13.3). Likewise, certain technologies cannot be exported to certain countries, and the U.S. also has embargoes on various countries at various times. Check your laws!

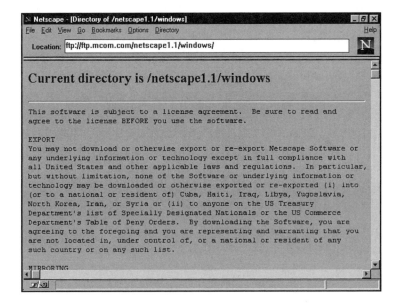

Fig. 13.3

The Netscape Communications export restrictions are displayed before you are allowed to download the software.

> **Note**
>
> Keep in mind that packaging may play an important role. Items packaged in a certain way may be allowed, while the same item packaged differently may be refused. Such is the case with many prepackaged foods. Depending on the packaging, customs may be required to open and inspect the contents.

Restrictions also exist for certain high-technology items, especially on encryption and decryption technology. Some countries may forbid you to send in certain intellectual, political, or entertainment material if it is censored by that country. It could be very expensive to ship goods to a country where they are illegal, because they probably won't be returned to you and will instead be destroyed.

Finally, when shipping to foreign countries, estimate customs delays as well as foreign shipping delays. If you are shipping perishable or time-sensitive products, these delays can become serious problems.

All of these factors must be brought into consideration when selling and shipping via the WWW. Just because it is easy to reach a worldwide audience doesn't necessarily mean that your product can be sent to that audience.

Handling Incomplete Orders

Invariably you will receive an order from a user who has given you only partial information. One of the first things you must do is ensure that the user did not submit the order a second time. In fact, you should do this with all orders anyway. If for some reason your response to an order did not go through, users might submit it again thinking that you never received it in the first place. Or, users may have realized that they forgot information and might have corrected the omission and submitted the form a second time.

Once you have an order that is incomplete, you have two basic options. First, if the users left any access information at all that is complete, such as a telephone number, address, or e-mail, you will be able to contact them in that manner to obtain the missing elements. This is pretty obvious.

However, most often what is missing is users' e-mail addresses and other contact information. In this case, you can either simply ignore the order or attempt to reach the users.

If you are going to attempt to reach users, here are some hints to help you:

- Most form remailers—or any mailer coupled with the WWW—will in general provide you with some of the server environment. What we mean here is that usually appended to each e-mail you receive from a WWW system, you will see information as to what the user's browser is (for example, Mosaic), and what the user's domain name is.

◀ See "Clients and Browsers," p. 35

- The domain name will often appear to be something like `*unknown*@domain.com`. `domain.com` is the user's real domain name, but `*unknown*` indicates that the user's e-mail address was not broadcasted. Most sites, for security reasons, will not identify a user by e-mail name.

So how does this help you? If you have the user's domain name and if the user provided his or her real name, you have a very good opportunity to reach that person with one or two small attempts.

First, use the Finger capability to see whether anyone at that domain exists with the last name provided in your incomplete order. For example, suppose the user said his name was Bob Jones and the e-mail showed a domain name of playroom.com. Likely user names might be:

bobj@playroom.com

bjones@playroom.com

bob@playroom.com

jones@playroom.com

Using the Finger command will often match more than one user because they will match against the user's real name as well as their e-mail name. Therefore, if you finger bob@playroom.com, you might receive all the users named bob at that site. Next, simply look at the list and see whether Bob Jones is included. Once you find him, send him a copy of the e-mail order and ask your questions.

Tip
Don't forget to try derivatives such as Robert.

> **Note**
>
> For more information on the Finger command, refer to Que's Special Edition *Using Internet E-Mail.*

By using these methods, you can usually determine within about five minutes if you can find the user. If this fails, we recommend just ignoring the order. If your number of incomplete orders becomes excessive, you should possibly consider changing your pages to make the information requirements more clear to the user.

You should probably assign someone to be responsible for handling incomplete orders. This way, any incomplete orders you receive will not fall by the wayside, due to it not being anyone's assigned task.

User Receipts and Feedback

We have indicated throughout this book that user receipts and user feedback are very important. This small item will make the most difference in user confidence and satisfaction.

When you place an order, a primary goal is to immediately return to the user a confirmation that the order was received. The response should specifically confirm that the user's order was received and understood. At the very best, you will want to provide a receipt, as understood by your software, to the user.

Users tend to have a nagging suspicion that the information they typed in will not be understood by the software or people at the other end. Good ordering systems will send a receipt back to the user which looks different from the one the user submitted. By this we mean that it will be organized differently, making it obvious that the computer read their original order and produced the receipt, not just bounced their information back to them. This confirms the order within the user's mind.

Another factor in sending the user a receipt is to place a unique order number on the receipt. This provides the user with a method of tracking the order should something go awry. The order number can easily be fabricated by your receipt-generating software as part of the receipt and also echoed to you when the order is sent to you. This allows you to easily match a user calling in with questions against the order in question.

Extra-smart systems might even return to users a new form with the correct information already filled out, only prompting for the incorrect or missing information. Users would then be led through any problems or errors they have made, ensuring that you get only complete forms on your end.

As we have also mentioned throughout this book, you should attempt to send receipts and feedback not only via the WWW system in response to users' submissions, but also via e-mail. Giving users double confirmation only serves to increase their level of confidence in your order entry system.

> **Note**
>
> You should not think only of user receipts, however, when considering user feedback. In particular, orders that are incomplete can be flagged by the receipt-generating software, and the user can be told what to change. Because the user's browser will have kept the previous page, which will be the form submitted by the user, the error message returned by the receipt software can include instructions for the user to return to the previous page (via the browser's capability to go back to the previously displayed page) and correct the incomplete form.

Handling Bouncing Mail

The term *bounced mail* has to do with e-mail that for whatever reason did not reach the intended recipient. When the mail is returned to you, it is called *bouncing*. Bouncing mail represents a real problem for order entry systems, especially for totally automated systems. The problem comes when users have supplied either an incorrect e-mail address, or an address which is either temporarily not accessible or sits inaccessible behind a security system (such as a firewall). In this case, users may not be aware that they are not accessible from outside of their company.

▶ See "Working with Firewalls, Wrappers, and Proxies," p. 441

For these problems, you rely on the fact that users have received their receipt via the returned WWW page. However, in the event that your users did not, you need to contact each user in some manner.

Hopefully you have alternative contact information from each user, such as a phone or fax number. If you do not have such information, addressing e-mail to either **root**, **webmaster**, or **postmaster** at the user's domain will usually get you in touch with the administration at that site (for example, root@somewhere.com or webmaster@somewhere.com). You can then explain briefly the problem and give the site administrator the e-mail address you have been attempting to contact, along with the user's name. The administrator should be able to forward to you either the user's correct address or contact the user and ask that person to contact you concerning your problem.

> **Note**
>
> Before resorting to contacting a site administrator, you can try to resend the original message several times. Often systems are down for routine maintenance, or some other network problem may have occurred, which makes it impossible for your original message to have made it.
>
> We recommend that you try to resend your message once or twice per day over a two or three-day period. If it still refuses to go through, try to contact the site administrator.

One of the biggest problems with bouncing mail is that it can end up in an infinite loop within the mail system. This will make your system administrator very unhappy.

▶ See "The HTTPD Log," p. 342

A user submits an order to you which is e-mailed to your machine. Since the e-mail is actually submitted by the HTTPD remailer, it will often have the username of "nobody" at your domain name (nobody@domain.com), which is the username that most WWW servers run as. When a mail message bounces, it does not bounce to you but back to "nobody" at your domain name. You need to work with your site administrator to have some policy of periodically forwarding the bounced mail from "nobody" to you.

Obviously, many other shops and users may be using the form remailer; therefore, the administrator cannot simply forward all mail addressed to "nobody" to you, because you will get other mail as well. Often, the local webmaster will be helpful in resolving this issue.

Advanced order entry systems can spoof the form address. These systems can be set so that bounced mail will return to you, not to "nobody." However, these systems need to work together with the system administrator, because they often need special system privileges to be able to fake—or spoof—the return address to the mail system.

> **Note**
>
> The term *spoofing* refers to the ability to pretend that you are somebody or something that you are not. When software such as an order entry system spoofs an address, it does so to make the order appear to actually have come from the sender. This facilitates responding to the message using the traditional e-mail capabilities and can cut down on order processing overhead by allowing traditional e-mail tools to be able to handle the order process.

Spoofing is one of the best solutions, because it can make the order system truly effective by making the remailer process itself invisible. But spoofing cannot be used lightly. You must ensure safeguards so that users cannot make it look like the order came from the president of the United States. Simple domain match-ups help to ensure that the user at least comes from the same machine.

The best advice we can offer is that you should work with your site administrator to see what policy he or she wants to maintain for bounced e-mail within your shopping system.

> **Note**
>
> You always want to provide voice access information in your pages. Users who have not heard from you in some way can at least contact you. Make sure to include your office hours and location information so users around the world know when to contact you.

Order Fulfillment

Order fulfillment offers you another area in which you can help build user satisfaction. When the order is ready to go out the door, you should again send an e-mail message to the user indicating that shipment has begun. Little things like this will go a long way toward establishing loyal customers.

Sending the order to the user is a good time to hook newer users into using the Internet service again. First, be sure to thank them for their Internet order. This helps to remind users that they received this order via the convenience of the Internet. You are not only helping to remind them to use your service, but you are also helping the Internet community as a whole.

It's also an excellent time to offer them an incentive to shop at your store again. Giving them a small discount on their next order is a great way to encourage them to come back. Because most order entry systems implement some type of membership system, you have an excellent opportunity to remind them of discounts and other specials or rewards. Providing a place on your form where coupon and award numbers can be entered not only goes a long way toward hooking the first-time users who know they will receive a discount after their first order, but also helps keep the repeat customers.

III

Products and Services

Make sure that your forms support some method for the user to specify quantity, as most shopping systems do have quantity discount pricing capability. This method can let you get the most out of your pages and also allow you to offer more substantial discounts. Both you and the user can save in your fulfillment costs in both shipping and packaging, as well as inventory.

In situations where fulfillment becomes impossible—due to out-of-stock inventory, discontinued merchandise, and other problems—have a mechanism in which you can e-mail users and tell them of the problem. Users respond by telling you how to resolve the problem.

Internal and User Tracking

▶ See "The HTTPD Log," p. 342

You have many tracking mechanisms available to you on the Internet and WWW. These mechanisms can be used not only to aid in decreasing your cost and building user confidence, but also for helping you create better pages.

Most order-entry software generates an electronic transaction number and attaches it to each receipt. This number is unique for each and every order sent out. On the users' end, the number serves as an identification to the users' order. On your end, the number serves as an identification to not only the users' order, but to the users themselves.

By craftily creating your order number transaction ID, you can make a single identification tell you the user number, the receipt number, and the transaction date. For example,

```
52fa2911-5223-95C23-1
```

could indicate the following:

- **52fa2911.** The user number (a hexadecimal code with billions of possible combinations).

- **5223.** The product number.

- **95C23.** The year, month, and day—1995, March (A=Jan, B=Feb, C=March), 23rd.

- **1.** The first order on that day.

Note

Users will be e-mailed this number as part of their receipt, but should never need to refer to it unless a problem arises. (We realize our example is big, but it gives an idea of what you can do. More efficient codes are possible as well.)

Because you are storing these numbers into a database along with the receipts themselves, you have an interesting and powerful mechanism at your disposal for tracking user orders. You can, for example, enter a user's number to find out what that user has bought during any period of time. Likewise, you could type in a product number and get a cross-listing of people and times when products have been purchased. Finally, by listing dates, you can examine when buying trends increase and decrease and discover ways to make your pages more effective.

Likewise, users have access to the same information about themselves. Users could easily enter the tracking number to have it return information about the order. They could look at their user profile, which would outline their orders for any period of time they desired. This system can easily be managed with a few simple databases, and the correct forms and WWW software.

From Here...

This chapter showed you how to set up and implement an online order fulfillment and tracking system. Such a system can be new and unique to your business, or it may tie into your existing system.

Many issues were explored that you will have to handle when you develop such a system. Some of these issues include taxes, foreign orders, and incomplete orders. How you decide to handle these issues will depend on the size of your company and personnel considerations, among other things. Remember that your online order fulfillment and tracking system is supposed to streamline your efforts, making it easier for your employees and your customers, and save you money. If it doesn't, you will need to fine-tune your system.

For more information, refer to the following chapters:

- Chapter 4, "Planning a Web Site," offers general concepts when setting up a Web business.

- Chapter 9, "Information on the Net," provides further information for tracking down users whose orders bounce.

III

Products and Services

- Chapter 11, "Order Taking and the Net," teaches you the basics on order-taking systems.

- Chapter 14, "Subscription Services, Virtual Malls, and Instant Products," introduces you to innovative ways that online fulfillment systems can be used.

Chapter 14

Subscription Services, Virtual Malls, and Instant Products

Certain aspects of conducting business on the Web are unique to the WWW and offer fantastic opportunities to anyone with a good idea. Subscription services, instant products, and virtual malls are all new business avenues that have opened up with the advent of the World Wide Web.

In this chapter you learn

- How to set up and manage subscription services

- Pointers on managing subscription services

- What an instant product is and how to create, market, and sell instant products

- Special points to remember when dealing with instant products

- What a virtual mall is and how to implement one

- Using databases for large systems

Subscription Services

Of the many ways to make money off the World Wide Web, subscriptions services offer an amazingly easy method for making money. Little or no overhead is involved. A good service will be self-maintaining, requiring a minimal amount of time from you. All you have to do is set up a system that contains information and/or services that people will pay a monthly fee for, and then sit back and collect the checks as they pour into your mailbox.

Services that can be offered are limited only by your imagination, what the market will pay for, and in some cases, applicable laws and government regulations.

What is a Subscription Service?

To help you understand what a subscription service is, you need to understand the following:

- Subscription systems allow users to enroll interactively and instantly.

- Subscription systems track a user throughout the user's session.

Subscription systems may be free or may be designed to cost money. As a free system, you may want to limit memberships for a number of reasons:

- You may want to restrict the number of people accessing your system. This would reduce the load, making the system faster to use as well as allowing you to choose who can and who cannot access the site (perhaps based on information provided to you in a form filled out by the user).

- By requiring that a user log in to your service, you can determine just how many people are using it simultaneously and limit what they can and cannot access. For example, such a system could limit a user to downloading only a certain amount of information each day. This would allow more people fairer use of the system on a daily basis.

- You want to offer your members specialized services. The services may be "free" (as part of their basic membership), but you may require them to log into the service. This would keep non-members from using your system and taking resources away from your desired users.

As we indicated, you can also accept money for your subscription system. Pay systems can be very profitable if you are offering a service which people expect to cost them money. In a pay system, a user registers for access and provides some payment mechanism such as a credit card or billing address. Once registered, the user is allowed to access your system at any time.

> **Note**
>
> Any system can be a pay system, but not any system will work as a pay system. People won't use a pay system where they expect the "product" to be free.

As an example of a pay system, consider a stock broker service. Your service might provide free, one-hour-delayed stock quotations to any user who accesses your system. However, registered users might get instant stock quotations. For this non-delayed service, registered users may pay a yearly, monthly, or even a per-quote price. A subscription system will handle this flawlessly, allowing users to register and make use of the system instantly.

Whether a subscription system is free or pay depends entirely on you, your business, and how you intend to make money.

> **Note**
>
> Attempting to get users to pay for services which are traditionally free or available from some other location on the Internet for free is a bad idea. To make money from a subscription service, your product should be unique, at a discount, or in some way add value.

Attracting the User To a Subscription System

You can attract users to subscription systems in much the same way that you attract them to any home page—by advertising yourself in What's New lists and with robot searchers. However, once users reach your site, how do you encourage them to actually become a member?

In general, users are reluctant to pay for something they cannot see first. Unless you are a big-name company or have a prominent product where users have no question as to what they will get, you should provide at least a sample of what you have to offer.

◄ See "How To Advertise on the Net," p. 227

Providing a sample may or many not be easy to accomplish, depending on what your product is. However, most subscription systems have some way in which users can get an idea as to what their benefits are.

At the very least, you should describe your system in detail to the users. The description should be complete enough so that users have a good idea as to what you are providing. You should also give complete pricing and billing information, so there is no question as to when and how they will be billed and how they can expect to receive their service.

As simple as this scheme is, making it work in a free and easy manner requires care in your design. In particular, your information page should be organized such that you don't overwhelm users, who are reluctant to wade through huge documents. Additionally, you should be careful to have a good index where it is clear how users can find items they are searching for.

To help you best present your information, our recommendation is to divide your description into the following categories:

- *How Our Services Benefit You.* The first category outlines what users will get from your subscription service. The contents should be concise and fairly short. You should attempt to make all the important points first, at the top and in a bulleted list. This way, users don't have to read through the entire category to find out why or how the service benefits them.

- *How Billing Works.* This second section should provide users with the price for your service, as well as all the information as to how they will be billed and how you expect payment.

- *Frequently Asked Questions.* The third section should be presented in a simple question-and-answer arrangement. Here you should place the most common questions and answers that you receive. This will help to reduce the amount of e-mail and voice support you will need to do.

- *Signing Up.* The fourth section should take users to the form which allows them to subscribe to the service. It is important that this information falls beneath the others, because you want to lead the users through the questions before you present them with the form.

- *How To Find Us.* This last section should provide access information for users to locate and talk with you. In here, you might want to provide phone and fax numbers, as well as your e-mail address and perhaps a form with an area for questions for users to fill out and submit.

Tip

When designing a subscription service do not forget to provide information which tells users how to disconnect the service, as well as what happens if payment is not received.

Tip

Effective designs lead users through all the information they need to know before requesting them to join. Doing so gives you a better-informed user who has fewer questions.

Looking at this scheme, you should be able to see a distinct path that users take to find out about your service. The path is designed to be as simple and non-confusing as possible, while drawing users into your services in such a way that minimizes the amount of support you need to provide.

> **Note**
>
> A good page design will have a link—in larger text than the surrounding text—which directs the user to log in to the subscription system. Below that link, you can place the information for people who want to join. In this way, your current members can go directly into the subscription system, without having to visually find the link beneath the information to new users.

If your subscription system can support a live demo of what the user can expect, you will be guaranteed to attract even more users. Hands-on demonstrations are one of the quickest ways to help users make up their mind to buy.

There are many ways to show live demos. If your subscription system is product-oriented, you could show product shots. For example, if you are marketing software at a discount to subscribers, you can easily show pictures of the software packaging and screen shots. This can be done with any physical product which has visual appeal.

If your product is a service, you might want to offer a sample of that service. For example, if you generate reports, you could show sample reports. Likewise, if you offer stock quotes, you could show delayed quotations.

If it's difficult for you to demonstrate the product without the user being a subscriber, consider allowing users to join with reduced functionality until their full membership is approved. In these cases, users can actually begin to use some of the capabilities, as well as see what they will have access to once they become a full subscriber.

Figures 14.1, 14.2, and 14.3 show various stages of a subscription system. In this case, *Wired* Magazine maintains a site on the Internet named *HotWired*, which requires users to subscribe, much like a magazine except in this case the subscription is free. Figure 14.1 shows the first page you receive at the point of entering the subscription system. Figure 14.2 shows the new member form, and 14.3 shows the first page once users have successfully joined.

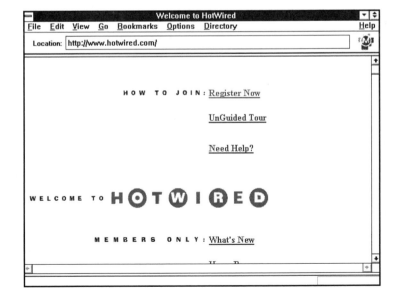

Fig. 14.1
The first page of the *HotWired* subscription system draws members and non-members into their appropriate areas.

III

Products and Services

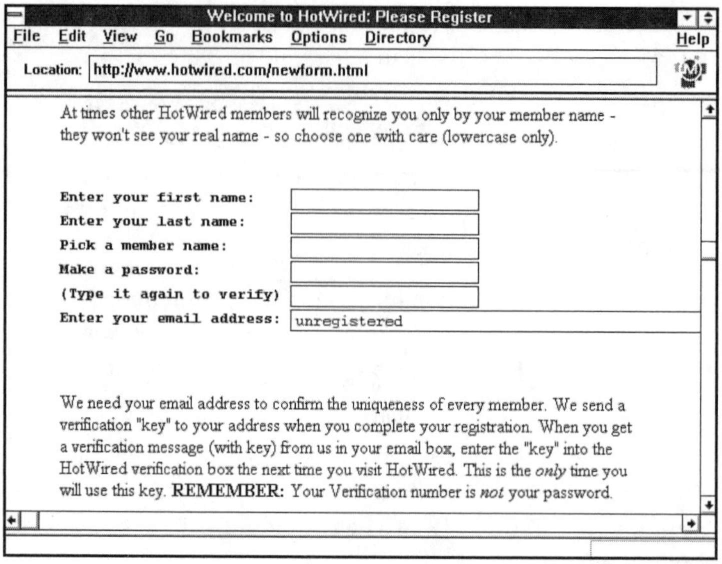

Fig. 14.2
New members
receive the
HotWired new
membership form.

Fig. 14.3
The *HotWired* site
appears once a
user has success-
fully logged in via
the subscription
system.

Pros and Cons

There are several considerations to keep in mind when designing subscription systems. First and foremost is the cost. Subscription systems cost a considerable amount to implement.

The reason for the higher cost for subscription systems is that they have to track users as well as keep pages secure. It would not be good if, once users entered a subscription system, they simply accessed HTML documents via URLs. If that were the case, users could simply enter the URL into their hotlist and jump there at any time after that, bypassing user authorization altogether. Because of this, subscription systems must not only track users but also hide URLs.

> **Note**
>
> While most servers have some form of user authorization built in, many subscription systems must be custom designed, because the simple server-oriented user authorization simply does not have enough features.

The benefits to a business with a subscription system include the ability to collect demographics and track demographic groups, as well as to sell products and services to a desired clientele. Additionally, cost savings on throughput can be realized because you are narrowing the scope of users who can access your pages, which may be heavy in size and thus expensive to transmit.

Finally, because subscription systems naturally include membership systems and tend also to include some form of cash handler, they are all-inclusive and can often handle many different aspects of business online. For example, since a subscription system takes money, it is probably a trivial extension to make it act as a shopping system. Likewise, since it already takes membership information, it probably has the ability to route any form to you via e-mail. All of these strengths add up to additional capabilities which make the system easier for users to operate, as well as more efficient.

Instant Products

Instant products offer another unprecedented means for making money on the World Wide Web. As you discover in the following sections, instant products are easy to implement and can make outstanding sums of money with very little investment.

The Unbelievable World of Instant Products

It should be fairly obvious by now how to use the WWW to make money from existing products and services. However, the WWW offers something that few mediums do—the ability to actually create new products from nothing more than a simple idea.

The WWW itself is a product, and as such has an incredible potential for making money. The basic idea here is to create a service or product, using the WWW, which cannot exist without the WWW (or at the very least could not exist in the manner in which you present it).

Since the product itself is the WWW, it is virtual. This means that cash will come in based on the value of the service, as opposed to the physical dispensing of a product. In fact, to qualify as an instant product, a WWW service must conform to the following restrictions:

- The product must be information- or service-based and in digital form.

- The implementation must be self-managing and self-running.

- The product must involve a subscription system.

As an example, one of our first instant product ideas was Virtual Secretary. The idea behind Virtual Secretary is that you could access your appointment schedule and address book from anywhere in the world. Additionally, users could fax documents and send e-mail, as well as make overnight deliveries from anywhere in the world. These last two additions are attractive because they are potential money savers. People in Europe can fax to the U.S. without an international phone call. Likewise, you can overnight express a letter without customs delays or international shipping charges.

To encourage use, the system could be affordably priced at, say, $10 per month, with faxes and overnights being provided for just a few dollars more.

Now, consider this system. With an Internet population of more than 35 million users (at the time of this writing), if even a small fraction—say, 1000 people—found this service useful, it would generate at least $10,000 per month, or $120,000 per year in income. And if 10,000 people used it (still a very small amount of the total Internet population), we would see $100,000 per month, or $1.2 million at the end of a year—all from just the minimum fee.

Additionally, such a service is totally self-running. The only component that requires a human is the overnight printing and delivery, which requires someone with enough brains to take a printout and put it in an envelope and address it correctly. Not exactly rocket science.

Figures 14.4 through 14.7 show various screen shots of the Virtual Secretary system.

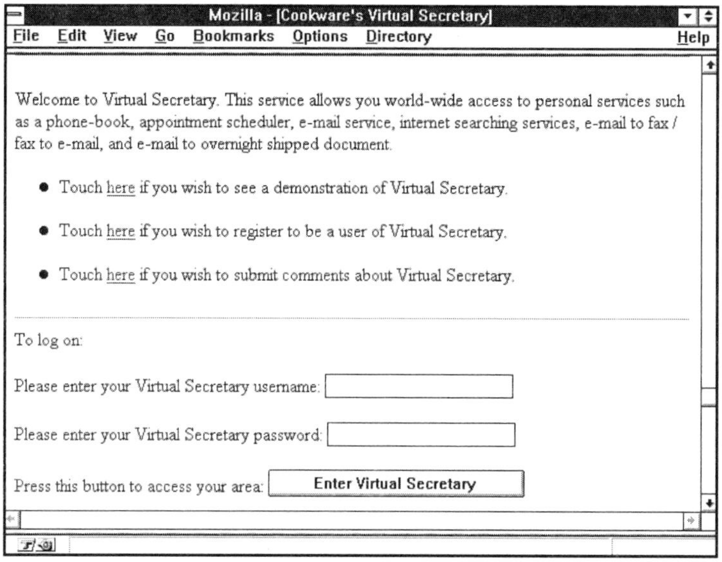

Fig. 14.4
The Virtual Secretary login screen provides various options users can choose to find out more information, and an area where users can log on.

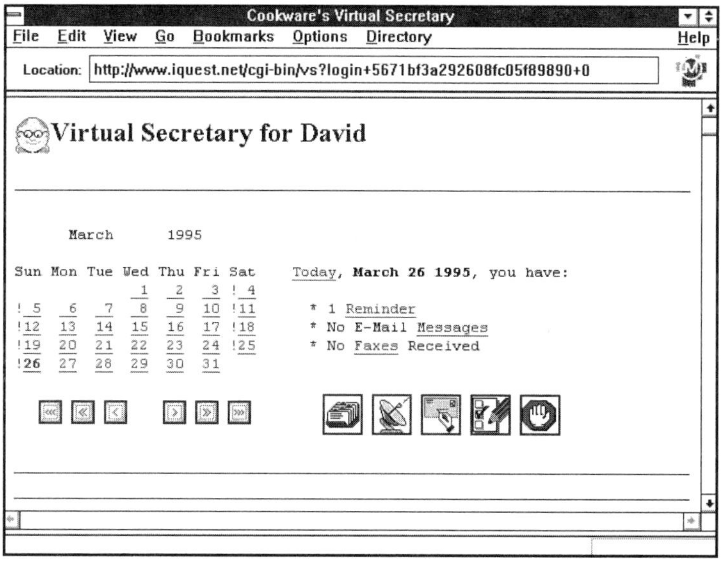

Fig. 14.5
The Virtual Secretary main screen shows the current calendar on the left and the user's choices on the right.

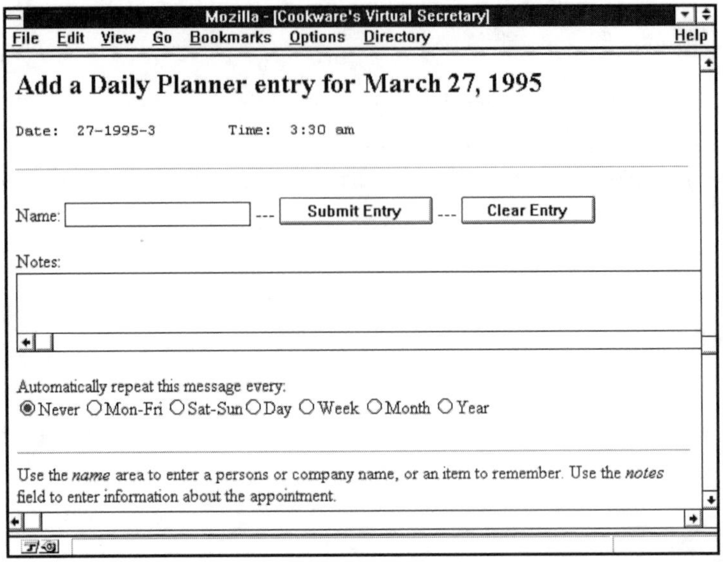
Mozilla - [Cookware's Virtual Secretary]
File Edit View Go Bookmarks Options Directory Help
Add a Daily Planner entry for March 27, 1995
Date: 27-1995-3 Time: 3:30 am
Name: --- Submit Entry --- Clear Entry
Notes:
Automatically repeat this message every:
Never Mon-Fri Sat-Sun Day Week Month Year
Use the name area to enter a persons or company name, or an item to remember. Use the notes field to enter information about the appointment.

Fig. 14.6
The Virtual Secretary appointment schedule screen appears for a single entry. Note that users can edit and delete their entries.

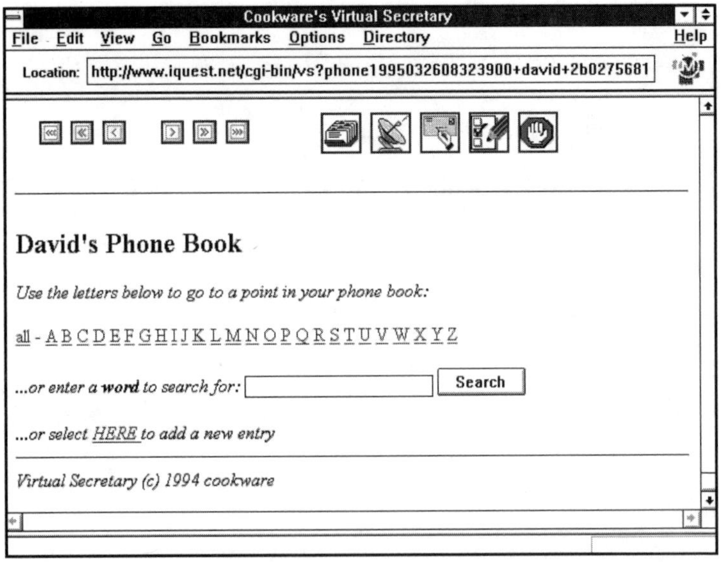
Cookware's Virtual Secretary
File Edit View Go Bookmarks Options Directory Help
Location: http://www.iquest.net/cgi-bin/vs?phone1995032608323900+david+2b0275681
David's Phone Book
Use the letters below to go to a point in your phone book:
all - A B C D E F G H I J K L M N O P Q R S T U V W X Y Z
...or enter a word to search for: Search
...or select HERE to add a new entry
Virtual Secretary (c) 1994 cookware

Fig. 14.7
Selecting the Address icon on the main page brings you to the Virtual Secretary address book screen.

Getting the idea? Now, suppose it takes us about two weeks to come up with an instant product idea and implement it. The idea may or may not take off. However, the investment is minimal, and the medium allows us to experiment heavily with the format, pricing, and structure. How many instant products can we come up with in a year? And if even one out of every 10 is successful, how much are we making? And if more than 10,000 users like it, what then?

Welcome to the wonderful world of instant products!

> **Note**
>
> With the current Internet population at more than 35 million and growing fast, the right idea can net an amazing amount of money with just a simple two-week investment of time.

Instant products can do much more than just make you money. For example, you can create an instant product that allows others to make money, as well as you. One such instant product is our Conference Room system.

Figure 14.8 shows the front page of Conference Room. This system allows you to become a moderator of your own talk room. Moderators are charged for their rooms, but may in turn charge their users anything they wish. This means that moderators can make money off the user.

◀ See "Appealing To the Largest Audience," p. 178

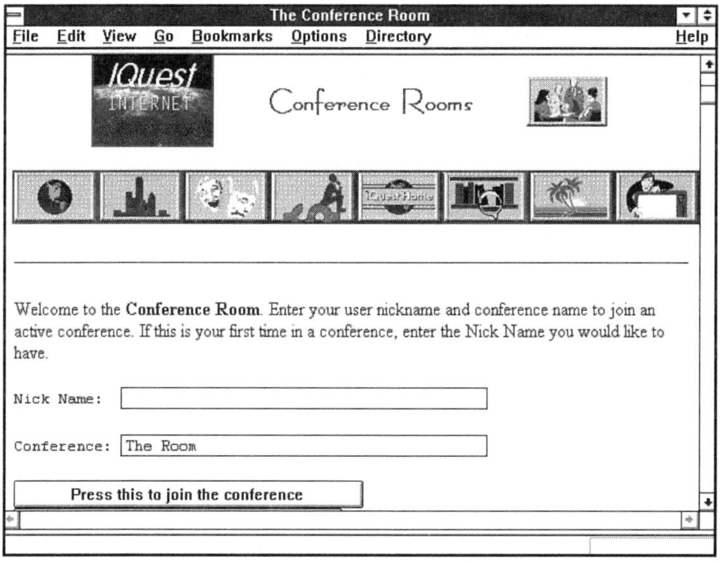

Fig. 14.8
A user arriving at The Conference Room site sees the first page.

Figure 14.9 shows the Moderators Lounge, which explains how to become a moderator and its benefits.

Fig. 14.9

Moderators can visit the Conference Room Moderators Lounge to find out the latest information that pertains to them.

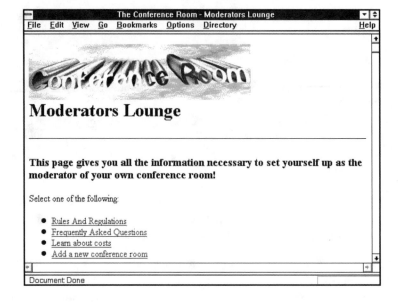

Figure 14.10 shows an actual Conference Room, with messages in it.

Fig. 14.10

The inside of the Conference Room welcomes the new user and provides helpful instructions for moving around.

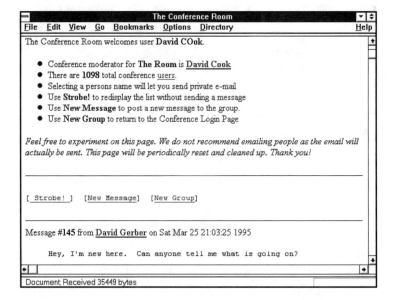

Because Conference Rooms were designed so that they could be private, it's possible for moderators to create a hidden conference room for only the people they want to invite in. What this then becomes is a subscription system within a subscription system. A user decides to become a moderator and subscribes to our service. The moderator then attracts other users who subscribe to the moderator's room. We bill the moderator for his or her usage, and the moderator bills the users. Everybody makes money and everybody receives a benefit.

Once you get the hang of subscription systems, it's hard to stop. For example, consider a classified ad subscription system. It would be simple to set up a page which accepts classified ads for $5 a month. The ads would be small, for example, no more than five lines. For an extra $10 a month, you could get a picture added to the advertisement. Again, with more than 35 million users, how many would find inexpensive worldwide classified advertising to be a benefit? Extending the classified ad idea to personals would be trivial, and so on and so forth...all the way to the bank!

Creating Instant Products

Now that you have an idea as to what instant products are, you probably are interested in creating your own instant product.

The first step in creating an instant product is figuring out what product and/ or service to offer.

As discussed earlier, there are many possibilities in creating instant products. Some of your ideas will probably revolve around your own company's products or services. Others may be completely novel. It really doesn't matter. In fact, the only thing that does matter is that other users will find it both affordable and useful.

With this in mind, you should attempt to create an instant product that you feel the Internet population would benefit from.

> **Note**
>
> This is the one area of this book where we will not help you, as any ideas we have we would rather implement ourselves (considering the potential worth of each idea of this nature).

Once you have identified your service or product, you should begin the implementation. Almost all instant products will involve some form of subscription system. This is required in order to keep people from using your system if they are not paying for the service. Therefore, one of the first jobs will be to design and create the subscription system.

Secondly, there will most likely be some form of cash handler, because people will not only be joining your system, but may also be purchasing items within your system.

Finally, there must be some mechanism by which the product or service is dispensed to the user. You can dispense it in the form of e-mail, WWW pages, postal mail, or any other mechanism that you care to dream up.

Self-Managing Products and Services

As you probably suspect, instant product systems are usually more complex in design and capability than subscription systems. One reason for this is that because you are going for quantity (of users), you want to minimize your support and user interface requirements. Ideally, the service should run itself with little thought from you, including billing! All you should do is occasional maintenance and driving once a month to deposit the checks in your bank account.

In order to realize this dream, one of the primary goals of an instant product is to make it self-managing. A self-managing product is one which, after it is created, runs itself with minimal human intervention.

Subscription systems themselves tend to be self-running. They handle registering users and managing the systems. However, making an instant product self-running requires a little more effort. To see why, refer back to the classified ad example.

In the classified ad system, you have a design where anyone on the WWW can come in and browse classified ads. No subscription system is required for that effort.

However, in order to post an ad, the user must subscribe. The user does so through a page which displays a form asking for billing information as well as desired payment mechanism. It also accepts at that time the user's classified ad.

Once the form is submitted by the user, it goes to the server where it is analyzed. Incorrect forms are sent back to the user for correction. Correct forms are entered into a user database, and the classified ad is entered into the ad database.

Since ads are only allowed in the system for a set period of time before further payment is required, the instant product should also take care of sending e-mail to subscribers to let them know their ad is about to expire. The same system can accept e-mail back from users indicating whether or not to keep the page and how further billing is to be accomplished (this information can alternatively be taken via the WWW).

Finally, the same system should be capable of generating a report on demand of the system's activity for a daily or monthly basis. This allows you to track the activity as well as assure yourself that billing is operating correctly and that people are not taking undue advantage of your service.

Note

Well-designed self-running systems should include report generation capabilities, which allow you to monitor the health and growth of your system without having to actually deal with the data or day-to-day operations.

All of this indicates a fairly complex and integrated system, which means that instant products—and especially self-managing instant products—cost more than a simple subscription system to create.

However, the return on your investment for an instant product should be fairly quick, as the creation costs are most certainly one-time and up-front (and if they are not for an instant product, you have picked the wrong contractor!).

We alluded earlier that an instant product takes only about two weeks to put together. The actual time it will take to create a particular product varies, depending on the complexity of the service being provided. However, the meat and potatoes of the job—basically that of the subscription system, cash system, tracking system, billing system, and reporting system—are all doable within a fairly short period of time. The actual functionality of the product you are dispensing will, of course, be the one factor which we cannot predict.

To help illustrate this, consider the functionality of the classified ad project.

Suppose you create an instant product which allows people to submit text and simple instructions, and have them arrive next-day mail as beautifully constructed business slides. You would give people overnight production of charts, graphics, and other slide visuals—certain to be a popular item among many people. Such a system would be much more complex in design than the simple example of the classified ad system. However, upon examination, you notice that most of the components are identical. Both systems have fairly identical subscription systems, billing systems, reporting systems, and tracking systems.

III

Products and Services

Where the two systems differ is in functionality. The classified ad system merely needs to add the text copy to a database, which is a fairly easy and straightforward task. The slide production system, on the other hand, needs to take text; figure out proper orientation, sizing, font information, backgrounds, colors, shadows, graphics, and many other factors; and produce high-quality visuals. You need to invest a huge amount of time and coding to make the entire system run flawlessly.

So, where both systems contain basically the same components, except for functionality, you can expect that the slide system will cost much more than the ad system, due to its complexity.

The bottom line here is that, assuming your idea is sound and your price is right, instant products are a very good way to create, market, and sell a service. The return on investment can be both staggering as well as quick.

Virtual Shopping Systems

A virtual shopping system is shopping in the 21st century. It combines the best of catalog shopping with television shopping. Users can access the products they're interested in without having to wade through pages and pages of catalogs and without having to listen to idiotic TV spiels while they wait for the one product they want to finally be featured.

Virtual shopping systems offer users the ability to shop with unprecedented convenience. Whereas many current systems require the user to jot down a product number or order items separately, virtual shopping systems are integrated and make purchasing items as easy as simply pointing at them.

This section explores the different types of shopping systems and their pros and cons, as well as implementation considerations.

What Are Virtual Shopping Systems?

◀ See "Membership Systems," p. 284

Virtual shopping systems combine membership systems with simple product selection, ordering, and purchasing systems. This section shows in detail how such systems are created.

To help you understand what virtual shopping systems are, consider a music store which sells CDs. Suppose that this particular store has more than 10,000 titles. How do you effectively sell these titles in such a way that the user is encouraged to purchase? How do you ensure that the act of purchasing itself is just as easy when selecting one product as it is when the user selects 100 products?

You can imagine that the solution contains a membership system, since it reduces the number of times the user needs to enter items such as credit card numbers and shipping addresses. However, membership systems simply provide the convenience for us to know the user's identity and billing information. They do very little to help in the selection of products.

Going back to the CD store example, you can imagine that the store could list its titles in pages by categories. Users could select the category they want and would then be taken to a page containing the titles, product numbers, and short descriptions of the CDs.

At the simplest, you could have users jot down on paper the product number they were interested in. When users are finished, they could go to a form where the membership system accepts their membership ID and product numbers, and the order is placed. This would certainly work and would require nothing more than a membership system that could take an order form.

However, this mechanism puts the burden of purchase on the user. You can easily imagine that, after jotting down a few products, users might become inconvenienced. If you want users to purchase more, you must make the purchase mechanism simpler.

> **Note**
>
> The idea of a virtual shopping system is to make the job of picking products as painless as possible. In essence, we want the user to do no more than simply point to a picture or word to purchase the item.

For example, a small picture of a person holding a stack of CDs could serve as a purchase icon. Placed next to each item, users can simply click the icon to add the item to their shopping cart. The item then appears in their cart. Users go on, pointing to items they want to purchase, which are automatically placed in their cart. Click, click, click...

When the users are ready to purchase, they simply go to their shopping cart and complete the membership information to complete the purchase.

This mechanism makes it easy on users, who are actually encouraged to purchase more. They can place items in the cart even if they are unsure about them, and can decide later if they want to purchase them while shopping for more products.

III

Tip
The shopping cart is usually found at the bottom or top of the page or available by selecting a link at the bottom or top of the page.

Products and Services

Shopping systems of this nature can be designed to span store boundaries, allowing users to enter virtual malls with many shops, and browse and select items in each shop. Users would pay only when they left the mall, making it truly one-stop shopping with the most convenience.

Databases and Virtual Shopping Systems

Before you learn methods for implementing virtual shopping systems, you should examine alternatives in packaging the data. Using the CD store example in the last section, consider again the 10,000 titles.

We already mentioned that one design could consist of a page containing all categories, which then led to pages that contained all the information for the CDs under that category.

You can imagine that each category of CD would contain perhaps 1,000 titles with short descriptions. You could easily split each category into 10 pages of 100 titles. This wouldn't be too bad for the user to wade through.

However, upon reflection, this is probably not a good way to organize 10,000 products. And what if your store has 100,000 products? Even without the 10,000 product example, you can imagine that a page with 100 titles on it will not only take time for the user to download, but it will also take time for the user to read. Furthermore, users are perhaps only interested in one or two of the artists or CDs in the entire list, or perhaps the CD they are interested in is in one of the other 10 pages of 100 titles under this category.

What happens to your throughput bill while users are trying to find their CD? Each page is very long, and if you subdivide your pages to make them shorter, users are required to load more pages to find the item they are interested in.

You can see that normal WWW page design breaks down in systems that have huge numbers of products. It would be easier if you had a mechanism that enabled users to narrow their choices very quickly, say within a page or two. You would also like to make each page that comes up fairly short, so that data throughput is minimized both for the user as well as for your Internet bill.

Luckily, a fantastic solution is available. Consider a situation where users can select categories by selecting check boxes on a form or from a forms scroll list. Consider also that users can type one or more words into a form. When users submit the form, a database is searched for any items which satisfy the users' category picks and text search strings.

The next page that is shown to the user consists of a line per item that matched the user's request. Each line is a short description about the particular product that matched the search. The user can then easily scan this list and identify the product or products they want. Selecting the desired subject line returns to the user a page describing the product.

It should be fairly obvious that this mechanism is much more efficient at handling huge quantities of products than a linear page design. Instead of having to go through hundreds of pages at great throughput, users can go directly to any desired product within three pages.

> **Note**
>
> One way to look at a database/virtual shopping cart design is to view it as a traditional product catalog. The database takes the role of the catalog index and page numbers, and the shopping cart takes the role of the order form and delivery mechanism.

> **Note**
>
> Databases can effectively present huge quantities of data to a user with a minimum of throughput and searching. Efficient database designs allow users to zero in on needed data within three pages.

There are many other advantages to database designs:

- *Space*. Consider the amount of room you could devote to the CD title on the linear page system first described. In that system, up to 100 titles were on a single page, thus the amount of room you could devote to them would be limited by necessity of throughput and user patience.

- *Advertising*. On the other hand, the database design always narrows the users down quickly to a single page which describes the product they want to see. In this case, you have a whole page to a single product. This is enough room for entire explanations of great detail, pictures, imbedded forms, audio, movies, or anything else you want to put in it.

- *Ease of use*. By allowing users to search your database using any criteria, they can easily find products that relate only to them. This keeps you from having to place products with broad uses into categories where users might not find them.

In other words, databases can help you not only reduce your throughput, but also increase your advertising potential and product exposure.

Databases can easily be integrated into virtual shopping systems. The information returned by the database can either exist in HTML format or can be formatted on-the-fly by the database engine itself. Because of this, it is easy to scan the document for product information and imbed a link to drop the item into the shopping cart. This means that as users search for products, they can instantly point, click, and purchase the product.

Figure 14.11 shows an example of a product database. The product is the Online Career Center, a job search service where users can type criteria and have the software return jobs that match the criteria. The first page shows the form which allows you to enter your criteria into the database.

Fig. 14.11
The user has typed a query and is ready to submit it.

Figure 14.12 shows the results of submitting the query string shown in figure 14.11. The database has found more than one item which matched the criteria, and provided a listing of subjects for the user to examine.

Figure 14.13 shows the result of picking one of the items from the list shown in figure 14.12.

Database designs, integrated with virtual shopping systems, need not be limited to purchase designs. The same systems can easily dispense pamphlets, booklets, sales literature, or any other type of free and categorizable data.

In other words, whether or not you accept cash for your product, databases make a good solution for dispensing hundreds or thousands of items. When coupled with virtual shopping systems, a method of product choosing and eventual ordering/delivery is available, giving a complete shopping system.

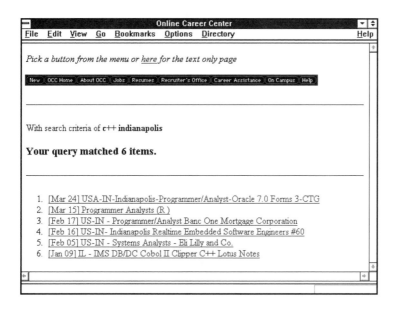

Fig. 14.12
After the user fills out and submits the query shown in figure 14.11, these results are sent back to the user.

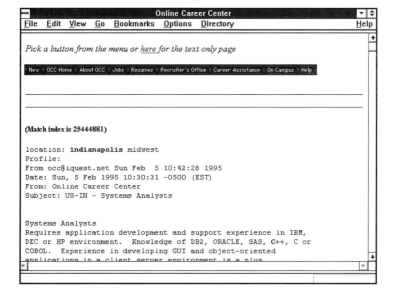

Fig. 14.13
The document is retrieved and displayed for the user to examine.

Implementing Virtual Shopping Systems

When implementing a virtual shopping system, one of the first questions to answer is, "When do I ask users for their membership information?"

You have two choices:

- You can let users come into your shop, browse and pick items to their heart's content. In this case, you are probably dispensing information about a product, such as descriptions and pictures. When users are ready to purchase, they then provide their membership information or become a member if they are not already. If users leave without paying, no products are shipped and no harm is done because you are only dispensing information.

- In some cases the information you are dispensing might be the product itself. For example, if you are allowing users to retrieve client reports over the Internet for a fee, you will not want to let them have the report before paying. In this case, you will want to take the membership information up front.

> **Note**
>
> Unless your product is being dispensed as information over the Internet, having users pay when they leave is the more preferable choice. It's the most convenient method for users.

Many times users may not expect to buy anything, but purchase on impulse when something unexpected strikes their fancy. If you require them to be a member before they can put the item in their virtual cart, you are giving them plenty of time to reconsider (as they fill out your membership form).

Instead, you would prefer that as soon as the impulse hits users, they have a nice big button to click to instantly put the product in their cart. Once the item is in the cart, they will naturally begin to develop an attachment for the product and it will emotionally be harder for the user to not buy the product.

Regardless of where you take the membership information, one of the harder things to do in a virtual shopping system is to track the items in users' carts as they shop. You might have tens of thousands, or even millions, of users over the period of a year. Many users may be online at one time and may browse and place items in their cart, but might not actually buy. Users might get up in the middle of their shopping, turn off the computer, and leave.

Likewise, users might have several shopping carts open to you at one time, each on a different window or terminal.

First, if you attempt to keep track of the users' orders by remembering the users' shopping cart items, you must either have the membership information up front or assign them a temporary membership ID until they purchase. In this case, when users first join, they are assigned a number which travels with them in each page they get after that. As users pick items, they are placed in a file referenced by the users' temporary numbers. From that file the contents of the cart can be created, on the fly, by the shopping cart software.

There are many problems with this scheme. However, the majority of shopping systems implement a similar, if not identical mechanism; it is one of the easier implementations. One of the problems that crop up under this scheme is what to do with users who simply get up and go away. You cannot tell they have left unless you remember the time of their last request. You then have to periodically scan all the requests that you know about and delete the ones which are older than a certain set time period.

Caution

This system is obviously filled with problems. It gets even worse if your site is popular, with tens of thousands of simultaneous users. With a significant number of them coming and going abruptly, you will quickly have a huge file system of remembered orders. If you set the cleanup period too short, users who get up to grab a snack from the kitchen may return to find you have timed out their order. If the time period is too long, you might not have enough disk space to handle all the temporary orders.

Another factor to consider is users who want to continue their shopping at a later date. You either must have a mechanism by which those users can specify to hold onto the data, whereby they can return to the order later by entering their temporary number. You could also simply prohibit them from shopping after a certain time limit. If you do let them specify to hold onto the order for continued shopping, what do you do with the users who never return?

Even though the majority of shopping systems handle their transactions as described, dipping in and around some of the problems outlined, there is a better, though far more complex method.

The alternative is amazingly devoid of problems, but can be extremely difficult to engineer. However, there are benefits to the alternative system:

■ Users are never tracked because they don't keep their information locally in a file; thus there is never anything to clean up.

Tip
In this type of design, the pages sent back to the user are encoded with the current shopping cart items. In this way, the pages themselves act as the user's own state.

■ Since users are not really tracked, there is no time limit placed on them for finishing the shopping. Not only can the user continue sessions days, weeks, or years later, but also you do not need to do anything to make it happen. Users can simply drop their session, at any time, into their browsers' hotlists and have it instantly returned when retrieved at any other time. In this case, the users' own hotlists are being used to store the items.

> **Note**
>
> The reason that this method is so complex is that it requires a lot of care and understanding of the entire HTTP and HTML process to handle all the possibilities that can crop up in such a design. Because pages hold the data and must relay the data back to the server on subsequent calls, the pages must be modified uniquely for each user. The engine that does this is extremely complex because it must simulate the entire HTTP protocol, as well as act in some very non-HTTP ways in order to fool both the browser and server into holding the appropriate information.

Unfortunately, a detailed description of this design is beyond the technical level of this book. However, within this book are many examples of systems which we have created that use this design, such as the Conference Room pictures in figures 14.8 and 14.9, the Virtual Secretary pictures in figures 14.4 through 14.7, and the Virtual Shopping Cart in Chapter 12. All these provide user tracking by keeping the users' current status, either in part or totally, in the pages returned to the users.

◀ See "Membership Systems," p. 284

Because of the high level of difficulty in creating stateless shopping systems, most designers opt for creating the slightly more restricted systems, and in general do a fairly good job of it. The resulting systems can usually handle the needed number of simultaneous users, and handle user tracking as well as order entry without too much trouble and with only some additional maintenance and administration.

If you are designing your own shopping system, you may indeed decide that this route is the most cost-effective for your needs. However, if you are contracting out a shopping system, you may want to request the alternative design which can reduce both your system requirements and administrative requirements. Certainly getting a bid for both types would allow you to determine which would be best for your company.

Note

You are probably wondering how much you should expect to pay if you hire someone to design your shopping system. It depends totally on the requirements of the system. We have off-the-shelf solutions here which go for around $9,500 but a custom-designed solution may be much more. We have bid custom-designed solutions as high as $2 million for a single design, and as low as $1,000 dollars—a very wide range.

As time goes on, more and more companies will begin to offer prepackaged virtual-shopping-cart-style solutions. As this happens, you will have more and more choices for implementation with less need for custom-designed solutions.

Pros and Cons of Virtual Shopping Systems

Since virtual shopping systems consist of membership systems, order entry systems, and often product databases, they can be more costly to create than simple form systems. In fact, the cost can be quite dramatic.

In general, a simple form-based order system will only cost as much as it takes to create the form. For example, an average price for a page with information and a form would be around $120 to $200. Getting the form routed to you as e-mail by subscribing to a service may cost a minimal monthly fee. In this case, users are expected to jot down the product numbers they are interested in; you are required to check and clear the order by hand.

Alternatively, designing a membership system requires a membership database, as well as the ability to check the accuracy of orders, route orders via e-mail or some other mechanism, select products, and track products in some manner, and potentially, the requirement to interface to a product database.

Full shopping systems, while more expensive than the simple form route, do offer significant benefits as mentioned earlier, and are not by any means unaffordable to larger companies. The primary benefit, besides added ease-of-use and satisfaction for users, is its automated nature, which greatly frees you from doing any administration beyond perhaps a monthly checkup, and of course, fulfilling all the orders.

Note

Full shopping system designs are more expensive than simple form-based solutions; however, they offer significant advantages which make them good alternatives.

III

Products and Services

As we stated earlier in this chapter, however, automatic shopping solutions are becoming more and more commonplace as more businesses are demanding integrated shopping solutions. Not only are prepackaged systems now available, but also systems which allow you to use them without having to purchase custom code, and in some cases, do not even require you to have your own server.

Finally, you should not think yourself limited to only the very simple or the very complex. Virtual shopping systems can embody many mix-and-match flavors, each offering strengths and weaknesses. When shopping for your system, keep in mind your basic requirements and find the system that most closely matches what you have in mind.

From Here...

This chapter covered the high-technology areas of the WWW. Instant products has shown an unlimited method for creating money with just a little ingenuity. Subscription systems give a path for implementing both virtual shopping carts as well as instant products. Virtual shopping carts provide ease of use for the user, as well as administrative and throughput benefits.

From here, refer to the following chapters:

- Chapter 11, "Order Taking and the Net," provides various ways to take orders from Internet customers.

- Chapter 12, "Methods for Collecting Cash," offers information about membership systems which accept money from users.

- Chapter 15, "Acquiring Demographics About Your Users," teaches you how to gather important demographic information about your customers.

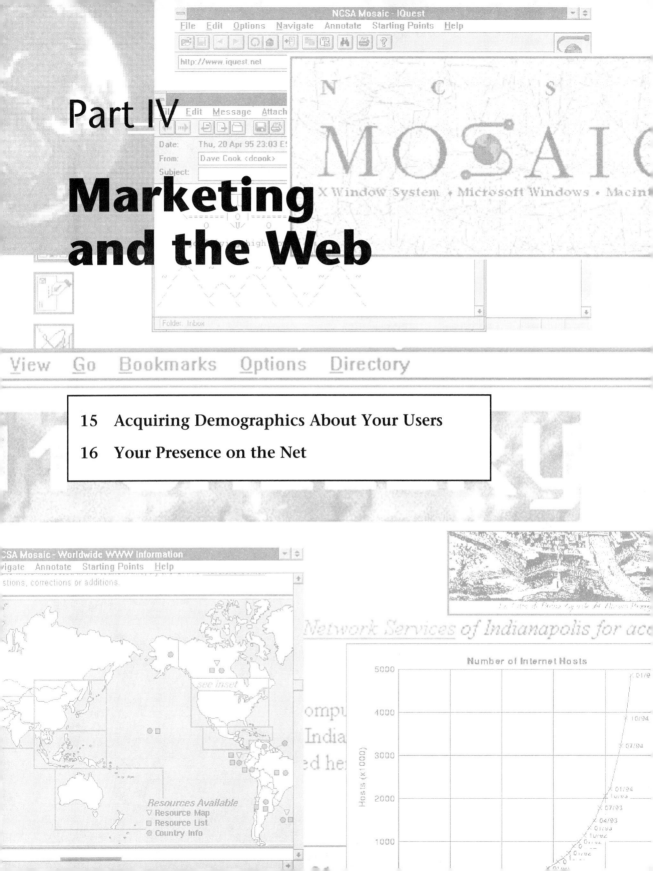

Part IV

Marketing and the Web

Chapter 15

Acquiring Demographics About Your Users

On the World Wide Web, it's pretty easy to get people to come to your site. Simply advertising your site in the many lists and robots will guarantee you a steady stream of interested people. However, of those who visit you, what percentage come back and what percentage actually purchase? This information would be very useful because it would act as a measure of how effective your site really is.

Demographics are one of the most important side benefits of the WWW. Demographics allow you to see how effective your advertising is, and also allow you to see which pages in your site are the most popular so you can adjust your site accordingly. Demographics also allow you to adjust your Net strategy to get the most impact for your advertising dollar.

Of course, if your Web site is a membership system or uses logins, you probably have a lot of the demographic statistics you will need. But the average Web site would benefit from knowing information like how many people are visiting your site at what times of the day, and what pages are most popular.

Of course you could just ask people for some of that information, but not everyone will fill out your forms; others may even try to feed you false information. You can, however, gain access to the type of information mentioned earlier without having to bother your users for it. More personal information can only be gained by asking the users to supply you with it.

In this chapter, you learn about

- Current built-in HTTP features that allow you to capture demographic information

- Other methods of capturing user access information such as page counting and sticky page tracking

- Special uses of standard mechanisms like forms and e-mail

- Tips for getting user information from forms and buttons

The HTTPD Log

One of the easiest ways to get statistics is to take them from the HTTPD log. The WWW server creates log files which record every access of every piece of data which comes in through the Internet, to provide information on such topics as security, demographics, and debugging. If you have access to the log, you have access to extremely detailed information concerning your site and how people are using it. The following sections explore the format of the HTTPD log and look at various demographic uses of it.

The HTTPD Log File Format

The format of the log file depends on which server you are running. However, the content of the log file is fairly consistent. As an example, we'll show you the format for the CERN server. It is a popular server and is the one we are most familiar with.

Each and every user that comes into the server has a record of his or her access stored in a log file. The log files record a single record (or line) for each access that is made. To understand what an *access* is, consider a page with text and three images. When the browser goes to fetch the page, here is how it works:

1. The first access brings the text of the pages across.

2. The second access brings the first image over.

3. The third access brings the second image over.

4. The fourth access brings the third image over.

Therefore, to completely load this example document, the browser makes four accesses of the server, and the server enters four records into the log file.

The CERN server logs the following information:

■ The domain name that the user came in on

■ The date (day, month, year) of the access

■ The time (hour, minute, second) of the access

■ The server command (GET, POST, or others)

■ The URL of the access

■ The return status

■ The exact number of bytes transmitted

As each access comes into the server, it is appended to the log with all the information listed here being supplied.

> **Note**
>
> Additionally, the log can be made to record the user's login name, if the user's machine allows reporting of that information. Most systems on the Internet do not allow recording of this information because of potential security holes in that type of request.

▶ See "How To Determine Whether Security Has Been Breached," p. 424

Look at what this information really tells you:

■ The domain name will either be the IP address or the actual name of the machine that the remote user is on when the request comes in. In the case of situations where the user is abusing your system, this is the one piece of information that you would use to help catch the user.

■ The date and time show the exact moment the user's request came into the system, and is recorded using the server's current time information (not the time and date where the user is).

■ The server command can be ignored for the purposes of demographics, as it serves only to instruct the server how the data is to be fetched.

■ The return status indicates the result of the request. It is a number which indicates an error or success status. The normal value for a valid response is 200, which means that the document was retrieved and returned.

Tip

The URL contains the actual location of the file that was retrieved. This lets you know where the user went and what the user asked for. It's useful not only for demographics, but also for billing.

- The exact number of bytes transmitted specifies exactly how many bytes were transmitted over the Internet to the requesting user.

Getting Access To the Log

If you are managing your own server site, you have total access to the log. However, if you are hosting your pages at a Web provider's site, the provider manages and maintains the log.

A good provider will not allow just anyone to access the log. In fact, a good provider should allow no one to access the log. There are two good reasons for this:

- The log contains information not only on the success of your site, but also the success of other sites. Allowing people to analyze the log themselves would give them access to the entire customer base at that provider site.

- Allowing people to poke around at the log could allow people to accidentally corrupt the log.

> **Note**
>
> Another problem with the log file is that it is often unmanageably big. We clean out our log file on the first of each month, so we start with an empty log file each month. By the end of the month, we usually have a couple of hundred megabytes of information in the log.
>
> We used to provide a program which allowed users to read the log anytime they desired and would display their complete page statistics. The program proved, unfortunately, to be extremely popular. People were checking their statistics all the time, which meant that a couple of hundred megabytes of data were being scanned on a constant basis. This activity crippled the machine, and we had to back off our service to generating the statistics every night and providing them to the user in HTML form the next morning.

Good providers will work with you to get you the information you need. Most providers realize the importance of needing to see how effective your site is, and analyzing the log is one of the best ways to do it.

Providers can perform log statistics for you in a variety of methods. First, as we already mentioned, a provider might give you an interactive program which would scan the log file and print out statistics whenever you requested it. You could do this only if the log file is relatively small or if the provider clears it out daily.

Another method of getting log information to you is to run—like we do—a program once a day that generates a document which is given to users. Users can access the document whenever and as often as they like without touching the log file or impacting the system performance.

A third method of getting the log information is to run the log program once a month and give users a formatted document of their monthly performance.

Finally, one of the simplest methods is to simply extract their log entries once a month and give them that file.

Caution

You will want to avoid getting a log file that is simply too big to use or that takes way too long to examine and analyze to be useful.

Using the Log File To Count Users

The log file, or log statistics, that is given to you by your provider can be used to determine the number of unique users coming into your site. Since each entry is stamped with the server's date and time, and domain name of the user, you can pretty much see who is going where and doing what.

One mistake made by many people is to count accesses the same as users. As we indicated at the beginning of this chapter, accesses handle everything from text to images; therefore, a single user requesting a single document might actually make several accesses as both the document and images are retrieved.

If you have an average of nine images in a page, there will be a average of 10 accesses per document downloaded (one for the document and nine for the images). Therefore, if you record 3,000 accesses in a day, you had approximately 300 users (3,000 accesses at 10 accesses per document equals 300 documents).

This number in itself is a good approximation of your users. However, some users may have come into your site more than once. It would be useful to know how many unique users you had in your site.

Unfortunately, this number is a bit more difficult to ascertain because there is no accurate way to acquire the user name of a user. Because you only get a domain name for the user, you cannot actually see who the individual users are.

Suppose that you run an art gallery on the Web. You are interested in the number of unique users coming into your site. However, on a particular day, an art class of 35 students from France all surfed your pages as a part of class. In this case, you get hundreds of simultaneous accesses from the same domain name. It becomes very difficult to try to figure out unique entries based on the time and files retrieved. The best thing you can do, using the log, is to simply estimate the number of users as we did earlier.

Another indication of the number of unique users is to count the number of users who accessed your home page and not your secondary pages. Using this method, you will receive a more accurate count of unique users than estimating your accesses per page, because pages may vary quite a bit between the number of accesses on each page. However, this method is still not totally foolproof because a single user may have come into your home page more than once, or a user may have skipped your home page by accessing one of your inside pages from their hotlist.

> **Note**
>
> Remember that most browsers cache pages during a session. Users who enter your site and move forward through your pages and then move backwards do not actually load the pages again as they move backwards, but instead access them from their cache. This helps to keep the unique user count a little more accurate because it reduces the number times the same user pulls the same page.

Using the Log File To Improve Your Pages

Another good use of the log files is to improve your pages. By examining what pages have been accessed and at what frequency, you can begin to build a profile of how users access and use your WWW site.

Tip
When rearranging your site, make major changes all at once or small changes occasionally. Making big changes over long periods of time discourages users from using your site because they always have to relearn it.

For example, you might discover that a page that highlights a new product is getting very low traffic compared to your other pages. This would be a good indication that you might move the page around so that it is in a more high-profile spot. Or maybe you need to highlight the link to that page in some way.

Because you get the ability to have near-instant demographics of your site, you can shift your pages around on a daily basis until you establish the optimum layout.

You should make sure to examine the statistics for more than a single day before making any decisions on changing your pages. The profile of access for a week can be very different each day to the next. This profile is also highly dependent on the product or services you are offering.

For example, we have noted that art galleries tend to get a low amount of visitors on Mondays. We attribute this to the fact that Mondays are often stressful and hectic as people return to work after a weekend. On the other hand, we have noted that job employment and search agencies have higher than average accesses on Mondays. We attribute that to exactly the same reason why the art gallery attendance is low.

Needless to say, Fridays seem to be great for art galleries (and so are Wednesdays, surprisingly enough), whereas Fridays are a bit slower for employment agencies on the Web (because people are looking forward to their weekends).

Determining your user access profile on both a weekly and monthly basis is a very good step to undertake before you try to reorganize the pages within your WWW site for the following reasons:

- It gives you an indication as to when the best time is to make changes. Obviously, you should strive to change during your low-traffic time and not in the middle of your high-traffic time.

- You can get an average access for each page. You might find that on one day, for whatever reason, absolutely no one went into a particular page, but when averaged out over the month, the page enjoyed the same traffic as the rest of your site. By taking an average over a period of time, you can smooth out the small variations that are bound to exist. This will help you make more accurate changes to your pages.

- Examining the log also lets you determine how many users are looking at your pages with graphics turned off. You can tell this because a domain only shows accesses to HTML pages, and does not show accesses to any other types of links.

> **Note**
>
> Make sure you examine more than what pages are being visited. If you have sounds, movies, or pop-up images, these accesses appear as well. If any of these aren't being accessed (which would be rare because sound files and visuals tend to be popular), you can remove the files and the links to them. There is no reason to pay for storage on files or throughput on links that no one is taking.

Tip

If you rearrange your material or delete some of it, make sure to update or delete the links pointing to the data. It's very annoying (not to mention unprofessional) to have links that go nowhere.

It is important to notice if users are accessing images on the first page they get to, but are then not accessing images on any other page they go to. This may indicate that users felt your site was too expensive graphically (for example, they didn't feel like spending the time waiting for big images to be loaded) and turned off graphics for the rest of your pages. If enough users are doing this at your site, you may want to consider reducing the size and complexity of your graphics.

Other Methods for Collecting Demographics

While the HTTP log offers you some of the best and most accurate demographics possible, there are other methods of tracking users and collecting demographics. The following sections outline some of these other techniques.

Page Counters

A *page counter* is simply a number which increments each time the page is downloaded. Because each page can have its own counter, you can easily see how many times each page has been accessed. You probably have seen page counters on various pages throughout the Web. Figure 15.1 shows a site with a page counter on it.

Fig. 15.1

This page counter on the Rolling Stones page tells the user what caller number the user is. In this case, the user was caller number 405,662.

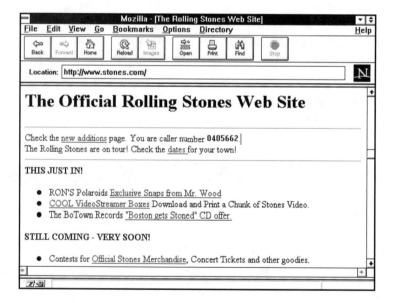

Page counters have another advantage: they tell users how many people visited the page before them and what user number they are (for example, You are user number 100,000). This technique can inform your users that you have a busy site; you can build a perceived value in their minds (you know, a million people can't be wrong).

If you recall from the previous sections, one of the drawbacks to analyzing the log files is that it is somewhat difficult to separate page accesses from all accesses in general. With page counters doing the job, it is much easier because a page counter counts only HTML pages.

Caution

It isn't possible to count pop-up images, sounds, movies, or any other type of download with the standard page counter mechanism.

Page counters involve some special programming, but shouldn't be too hard. Page counters may be implemented in one of two basic ways.

First, the page containing the counter can be unchanging, but can point to a GIF picture which contains the access count or user number. Modifications to the server can cause the picture to be regenerated each time the page is accessed. As the page is accessed, the GIF is regenerated with the proper number in it and sent back to the user as the page counter.

The second method is to access a cgi-bin program instead of a document. The cgi-bin program increments the page counter for a requested page and fetches the page from disk. The cgi-bin program then examines the page and inserts the proper count at some known point (designated by you) within the page and returns it to the user.

▶ See "How Forms Work: An Introduction To cgi-bin," p. 539

You may find cgi-bin programs that do page counting on the CERN and NCSA sites. These programs are already set up to help you incorporate page statistics directly into your HTML pages. However, these programs only help you if you are hosting your pages on your own server.

Note

NCSA maintains an FTP archive of cgi-bin public domain programs such as page counters. You can access this archive by pointing your browser to

ftp://ftp.ncsa.uiuc.edu/Web/httpd/Unix/ncsa_httpd/cgi/

If you are hosting your pages on a WWW provider site, you should contact your provider to see whether they have any page-counting capabilities. If they do, you can work with them to get it running.

If your provider does not have page counting, you might want to suggest its benefits and the sources for finding public domain page-counting programs.

Finally, our own GATE technology lets people access page-counting capabilities as well as other useful functions, and is available to anyone who does not have a server that will allow it. GATE can be seen at

http://www.iquest.net/cw/gate/extension.html

Sticky Pages

Sticky pages offer unprecedented capabilities to users of the Web. Through the use of sticky pages you can do the following:

- Keep your company logos at the top of users' pages regardless of where they go in the Net after visiting your site.

- Implement customized sticky menus which give user functionality throughout your site (such as shopping systems, databases, and more).

- Bring advertising to users, instead of making users go to the advertising.

- Track users no matter where they go after leaving your site.

Looking at this list, you might think that very few of those items have anything to do with demographics. However, the entire sticky page concept is itself an experiment in demographics gathering.

The basic concept works like this. A user arrives at your site. One of the pages accessed (usually the home page) is a sticky page. This means that portions of the page have been designed to attach to the user. As the user moves to the next page, the sticky portion of the previous page stays with the user. Even when the user leaves your site, the sticky portion of your page still stays with the user.

Users can drop their link into a hotlist and pull it out at any time, and your information will still be stuck there.

How do sticky pages help you with demographics? As long as users have some of your information stuck to them, you have the ability to find out where they are as they move from site to site. You can use this to develop databases of other URLs that are frequented by your users and develop user profiles, which you can use to tailor and change your site.

A sticky page can be overt, in that it can actually put information, like your logo, into the user's screen. Or a sticky page can be invisible, simply watching and recording without letting the user know that it is there.

> **Caution**
>
> You need to be careful when using sticky pages in this manner. Whether or not this behavior is ethical depends on its use; for example, using a sticky page to build a database of URLs might be okay.

You are probably wondering what the general user reaction is to sticky technology. Many users do not realize that they use similar technology all the time.

Virtual shopping carts, which allow users to purchase products by clicking the product and purchasing after all products that the users want have been collected, are forms of sticky pages. Even popular searchers such as Lycos, Webcrawler, and other robots and worms are types of sticky systems when they go off at night to collect more URLs. These sticky systems may not be following you when you leave their sites, but they are sticky nonetheless.

◀ See "Virtual Shopping Systems," p. 328

But this still does not answer what the public reaction to sticky pages is. In general, following others without their knowledge and placing your company information on top of other company information is probably not going to be met with a great deal of enthusiasm.

However, there is an advantage to sticky pages that will allow users to buy into the capabilities while allowing you to collect your demographics. To show this, consider the following example.

Suppose you have an area in your pages where users can customize a small menu. Users can pick up to seven functions that they want to have attached to the top of their screens. The seven functions could be selected from a list of 40 or more functions offering great variety. The list of 40 functions can contain things for businesspeople, students, children, lawyers, government people, and so on. A button represents each item that brings you to a useful Web service with a simple click.

For example, a businessperson might pick the following seven functions from the list of 40:

- Appointment scheduler
- Phone book

- 15-minute delayed stock quotes

- World news service

- E-mailer

- Link to What's New

- Link to Lycos

When the user is finished selecting the seven choices, the selected choices appear as nifty buttons across the top of the screen. No matter where the user goes on the Internet after that, those buttons stick to the user, giving him or her the advanced capabilities behind the buttons.

In return for this service, you can also place a small paragraph at the bottom of each page which contains one small advertisement for some site on the Web, along with a hyperlink (no graphics). No matter where users go, the menu is at the top and the small advertisement is at the bottom, with the actual content from the users' current site sitting in the middle.

For example, the user leaves your site and goes to the White House. At the top of the White House page would appear the nifty, custom menu bar and at the bottom of the White House page would be the one small advertisement. The White House page is not actually modified, only the content of what is returned to the user.

We can select the advertisement from a pool of random ads that we are paid to run for various companies. Because the ads are small and random, they are rather enjoyable, giving users something new and different to check out each page they go to, even if they have been there already.

They can touch their nifty buttons at the top and instantly get their stock quotes, news, or searching capability, providing them with very convenient functionality.

Will users accept the page with the small advertising at the bottom? Will they accept it without the advertising at the bottom? The answer is yes to both questions, and for users who want to be detached from the sticky page, you should offer a quick way to turn it off. Users should always be able to turn it off. Not being able to turn it off may invite the ire of your users.

Now for the demographics. We have presented a wonderful system for advertising. It has major advantages which the normal Web is without. For example, this is one of the first times on the Web that advertising comes to the user, not the other way around. Is that a good thing?

You can use sticky pages to hook users into your services because you can offer them value-added capabilities. In order to make sticky pages work, you must have a server to route the pages and maintain the sticky information. The server keeps track of the users' movements through the Internet, and is constantly aware of where they are (it needs to be because it needs to serve the sticky information to them).

You might point out that this would be an invasion of privacy. However, we do not know who the individual user is. The user is fairly anonymous, since only the domain name is known.

Note

If you are the only person on your domain—that is, you have your own domain name for your business or home—users can find out who you are if they have your domain name.

Demographics is not collected on the actual users but simply on the movements of browsers throughout the Net. We do not necessarily know that a user is moving from point A to point B, but rather that the user just happens to be now at point B. It's the same as saying that we know how many cars are in a particular city, without knowing who the drivers are or where the cars came from.

By collating the number of cars in each site, you can determine which sites are popular and which are not. You can begin to build profiles of what type of information users like to see on the Web. This type of information is invaluable because it is unsolicited and it shows trends. And since the users originated at your site, it shows trends of users that frequented your site. You can use this information to build your own databases of favorite sites for your users based on the likes and dislikes of the population at large, or use it internally to help tailor and improve your own Web site.

Note

Just as mailing lists are now sold, in the future there may be a market for Web demographic information. Because demographic information not only tells you where the user is (via the domain name) but also what is popular and what is not, we foresee a market for these statistics.

The majority of sticky pages do not track user movement off a server. Doing so involves very advanced technology and is a rather large drain on both bandwidth and computing resources. However, for the large company that wants to offer fantastic capabilities to its users, this mechanism offers advantages that are hard to come by any other way.

▶ See "Benefits of Networked Information Kiosks," p. 460

This mechanism also offers advantages in kiosk design, where you want to have certain buttons always available no matter where on the Web the user goes.

Finally, the virtual mall owner will also find this a useful capability. By attaching a sticky page to users when they enter your mall, they can travel freely from store to store with a virtual shopping cart. Your mall logo, nifty blurbs about other stores, and the ability to go back to the mall main door with the click of a button are also included in the sticky page. As the mall owner, you get demographics about how the users shop at the various stores. The individual store owners get the advantage of not having to modify their pages but still getting your sticky capabilities. And your users get an easy way to do their shopping.

Demographics Through E-Mail and Forms

This chapter has provided several methods for collecting data from logs and access statistics of your pages. However, there are other ways to collect demographics about your users. The following sections cover those uses.

Using Forms To Solicit Demographics

Forms have many uses for generating demographics. Most obvious is the fact that you can ask questions in a form, which a user fills out and submits to you. You can then collate the information and use it any way you like.

There are many types of demographics that you can solicit in this manner. You can ask questions about improving your site—whether it is too slow, does not provide enough graphics or too many graphics, is easy to use, or any other questions you care to ask that will help to make your site a better place.

You can also begin to collect demographics from your users concerning your products. Asking questions about the perceived uses, quality, needed functionality, and any other items can allow you to build a database of future direction.

Likewise, you can use forms to find out more about your users themselves. Requesting information such as level of education, career, family size, and other similar questions allows you to build generic user profiles. This in turn can better help you understand your clientele, letting you build better products and services.

You can also use forms to help you indicate where users are going on your pages. If you cannot run a page counter and your provider does not provide you with system log information, you can use this technique to help you gather some information about what your users find interesting and where they are going.

As you will find out in the Appendix, each element in a form (for example, TEXTAREA, RADIO buttons, and CHECKBOX) has a name associated with it that is used by the server to figure out what form data is what. To show how this works, suppose you have a form with two items, a text area for the user's name and one for the user's e-mail address. You might specify that the user's name goes to the server under the reference "full_name", while the user's e-mail address goes to "full_email". You can use this information because, in general, form remailing software hands you back those names when you receive the form the user has filled out.

For example, you might get the following e-mail sent to you via a form remailer shortly after a user fills out and submits a form:

```
Full_Name:     John Q. Public

Company:       XYZ Company

E_Mail:        John@baton.org

Comments:      Really liked your site but it's a bit slow.
```

As mentioned earlier, the names on the left were assigned in the form, and serve to identify the fields so that you (or your server software) can figure out what data is what.

How can you use that information to your benefit to see what pages are most interesting to what users? If you put a small form at the bottom of each page, simply asking for an e-mail address and providing a `Click here for more information` choice, you could use the form to do more than collect addresses for sending more product literature. For example, the number of people who submit the form to you will be a direct indication of the effectiveness of your pages.

Tip

By careful construction of your forms, you can use them to collect more data than just what the user types in.

▶ See "Adding Forms To Your Pages," p. 539

By making the name of each field unique for each page, you can tell what page users were on when they filled out the form. For example, your first page could use the fields 1_E_Mail and 1_send_info. Your second page could use the fields 2_E_Mail and 2_send_info, and so forth. When you receive e-mail from users, you know instantly what page they were on when they submitted the form.

Caution

You don't want to overload the user with too much information to enter, because that might limit the amount of forms they will want to submit. Asking for an e-mail address for more information, or asking a question such as

```
Click here if you thought this page was well-
organized, or click here if you thought it could
use improvement
```

should be all you need to do to make this work. The form would include only one or two buttons at the bottom of the page, making it far more likely that the user would use them.

While collecting this information, you might find that you never get input from a certain page. You can use this fact to determine that the page is simply not effective and you can take steps to improve it.

Note

If you do not have form handling capability on your server, you might want to look into the various form remailers commercially available, such as ours at

http://www.iquest.net/cw/web/forms4u.html

These kinds of services let you use forms and receive the output as e-mail for a low monthly fee.

Using E-Mail To Solicit Demographics

The e-mail system can be used to solicit information about your users beyond the use of forms mentioned in earlier sections.

As your business presence on the Web begins to grow, you will begin to re-ceive more and more general e-mail about your company. In our situation, about 70 percent of our new user requests come in via our forms; the other 30 percent come in directly from e-mail. These users may not have form ca-pability in their browsers, or may jot down our e-mail address or print our page to look at later. Then, when deciding to contact us, they simply send e-mail as opposed to bringing our forms up again.

When you receive e-mail routed to you from a form remailer, you do not get information about the user beyond the questions you asked in the form because the server is actually sending the e-mail, not the user.

> **Note**
>
> HTML has a mailto: feature which allows you to send e-mail directly from a WWW page without needing a form remailer or handler. While you can certainly use this mechanism to solicit information, it is not recommended as your only method because a large number of browsers do not handle that type of input, whereas almost all browsers handle forms.

However, when users e-mail you directly, you receive a wealth of information that you might not have otherwise received. This information is found in the mail header attached to the e-mail by their computer and your computer.

First, you receive information about the user's location. If a company field is present in the header, it contains the company name and, perhaps, address. If no address is given, the domain name of the user is always available. Typing **whois** for that name will identify the location of the server, which in general is usually fairly close (within a local phone call) to the user.

If you want the user's mailing address, a phone call to directory service for that metropolitan should give you the phone number. A call to that number will give you the address, because most businesses give their mailing address to anyone who asks. If you feel you need an excuse, just tell them that you would like to add them to your mailing list, and you need their mailing information.

> **Note**
>
> Information about the user's server location is useful because it gives you an indication of your penetration to a worldwide market. If you are primarily selling your products to the U.S. market but begin to see more and more e-mail routed from Europe and Asia, you probably need to think about expanding your other marketing efforts to include those demographics areas.

The other main benefit that you receive from e-mail over forms is a guaranteed user name and e-mail address. Nothing is more frustrating than getting a potential great lead who forgot to leave his or her e-mail address or left it incomplete. This doesn't happen in e-mail.

◀ See "Other Alternatives for Order Taking," p. 270

Listservers are also interesting tools for collecting demographics from users. Listservers hand out information automatically when contacted to do so via e-mail. A user might send a message to your listserver to send a packet of information. The listserver instantly responds with the requested package automatically via the e-mail system. The listserver can also at that time record the user's location and e-mail address.

Again, the user's e-mail request to the listserver can be used to generate a user profile which not only includes geographic demographics but also interest demographics (based on what the user requested from the listserver). Since listservers are highly dependent on the provider, contact your provider if you are interested in these capabilities to see what options are available for you.

From Here...

For the Web business, just as with any other business, customer demographics is an important key to implementing and running a successful business. You need this type of information to know who your customers are and what they need and/or expect. You can use this information to make sure you are reaching your target audience. You may even find out your audience isn't who you thought it was. It will influence how your World Wide Web site looks; what information, products or services you offer; and where and how you advertise your WWW site.

In the future, there will undoubtedly be developments which collect more user information in an unobtrusive manner. Until then, the best ways to do so are through HTTPD logs, page counters, sticky pages, forms, and e-mail.

Businesses who need extremely detailed and confirmable user demographics will want to implement a membership or login system where individuals are identifiable. Information important to your company—maybe the gender of the user or income level—can be confirmed.

From here, refer to the following chapters:

■ Chapter 3, "Why the Net is Good for Business," re-examines the broader concepts of the benefits of the Web to business.

■ Chapter 4, "Planning a Web Site," shows you how your demographics affect the design of your WWW pages.

- Chapter 12, "Methods for Collecting Cash," provides information on membership and subscription systems.

- Chapter 14, "Subscription Services, Virtual Malls, and Instant Products," teaches you how subscription services can be used to acquire demographics.

- Chapter 22, "The Future of the Net," shows you how the future of the Net will impact you.

IV

Marketing and the Web

Chapter 16

Your Presence on the Net

On the Web, as in everyday life, first impressions are important. Different types of businesses will find different ways of putting their best foot forward, depending on their target audience, field of business, and marketing strategies. Deciding early what sort of image you want to present on the Web will help your market penetration and awareness, as well as save you money in the planning and development stages of your site.

As you consider your presence on the Web, you may find yourself going back to Chapter 8, "Etiquette and the Net," for information on Net culture. You should make sure that the image you choose not only represents your company well, but also represents you well to the Net community. Keeping track of the meanings of certain words and phrases on the Internet will also help to make sure that what you are saying to your users is what you think you are saying.

In this chapter you learn

- Methods for generating the image you want for your company

- Components of good home page design

- How the stability of service reflects your presence

- How to make sure your company's image is the one you want

- The importance of being unique on the Net

- How to stay current with Web trends

Everyone Looks Good on the Net

"On the Net, nobody hassz to know you're a dog" and "On the Net, no one has to know you work in your garage" are two phrases that point out this aspect of the Web. They relate to the fact that much of the business conducted on the Web is conducted solely on the Web. Your customer or client never comes to your place of business. They never see you face to face.

While not working face to face does have some disadvantages, there are some real benefits from this sort of invisibility that every business should be aware of and consider using when applicable.

High Profile Invisibility

How can you be high profile if you are invisible? By *high profile invisibility*, we mean that while your WWW site is widely advertised and known, it acts similar to a mask. While you are busy being a dog or working in your garage, you can look to the outside world like a big company. We are not suggesting you become invisible to commit fraud. But realize that you can represent your company in a variety of ways and that presenting the same information in different formats can create very different opinions. It's up to you to present the information in the manner that is most beneficial to you.

For instance, in a background summary of your business, you could say, "We have been in business for two years," or "With years of experience." Basically, you are saying the same thing; one, however, makes you appear more established.

Tip
You can make your phone number appear as if it's part of a larger trunk system. Request from your phone company a number that ends in `00` or `000`. It may cost a little more, but it's worth it if you are trying to achieve a certain image.

This type of marketing strategy is very common, and most people will know that "years of experience" really means anything greater than one. If it's important to your customers exactly how many years of experience you have, they will ask. But in the meantime they have to contact you, and if they do, you have the perfect opportunity to make your pitch. Maybe after you've talked with a potential client and made them see how good you are, your "mere" two years of experience won't be so important.

You may decide to create a higher profile by maintaining more than one discrete site for your firm.

How To Make Invisibility Work for You

There are two aspects of invisibility you will want to use to make sure that your company presents an image that will attract customers:

- A site that is well-designed and complete.

- A site that is widely advertised.

The primary strategy for making invisibility work for you is to provide as professional and complete a site as possible. You basically have to ask yourself the following question: If you are presented with two sites from two competing companies, and one site has a single page with an access number and the other has customer support, FAQs, online ordering, "meet the staff" information, and links to other useful sites, which company's pages are you going to go to?

The answer you make will probably be based on your impression of the site, not the size of the company. The company with the small page may be unsure as to the market potential and may have only stepped into the Web to experiment. Even if the company is huge, it will still appear small on the Net.

Conversely, if you have only one employee—yourself—and you ship out of your garage, handle all the phone calls, but still have an impressive site, you appear on the Net as a substantial company.

This technique has worked well, even for ourselves. We are not a large company by any means; however, our Web presence is not only large, it is very complete and very professional. This presence has helped us not only attract large corporate accounts, but also helped reduce the amount of work we need to do by providing detailed answers to the many questions we receive daily. We have steadily reduced the amount of support and education we need to land a new account, and have increased our client base.

The second thing that you can do to have high profile invisibility is to place your site in as many lists, searchers, and malls as you possibly can. When people see you at every turn and in every mall, you again appear very large. People cannot help but notice you because you're everywhere.

Note

Remember, however, that your real company presence should mimic your virtual presence as much as possible. If you have an extremely professional site but you don't answer your phones until one in the afternoon, a sleepy "Hello" will undo most of the prestige your site has built for you.

The Pitfall of Invisibility

One definite pitfall of invisibility is what happens if you cross over the lines of legality when you create your Web presence. Declaring professional credentials, especially if they relate to law or medicine when you don't have them, can land you in jail. Other lesser misrepresentations can result in losing your Internet access or having your reputation on the Internet ruined.

The following are some guidelines to follow:

- The use of the term "years of experience" can mean more than one or it can mean 20, but the phrase "in business since 1913" means exactly that.

- Don't entice customers with fuzzy phrasing that might make them think you have credentials you don't. This includes college degrees and board or technical certification. Certain trades such as plumbers, electricians, and legal and medical personnel must be licensed even just to use the title. If you are a handyman who can do minor electrical repairs, that's how you should represent yourself. Calling yourself an electrician could get you in trouble.

- Don't promise what you can't deliver. In the case of selling a product, if you advertise that you have a product at a certain price and then don't have that product, it could be considered a "bait and switch scheme" which is illegal in every state we've ever lived in.

- Don't enter into agreements or set up your sites such that it might be considered *price fixing*. For example, if you have five Web sites for your office supply company, you might be contacted at more than one of your sites for competitive bids on stationery. Is it really a competitive bid if you are bidding against yourself? What if the customer goes to the trouble of contacting five different companies for bids and all five are your company? Be careful that you don't break any laws.

Your Home Page

◀ See "Home Page," p. 97

On the Web, your home page is your face to the world. Only on the Web, you have much greater control over how your face looks.

Making sure that you look your best on the Web involves the following:

- Use of good graphical design concepts.

- Proper attention paid to how your users will travel around in your site.

- Making sure your Web image matches your business image.

When designing your home page, you will use many tools to convey your image. Although the actual HTML code to implement these tools is contained in the Appendix, we discuss some of the terms here:

■ *Text.* Currently, some browsers allow end users to change their font style; this is only applicable to individual monitors. Text will appear in whatever style it is going to appear in (see exceptions that follow). However, text can be manipulated in terms of size, bold, or italic. The latest release of the Netscape Communications browser can even allow text to blink on and off, have different colors, or appear against a colored or textured background. Non-standard text can be created using fancy, graphic fonts and transparent GIFs or overwritten on top of other pictures.

■ *Graphics.* The current standards are GIF and JPEG. Each has its own advantages and disadvantages and are discussed in detail in the Appendix. Of more importance when designing home pages are invisible GIFs. (Other graphics such as buttons and icons are discussed separately later.) Invisible GIFs remove the square boundaries of your image by causing the background of your image to be transparent to the background of the browser. The result gives the impression that an image is floating over the browser, or embossed into the browser surface.

■ *Horizontal ruling lines.* These lines are offered in HTML programming which create a horizontal line across your page. Some people have created their own horizontal rulings in the form of inline images. They range from simple rainbow lines to a series of linked images that span the screen. The purpose of these lines is to create separation between material.

■ *Links.* Links allow you to send the users to a different page or different portion of your page. You can use links to guide your users through your material. Any object may be linked, including words, sentences, images, sound icons, and movie icons. Pointing to an image could bring up a bigger version of the image, a document describing the image, or a sound. The possibilities are limitless.

◄ See "Using Hyperlinks and Other References," p. 242

■ *Forms.* Forms contain fields that users can type into or pick from. When filled in and submitted, the information in the form is sent to a forms processing program. Many commercial services exist to help you take the output from forms and convert it to useful data, product orders, or messages.

► See "Adding Forms To Your Pages," p. 539

New advances in browser design even add to the ability to change pictures without the user having to ask for another picture. Server Push and Browser Pull, implemented in the Netscape Communications browser, allow documents, pictures, and sounds to be retrieved at preselected intervals. These capabilities allow pages to act as slide shows, slow animations, or one of many other motion effects.

Home Page Design

Many people may feel they don't have the artistic skill to design and create an attractive home page. If you have free access to a graphic artist or can afford one, you may want to pay the money to have the artist create artwork for your WWW site. However, you can follow these guidelines to design, create, and implement a first-rate Web page:

- Don't crowd too much information into one space. Break it up with titles and headings, horizontal lines, or simply blank space.

- Stick to one or two font sizes for your page. Rather than creating interest in your pages, lots of different font sizes actually makes for an awkward design. The viewer's eye is pulled in many directions at once, instead of flowing down your page.

- Make good use of color to create pages that are vibrant and eye-catching, but make sure that the colors don't clash. Sticking to one or two colors can avoid this problem. Using different shades of the same color can also be used effectively.

Fig. 16.1
This particular home page is aesthetically pleasing and shows some good design elements (**http:// www.artsci. wustl.edu/ ˜hussain/index- old.html**).

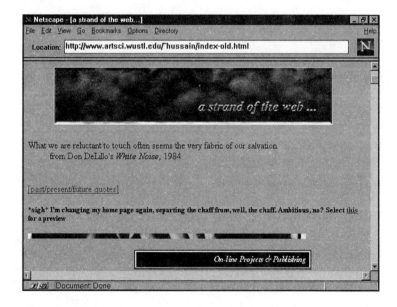

- Choose graphics that blend with the text style you've chosen, the colors you've chosen for any special text (via invisible GIFs), and the message and image you are trying to present.

- Make sure that your graphics are easily identifiable. If your viewer is looking at your page thinking, "What the heck is that?" you may not be making your best impression.

- Check your text for spelling and grammatical errors. Such errors are definitely unprofessional.

Also when designing your page, it can be helpful to have someone else's opinion. Get your secretary, boss, teenager, or anyone who will take the time to look at your page. A new pair of eyes can sometimes see what you have overlooked. It can also be a benefit if you get a wide variety of people to look at your page. A secretary might be good for picking up technical errors, but a high school or college student will be able to point out recent trends in slang that you might not be aware of. Get someone who doesn't use computers to see if it's easily understandable to people new to the Internet and WWW.

> **Note**
>
> When choosing people to proofread your page, try to find at least one that has a good eye for detail. This type of person will usually be best in picking out such things as spelling and grammatical errors and consistent use of font size for headings and subheadings.

Another very important factor is to try your page in different browsers and on different platforms. Sometimes, the way you write your HTML may work on most of the browsers, but fail on one or two. Making small changes in your HTML will make them work universally. For example, some browsers are less than forgiving when it comes to quotation marks which have been started and not stopped. These browsers will make serious mistakes when displaying pages with this error in it. Other browsers are smarter and ignore the quotation marks. These browsers can handle missing quotation marks.

> **Caution**
>
> Make sure to test your pages in multiple browsers. If you don't, you might not be aware of any mistakes until it is pointed out to you by a user.

Tip

Try to choose colors that are distinguishable by color-blind users.

IV

Marketing and the Web

Note

If you need people to help test your pages in a variety of browsers and platforms, try the IRC group **#www**. Webmasters sit ready to assist you in testing your pages or help you through particularly tough problems. But don't forget to RTM first (Read The Manual).

Now, put some of these components together to make your own home page:

1. You need some sort of title or name for the site. Place this information at the top. You want to draw your user's eye to this information immediately. Make it larger than the text of the rest of your page.

   You can also use italics or bold to call attention to it. If you want something really different, create a transparent GIF in some attractive font style. You can also use a transparent GIF for any image that you don't want confined to a square format—your company logo for instance (transparent GIFs allow the background of the image to be transparent to the browser's background color).

2. You may want to follow the site name with a brief description of your company or Web site. You can also put your company contact information here, such as mailing addresses and phone numbers. The other spot commonly used for this information is at the end of the first Web page. Providing contact information outside of the Web can be important in presenting yourself as an established business. If you are so inclined, include every way you can be contacted—mail, phone, fax, data line, e-mail. All help to establish your credibility.

3. Next, you need to create the body of your Web page. It can include text, photos, a linked table of contents, or whatever you want. If the body of your Web page consists of text, you may want to divide it into sections and subsections.

   Text can be free-formed or formatted using indentation and centering commands.

   Create additional delineation by specifying the text of headings and subheadings in different sizes. Also in all text pages, you may want to use simple graphics to create extra visual interest.

4. Within your page body, there may be links. Links are a very valuable tool for leading your user through your material. If you have lots of

information, you might decide to set up your initial home page as a table of contents. In this case, a good use of links would be to link each item in the table of contents to other Web pages that cover that item.

In another instance, if you are selling a product, you may want customers to read company and product information before they get to the page that contains your actual order form.

In a well-designed system, the number of steps from the front page to any choice within the system should be as small as possible. Likewise, the size of the documents being retrieved at each step of the way should be as small as possible.

People with huge quantities of data might want to make use of databases, which can help alleviate this problem by allowing selection based on search criteria.

> **Note**
>
> Web pages that contain no links are sometimes called *cul-de-sacs* or *dead ends*. Although, on the other hand, if you have too many links, you will probably generate criticism for confusing your audience.

5. If you have any acknowledgments (for example, software assistance or hardware donations), they are usually placed discretely at the bottom of the first page with links to the pages of the appropriate company or individual.

6. The addition of simple forms for online ordering or customer support can go at or near the bottom of the page—a better choice is usually on a different page connected by a link.

Your Corporate Look

If you are an established firm, you more than likely already have some sort of corporate style or look. Your goal will be to find the best way to translate that style to the Web.

If you are a new business, you have the opportunity to make up that corporate look. You can be daring and innovative, or you can be traditional. It will all depend on what your business is and who you are targeting. Figures 16.2 and 16.3 both show corporate sites that use appealing graphics.

Tip

Links can ensure that your users get to the information they want to access without having to wade through a bunch of text they don't need.

◀ See "Databases And Virtual Shopping Systems," p. 330

Tip

Links can also save you throughput charges by reducing the amount of information on each page.

IV

Marketing and the Web

Fig. 16.2
This home page belongs to the Sony site and has a very appealing graphic to draw the user into the different areas (**http://www. sony.com**).

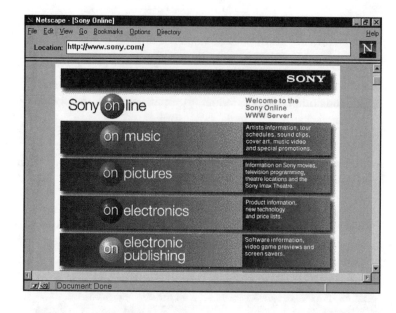

Fig. 16.3
The Zima home page uses graphics specifically geared to the young adult audience (**http:// www.zima. com/**).

Your corporate look will probably include a logo, pictures, or some other form of graphics. If you don't have a logo already, maybe now is the time to design one or have one designed for you.

> **Note**
>
> When designing a logo, remember the considerations of the computer screen and avoid those styles which might exaggerate the jaggies.
>
> If you already have a logo, you might need to alter it slightly so that it shows up best on the computer screen. Use of restricted colors and designs that are not too detailed help translate the image more faithfully than full-color logos or logos with extremely detailed design. Remember that it will be reproduced on various computers and video monitors of various quality.

When creating your corporate look, consider the impression it will create in your customers' and clients' minds. You may have always liked a leather and metal look, but is that the type of look that is going to make your customers want to give you their money? It might be if you are selling motorcycle accessories, but perhaps not if you were advertising your legal services.

Imagine the textures and colors that you feel embody your corporate style. Is it natural wood grains and tweed? Flowers and lace? Brick walls and spray paint? Highly polished marble and chrome? Is it Deco? Gothic? Dada? Neo-classical?

Think about colors. Are you a hot color or cool color company? Or maybe neutrals would best suit your company image? Perhaps an elegant palate of just black and white with a touch of silver? Choose the color scheme that best represents your company.

Answering these types of questions will help you decide exactly what look you want and need. It will also help you achieve this look, because now instead of aimlessly trying out things that you think will look good, you have direction. You can go out and get the specific images, textures, and font styles you need for your look.

A search of online archives for images and textures may supply you with what you are looking for. You could opt to create them yourself using a paint package. A third option would be to have a graphics firm design your graphics for you.

If you are having your site created for you but are creating the graphics internally, you want your graphics department or graphic artist to work with the webmaster to ensure that the best quality can be achieved for the best value. The webmaster should have suggestions for how to format and transmit the information for incorporation into your site.

The Stability of Your Service

One aspect of putting your best foot forward is making sure your customers can get to your WWW site. The greatest Web pages in the world are of no use if your customers, clients, and other users can't access the pages. Instability of service can come from a provider that can't handle throughput loads, problems with your HTTP address, and errors in your HTML code. Another hindrance for users is links that don't go where they are supposed to, or too many "under construction" signs.

Caution

Make sure that every link in your home page is checked regularly. Often sites will change the location of their pages and your link will break. Broken links are not beneficial to your Web image.

In all these cases, your user is faced with some form of error and difficulty in accessing your WWW site. You can lose sales from customers who get fed up trying to access your site and go elsewhere to make their purchase, or from angry clients who can't access services they have paid for.

The Consequences of an Unstable Service

An unstable service, at the very least, results in lower sales and an uncomfortable clientele.

In the worst case scenario, an unstable service will flood you with messages from users having problems. This occurrence is exactly what using the Web is supposed to avoid. If you spend all your time apologizing and running shotgun, your investment was applied in the wrong place.

Unstable service can show up in many places:

- Unstable service can show up in the provider's connection to the Internet. If the system is too slow or not connected well enough, you will have users who either cannot get in or get miserable response time. These problems will be a big deterrent to your users who will opt for a faster site.

- If you frequently get a busy signal when you call your provider, it may mean they don't have enough phone lines to accommodate all the people they have sold accounts to. Besides being irritating to you as a user, it indicates that a provider may be in trouble.

■ Another place where the service could become unstable is in the routing of e-mail messages. If your provider has a slow, unstable, or misconfigured e-mail system, you might be missing orders and messages from clients.

> **Note**
>
> Even the service from a good and stable provider can be expected to fluctuate. Because of the extreme popularity of the Internet and WWW, growth is occurring at an incredible rate. It's difficult for a provider to predict their growth needs because no two users are the same. For example, one user's WWW site might get hit a few thousand times in a month, generating a few megabytes of transfer. Another user's pages might get hit tens of thousands of times a day, accounting for many gigabytes of throughput and resource drains.
>
> A good provider is one who gives stable service most of the time, and addresses problems within one to two weeks of their appearing.

Maintaining a Stable Service

Your biggest key to guarantee stable service is to put your Web site on a provider that has at least enough power to handle an upgrade path. While this isn't a totally foolproof method, it does help.

Many of the ideas to be taken into consideration that were covered in Chapter 6, "Placing a Business on the Web," we outline again here. Your Internet provider should have the following:

■ Big enough computers to handle storage and throughput. Sun, Silicon Graphics Inc. (SGI), and Hewlett Packard are manufacturer names to look for. Also, most large providers will have more than one computer for their system, and in many cases will have multiprocessor systems.

■ Lots of high-powered communications lines. It's not uncommon for large providers to have hundreds of T1 lines coming into their system and at least one or more T3 lines.

■ A well-trained staff with some form of 24-hour contact.

■ Proper security measures in place to protect from crackers and pirates.

■ Protection from electrical storms and electrical generators for back-up.

If you are setting up your own server site, you will want to keep these points in mind. Although you may have budget constraints that keep you from deploying each of these points, you should do the best within your means. For instance, your 24-hour staff may be as simple as having your business phone forwarded to your home (you will enjoy the calls at 3 a.m.).

You should keep in mind that in any type of growth, some downtime is to be expected. However, a good provider should minimize the downtime, and your pages should be available around the clock, around the world.

What To Do in Rough Weather

There is one case when you will have to disconnect your service voluntarily—when there is severe electrical activity in your area. Direct lightning strikes to the building you are in or to the phone lines that connect to your computer will fry your machine. We have yet to see a surge protector that can handle millions of volts of high amp electricity of a direct lightning hit.

Very large Internet providers have invested in hundreds of thousands of dollars' worth of specialized equipment, including isolation transformers, which are beyond the investment scope of most businesses. Often these large providers can stand fairly direct lightning strikes as well as power outages of hours to days.

If you are running your own Web site, you might put a disclaimer in the beginning of your pages which notifies users that in the case of severe weather, the site will be down. While this won't help first-time users, your repeat users should understand your situation and try your site again in an hour or so.

> **Caution**
>
> The outcome of not unplugging your computer from the wall and your computer from your phone lines is hardware that can quite literally be melted together. It can also result in loss of data or software.

> **Note**
>
> While most insurance policies will cover your hardware loss, software and data losses are harder to prove. You'll also have to consider loss of business. Many businesses may find it impossible to ride out the days, weeks, or months it can take to replace equipment and software, reconfigure systems, and reconstruct data bases.
>
> Unless you are *very* well protected, it is better to avoid the whole mess together and unplug your machine. Also, if you plan to be out of town and leave your system up,

especially during thunderstorm season, you might want an employee, business associate, or computer-competent friend to monitor potentially dangerous weather systems.

You should be careful to completely unplug your system and all its components. If you unplug your computer, monitor, phone line, and modem, but leave the printer plugged in, the lightning strike can go through the power cord of the printer, throughout the printer electronics, and down the data cable to the computer.

Another consideration is that nearby lightning hits (and we mean *nearby*) can erase data on magnetic media. You should always keep good and stable backups. Isolating your computers within a metal-walled room also helps isolate the electromagnetic effects of nearby lightning strikes.

Ensuring Accurate Information

Although correcting information in a Web site is much easier than correcting a print ad or a television commercial, it's still something you want take steps to avoid. Incorrect information can result in loss of sales, a poor market image, and, in severe or negligent cases, lawsuits or other legal actions.

Incorrect information, such as a wrong address, can result in more than just the loss of business and poor image. If the incorrect information is the wrong rating for an electrical part your company sells, any damage or injuries caused by your equipment could be financially devastating.

Having people other than the designer double check the information helps to make sure the data is accurate. If you have your site designed for you, do not rely on the webmaster to ensure the data is accurate. It will be difficult for that person to have access to the information necessary to ensure accuracy. You should make sure someone internal handles this task.

Tip

The more sensitive, crucial and/or technical your information is, the more care you will need to take.

The Development Cycle

When designing your own Web site or having one designed for you, the first step after the creation of the specification is the development cycle.

◀ See "Specifications Document," p. 104

In general, Web development cycles are fairly short. The basic page information begins to appear first and can be critiqued as it comes up. Changes to the design should be made as soon as possible so that the amount of redesign can be minimized.

◄ See "Imple-
menting Vir-
tual Shopping
Systems,"
p. 334

Advanced techniques such as conference rooms, shopping systems, databases, and form handlers are then designed next. These systems can be brought up using a minimal set of data, so that the creation of the software is not waiting on the completion of data acquisition or formatting.

► See "Adding
Forms To Your
Pages," p. 539

As the pages near completion, more and more data can be added to the system databases, making it more complete. At this point, you should begin an in-depth testing cycle.

The Testing Cycle

You do not want to begin your testing cycle too early, otherwise you will test components that may change. While there will be internal development testing going on to ensure that the support software and mechanisms work properly, testing of the full site should begin only after about 75 to 80 percent of the site is complete.

The testing cycle is twofold:

1. First, you want to test the software thoroughly in many real-world situations by having as many people as possible use the system.

2. The second testing cycle verifies that users can actually use the system. Observing users interacting with the system is the best method. Relying on their input is also important, but you should realize that users will adapt to a situation and may have mentally assumed that a "solution" was not possible.

Here is an example of this type of thinking. We visited a production studio in New York a few years ago. The artist at the graphics workstation was using a primitive paint package that did not support curves or circles. We asked the artist how he created a circle. The artist quickly picked up a straight line tool and drew the approximation of a circle using little straight lines. The artist then took a small erasure tool and started nicking away at the sharp corners of the small lines. When the artist was done, he had a beautiful circle which took him about five minutes to create.

We were appalled. We asked the artist that if we could give them a curve tool, which would simply draw perfect curves of any size, would he use it? The artist pondered the question and said, "Well, I don't think it's possible to make a curve tool." We assured him that it was possible, to which he replied, reluctantly, "Well, I suppose that I might use it, but the method I use now is really fast."

The point here is that the user did not really know what was possible, and had adopted the best solution that he could with the tools he had. Even when confronted with a far superior method, the artist was reluctant to abandon the old method that he knew so well. Only by observing the artist could we identify a major flaw in the system (the lack of a circle tool). Our observations revealed a process which was taking five minutes, when it should have taken only five seconds.

The testing cycle must have a feedback loop to the developers. Any problems which are identified must be solved as quickly as possible to ensure that testing can continue on schedule. You want to avoid having people test with known problems, since it just slows up the testing process. Once a problem is solved, it must be retested to ensure that the solution did not uncover or create new problems.

Implementation and Verification

Once your site has been developed and tested, it is time to implement the site.

Implementation of a site includes announcing the site to the various lists and search engines. This is the only way that people will find you out on the Web.

◄ See "How To Advertise on the Net," p. 227

Once you have advertised yourself and placed yourself in the proper malls, lists, and robots, you should verify the site. Test it yourself, and also examine the log to see how many other people are using the site.

Make sure that all the pages are being accessed. Look at the log on a daily or weekly basis for the first few weeks to ensure that people are finding your pages. This is the perfect time to make last-minute changes in your site. Working with your log can help you determine just what you need to change.

◄ See "The HTTPD Log," p. 342

You may wait to announce it and have a large, trusted network of users—instead of your testing group—access your site from outside your immediate group. Upon their approval, you could then turn on your site.

Being Unique on the Net

Being unique on the Net can mean one of two things:

- You offer a service or product that no one else is offering.

- You present yourself in a way that no one else does.

With the recent rapid advances being made in graphic presentations that are available in Web browsers, being able to present your company in new and original ways is becoming easier and easier. (For an example, when we starting writing this book, the blink option for text was not available. Now it is widespread enough that Web lists won't let people use it when placing a listing.)

Why Being Unique is Important

When you use the latest advancements in HTML and when you use these advancements in exciting and new ways, you will have a site that is very popular. People will come to your site just to see what you've done. They will also list you in their hotlists and tell their friends about it—great for word-of-mouth advertising! This can be very important in generating the Web-equivalent of a walk-in business.

Currently, the Web is composed of more than 2.5 million unique places to go. By the time you read this, the number should increase to well more than 3 million URLs.

> **Note**
>
> Just to show you how fast the Web is really moving, about four weeks after adding this comment, the Web now has 3.5 million unique URLs.

With all these places to go, why would someone hang out in your site?

When people come by your site, they are looking for something. If you are providing nothing interesting or nothing unique, users will just look around and leave. At the most, they will have wasted some time and your bandwidth.

With so many places to go, if users don't see something that totally hooks them, they will not be back. If, however, they come to your site and are amazed at the look or the depth of the offerings you have, they will not only be back, but will tell their friends and acquaintances to go check you out.

This is the type of site you want to have.

Having Fun on the Net

One of the best ways to attract people into your site and have them stay around is to entertain them.

Having games, jokes, cartoons, poetry, fiction, interactive chatting, and similar activities would all be big draws into your site.

You should make your entertainment relate to your site so that you do not attract the wrong set of people. Providing entertainment is one thing, but when you are trying to sell cars, hosting a children's magazine online may not help you as much as hosting something like an antique auto trivia contest. You should make your entertainment an effective pulling mechanism to attract people to come to you to view your services and products.

Another way to make a site fun is to change it frequently. Users are always entertained by new graphics and layout that greet them weekly or monthly. Keeping your material fresh is extremely important, though you want to make sure not to change your layout too drastically. If you always require that your users learn a new organizational scheme, they will quickly become irritated. The best way to make changes is to modify the graphics but keep the position relatively the same. Small shifts in position of some items, or addition of new items, is fine from time to time, but making sweeping changes to layout often means that users need to learn how to traverse your site all over again.

Staying Current with the Trends

Of course, the best way to design a Web site is to go out there and see what's being done. We don't mean ripping off other people's ideas, but adapting them and modifying them into something that can work for your site.

Viewing the Competition

You definitely want to make sure to visit all your competitors' sites. It may be important to your business to offer at least the same services as they are. Seeing what information they provide about themselves and special services they offer (such as online ordering or feedback forms) can provide indicators on what your customers and clients expect.

If they do offer such services, you might want to shell out the bucks and try ordering a product. Does their system work? Did the product arrive when it was supposed to? If they offer online services, do they really work? Were you able to get access to the proper personnel? Was the information correct and did you receive it in a timely method? The answers to these questions could be important in planning your Web market strategy.

Also, take a look at the image they are trying to project. It may give you some ideas as to how you want your site to look (or not). For instance, if your competition has a really far-out site, you may decide to make your site more conservative, trying for the more mature or serious client. Or you may decide they have the right idea and design a page that is even more innovative and provocative.

While you are visiting, not only can you see their site but also the HTML code used to create their site. When you're at their site, click the View option on your browser's command bar. Clicking Source will give you the source code for the page you are currently at (the method to do this will vary slightly based on the browser you are using). There's nothing illegal about it. You can even use parts of the code you find there.

Caution

Lifting an entire site verbatim is definitely not a good idea. And using copyrighted graphics, logos, or text for which you don't have the rights is against the law.

Spending Time as a User

Beyond visiting your competitors, you should make an attempt to see what's new and interesting out on the Web. You can start by cruising sites on topics that interest you. When you find one that is visually interesting, see who created it and if that company lists any more of its sites.

Also, check out these people's hotlists because if you liked their site, you might like the sites they liked. This is a hit-and-miss method. You'll find sites with no imagination at all, just plain text on a plain background. You could also find links to esoteric sites. After you randomly cruise the Web for some time, jump back into your page and look at it. Try to see it as a new user would who, just like a real user, had just come in from other sites. How did your site compare with the other sites you were at? Better? Worse? Can you make improvements?

> **Note**
>
> We promote stream of consciousness surfing of the Web. Whether you have an extra hour or an extra 15 minutes, take a spin around the Internet. If you let it lead you, you'll be surprised where it will take you.
>
> Surfing the Web this way can have a synergistic effect. You may find solutions to problems you thought you had to live with, and answers to questions you forgot you had. This is due, in large part, to the interconnectivity of the Web. When you (figuratively) step around the corner to price a widget, you may find yourself halfway around the world getting the recipe for a dish you had on your last vacation.

Some magazines that focus on the Internet, such as *Wired* and *Internet World*, list interesting spots. You can also check out the NCSA What's New selection at

http://www.ncsa.uiuc.edu/SDG/Software/Mosaic/Docs/whats-new.html

This place lists new sites as they become available. Looking here will show you the very latest sites, which often use the latest features and capabilities.

Even non-computer related media are becoming a more popular place to find out about Web sites. Lately, as the Internet and Web have become more mainstream, we have seen HTTP addresses in popular magazines and on TV. At the last concert we attended by the performance artist Laurie Anderson, the address for her Web site appeared in the concert program.

Remember, by not restricting your Web cruising to merely your competition, you'll also be able to find out about trends and new functionality as they arrive on the scene. Perhaps you'll become the trendsetter for your industry.

Predicting the Future Through Related Media

No matter what your corporate image is, you'll want to stay on top of trends in the Internet and the Web when they apply to your business. This may involve some guesswork on your part as to where the Web is heading.

▶ See "How the Future Net Will Look," p. 499

Magazine, newspaper, and journal articles may provide some clues as to the future of the Web. Remember that most publications' first goal is to sell copy. Quite often newspaper articles and magazines will go for more outrageous predictions, including those of crash and burn (the death of the Net due to one ridiculous reason or another). Most unreliable are non-computer magazines which often reprint rumors or opinions which are simply not true.

When a large enough magazine does this, it can impact negatively on the general public's impression of the Net and Web.

Another interesting way to predict the future of the Web is to read some of the science fiction books which are beginning to appear. Science fiction has always had the uncanny ability to predict the future of social and technological changes. This ability extends amazingly well to the Internet and Web as well. Several science fiction books weave the Internet and Web into their story lines. Two of our favorites are Neal Stevenson's *Snow Crash*, which portrays what we feel is an extremely realistic view of the near future of the Web, and *Rim* by Alexander Besher, which has an interesting (though less realistic) view of the future of the Internet and Web.

From Here...

This chapter covered many diverse factors that come into play when you create a company image. Factors such as how your page looks, its ease of use, and the reliability of access to your page are all crucial when shaping a Web site.

Realize also that when you create a Web site, if you don't pay attention to your image, whatever hodgepodge impression that is created by your page will be your corporate image. It is better for you to decide on your own image than to have it decided for you.

From here, refer to the following chapters:

- Chapter 4, "Planning a Web Site," helps you determine who your intended audience is and the best way to reach them.

- Chapter 6, "Placing a Business on the Web," shows you how to locate Internet providers in your area and integrate the Web into your business.

- Chapter 7, "Picking a Name for Yourself on the Net," offers information about domain names and tips for picking effective names to use on the Web.

- Chapter 10, "Advertising on the Net," teaches you the best ways to promote your Web site.

- Chapter 22, "The Future of the Net," helps identify other trends you should keep in mind when putting your company on the Web.

- Appendix, "An Introduction To HTML," shows you the nuts and bolts of creating a Web page.

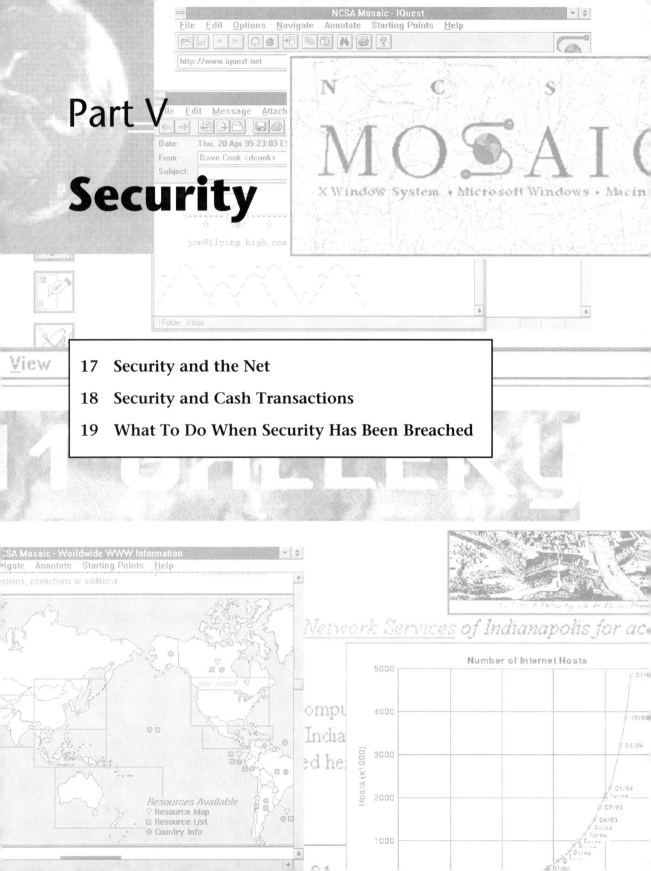

Part V

Security

Chapter 17

Security and the Net

All over the United States and the world, people are having to take more precautions to keep themselves and their property safe. The Internet and the Web aren't exempt from these problems. As time goes on and the Internet becomes more complex and populated, you can expect to see more and more people looking for ways to use the Net dishonestly. This chapter explores Internet crime and the people that commit Internet crime.

In this chapter you learn

- The types of crimes that are common to the Web

- Ways to protect yourself as a consumer

- Important security facts for companies

- International law and security

- Ways that the Internet protects itself

Crime and the Net

The Internet is a huge place that hosts over 35 million people. Unfortunately, not all of them are honest. As in any city, when you walk the streets of the Internet, you must be careful.

Statistics show that only 10 percent of computer crime is reported, and that only 2 percent of reported crime results in convictions. Losses from computer crime rose more than $40 billion in 1994. Given the growth rate of the Internet, these numbers will only get worse.

The following sections examine some of the issues, myths, and truths behind computer crime as it relates to the Internet and the World Wide Web.

Meet the Criminals

Two basic types of criminals stalk computers:

- The user who is trying to understand and learn the various systems and capabilities. This person is not seeking to do damage or to steal, but is merely seeking knowledge of how things work and perhaps going about it in a way that is slightly wrong. Sometimes such people are like teen-agers, who see how far they can go without getting caught.

- The hard-core computer criminal who uses the Internet and Web to profit illegally. Such criminals often know all sorts of hints to hide their activities and may even band together to share the fruits of their illegal endeavors.

Generally, you need not be concerned with the first type of criminal. These irritants soon tire of their games, and either mature or go on to understand the system and then design better systems (they don't necessarily have to be mature to do so). In other words, these people are not threats.

The second group, however, *is* a threat. These people enjoy stealing software, computer time and memory, and payment and phone information, as well as cause damage to equipment or data.

As you can imagine, a system as large as the Internet has many holes and crevices in which a determined person can easily find data spigots more than happy to spill all the data it can.

Before you begin to learn about the specific crimes, you need to be familiar with some terms for the criminals themselves. Unfortunately, the media-hyped term *hacker* is often used inappropriately. In computer circles, a hacker is simply anyone who is good with computers. Hackers prefer *cracker*, *phreak*, *phracker*, and *pirate* as the proper terms for the people who participate in illegal activities involving computers and telecommunications systems.

A cracker is someone who specifically breaks into computer systems by by-passing or guessing logins. Such criminals are a severe threat, because if they can gain access as a privileged user, they have access to incredible amounts of billing information, credit card numbers, and other highly personal data.

Phreaks, sometimes called *phone phreaks*, are people who hack phone systems. These people are specifically trying to scam long distance time, control phone switch capability, or hack company-automated PBX systems to scam free voice mail accounts or raid companies' existing voice mail messages (PBX refers to digital phone systems found in many offices).

> **Note**
>
> Voice mail phreaking is a minor threat unless the phreaker is selling stolen message data to your competitors. However, scamming long distance phone time can involve stealing and trading in calling card numbers and other illegal activities, and can be very damaging. Currently, phone companies report more than $50 million per year in losses to phreaking.

A phracker is a combination of a phreak and a cracker. A phracker breaks into both phone systems and computer systems, and specializes in total network destruction. Generally, phrackers tend to be worse than phreakers because they have more knowledge of advanced systems. Not only can phrackers bypass phone systems, but they can also bypass computer systems.

Finally, data pirates tend to be computer oriented. Their forte is to steal commercial software, modify it to run without needing serial numbers or other startup keys, and post their data in warez sites. A *warez site* contains stolen software set aside for the downloading pleasure of all the pirate's friends and clients. Pirates place most warez sites on innocent company computers from the outside, which makes it hard to find and catch the pirate. Not only do these pirates steal money from software companies by giving away their software, but they also jeopardize company computers by making them host to stolen software and by consuming the host computer's general resources.

> **Tip**
>
> Generally, phrackers tend to be worse than phreakers because they have more knowledge of advanced systems.

The one group that is missing is the "professional criminal" that you experience in the real world. Such criminals have now begun to use the computer. They still are in the minority, probably because of the sheer amount of knowledge that you need to have to pull off any real computer crime. Because the amount of information is so complex and varied, only geeks who have gone bad tend to be computer criminals. However, as time goes on, the professional criminal also will be surfing the Web, looking for potential victims.

Misrepresentation

Two crimes are sure to grow in popularity: misrepresentation and fraud. Although currently little fraud occurs on the Internet and Web, much more is certain as time goes on.

One of the major reasons that misrepresentation will become a problem is that, on the Net, it is so easy to appear as anyone or anything you want. The Net makes it easy for legitimate, trustworthy "mom and pop" businesses to sell to the world, but at the same time makes it easy for users to present themselves as someone they are not or to sell something that isn't all they claim.

Certainly some harmless misrepresentation goes on now. After all, advertising is advertising, whether it's on television or the Web. But although fledgling companies may present themselves as being bigger and better than they really are, no one (to my knowledge) has created a site that is purely a scam.

> **Note**
>
> When doing business or negotiating other transactions on the Web, the rules of traditional business apply. If you are looking for the best price, shop around. If a deal involves trust, do a background check: call the Better Business Bureau or the attorney general's office for the appropriate state, get references, and call them. In many fraud cases, the victim asks for and receives references, but fails to actually check them out.

Creating a scam site is not as easy as it might seem, primarily because you must host your pages somewhere, which makes the provider responsible for the content. For this reason, most providers examine sites and have access to information about you. And although you can quickly and easily put up and take down a site, you can also easily and within a few seconds trace a location right to the provider's door.

However, in the future, the number of fraud cases in which perpetrators create their own provider site will increase. For this reason, it will be increasingly important for Web users to protect themselves.

You can avoid fraud in several ways. First, a company trying to commit fraud usually doesn't take the time to create proper cover. If you are shopping at a company, glancing at the URL can often be most revealing. Most large and medium-sized companies have their own domain names.

◀ See "Domain Names," p. 159 Likewise, companies committing some type of fraud usually have little noncomputer access information in their pages (such as telephone numbers and addresses). Most legitimate companies advertise as much access as possible, and should have e-mail, fax, phone, and address information. An 800 number is another good sign, although many small companies do not provide this service.

If you are unsure of a particular business' stability, call the company's area code and check whether the business is listed in directory assistance. If the business is a fly-by-night operation, it probably hasn't been around long enough to be listed. If it is listed, call the area's Better Business Bureau and ask whether the company has had any complaints against it.

Finally, a call to the company itself will tell you a lot. If you ask the business to fax you information, you often get an indication of its professionalism as well as more information about its services.

> **Note**
>
> Just because a business chooses not to list a phone number is no reason to assume they are not legitimate. Many businesses use the Internet to help cut down on phone support. Such businesses rarely have their phone number listed. Use common sense to determine if a business is suspicious. If unsure, ask questions via e-mail and judge the quickness and quality of the response.

> **Note**
>
> The UNIX WHOIS command is very useful. If you need to contact an administrator of a site in an emergency, typing **whois** followed by the site's domain name accesses the InterNIC registry and returns the contact information for the system administrator of that domain. Many PC and Macintosh Internet software systems also have the WHOIS capability.
>
> For more information on the WHOIS command, refer to Que's Special Edition *Using Internet E-Mail*.

Theft

Theft can take many forms on the Internet. Phreakers or pirates could take space on your server for themselves. A cracker might raid your password file and break some of the more common names, gaining access to your system. Alternatively, a phreaker or phracker could steal credit card numbers and use them to make illegal purchases. Another form of theft is to steal someone's access codes in a private WWW site, log in as that person, and steal data.

Still another form is to intercept your communications between servers. This type of computer crime is perhaps the most feared, but is actually quite difficult to commit. In fact, the other forms of theft are the most common.

Everybody seems to fear having their credit card information stolen when they type it into the WWW. Often, users type into a field such sensitive data as a credit card number and then continue their Web session. If the user then leaves the computer turned on and unattended, anyone who walks by that computer can go back through the user's pages and see what the user was entering, including the credit card numbers that were typed.

To avoid this problem, two solutions are available:

- Use your browser's ability to go back to previous pages until you reach the page that contains the sensitive data. Go forward from that page to any non-sensitive page. This effectively changes your cache's branching.

- You can use the Clear Cache command that many browsers offer (look in your browser's option or Preference drop-down menu).

A good alternative for people setting up credit card handlers on the Web is to make the area for entering the credit card number a password field so that the card number is never visible on-screen. If you employ this alternative, users will not be able to see whether they made a mistake when entering the number, so you probably will also have to require that users verify the number by typing it twice and then using software to compare the two to make sure they are identical. (Allow the user to try again if the two differed, because that indicates the user made a mistake.)

▶ See "Form Elements That Accept Typed Data from Users," p. 542

The weakest links of the system are in the user's and the store's provider. At these two points, the information is cycled internally through the mail system. Between these two points, while whizzing throughout the Internet, the information is fairly secure.

The information is secure because most of the data routing is performed by machines called, not surprisingly, *routers*. These machines do not possess much intelligence, but merely pass data as fast as possible. Data sent via routers are broken down in discrete chunks of data called *packets* and interspersed with other packets from other messages. When you are not the receiving computer, reassembling these chunks is not always straightforward.

Furthermore, to be a site acting as a router, your neighboring sites must have a high level of trust in you, and you must prove yourself to be technically advanced. After all, you will be routing their data as well as general Internet data. If unscrupulous persons set themselves up as routers, they would be quite visible and thus easy to catch.

> **Note**
>
> Because the weakest section of the whole Internet scheme is at the user's and the store's providers, you should pick providers who have firewalls running and know about secure e-mail and other methods of keeping data secure.

Another form that theft can take is *plagiarism*. Taking text, sound, or images from a nonpublic domain source and using them without proper credit or permission is illegal. This type of theft is simple on the Internet, where copying a file is a matter of a click of the mouse and a few seconds of time.

▶ See "How To Determine Whether Security Has Been Breached," p. 424

The Web itself is especially vulnerable to plagiarism attacks. If plagiarists see a neat graphic or technique at a site, they can easily copy the graphic or "borrow" the technique. We have fallen into this form of plagiarism by using an image openly available on the Web (which we thought was free and clear), only to be contacted by the image's creator, who was not terribly happy.

> **Caution**
>
> It is the best policy to either create your own artwork or purchase it from clip art libraries or artists. Using preexisting artwork from the Internet itself could be mean accidentally using copyrighted material.

The major problem is that it's often difficult to determine whether images or data on the Web are copyrighted. Often, the files simply offer no indication, but sometimes they have been stolen and then presented as copyright-free material.

What should you do if your information is lifted?

1. Document the theft's occurrence, so that you have solid proof. Documenting such theft can be as easy as printing the offending pages or showing someone else what you have discovered. You also must be able to prove that your version of the data is the original. You can do so by presenting your prior work leading up to the data, file dates, document dates, or the knowledge of others who witnessed the data.

2. After you are armed with the proper proof, a simple call to the offending party should be enough to begin a dialog. You should point out to the offender that you have ownership and you would appreciate an immediate halt to their use of your data. If this notice does not immediately bring the offense to a halt, simply take it up with the offender's lawyer. If you have the proper proof, you should easily obtain a settlement.

But what if you are the plagiarizer?

Simply acknowledge your mistake and rectify it as best as possible. Often, you will not be aware that you are taking information that is not in the public domain. For example, many icon and image sites exist, but not all the images in those sites can be legally distributed. The sites are in violation, either consciously or unconsciously, but you are also in violation if you pull the data, even though you had no way of knowing of the legal restrictions.

> **Note**
>
> The best rule for determining whether you can use an image or other piece of data for your own use is simple: don't. It is far better to fabricate the data yourself or have someone create it for you, than to take it and find out later that it belongs to someone else. This is especially true of graphics created for your Web pages. By creating your own graphics, you ensure that no conflict of ownership arises. Another solution is to use reputable clip art libraries and image banks. But be aware that most clip art libraries limit the number of images that you can use per "project." Read your documentation carefully.

Illegal Transactions

Currently there is a huge cry for secure servers that will make credit card transactions supposedly safe. But safe for whom? Although such servers might protect consumers from having their credit card information ripped off in midstream, they would do nothing to protect the store owner from criminals who use fraudulent credit card numbers or false identities to purchase products.

Unfortunately, store owners have little protection from the use of fraudulent cards or identities. However, the same problem exists for businesses who accept credit card orders over the phone, which is a common everyday practice. The rule of thumb is to use the same safeguards on the Internet that you use with a phone ordering system.

Tip
The more data you have, the more ways you have to confirm the order.

It's rather shocking, but all that you need to clear a credit card on the Internet is the card number, expiration date, and user's name (though regulations are being formulated within the U.S. to help change this). You need not confirm addresses or anything else. In fact, often you don't even need the expiration date or user's name. However, you should insist on as much data as possible in your order.

One of the simplest ways to safeguard against illegal transactions is to have your order-entry system check credit card numbers against the credit card checksum standard. You can run this algorithm on any credit card number to determine whether it belongs to the valid sequence of numbers. Although the algorithm does not tell you whether the card is *really* a credit card, it at least prevents people from typing **123456789** as a credit card number and having it work. The user would either need to be familiar with the formula or be extremely lucky and guess a viable number. This chapter doesn't offer such a formula (that would defeat the purpose, after all), but be aware that good order-entry software should have this capability built in. Alternatively, if you are creating your own order-entry system, you can gain this capability from the appropriate channels.

The Net and International Borders

Because of its open nature, the Net transcends national and regional boundaries. For this reason, you may already be a criminal without knowing it. Because different countries have different laws concerning international commerce and transmission of data, the legality of products and services may differ. This section explores how such differences occur and steps that you can take to avoid problems.

The Net Knows No Limits

Because of the Net's ability to pull, integrate, and route data from anywhere, the user is never sure where the data is actually coming from. The Net reaches everywhere and thus violates some interesting laws.

In particular, many countries have laws about what can or cannot be brought into the country. These laws extend to printed material and other intellectual property. Not surprisingly, most Internet users break these laws daily.

A good example of such law breaking involves the U.S. laws concerning encrypting software. As other parts of this book have stated, the U.S. government considers encryption software to be munitions (see fig. 17.1). Therefore, to export encryption technology is an act of treason. However, many other nations do not have similar restrictions and the most sophisticated encryption is readily available. If you download such software, you could be committing treason. More importantly, in the United States, just having on your machine such information or software—even if you have obtained it legally—may be a legal problem. And if you let users anywhere in the world copy such information or software from your machine, you are committing a crime that is as bad as copying the information or software yourself.

V

Security

Fig. 17.1
This FAQ page
from RSA Data
Security Inc.
discusses the U.S.
cryptography
laws (**http://
www.rsa.com/
faq/faq_gnrl.
html#Is-
cryptography_
exportable_from_
the_U.S.**).

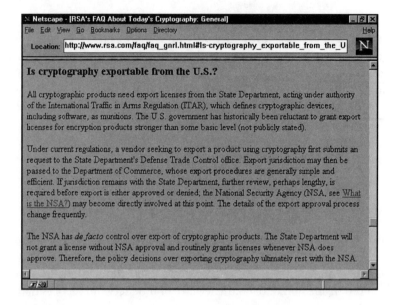

Another problem concerns the routing of data. If a user in a North American country other than the United States requests the information legally from a legal site in Europe or Asia, computers in the U.S. will likely route the data at some point. Under recent suggestions made here in the U.S., the owners of the routing machine could be considered in violation.

However, there are no legal systems anywhere in the world which are set up to deal with the dilemmas caused by the accessibility of data on the Net. Although the U.S. government has not yet prosecuted anyone for having encryption software on a machine, some people suspected of allowing such software to get outside the U.S. borders have been watched and hassled.

The problem becomes more difficult for secure browsers and servers. Cash transactions systems that rely on encryption technology do not work outside of the U.S., nor can users outside of the U.S. use secure transactions with servers within the U.S.

This is just one example of restricted information. Many other examples exist, and as the next section reveals, political and cultural taboos can create quite a mess. If nothing else, the Internet will certainly affect political, cultural, and social boundaries and laws.

The Net and Cultural Taboos

All countries and societies have their own moral and ethical codes. What is taken for granted as acceptable in one country may shock people in another country. Because the Internet and Web remove national boundaries, you have a sudden, worldwide mixing of philosophies. As with other media forms, like television, this mixing can have drastic consequences for cultures not yet ready for the surge of new ideas that can shake traditional morals and ethics.

Primarily for this reason, some countries have refused Internet connectivity. Communist China is one good example of a society which recognizes the benefits of the Internet, but is hesitant to allow full access to its people. While recognizing that the Internet can be extremely useful, the Chinese government is also reluctant to introduce its citizens to the influence and ideals of other countries. Although some Internet providers operate in China, they are few and strictly regulated.

Other countries such as Germany and Japan are fighting political and commercial wars for control of the Net. These countries still have not determined who owns the Net and who can play the Net game. In these cases, government agencies are fighting among themselves over the issues of releasing the power of the Net to their own citizens. Unfortunately, because of this infighting, users in these countries can find it both expensive and difficult to gain Internet access.

But nowhere are the cultural implications more important than in sexual taboos. The laws and views of sexual issues vary incredibly among countries.

For example, recent rulings in Canada have made it illegal to possess artwork or text that demoralizes women or children. This ruling extends to fictional works of art, including artists' drawings. Therefore, if you are an artist working out some early childhood frustrations and are providing your work on the Internet, you could be violating Canadian laws if you display your work via Canadian servers. And under the current laws (as they are currently understood), a Canadian citizen who accesses your information, no matter where it is stored, is violating these laws.

Similarly, United States pornography laws extend to the local level. What is legal in one town might be illegal in another. Just because you can run an adult site in your town does not mean that you cannot be arrested for violating pornography laws in another town or state. If someone in a town with more stringent laws than yours accesses your information, you can be hauled to jail for transporting pornographic material over state lines—even though the transportation was done privately and in the form of electrons. The same danger applies to international sites. Accessing adult information from a server in Holland, where sexual taboos are less strict, could cause major problems for you at home, depending on the laws of your city and state.

V

Security

> **Caution**
>
> As you create your Web pages, keeping in mind all the taboos of all the various cultures is difficult. In fact, even being aware of all potential taboos may be impossible. For example, few people are aware that a picture of someone waving with an open hand may be considered obscene to a Greek Web surfer.

However, you should not have to go to extremes to sugar-coat your pages. Present your information in a manner that is correct for your upbringing and society, and try to make your pages usable to everyone. For most business applications, you should definitely go out of your way to avoid topics and material that may be unacceptable to an audience of all age groups and from all over the world.

Keep in mind that most of the Internet audience is well aware of the international aspects and impact of the Internet and thus will tolerate other views. Indeed, many people cruise the Internet just for that reason, because it *is* a place where you can find and get most anything. It is the ultimate culturally integrating experience.

Staying Aware of Local Laws

You can bet that new laws to regulate the Internet will be put into effect quickly. We are entering a period of major confusion and fighting within the courts, as the new freedoms of the Internet and Web are ironed out.

The most critical issues facing the courts today are the following:

- What does *privacy* mean with regard to the Internet?

- What does *copyright* mean with regard to the Internet?

- How do courts handle the fact that the Internet has no national boundaries?

- What is freedom of expression and what is harassment and libel? And how do these expressions or offenses extend to the laws of other countries?

- What constitutes obscenity versus art?

Note

The issue of privacy is one of the most critical. This issue involves what you can and cannot view over the Internet in the privacy of your own home. The issue also covers what others can view of your information, which extends to digital signature and other forms of encrypting and protection, and includes what you can or cannot sell.

The court battles have already begun. As they continue, you will have to keep up with the resulting laws and decisions. You can expect the laws to vacillate, because the Internet is a very hard beast to move.

▶ See "Can Internet Cash Transactions Ever Be Safe?" p. 403

Think of the Internet as a huge, collective consciousness. It is a society unto itself and has a law of its own. It embodies intellectual freedom, which when carried to the extreme, tends to violate local laws. The localized efforts of passing laws will have but a Lilliputian effect on the huge Gulliver of the Internet. Short of physically forbidding the Internet or dramatically hiking the price, you can't do much to restrict access or content in the United States.

Imagine trying to remove television from America. The Web is like television, but with a million good channels. The more people are exposed to the Web, the more difficult it will be to change the media, and the more likely that the media will change society.

Nevertheless, you can expect new laws and much confusion. If you want to stay on top of the changes, the best place is, not surprisingly, the Internet and Web themselves.

NetNews, IRC, Web sites, and magazine articles brim with discussions of all these issues. Because laws that affect one area of the Net concern the entire Net community, these sources discuss such legislation with great passion.

Also remember that the technologically sophisticated portions of each country are the first to populate the Internet. High technology tends to embody big business, which also means big political clout. Although local governments will certainly pass laws regarding such issues such as pornography and other moral and ethical situations, the big businesses that seek to use the Internet will protect its overall freedom.

V

Security

Spies and the Net

This chapter may be creating an impression of a wild, wild Web. You might view the Web like the Old West—a lawless frontier of vigilantes and outlaws wrecking havoc with every byte transmitted.

This view is simply not true. The Internet, like any large society, has both good and bad factions. Most people walk the streets of the Internet safely and never run into a serious security incident.

However, you also should not be naive as to the nature of the Internet and Web. This same mass of social mingling is of great use to others outside the business world. Government has found the Net's freedom of expression an excellent way to control high technology bandits. As this section describes, many capabilities exist for catching the outlaws of the digital frontier.

Net Snitches and Net Police

You might be startled to learn that the Internet is fairly well watched. Internet activity is observed on many levels, and automatic traps have been set to catch and snare unsuspecting computer criminals.

> **Note**
>
> Government personnel constantly monitor the many IRC groups that deal with stolen software (such as the **#warez** groups), cracking (**#hack** and others), and phreaking (**#phreak** and others).

◀ See "IRC," p. 46

Also, NetNews is often filtered for content. Such content filtering is extremely easy, requiring only a program that searches each news item for certain words. Documents that include such words are shuttled away for more advanced analysis. Many moderated groups use just such a filter to remove unwanted postings.

◀ See "NetNews," p. 39

But the best snitches are the software "watchdog" programs that system administrators place on their systems. Many crackers attempt to penetrate a site at its weakest link to the outside—the Internet connection. This connection provides crackers with many "holes" through which to enter a machine. System administrators cannot afford to plug all holes, because some are required to keep the Net operating smoothly (in other words, if they plug certain holes, things will start to break).

So, system administrators watch such holes instead of plugging them. In this case, the hole becomes a trap. Whenever unsuspecting (or naive) crackers try to enter a system through a watched hole, they are quickly brought to the system administrator's attention, and a full logging of the event, including the cracker's traced path, is available.

> **Note**
>
> Other mechanisms of automatic snitching and policing include wrappers, firewalls, and proxy servers. These mechanisms help to divert and mislead crackers. You can even set up these mechanisms to lead a cracker down a blind alley.

The major nongovernment group that handles computer security violations is the Computer Emergency Response Team (CERT).

▶ See "Working with Firewalls, Wrappers, and Proxies," p. 441

Government Watchdogs

The previous section introduced you to several government watchdog groups. Several groups constantly monitor communications such as e-mail, NetNews, and IRC. Some governmental departments have set up teams not only to scour BBS sites looking for illegal activity, but also to pose as pirates, crackers, and phreaks in IRC and other talk groups and infiltrate the inner sanctum of elite warez sites.

▶ See "Soliciting Help," p. 431

Likewise, the government has set up some FTP and Gopher sites that are in fact traps, containing material desirable only to the undesirable. Accesses to such sites are logged.

In the U.S., legislators have proposed laws that would make providers responsible for the content of the data on their machines and the data routed by their machines. If passed, such legislation will require all providers to scan for illegal use. (We have major doubts that the government will successfully pass such legislation, but you never know.) Already, some of the larger providers do some scanning to keep illegal use in check.

> **Note**
>
> If you are concerned about privacy and want to make it more difficult for others to read your data and messages, use a package such as *PGP* (*Pretty Good Protection*). PGP is a digital signature system designed by Phil Zimmerman. Although the code is considered encryption and thus cannot be sent out of the U.S., data encrypted with the method can be sent anywhere. PGP is available outside of the U.S., so you can use the method to ensure secure and private messaging.
>
> For more information on how to use PGP, refer to Que's Special Edition *Using Internet E-Mail*.

V

Security

Keep in mind that the government has a huge quantity of data to monitor. Even with supercomputers, the amount of data is quite large and growing daily, and the amount of Internet content that is open to scanning is unknown. While government watchdogs are not scanning every message, you should treat all your messages and correspondences as though someone is watching.

Industrial Espionage

When being placed on the Internet, large companies are often most concerned about security. Once on the Web, these companies fear that outside crackers will break in and destroy or steal important company secrets.

Usually this fear is mostly misplaced. Although security problems are in fact a significant threat and risk, a simple, foolproof way exists to ensure that crackers do not breach the security of internal company computers: don't hook your secure computers to the Internet. By keeping a total division between those computers that service the Internet and those that handle secure internal information, you ensure that crackers have no way to access one from the other.

Nevertheless, corporate espionage is not to be taken lightly. Unfortunately, statistics show that insiders perpetrate the majority (more than 80 percent) of computer theft and destruction. Therefore, regardless of whether you connect your computers to the Internet, security is still a problem.

One of the simplest ways for a cracker to find out about your internal company data and codes is simply to go through your garbage. By finding printouts, sticky notes, telephone memos, and other documents, crackers can easily breach most systems' security.

Another simple way for a cracker to enter your system is to guess the system's passwords. An insider can do this much more easily than an outsider. Why? Insiders potentially have access to more personal data about users such as data that may have been used to create passwords. In choosing passwords, users commonly use such items as birthdays, names, pets, PIN numbers, and so on. Usually the less computer literate a user is, the bigger the chance that he or she will choose a guessable password (such as his or her name). Insiders armed with this advantage can either simply guess the password within a few tries or casually observe someone logging in to see whether they reach for numbers or letters first (helping to narrow down the possibilities for names).

> **Caution**
>
> One of the most amazing ways for companies to lose their data is to sell it outright to their competitors. When updating computers, businesses often sell their old equipment at auctions. This old equipment often has not been properly cleaned and thus has quantities of data remaining on the hard drives. Even after the owner deletes a drive, crackers can often recover the contents by using an undelete tool. Always be sure to destroy your data before selling your old equipment!

The best way to combat corporate piracy is to do the following:

- Insist on a regimented method for destroying documents.

- Train employees on proper privacy precautions. Employees should change passwords periodically, perhaps once a month.

- Remove any accounts that users access less than once a month.

Crackers and the Net

Instead of physically attacking your system, most crackers rely on remote attacks through your computer network. Crackers will try to log into system administration, guest, demo, FTP, games, and root accounts. They try using common first names.

If the targeted site is a provider, crackers often get an account at the site. From within the site, they can examine files and logs. Although a good administrator will have protected the sensitive data, a determined cracker can still obtain far too much information.

One of the most harmful things that a cracker can obtain is a copy of your password file. The cracker can run this file at his or her leisure against a program that tries to break the passwords. If the program breaks even one password (and the standard programs are quite good at breaking passwords), the cracker has gained access to a forbidden area.

> **Note**
>
> System administrators often run the crack password guessing program (available at CERT and other sites) against their own password files. If this program breaks any of the passwords, the administrators contact the passwords' owners and ask them to create more secure passwords. This program can go a long way toward making the system more secure.

V

Security

◀ See "FTP,"
     p. 41

Finally, one of the easiest ways to get into a system is through the FTP mechanism. If you are offering FTP capability, make sure that you restrict your FTP mechanism and that it does not enable the user to go past the root FTP directory. Check your FTP manual pages to find out more about FTP-restricted access.

From Here...

This chapter briefly described the types of security problems that are possible on the Web. For many business applications, such as simple advertising and promotion, you probably will never have to deal with security precautions. But if you allow users or employees access to sensitive data, you definitely must take steps to protect yourself and your data.

For more information, refer to the following chapters:

- Chapter 18, "Security and Cash Transactions," explains how to set up your Web site.

- Chapter 19, "What To Do When Security Has Been Breached," provides strategies for handling security breaches.

Chapter 18

Security and Cash Transactions

Much of the talk today in the press and on the Web is about the arrival of secure servers and secure transaction handling on the Net and Web. This topic is important because increasingly more people want to transfer secure documents and credit card information without the fear of pirates and crackers.

This chapter explores these issues and provides a basic overview of encryption and digital signature techniques. The chapter also briefly discusses some higher-end security concerns and their solutions.

In this chapter you learn

- How to increase the security of cash transactions on the Net

- Data encryption

- How to create a digital signature

- How to retrieve, display, and retransmit data securely

- Restrictions on encryption across international borders

Can Internet Cash Transactions Ever Be Safe?

The question of Internet security and cash transactions is one of the hottest topics on the Internet today. The quest for secure transactions includes not only cash transactions but any type of transmission in which privacy of the data is desired.

Chapter 17, "Security and the Net," described how a perpetrator can access your data. With all the ways available to steal data, how can you make your data secure?

The entire security issue, however, is a sheep in wolf's clothing. As Chapter 17 pointed out, pirating the data between the browser and the server is not nearly as likely as simply pirating the data at the server itself. To intercept data, a pirate must position himself to do so while the data is being routed, which requires that the pirate expose himself. The pirate also stands to lose much of your data while it is being routed.

◀ See "Crime and the Net," p. 385

This is the big joke with the secure server discussions. While everyone is clamoring for secure servers, they protect only one half of the picture.

Secure servers attempt to encrypt the data between the browser and the server. Pirates have many ways that they can try to intercept the data. However, each method requires that the pirate operate within a trusted loop, have significant technical expertise, and risk exposing his or her identity.

Sometime during the shopping cycle, after the data reaches the secure server, the system must decrypt the data. Even if the data is decrypted only for an instant, the information could still be intercepted. The most sophisticated software handles this decryption using the quickest and most uncrackable mechanism possible. Nevertheless, creating a system in which information remains encrypted throughout the cycle is practically impossible.

Products that try to address this problem are beginning to appear, such as Netscape Communications' I-Store. This product tries to make the system 100 percent secure by connecting the store owner to a commercial bank that clears the credit card information. The system sends the credit card information directly to the bank in an encrypted format. The data is then decrypted in the bank's secure system.

Such bundled solutions are interesting and useful to the new store owner, but often fall short of the needs of store owners who can already clear their own credit card information. In such cases, the system must route the credit card information directly to the store owner. Often, the charges of the bundled service may be greater than the store owner's current service.

Regardless of whether the system routes information to the shop owner or to the bank, the credit card information can actually remain encrypted until the last possible moment. However, at some point, the system still must convert the information so that the shop owner can read it. At that moment, the information is crackable.

The most secure setup is one that transmits the information to the shop owner in encrypted format, moves the information to a computer that is not on the Net, and then decrypts the information (as shown in fig. 18.1).

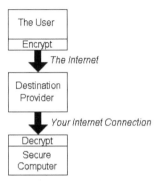

Fig. 18.1
Keeping your data encrypted until it is on a secure system gives you the best possible protection.

Many professional mathematicians and theoreticians foster the belief that modern encryption technology is totally unbreakable. However, although many recent breakthroughs in encryption technology have been achieved, there have also been concurrent breakthroughs in decryption technology.

> **Note**
>
> Recent advances in distributed prime number calculation have broken security keys previously considered unbreakable. No longer are supercomputers required to break encryption systems. Instead, the problem can be split into millions of little problems and distributed throughout a network. In this way, the problem can be solved with alarming efficiency.
>
> This is not to say that any Nintendo-waving kid can break encryption. In fact, it took a team of mathematicians and cooperation among several institutions to prove that the decryption theories worked. Of course, the security community was quick to respond with new keys that are harder to break. Still, the team's achievement demonstrates that no matter how secure a mechanism is, some method or technology that can break the mechanism will eventually arrive.

The bottom line is that although secure servers do much to make people feel secure, much of that security is merely in the user's state of mind. Users should feel reassured knowing that the flow of data from the user to the server is secure. Also, you can take steps to hide the data as long as possible within the sever itself. These techniques include putting the data in hidden directories or in files that are mislabeled. For example, don't put credit card numbers in a file called cards.txt; put them in grocery.txt. Each step you take reduces the chance of a pirate plundering your data.

V

Security

Regardless of the steps you take, however, you should be aware of the issues of monitoring for and handling any security breaches that occur.

Encryption

Encryption is a technique for hiding data so that it can be seen only by those for whom it is intended. Simple encryption schemes exchange one character for another. For example, the word "bqqmf" is an encrypted form of the word "apple," where each letter is simply incremented to the next. Obviously, this type of encryption is not very secure. Given a sufficient number of words in an encrypted message, you could quickly deduce the message's meaning simply by playing with different substitute letters.

As you can imagine, many more secure schemes exist. For example, the number sequence

```
0 1 1 616 12 0 5
```

is also an encoded version of the word "apple." This example is fascinating because the encoded version contains more numbers than the original version has letters, and also because the encoded version apparently includes two sets of repeated numbers, whereas the word "apple" has only one set of repeated letters.

To decode this example, simply place the numbers in pairs of two ("01 16 16 12 05") and then replace each pair of numbers with the corresponding letter from the alphabet ("a" is the first, "p" is the 16th, "l" is the 12th, and "e" is the fifth). This method enables you to express the same word many ways. For example, the following sequences all represent the word "apple":

```
0 1 1 6 1 6 1 2 0 5
0 11 6 16 1 2 0 5
0 11616 1205
```

In fact, you can easily extrapolate this method into a nasty little scheme. For example,

```
a01(g1LZ6&@16SAL1JS20FSD@*5!(>S
```

is also the same form for "apple"—if you simply ignore the letters and special characters. Unless you are aware of this rule, however, such a scheme makes it difficult to distinguish the garbage from the pertinent code.

Of course, now that you know the secrets of this coding scheme, you can easily decrypt any message that uses it. In fact, you probably could also quickly figure out variations on the code. This method is not very secure, because you can guess the code with a bit of effort.

> **Caution**
>
> Simple substitution codes like those described are bad because in large messages, the number sequences will repeat for the most frequently used letters of the alphabet. By comparing the frequency of certain patterns against the most frequently used letters, you can begin to deduce the meaning of a coded message.

Computers, with their amazing speed and relentless pursuit, can be easily applied to the duty of decryption. They can sift through millions of patterns and combinations looking for results that make sense. Therefore, most codes quickly become useless when scrutinized by even moderate computing power.

Codes that cannot easily be broken consist of messages created without repeating patterns. For example, in the previous scheme, you could encode

```
apple apple apple
```

as

```
0116161205 0116161205 0116161205
```

However, in a more complex scheme, you might encode it as

```
abcdefghijklmnopq
```

In this case, if each position in the string derives a different algorithm for encoding the position, determining the message without knowing the encoding scheme is almost impossible.

However, this scheme also fails because it depends on a constant method of encryption. Even if the encryption is position-dependent, it is still constant for that position. Therefore, this scheme is secure only as long as the actual algorithms for encryption do not fall into enemy hands. If three employees—Sue, Pete, and John—all use their employer's algorithm to encrypt and decrypt all messages, John could decrypt a message sent between Sue and Pete, which could create a security problem.

How can you create an encryption scheme that enables Sue and Pete to trade messages without John being able to read them? One mechanism is to require some third piece of data to decrypt the code. This third piece of data is called a *key*, because it acts much like a key to a lock.

Sue and Pete can use the key and the encryption algorithm to decrypt messages transmitted between them. Even if John knows the encryption

V

Security

algorithm, he cannot deduce the meaning of an intercepted message without the proper key. If the key is sufficiently complex, John will not be able to guess the key in a reasonable amount of time.

For example, suppose that your encryption algorithm is a simple replacement code, which replaces one letter in a string with another letter in another string. Here is an example of how such a scenario would work:

1. In addition to using the standard company encryption algorithm, Sue and Pete agree ahead of time to use the following key:

   ```
   zyxwvutsrqponmlkjihgfedcba
   ```

2. Sue sends Pete the message

   ```
   zkkov
   ```

3. John intercepts the message and just gets garbage. He suspects that Sue and Pete are using a key, so he tries the following key:

   ```
   bcdefghijklmnopqrstuvwxyza
   ```

   This results in "bqqmf," which is not correct. John tries several other keys before giving up in frustration.

4. Pete receives the message from Sue, applies the key, and deduces that the word is "apple."

John is obviously pretty stupid if he could not guess the proper key in this example. But you can see how, given a slick enough encryption algorithm and a sophisticated enough key, you can generate a system that is practically invincible.

The preceding design has one major flaw, however: it works only if both the sending and receiving parties know the key. If the receiving party does not know the key, you have to send the key to that party, and when you do so, the key can be intercepted. For example, if Sue sends Pete the key and then the message, John could both intercept and decrypt the message.

This flaw can makes things very inconvenient, especially when you want to use encryption to do things like purchase from stores where you have never been. If you have to request the proper key from the store, you give ample opportunity for someone else to witness the same transaction.

Combating this problem leads you to the next step in encrypting technology—digital signature.

Digital Signature

The previous section outlined the basics of encryption and leaves you at the point where you need a solution for transmitting a secure key to another party. The solution is a technique called *public-key encryption*. Currently, the most popular commercially available public-key encryption system is offered by RSA Data Security of Redwood City, Calif. (see fig. 18.2 and 18.3).

Fig. 18.2
The RSA Data Security home page at **http://www.rsa.com/** has complete information about public-key encryption systems.

V

Security

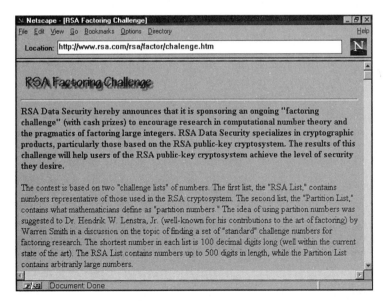

Fig. 18.3
RSA Data Security offers a cash prize for a computational challenge in encryption theory. If you're good with math, check out **http://www.rsa.com/rsa/factor/chalenge.htm**.

In a public-key encryption system, each user has two keys:

- a public key

- a private key

The encryption and decryption algorithms are tuned so that only the private key can decrypt data encrypted by the public key, and only the public key can decrypt data encrypted by the private key. Therefore, you can freely broadcast the public key to the world.

At first this system seems somewhat confusing, but it is actually quite simple. Consider the following scenario:

- Sue has a private key that only she knows.

- Pete has a private key that only he knows.

- Both Sue and Pete have public keys that Sue, Pete, John, and everyone else know.

Sue wants to send a secure message to Pete in such a way that Pete knows that Sue sent it but that no one else can read it. Sue encrypts her message using Pete's public key, which everybody knows. However, once encrypted, only Pete's private key, which only Pete knows, can decrypt Sue's message.

Sue sends the message to Pete, but along the way, pirate John copies it. John now possesses a message from Sue to Pete. John knows Pete's public-encryption key, which Sue used to encrypt the message. However, that key does John no good, because only Pete's private key can decrypt the message. Therefore, John cannot decrypt the message.

When Pete receives the message from Sue, he simply decrypts it with his private key and reads the message. Pete writes a responding message, encrypting it with Sue's public key, and then sends it to Sue. When Sue receives the message, she decrypts it with her private key.

As long as Sue never discloses her private key and Pete never discloses his private key, all their messages will be secure.

Secure servers and browsers use this type of scheme as follows:

1. A user fills out an order form and submits it.

2. The user's browser contacts the remote server. The remote server sends back to the user's browser its public-encryption key.

3. The user's browser uses the server's public key to encrypt the order form and then sends it to the server.

4. The server decrypts the order form using the server's private key, which only the server knows.

If a pirate happens to catch any of the transmissions—even that of the server's public key—the pirate cannot decrypt the transaction, because only the server's private key can do that.

At first, this scheme might seem incredibly secure. About the only way that a pirate can break the code is by guessing the key. And most systems use huge keys that supposedly make the possibility of guessing them absolutely astronomical.

Unfortunately, pirates are not quite that lazy. A pirate can easily pretend to be the server. In this case, the user's browser contacts the pirate thinking that person is the destination server (the pirate is spoofing, or faking, the server's IP address or has injected himself into the stream). However, the encryption folks have solutions for this and for many other mechanisms that pirates might use.

Receiving Secure Information

If you want to accept information in encrypted form, you should use some type of secure server. Such servers handle transactions from all secure browsers that know about the server's protocol.

However, some users do not have a browser that can interact securely with your server. Such browsers send you insecure data no matter what. Even if your policy is to refuse forms from such browsers, you still cannot stop users from using them to submit the form. Just the simple act of submitting the form is all that is needed to give pirates ample opportunity to retrieve the data.

> **Note**
>
> In your pages, you might want to mention that you can handle secure transactions. Offer a link for users to find the appropriate software or contact information so that they can begin to use a secure browser.
>
> You might also want to provide a link to a page that gives your public-encryption key. Then users who are encryption-savvy but still lacking secure browsers can at least use your public key to send you e-mail orders and other information.

If you are someone who receives secure information, such as a store owner who receives encrypted orders, you need to know how to handle the transaction. Depending on how you get your order, you see it in either encrypted or decrypted form. If the order is decrypted, it is already too late for you to take precautions.

> **Caution**
>
> Decrypting your order before you are ready to use it gives pirates more time to steal your data. Decryption should be the last step before processing the data.
>
> If the message is encrypted, you can take a precaution to keep the data secure: avoid decrypting the information on a public system. Instead, move it to a secure system (one that isn't hooked into the phone lines or some other network) before you decrypt the message.

For example, if you are on a network, as you receive your orders you might simply archive them in their encrypted state. When you are ready, you can transmit the orders to a secure system and then disconnect the link. With the secure system completely off the Web, you can then decrypt the information without worrying about pirates invading your dataspace.

◀ See "Credit
Card Transac-
tions," p. 275

◀ See "Virtual
Shopping
Systems,"
p. 328

> **Caution**
>
> When you receive an order from a secure mechanism, keep in mind that the sender isn't necessarily honest. You still cannot guarantee that such senders are who they say they are. This is particularly a problem if you use a secure server to accept login information for a subscription or membership system.

In a login system, the pirate can do a few things:

- Record the login sequence and then repeat it later. This enables the pirate to gain access.

- Misrepresent himself as another person.

Most encrypting servers and browsers have special capabilities that enable them to overcome these types of problems. The foremost solution is to timestamp each transaction. This totally eliminates the possibility of recording and then playing back a login session.

Encryption servers also use a technique known as a *certificate* to verify the user. Certificates act as a mechanism to stop pirates from using false IDs (that is, from using other people's names with a different key).

Certificates work by having a third party keep track of public keys and their owners. The third party must be a trusted party, similar to the InterNIC. The certificates the third party issues are encrypted with private keys.

Under this scenario, when contacted your server asks for the certification document, which the sender provides along with the sender's private key. You can examine the certification, which only the third party can encrypt, and compare the name and public key to the person who submitted the message. If they match, the user must be who he or she claims to be (as long as the third party's confidence is not compromised).

As you can see, the issues related to receiving secure information are complex. But although you cannot plug every security hole, you can plug up the vast majority of them. One hole that you cannot plug is that which enables a pirate to intercept enough of your messages to deduce the key (after much time and effort). In a world of supercomputers and corporate secrets, plugging this hole is not impossible or improbable, but does require an investment of both time and energy. You can, however, easily thwart such a threat by periodically changing your keys.

Storing Secure Information

Throughout this and other chapters, this book has repeatedly pointed out that the most insecure part of the Internet is not the Net itself, but the source and destination of users and computers on the Net.

First, as a user of the system, you should know where and how to store your data. Everything that you have learned about security applies to both the user and the administrator. While you are connected to the network, your personal system is vulnerable. Because of the nature of SLIP-style connectivity and TCP/IP networks, someone else could be probing your system while you work. (The type of software that you have may determine whether simultaneous access is possible.)

Note

Because most DOS or Mac style software doesn't multitask, it doesn't allow simultaneous access. However, some commercial software for Macs and PCs does monitor the SLIP connection for incoming information. These software applications can potentially enable someone outside your system to enter your system while you are hooked to the Internet. Check your software documentation.

Keeping Sensitive Data Encrypted

Decrypted data residing on your hard drive may be available to outside snooping. Remember, it's easier to pluck data from your machine than through the airwaves, just as it is easier to overhear a phone conversation by eavesdropping next door than it is to tap into the phone lines. As server and browser security increases, almost all pirates will be driven to breaking into the systems at the source or the destination.

The problem is that when your information is local to you, you rarely store it in encrypted format. Currently, storing your word processor documents, spreadsheet information, source code, and other information in encrypted format is simply not feasible. Having to do so would make it very difficult to use your information and software.

As telecommunications increase, you will begin to see more commercial software with built-in encryption and authorization. Until then, however, you must provide your own security.

This information, of course, applies equally to both the user and the store owner. Store owners must ensure that their product databases are secure. Furthermore, store owners should go to lengths to ensure that they encrypt archived transactions, as well as transactions in the process of being fulfilled.

> **Note**
>
> Probably not everyone will follow this security advice. In fact, we do not always follow the advice ourselves (except for any software that deals with credit card information). Again, providing total encryption of all information is extremely difficult, at least in today's computing environment. Often, you interface with mechanisms that cannot handle encrypted data. Other times, the cost of making a system totally secure is beyond the business owner's means.

The important thing to understand is that total security is not necessary for everybody. The small mom-and-pop establishment should merely be aware of the issues, keep the system as cost-effectively secure as possible, and monitor all appropriate logs and ports. However, the huge corporation and the company with a nervous clientele will want to invest in the most secure technology available.

Note

If your business can afford only minimal security, one thing that you can do is keep permissions of files hidden from prying eyes (ask your system administrator to "check the permissions"). To do so, put the data in a hidden directory. Consult your platform manuals for information on how to do this. You can also hide the data as junk (that is, under file names that seem routine and boring).

The primary thing that *all* security-conscious users of the Internet will want to do is to ensure that they keep their private-encryption key private. If a pirate can penetrate your machine and find your private-encryption key lying around, that person can then break your encryption security to the highest level. For this reason, hiding your data well and monitoring your system for security violations is important.

Protecting Your Data's Physical Storage

When you store your data, one critical choice is physical location. Most users overlook the fact that much of today's data is portable. Slipping files onto a floppy disk or taking a laptop on a trip is fine, except when you leave sensitive files on them. You can easily misplace them or have them stolen. If the laptop or floppy disk contains your private key or other sensitive information, you could be in for an unpleasant surprise.

Caution

When you travel by airline, be careful when you leave your seat. On a recent trip, I left my laptop in my seat with a floppy disk in its drive. Later I discovered the floppy disk was missing. Whether it had fallen out or been stolen, the floppy could easily have ended up in someone else's hands. Lock your computer in a case before leaving your seat, or at least take the floppy disk with you. Also when traveling, think twice about leaving your laptop in a nice, new, shiny rental car.

Even machines that you think are secure in your home or office can be broken into and have stored data destroyed, changed, or copied. Although mom-and-pop businesses don't have to worry about this too much, larger companies with aggressive competition might want to take precautions of either hiding or encrypting their data, even on machines not on the network.

V

Security

If a competitor wants your data bad enough and cannot hack into the system from the network, a well-paid pirate could easily get into your premises by posing as part of contracted maintenance, security, or cleaning crews. More importantly, a well-paid pirate can infiltrate your employee staff, either as a temporary worker or a new employee.

You might think that these "spy stories" of covert activities are as implausible as a Hollywood plot. In fact, many young pirates get their education from movies. Many pirates start by getting jobs with local telephone companies or giants like AT&T, Ameritech, Sprint, or MCI. Student intern, temporary, and full-time positions give pirates access to major information about network security, telephone switch technology, and protocols. Your competition can easily apply this strategy to gain access to your company's stored data.

Note

By keeping your data encrypted or secure, or even having a remote camera watching the computer setup, you can do much for your internal security. Also, don't forget to keep backups, because destruction of the data is also a potential sabotage possibility.

One of the best security measures that you can take for physically stored data is to have hardware password protection at powerup. Many commercial products provide this capability and often work well to keep your data secure.

Some laptop computers also have powerup password protection. Users who frequently travel with sensitive data might consider a laptop with this type of protection. Although such protection is not impenetrable, it can go a long way toward warding off the casual criminal who might steal your computer for the hardware and then try to forward your data to your competitor for an extra buck. Making it difficult to get at your data might be just the amount of protection it takes to keep your competitor from getting your data.

Note

If you work in a field that is prone to industrial espionage, the thief who steals your laptop computer may simply be committing a crime of convenience and may not necessarily be after your sensitive data. However, if the thief finds important information on your computer, he or she may decide to try to sell it to your competition.

Cleaning Discarded Hardware

When you sell or donate your old computer, make sure to have the drive cleaned. Too often, used computers are loaded not only with software but also with the previous owner's private files, company e-mail, and spreadsheet files.

This warning is particularly important when a business sells or donates its computers. Many companies don't stop to consider the information that a computer might contain, or may simply assume that any such information is too old to matter. However, if the computer was used by a sales representative, for example, it probably is full of purchase order numbers, credit card numbers, telephone numbers, corporate account numbers, and all sorts of other goodies that an enterprising cracker or pirate might find useful.

Simply deleting the information is not enough. Pirates can easily undelete previously deleted information. They can even unformat a formatted disk.

The best solution is to use something like the Defense Department's recommended secure delete program. Such programs are available in software archives throughout the Internet. Before marking the file as deleted, such programs first write repeating sequences of bits to each bit within the file. This ensures that the magnetic particles are toggled several times so that even faint magnetic signatures are not readable.

Another solution is to delete the files on the disk and then write a single, huge file that takes up all the disk space. After the disk space runs out, confirm that you have zero bytes available on the drive and then delete the program.

Tip

Before deleting files in the methods described here, make sure that you really want to get rid of them, because you can't recover them later. These methods delete the actual data, not just the file name.

Tip

After securely deleting your files, defragment your drive using any popular drive cleanup program. Such a program ensures that the original structure of the disk is reorganized, leaving no recoverable data.

V

Security

Retrieving, Displaying, and Retransmitting Secure Information

If you thought the last section started to get a little far out, you will really enjoy this section. You already learned how pirates can break into systems and even foil encryption schemes. You should also be fairly aware by now of steps you can take to keep your data secure when it is stored and when it is transmitted. However, at some point, you must actually view the secure information. And at that point, the information again becomes unsecure.

> **Note**
>
> The level of security that this section discusses is really only for companies that are dealing with extremely sensitive information. The average hacker, unless backed by lots of money, will not have the equipment to use the measures described in this section.

We do not yet live in a paperless society, so we still like to keep records. Printouts present especially nasty security problems, because they often provide information that you did not intend them to provide. For example, banners for printouts often contain account information and even key information.

Many users don't read the banners and therefore aren't adequately aware of the sensitive data they may contain. Or, they may simply forget that when they press the Print Screen button, the resulting hard copy includes the banner. Such information left lying around is an open invitation to the curious. This material can also be a possible security threat if you simply toss it into the trash where it can be easily retrieved.

You may be shocked to learn that the following type of pirating is possible. All computers and display devices emit electromagnetic radiation as they operate. In the early age of computing, programmers could debug programs by turning on a radio and setting it near the computer. The internal clock speed of the computer would oscillate like the radio station's, and thus they could "hear" the programming running. The programmers soon learned how to interpret the squawks, squabbles, and tones to determine what was happening in their program. If the program crashed, the radio produced a low sound or no sound. If the program went into an infinite loop, the radio might emit a constant, nonvarying, high-pitched sound—the higher the frequency, the faster the loop. (Remember, this debugging practice was common in the early days of computing.)

Incredibly, a type of technology and research called TEMPEST is available that can reverse this electromagnetic radiation into a reasonable reproduction of the original information. The U.S. government has classified most of the TEMPEST information, but although most of the information is not generally available, some information is known. Current theories hold that a poorly protected computer (the meaning of the term *protection* in this context is covered shortly) can be monitored remotely from a distance of 1K from the computer.

As an example of how easy this technology is to create and use, consider the following. Your video monitor uses a rigid video protocol to transmit video signals, which themselves create a field that extends for hundreds of feet. Microwave receivers can easily tap the wave of radiation coming from a monitor, even through walls. The receiver's output is sent to a monitor with an external genlock (the sync of the signal), which is slowly changed until the image appears.

To use such a device, the pirate pulls up a van a few blocks away from your building. He then positions a microwave receiver (which is about as small as a radar detector) in the direction of your computer. He then turns on his monitor and slowly adjusts the horizontal and vertical sync. At the right adjustment, his monitor picks up whatever is on your monitor, including color. His display might not be as clean and clear as your monitor's display, but the content is just as readable. This technique bypasses all security, because the data is displayed as decrypted on your screen and therefore also is displayed as decrypted on his screen.

Although this technique is probably not often used, it may be a concern for big corporations. However, you can actually do quite a bit to combat it. Currently you cannot stop all emissions, but you can reduce the emissions so that the van parked outside has to be right outside your window to pick up your information.

You can follow these tips to reduce your emissions:

- Buy only computing equipment rated as class B. Class A equipment is the standard, run-of-the-mill computer that you find in most homes and businesses. Class B equipment is rated to have one-tenth the amount of emissions and thus is less open to this kind of monitoring.

- Point the back of your monitors away from outside walls, because most of the emissions come through the back of the monitor. Also, to prevent potential health hazards, you should strive to keep the backs of computers pointed away from people as well.

- By using shielded powercords, video cables, and modem cables, you can help isolate the signals.

Tip

Find out from your equipment manufacturer whether your equipment is class A or B. Check if the manufacturer offers a line of class B equipment. Most companies who sell to the government carry class B computing equipment.

Encryption and International Borders

As you learned earlier, the U.S. has strict rules about exporting encryption technology. With all this discussion about servers and encryption, you might wonder how companies can export browsers with encryption technology.

The U.S. government is more concerned with encryption technology than with *authentication technology*. If you can significantly demonstrate that your clients can use your encryption product only for authentication and not for private encryption, you can usually export your product.

To the government, the difference between authentication and encryption is that authentication is built into a product and can be used only under the strict guidance of the product. General encryption technology, on the other hand, enables anyone to encrypt anything. The government does not mind people encrypting credit card orders and other material for the purpose of authentication with a remote machine. However, the government does mind encrypting for personal use.

Because the encryption of WWW browsers and servers is internal to the program and under strict use as authentication and digital signature, the government usually clears this technology for export. For this reason, the same encryption technology works around the world.

From Here...

Your security measures for computers connected into the Internet can be as complex as you want or can afford. Everyone should take the basic measures of creating secure passwords, not leaving printouts lying around, and keeping your hardware (laptops included) secure. Also, you should encrypt sensitive data (such as credit card information and account numbers for shipping companies) that you send over the Internet.

These basic measures should be enough to cover the average company. But remember to monitor your system. If you encounter any security breaches, you want to eliminate them and implement some of the more sophisticated security measures. Such measures are a must for any company with information that might be overly tempting and profitable for pirates and hackers. Particularly vulnerable companies include those involved in national security or those that have such companies as clients.

The key to security is vigilance. As the computing industry strives to build bigger and better mouse traps, the mice are getting smarter and finding new and better ways around the traps.

For more information, refer to the following chapters:

- Chapter 5, "Choosing Hardware and Software," provides tips for choosing the correct equipment and software for your needs.

- Chapter 9, "Information on the Net," describes how to find the information you need about security.

- Chapter 12, "Methods for Collecting Cash," deals with other specific security issues, such as how to clear credit cards and purchase orders.

- Chapter 19, "What To Do When Security Has Been Breached," talks about who you should turn to when the worst security breaches occur.

- Chapter 20, "Kiosks Made Easy," discusses security issues regarding kiosks.

V

Security

What To Do When Security Has Been Breached

The average user who hooks into the Internet via a home PC or Mac for a few hours every night doesn't have that much to worry about when it comes to security. However, many businesses have a dedicated computer hooked up to the Internet 24 hours a day, which increases the risk of hacking. If the machine has a multitasking platform (such as UNIX, NT, OS/2, Windows 95, and so on), then you have special security needs and concerns.

This chapter introduces you to some of the techniques used to help ensure a secure system on the Internet and Web.

The issues surrounding security are complex and require an understanding of system administration. Many books have been written on the subject and have much more to say about security than this one short chapter.

You might not need the information presented here simply because you will be hosting your pages at a provider's site. However, you should know how to identify a break-in, even within your data at a provider's site. Additionally, the information in this chapter gives you an idea as to what your provider should be doing to protect the site, as well as how to handle an intrusion should one occur.

If you are setting up your own WWW site, the information in this chapter will be extremely useful.

In this chapter you learn how to

- Recognize indicators that your security has been breached

- Isolate the damage

- Look for the cause of a security breach

- Solicit help for security problems

- Know who to notify when security is broken

- Create and implement a secure site

- Work with firewalls, wrappers, and proxies

How To Determine Whether Security Has Been Breached

Unless you are running proper firewalls, wrappers, and proxies, you might have difficulty determining if security has been breached (firewalls, wrappers, and proxies are discussed later in this chapter). In fact, if you are not constantly monitoring for intrusion, you might have intruders right now and not even know it.

If the system you are using is your own machine, you will undoubtedly be able to determine misuse with much less problem than if your machine is hosting many other users.

Wrappers and firewalls aside, one of the best indications of an intruder is excessive quantities of your disk space disappearing without any reason. Another good indication is increasingly slower telecommunications speeds.

Before learning how to check for intrusion, consider the following example of an intrusion that occurred about three weeks before writing this chapter.

At about two in the morning, we noticed a drastic decrease in telecommunications speed. Glancing at our throughput, we noticed that we were stuck transmitting data. This alarmed me because we knew that we weren't sending data, and by the looks of it, megabytes were flowing out of our machine to some remote user.

We quickly checked our FTP wrapper log and noted that a user had logged in to our anonymous FTP handler, which we keep for clients. Because the handler is empty except when a client is sending or receiving a file, we knew that the major amount of material being downloaded could not be our material in that directory.

We quickly went to our anonymous FTP directory and started examining the file system. We found—and this took some time—the following three directories in our upload directory:

```
.

..

..
```

Anyone acquainted with UNIX or DOS will recognize "." as the current directory, and ".." as the parent directory. But our FTP directory had an extra "..". This is not possible, and so we knew that a pirate had created a hidden directory.

The next step was to enter the directory. To do this, we needed to determine the actual directory name. We found that the user had created a directory with two dots followed by a backspace and then a forward space. This made it rather difficult to type from the keyboard, so we simply wrote a short program to move the directory to a new name. Once renamed, the directory could be entered.

Upon entering the directory, we discovered that we had been made a warez (pirated software) site. In fact, we were listed in the documentation left by the pirates as site #11, which meant that there were probably at least 10 other sites besides ours.

The directory was filled with more than 21M of pirated software, including programs from major companies. Directories were also set aside for the pirate's friends to use for requests for other software as well as general messaging. The pirate had also created a directory with advisories about certain software that reported itself as stolen via e-mail through the Internet.

All this was very well-done, all very illegal, and all being done on our machine without our knowledge.

The file date on the pirate directories existed for three days prior to the day we discovered the site, and thus the site had been running for three days without our noticing it! This meant that the pirates and their friends had been logging in to our system and uploading and downloading stolen software to their hearts' content for three days.

Tip

If you find illegal warez on your machine, do not run them! Not only are you running a stolen copy, but it also could be infected with viruses.

Needless to say, not only did it use system resources, but it put our entire system in jeopardy because it appeared that we were running an illegal warez site. Later, this chapter further discusses the steps taken to find the pirate and report the problem; but we discuss how we discovered the problem—basically by accident.

About four days after we found and removed the warez site, our system was again made a warez site. This time the pirate took no care in hiding the information. It was easy to find and examine the site. And again the pirate had completely filled up our hard drive space with stolen software. However, the pirate seemed to retaliate for my having removed the pirate's earlier site (especially because he put the new site under a directory named "guesswho").

My guess is that the new site was specifically left as a Trojan horse with the hopes that we would run some of the software in it. We suspect that it was a retaliatory measure and contained viruses that would have infected our machine if we ran them. For our protection, we simply deleted the material without examining it.

You can see by the preceding example that we did not take proper precautions to determine whether our system was being misused. It took the first offense for us to realize that we had a potential problem. We learned quickly and caught the second offense as it was happening.

You can actually follow an easy set of rules to ensure that your security is not breached:

- *Protect* (your system)

- *Monitor* (for intrusion)

- *Trap* (any intruders)

- *Report* (to proper authorities)

- *Destroy* (pirated data)

The first and foremost thing that you can do is protect your system. This is covered in-depth later in this chapter, but remember that with security in the 1990s, protection is everything.

The second most important thing to do when improving your security is to monitor your system. Monitoring is the only way that you can know if your system security has been breached. We discovered the pirate because we routinely monitor our communications throughput as well as our disk space.

Many indications of security breaches exist besides missing disk space or clogged communication lines. The system logs show login events as well as attempts to gain privileged user access.

Tip
Routinely examine your logs to determine if you have any users trying to gain access to your accounts.

> **Note**
>
> For security purposes, routinely monitor the following:
>
> - Disk space usage
> - Communications lines
> - Login files
> - Attempts to change user privilege
> - Network statistics logs

Another good indication is looking at the network statistics logs. These logs tell you about socket and port connections to your machine and should record who has used what socket and when. This information can not only help you find pirates trying to hack into your ports, but can also go a long way in tracking them down because domain information is provided as part of the statistics.

After you identify a potential break-in, you can attempt to identify and trap the assailant. This requires time and energy on your part, but is often rewarding because you can often at least identify the location he has come from. When you have an idea who the perpetrator is, you can then report him to the proper authorities and destroy the data he has been placing on your machine. All of these methods are discussed throughout this chapter.

However, as you discover later in this chapter, wrappers, proxies, and firewalls are the only real solutions to combating crackers and data pirates.

V

Security

Isolating the Damage

After you identify that you have a pirate or cracker hitting your system, take immediate action to identify and isolate the damage.

Caution

If you are trying to capture or trap the pirate, you want to be careful so that your action does not tip off the pirate.

After you identify the mechanism of entry, determine how much damage the pirates can cause with their current course of action. Because the break-in on our system came via the anonymous FTP system—and our anonymous FTP is highly restricted—we were not losing anything other than system resources. In other words, in that situation no damage was done. Because of this, we could afford the time to try to trap the pirate.

If, however, the pirate has free access to your system or you suspect that the pirate is roaming around in areas that contain sensitive information, terminate the user's connection immediately. You can do this in many ways, and the method you pick will depend largely on whether you have other users on your system.

Simple methods include terminating the user's session by simply killing the user's shell or FTP process. Other, more severe mechanisms include resetting your communications system or entire computing system (like hanging up your modem or turning off your computer).

Whatever method you use, be aware that pirates may not know they've been discovered. Indeed, in our situation after resetting the communications system, the pirate logged right back on and resumed transmission, evidently thinking that the line had been dropped for some natural reason. In other words, you might have to do something a little more drastic to make the pirates realize that you have caught on. (In our case, once we had identified the pirate we simply wanted him to leave our machine alone; we were not concerned that the pirate knew we had found him.)

We changed the default README of the FTP system (the information automatically displayed to users when they log into our system via FTP) with a specific message to the pirate. After resetting our communications system again, the pirate again logged right back on, but this time logged right back off.

> **Note**
>
> In cases of severe cracking or pirating, you should probably pull your system off the network and refuse user login until you have been able to isolate the damage. This ensures that other users, as well as the pirate, will not be able to disrupt the recovery of your system.

When the pirate is no longer on your system, you can begin to actually examine the damage. You should be very careful about doing this and document each step. Not only is this useful for you to reconstruct what happened, but it may also be necessary for law enforcement. If you simply remove the pirate's warez or undo the damage without documentation, prosecution of the pirate will be difficult.

Looking for the Cause

If you have a WWW page on a provider site and think that you have been accessed illegally, report it to your provider immediately. Your provider will help you isolate the problem and track down the pirate. If, however, you are running your own WWW site, the following information will help you track down the culprit.

When you begin to suspect that your system security has been breached, you will immediately want to know who the perpetrator is. Finding the suspect is rarely a simple matter, but one that does have several solutions:

1. If the user has penetrated via a known login, you can assume that either the password for that login was easy to break or that the user of the login has let the login information out. You can verify the user's password by either asking the user (which may tip off pirates if they are working with the user) or try to break the password yourself with a password cracking program.

   ◀ See "Crackers and the Net," p. 401

2. If the password appears secure, it's time to examine the user's logs. Look for unusual activity—for example, use during normal times as well as late at night might indicate that the owner of the account is using it during normal hours, but that the pirate is going in after hours. Likewise, being logged in more than once may be an indication of a security breach (although not always, as some users run multiple sessions).

V

Security

3. If the user came in via FTP, you can look at the FTP log. Make sure that the version of FTP you are using keeps accurate logs of user access.

> **Note**
>
> The WUSTL archives (**ftp://ftp.wustl.edu/**) provide quite a bit of public domain software, which is specifically built-in to log transactions. Check this archive site for the FTP and other Internet and Web software you need to do your logging.

Log files such as the FTP log and WWW log enable you to determine who has accessed your system, and some versions also track all the commands entered by the user.

Generally though, the user's actual name (or user name) won't be correct. Most pirates log in under a fictitious name; however, unless the pirates are extremely sophisticated, the listed domain name will be their correct domain name.

You can use this domain name to try to track down the user. Many tools can help you do this. The most powerful is the WHOIS command, which accesses the InterNIC database. With WHOIS, you can identify the user's domain and system administrator. This verifies that the domain is indeed valid, although it does not guarantee that the pirates are actually at that domain (sophisticated pirates know how to spoof domain names).

◄ See "Effective Order Filling Systems," p. 293

In many cases, pirates will, through a burst of ego, leave trails to their identity. In the break-in situation discussed earlier, the pirate actually left a file with the nicknames of all the pirates and the name of their group. This information can be used to guess user names at their domain name.

When you are armed with as much user information as possible, contact the user's site. If the site turns out to be fictitious, immediately take the steps outlined in the next section, because the user is a sophisticated cracker.

However, the majority of pirates can't spoof their domain names. Usually the pirate is on a commercial or educational domain somewhere, and typing **whois** will give you direct access to the system administrator.

Contact the system administrator as soon as possible. If a contact number exists, call it. Often, even at late hours, administration staff may be onsite. If you can't reach them by the phone number listed by **whois**, use the e-mail address listed or try sending mail to **root** at the domain name.

> **Note**
>
> The reason you want to talk to the site administrator as soon as possible is that if the pirate is dealing with stolen software or data—either yours or someone else's—the sooner the administrator of the pirate's domain knows about it, the sooner the administrator can examine his own system to see whether the data exists.

In the example involving my system, I noted that the perpetrator came in via a domain name of a nationwide Internet provider. The larger the provider is, the greater the chance that they have pirates as legal users on their system (pirating other systems from their system). I was lucky in that I also had login capability on this same provider. Therefore, I was able to log in while the pirate was downloading from my system and find him.

Because the domain name points directly to a single machine (not a site), I simply logged into the same machine and used the UNIX w command to view the users. Because the time of the incident was after midnight, relatively few users were on that single machine. As luck would have it, only one user actually was in FTP. This meant I had the user's real login name. I verified that it was the user by killing his connection and watching him leave FTP, re-enter FTP, and then, almost instantly, reconnect to our system.

After I knew the user's name, it was a small matter to report the incident to the system administrators on the user's machine. Often, however, you cannot determine the user's name for reasons already indicated. In these cases, rely on the system administrators to help you isolate the user. They will do this either by comparing system logs or by actually watching user activity while the pirate is accessing your site.

If the pirate has faked his or her domain name, or the security breach continues or is of a damaging nature, contact some of the agencies in the next section for help.

Soliciting Help

Many organizations stand by to help you with your security needs. These organizations exist all the way from the federal government level down to the private sector.

The most respected organization on the Internet for issues of networking security is CERT. CERT was created in 1988 by DARPA to address computer security incidents. CERT is currently run out of Carnegie-Mellon University in Pittsburgh, Penn.

◀ See "Net Snitches and Net Police," p. 398

> **Note**
>
> You can reach CERT by contacting them at
>
>   CERT Coordination Center
>   Software Engineering Institute
>   Carnegie-Mellon University
>   Pittsburgh, PA 15213-3890
>   USA
>
>   Internet: **info.cert.org**
>
>   E-mail: **cert@cert.org**
>
>   24-hour hotline: 412-268-7090
>
> They would probably appreciate it if non-emergency calls were kept between 8:30 a.m. and 5 p.m. EST, when they are normally staffed.

CERT runs a server that can be found at **info.cert.org** via FTP. This FTP site contains copious quantities of advisories on various computer systems and their security holes. Also included is advice and instructions for plugging the holes. I highly suggest that you visit this site because you know the pirates have. The site also includes question-and-answer files that contain advice on determining whether your system is secure, as well as programs that analyze your security and help you identify holes.

> **Note**
>
> It is highly suggested that you visit advisory sites and institute the procedures they recommend for plugging security holes. These are open sites, and you can bet that the pirates have visited them. You should at least secure your site from the published security holes.

In addition, CERT's 24-hour hotline gives assistance for anyone with an emergency situation. Furthermore, their advisories are available via NetNews and can be found in the **comp.security.announce** newsgroup. CERT also maintains several mailing lists that you can be added to in order to receive constant updates on security issues. Information on how to get on the mailing lists is available at the CERT site.

Many organizations that deal with security issues post and read the various security NetNews groups. The following groups have information that you can read concerning security issues:

- **alt.security**

- **comp.risks**

- **comp.security.announce**

- **comp.security.misc**

- **comp.virus**

These groups are also excellent places for you to post your own questions or to relate your own solutions.

The FBI, not surprisingly, maintains a Computer Crime Squad. You can report any serious intrusion to them. We recommend that you first report your intrusion to CERT, and then if advised by them, also file a report with the FBI. When we called the FBI to report the intrusion on our system, we were told that an agent would call us right back; but nobody ever did. CERT, on the other hand, was very informative and helpful.

> **Note**
>
> The FBI Computer Crimes Squad may be contacted at
>
> > FBI National Computer Crimes Squad
> > Washington, DC
> >
> > Telephone: 202-324-9164

Other groups that examine the Internet and security issues include the following:

- The Internet Better Business Bureau (IBBB)

  http://ibd.ar.com/IBBB.html

- The Internet Society

  http://info.isoc.org/home.html

- The Electronic Commerce Association

  http://www.globalx.net/eca/

Additionally, there are many places on the WWW where you can find security topics and discussions. Figures 19.1 through 19.4 provide four such locations.

Fig. 19.1

The Security Newsgroups page at **http://mls. saic.com/news. html** lists many news sources for security topics.

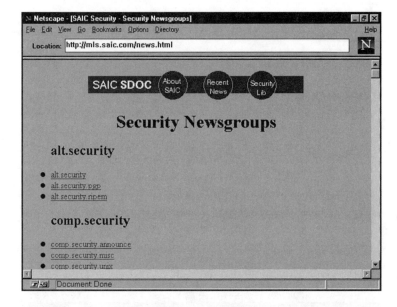

Fig. 19.2

The Security Locations page at **http://www. cycon.com: 8080/cycon/ security.html** lists many non-NetNews sites with security oriented discussions.

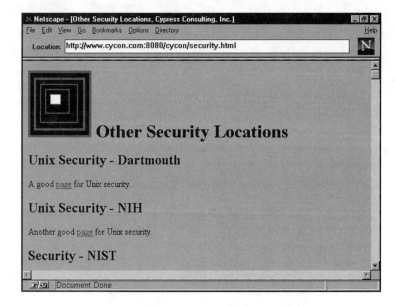

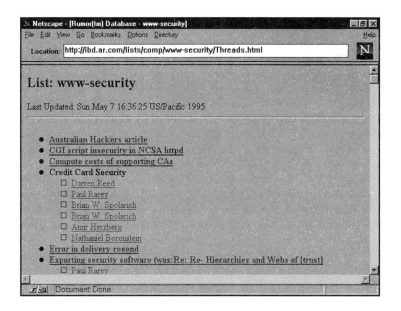

Fig. 19.3

The WWW-Security site at **http://ibd.ar.com/lists/comp/www-security/Threads.html** offers many references to security including topics such as credit card security.

Fig. 19.4

Trusted Information Systems, Inc., at **http://www.tis.com/Home/NetworkSecurity/Consulting.html** offers consulting services for security issues.

Notifying Others

This chapter has so far discussed contacting professional agencies such as CERT, the FBI, and system administrators. However, you should also notify some other people in case of a break-in.

> **Note**
>
> If the breach caused an inconvenience to any of your login users or regular WWW users, you might want to send them an e-mail explaining the situation and outlining your solution. Notifying your users of a breach goes a long way in keeping user confidence high, because it assures them that you are at least on the ball.

You should also discuss your situation when the opportunity arises with other system administrators or WWW page owners. Far too much of the current security problem is that, as with other forms of white-collar crime, people do not want to discuss it. Because of this, many people are not aware that their systems may be insecure. By spreading the word, you help increase awareness, which helps combat the problem.

After the break-in, our consciousness was raised, and we began to scour our system. We identified more than four severe security holes. During the course of this investigation, we also identified that a major portion of our file system had been remote mounted by a certain user at a university (meaning that this user could access portions of my disk as if it were the user's own disk). Although our security had been high enough to prevent the user from accessing sensitive client material, it still shocked us to realize that we had been violated so blatantly.

However, we immediately shared the information with an associate who runs a similar system. Working together in a couple of hours time, we identified even more weaknesses. By sharing the information instead of keeping it quiet, we were able to improve not only our system, but other systems as well.

> **Note**
>
> Many sites refuse to discuss security problems that they have had. They think that it shows their weakness. However, the more you share, the more you learn. By not discussing security breaches and solutions, you are simply making it easier for the problems to persist.

Implementing Solutions

Once you find that your security has been breached, you will immediately want to implement solutions to close your holes.

Wherever possible, attempt to close your security holes. However, many times you might have been penetrated in a way that you do not want to fix.

For example, if the pirate takes your system space via the FTP mechanism, you might not want to turn your FTP mechanism off. In our case, we offered anonymous FTP to our clients as a service; to turn it off would have been an inconvenience, and added scrutiny of the FTP file space was in order. We set up a schedule of periodic sweeps of the files in our system. The sweep only took a few seconds and could be run every day or two. The sweep can be automated, or can be done by hand by just simply looking in the directory or quickly going through the logs.

However, one of the best ways to handle pirates is to hit them in their weakest spot. Pirates and crackers exist by staying hidden, and if you expose them, they will quickly leave you alone.

The pirate site on our system had been broadcast to the pirate's users around the world. We were getting hundreds of logins a week into our FTP system to find the files. To combat the problem, we simply placed a short README document and automatic message that displayed every time a user logged in. The message simply said the following:

```
Dear pirates and crackers. The recent invasions of this system have
been discovered and tracked. We have reported these accesses to the
proper authorities and will continue to do so.
```

Remarkably, the number of logins very quickly decreased to zero. This message works well to persuade most crackers and pirates to leave your site alone. Most do not want to risk the chance of being caught. The notice served the same functionality as the alarm company stickers you see in windows and doors of businesses. They tell the pirate that you monitor and report; pirates would rather hit a system that does not monitor. With more than 16 million computers on the Net, pirates don't need to take the risk with your machine.

The preceding suggestion is a very low-tech solution, but it works amazingly well. It is, however, no replacement for constant monitoring and certainly no replacement for creating a secure system in the first place.

The following section gives tips and suggestions for creating secure systems, which helps to prevent problems.

V

Security

Creating a Secure System

The advantages of creating a secure system before you are pirated should be obvious. Prevention is the best medicine, and this applies equally well to computer security.

The first step is to keep the security of your data files such that only the right people can see them. This is especially crucial for any of the following types of data and files:

- User passwords
- Billing files
- System and user logs
- Credit card information
- Trusted remote system information
- Compilers
- Administration tools

Caution

Be sure to make the permissions of these files such that general users cannot get into them. The only users who should have access are trusted system administrators. If pirates or crackers can get to billing files or credit card information, they can use that information to do their own transactions.

User passwords and usage logs should be kept secure to keep pirates from looking at those files to figure out how to gain further access to your system. Keeping your password files shadowed or hidden keeps pirates from remotely acquiring your file and then running password cracking programs on the file in their own time.

Trusted remote systems are important to protect because you are protecting those whom you have a working relationship with. For example, you might have your credit card billing information handled by an external system. You would transmit credit card information to the remote system, which would in turn verify and handle the debit. If you keep access codes and other verification information to the remote system in files accessible by pirates, you are inviting them to use your service for free (at your cost).

Finally, be sure to protect administration tools as well as compilers. General users to your system should not have access to these tools because, if they fall into the wrong hands, the tools can be used to create programs that aid the pirate in breaking security.

Many pirates penetrate the systems from the inside out. It is much easier to buy an account on the large provider than to try to break into that system from the outside. A $10 or $15 month Internet account can be easily acquired giving the user—if the provider doesn't have proper security—full access to much of your system. Don't make it easier on the user by leaving the tools for your destruction around for them to find.

Systems may also be violated through their WWW servers. It's amazing how many servers in the world do not have directory protection turned on in the WWW server. In a system without directory protection, specifying a URL that points to a legal directory but not to a file will cause a listing of the directory to be displayed. The user can then use the **cd ..** command to move up and down your directory tree.

This capability enables even the most naive user to not only look at non-WWW files on your system, but also to download them by clicking them with the mouse. Servers have a simple mechanism in their configuration files that turns off the directory search mechanism. This one factor, which takes about 10 seconds to do, keeps users from cruising your directory space.

> **Note**
>
> If you are running your own WWW server, you should look at your server's configuration file for the DirReadme Off selection. If DirReadme Off is not in your configuration file, add it. Adding this feature enables you to turn off your directory searching capability and increases your WWW security.

Make sure that your users, both WWW and general system, know how to create secure passwords. The Web has the advantage of allowing passwords to be any length and contain spaces and other special characters.

Tip

Both Web and general computer users should use non-personal names, phrases, and terms.

V

Security

One of the best ways to pick nonsense passwords is to use a mnemonic scheme. For example,

```
This Is My 5th Password
```

would be

```
TIM5thP
```

Tip

Educating users about password security can easily be done with information contained in your login screens on how to pick passwords.

Likewise, on the Web (because passwords can be any length), you could have used the full sentence for your password.

On extremely secure systems, you might want to encourage users to rotate their passwords periodically. Most systems have this capability built in enabling this to occur, and Web systems can be designed to handle it.

You will also want to follow closely the newsgroups which discuss security and the CERT advisories. These forums are designed to help the security conscious system administrator.

> **Note**
>
> Security information can be found in the **comp.security.announce** newsgroups as well as the CERT advisories at **info.cert.org**.

The CERT site is especially useful because it contains may tips and techniques for creating a secure system. Besides text files that cover FAQs and simple solutions, you also find advisories that discuss known holes on different platforms and suggest changes to make them more secure.

Tip

Several programs are available for free on the Internet that can help you find security flaws in your system. Three such programs are crack, cops, and satan, and are available at many sites, including the CERT site.

If you discover new techniques or have experiences of your own to share that will help improve security, feel free to discuss it within the proper newsgroups. Others may have answers for your questions or may appreciate your insight into a situation.

One technique you can use to design a more secure system is to play the pirate yourself. See if you can break into your own system or gain access to your own data. To help you with this, you will find at CERT and other sites software that identify weaknesses in your system.

Programs such as *crack* try to break your password files and identify users with insecure passwords. You can then ask them to change their passwords. Make sure that you show them how to think up secure passwords.

Another useful program is *cops*, which analyzes a system and identifies weaknesses based on known holes in system design. You can run this program monthly to ensure that your system is in tip-top condition.

Satan is a program that examines the security of any system on the Internet, including systems that are not yours. It is designed to find security problems and report them back to you formatted nicely as HTML pages.

> **Note**
>
> Not only do system administrators use programs such as crack, cops, and satan, but so do pirates and other computer criminals. The same programs that can be used to protect your system can be used by others to infiltrate your system.

Credit card and other personal information should be encrypted at all times if at all feasible. Keeping credit card information around in decrypted form only invites easy picking. Although many order forms use simple form remailers that cannot use encryption technology, custom-designed shopping systems can be created and used to route sensitive information in a secure manner. Additionally, secure servers and browsers are beginning to appear that help address these issues.

◄ See "Virtual Shopping Systems," p. 328

◄ See "Encryption," p. 406

Finally, many good books, such as Que's Special Edition *Using the Internet*, cover the topic of security with more accuracy and in better depth than this chapter can here. Also examine the manuals that have come with your system and the documents at CERN and NCSA dealing with Web security.

Working with Firewalls, Wrappers, and Proxies

Firewalls, wrappers, and proxies offer a good line of defense for WWW server owners and system administrators.

Firewalls can be either software or hardware that protects your ports and keeps pirates from penetrating your security. The concept of a firewall is to only allow certain trusted domain names to access your system. Other domains are simply not allowed in and get a `Connection refused` message.

By restricting the millions of domain names such that only one or two get in, you are instantly restricting access to your system from the outside.

Firewalls can be configured to run on certain ports and not on others. This allows you to have security on all your systems except the areas where you don't want it. For example, you might want users to access your Web site from anywhere, but not ftp or telnet in. In this case, you would not have a firewall running on the Web port, but would have one running on your FTP and Telnet ports. Users from anywhere could access your Web information without any problem, but attempts to ftp and telnet would be refused unless they were coming from a trusted user.

> **Note**
>
> Maintenance of firewalls and other computer security systems is just as crucial as the initial setup and installation. Additionally, you should stay current with updates to your security software and trends in security technology.

Firewalls do little, however, to keep pirates internal to your system at bay or to keep out pirates sophisticated enough to fake (or spoof) a trusted domain name.

The second line of defense helps address this problem. Wrappers are available from CERT as well as other Internet archives. *Wrappers* run as a layer of software around your other software. In other words, a user ftping to you would first get the wrapper, which would then engage FTP. The user does not know that the wrapper exists and cannot detect any difference in the system.

Wrappers are interesting because they are flexible. Wrappers can act as firewalls and can actually refuse users based on their user names as well as their domain names. Second, wrappers log all accesses and thus can serve as a good indication of whether your security is working correctly.

Wrappers also enable you to create "blind alleys" that help to trap pirates. These can be tied into alarms that alert you to penetration of certain directories that you set up to look like juicy archives of all sorts of good information. While the pirate is busy downloading basically garbage (made to look like valuable data), you have ample time to trace the user.

Tip
Wrappers, like firewalls, are available from CERT and other security-related Internet groups.

Wrappers can be set up to track and trap FTP users, users probing your system by typing **finger** or **who**, or any other of an assortment of Internet probes. At the very least, they can print domain and user information (the user information may not be entirely correct because it is based on information supplied by the pirate) to the console or log, which allows you to monitor users accessing your system. Set up correctly, a wrapper can be a pirate's worst nightmare.

Firewalls can often make it difficult for your own users to get out to the Internet. This may be especially true if you are running a Web server behind a firewall. Web servers run in proxy mode can help to solve this. Proxy servers also allow you to hide data in a most convenient manner.

Proxy mode is most useful for users behind a firewall. The users set their browser's proxy address to point at your Web server. The Web server then handles the actual direction of data to the outside world. This narrows the direction the users are taking when they leave your system, enabling you to route data through holes in your own firewalls. The other major advantage to this is that the requests can be filtered by the server software. By filtering the information, you can restrict the content and track the usage as well as modify the information on the fly.

Tip
Proxies are built into WWW servers. Look in your server manuals for information on setting them up.

Proxy servers can also be pointed to other proxy servers, which allows them to effectively hide data. The actual data can sit on machines far away from the server itself. The server accepts the contact from either a local or a remote user. However, instead of simply fulfilling the request, the server in turn sends the request to another server. The second server sends the requested information back to the primary server, which is then sent back to the user. The user never knows where the information actually comes from.

One other advantage to proxy servers is that each major service—such as FTP, Telnet, Gopher, NetNews, and so on—can be routed to different servers. This enables you to distribute your various WWW server loads to different physical servers. Not only do you benefit from data hiding, but you also benefit from reduced server load.

From Here...

This chapter covered various issues in creating secure systems. You learned that although pirate and cracker attacks do occur, many mechanisms exist that if applied correctly can keep your system secure and your users happy.

From here, refer to the following chapters:

- Chapter 17, "Security and the Net," offers detailed information about security and the Internet.

- Chapter 18, "Security and Cash Transactions," provides information specific to handling cash transactions and private data in a secure manner.

V

Security

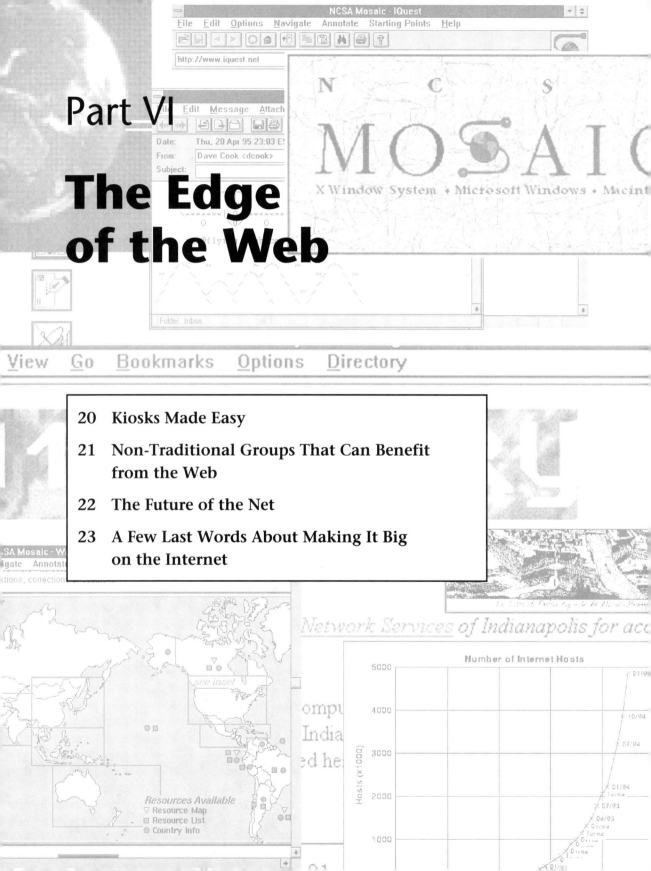

Part VI

The Edge of the Web

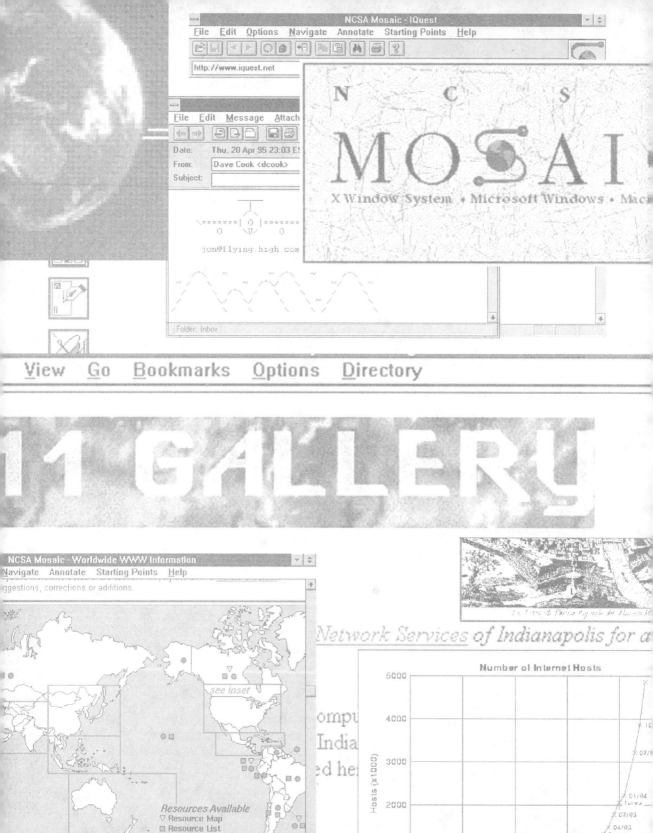

Chapter 20

Kiosks Made Easy

The effect of the Internet and the Web on kiosks is a lasting one. Because many kiosks already feature some level of computer interaction (sometimes invisible to the user), integrating the Internet with kiosks is natural.

In the future, you can expect to see Internet-based kiosks in libraries, hospitals, malls, and airports—basically any place where people congregate. These types of kiosks will offer products and services and even access to the Internet. Some kiosks will offer products and services for free as a strategy for getting more customers into a store or mall. Other kiosks will charge for services and products, collecting money through a variety of mechanisms ranging from credit cards to membership systems.

The business potential for kiosks is enormous. You can use the ideas covered in this chapter or come up with one of your own. Remember, though, that the startup capital for a kiosk-based system will be higher than some of the other ideas in this book. The costs for creating the physical kiosk, as well as providing the computer for each kiosk, are much greater. Despite this fact, kiosks will remain for many users a gold mine of opportunity along the Information Superhighway.

This chapter covers the possibilities for kiosk-based businesses that use the Web. In this chapter, you learn

- The definition of a kiosk

- Ideas for kiosk-based ventures

- Good locations for kiosks

- Benefits of Web-based kiosks

- Design considerations for kiosks

- Kiosk security

VI

The Edge of the Web

Kiosk Basics

This section introduces the basics for traditional kiosks. Kiosk hardware and software are discussed, as well as a new design for kiosks using the World Wide Web. The rest of this chapter is devoted to a closer look at kiosks and the Internet.

What is a Kiosk?

A *kiosk* is a stand-alone device for dispensing products and/or information. Users can simply walk up to it, conduct their business, and then walk away, leaving the machine open for the next transaction.

A kiosk must be able to present its products or services in such a manner that the average person can understand and use the device. This need will impact the design of the user interface for the kiosk. For instance, the reading level of a kiosk must be geared to an eighth-grade (or often less) level.

Kiosks also must serve users in all physical conditions. The kiosk must not be too tall, nor too short. Good designs accommodate physically handicapped users; some even offer Braille menus and audio prompting. Considering that a significant portion of the population is color blind, care must also be taken when choosing colors and designs.

Tip
Kiosk screens should use the design concepts outlined throughout this book.

◀ See "Your Home Page," p. 364

Kiosks often use icons, colors, and sounds to help attract the user, which also helps reduce the amount of reading and understanding necessary to interact with the kiosk itself. For example, a picture of a stop sign is far more recognizable in more languages and to a much wider age group than the plain word, "Stop." Figures 20.1 through 20.3 show various WWW-oriented kiosk pages and examples.

The kiosk works by automatically running a program from its local hard drive. The program displays opening screens and attraction loops, which help to draw in users. *Attraction loops* may consist of animations or videos and are often accompanied by music, sound effects, and vocal greetings.

When a user steps up to the system, instructions on or near the screen gets the user started. In most cases, the kiosk uses some form of touch screen for input and may rely on either an on-screen keyboard or a physical membrane keyboard for inputting of names and other text data.

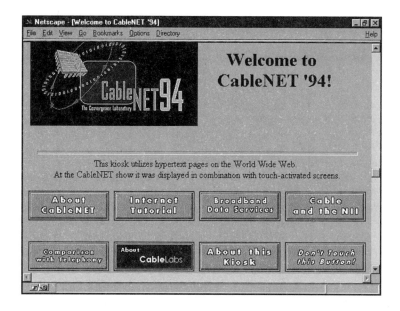

Fig. 20.1
CableNET '94 is a WWW-based kiosk site which was shown at the 1994 CableNET show. The project used touch screens for user input (**http://www. cablelabs.com /cablenet/kiosk /cnethome.html**).

Fig. 20.2
The Rocky Mountain Multimedia site offers a great deal of information and screen shots of various kiosk projects (**http://www. rockmedia.com /multimedia /#kioskPics**).

Fig. 20.3
ParkBench, at
**http://found.
cs.nyu.edu
/CAT/projects
/parkbench
/parkbench.
html**, offers
public-accessible
kiosks throughout
Manhattan, all of
which use the
World Wide Web.

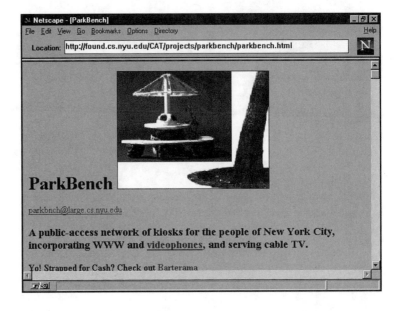

The user interacts with the kiosk by selecting from the choices presented on
the screen, usually by touching the desired choice directly on the monitor.
Each selection can access another screen of information or cause some event
to occur, such as printing the current screen, accepting a credit card, playing
a video or sound clip, or other similar event.

To handle users who walk away from the machine during the middle of a
session, the device will—after a predetermined set time with no user input—
return to its opening attraction loop and wait for the next user.

As self-contained units, traditional kiosks can be wheeled up practically anywhere there is power and perform their function. Because of this, kiosks have
become popular sales and advertising tools. In many cases, it is far cheaper to
dispense products and services by placing a kiosk in a mall, rather than to
incur the overhead of staffing a real office at each location.

However, as the next section explores, the capabilities of the World Wide
Web are beginning to change the efficiency and effectiveness of kiosks and
kiosk design.

Traditional Kiosks versus Net Kiosks

Traditionally, kiosks have consisted of the following components:

- Computer

- Video card

- Touch screen

- Keyboard

- Laser disk or hard disk

Information and programs to run the kiosk are stored on the laser or hard disk and are usually updated in the field (that is, at the kiosk's location), by physically changing the disks or drives. This means that if you have 100 kiosks, you must send someone to each of those locations each time you want to update your information.

In more advanced designs, the kiosk may sit on a network or be connected via a telephone line, allowing for remote update of content.

A Web-based kiosk consists of the following:

- Computer

- Video card

- Touch screen

- Keyboard

- Hard disk

However, the Web-based kiosk also contains a high-speed modem port. This connection by modem to the Web plays a crucial role in the future of interactive kiosks.

The basic difference between Web-based kiosks and traditional kiosks is where they store their content and how they can be controlled.

You can guess that a Web-based kiosk stores much of its information offsite. With the information stored at a centralized location, simple changes to a single piece of data results in each of the kiosks instantly being updated.

VI

The Edge of the Web

Tip
Web-based
kiosks can save
personnel costs
related to updat-
ing information,
maintenance,
and repair.

Further advantages include the instant availability of user statistics and demographics, as well as remote maintenance and testing. All these advantages
and many more are discussed later in this chapter.

Of further interest to businesses is that traditional kiosks are often more expensive to build than the new breed of Web kiosks. Why? Larger local storage
is required for the traditional kiosk. This storage, used to keep the content, is
not required to be nearly as large for the Web-based kiosk because most of the
content is housed offsite.

Another reason for lower costs of Web-based kiosks is in credit card handling.
Because credit card information was traditionally housed internally within
the kiosk, the kiosk needed to be made more physically secure. With the new
Web-based kiosks, transactions can instantly be forwarded to offsite servers;
the local kiosk remembers virtually nothing about the current transaction.

Examples of Good Uses for Kiosks

The following sections list uses for kiosks within various institutions. These
examples are given with networked kiosks in mind.

> **Note**
>
> While reading this section, keep in mind that these examples represent only a very
> small subset of where kiosks can be useful. As you will notice, the one thing that all
> the following examples have in common is that they provide access to information in
> locations where information access has traditionally been hard to obtain.

Malls

Kiosks and malls were made for each other. First, as indicated earlier, kiosks
are ideal for shops that want a presence in a mall without having to incur the
overhead of mall leasing.

For example, most malls do not have much in the way of service-oriented
stores. You're probably already familiar with the post office kiosks and bank
machine kiosks that are in malls everywhere, but other service-oriented
kiosks are beginning to appear as well. For example, kiosks have recently
appeared that can make instant business cards and invitations. Other kiosks
can create customized greeting cards.

Each of these kiosks is dispensing not only a service, but also a product—all without employee overhead and with little more than a water fountain's worth of space. With a little thought, anyone can come up with a half-dozen good ideas for services or products that can be dispensed through kiosks. Here are a few examples:

- A photo booth that allows the addition of simple computer clip art or text

- A personalized horoscope

- Access to consumer product information

- Record or movie reviews

A businessperson can make money through selling the product or service, as in the photo booth and horoscope; that person may also profit from selling or leasing the kiosks. For instance, although it might be difficult to sell a record review to a shopper, a record store might want such a kiosk to provide as a service to its shoppers.

This is wonderful for the store owner, but what about the mall itself? How can the mall use Web-based kiosks?

All malls have store directories. In many malls, this directory is already beginning to take the form of an interactive kiosk. The kiosks work well as directories because they can be easily changed when stores are moved or changed. Special functions can be added to provide information about sales and promotions. Searchable data bases could not only give information about what stores sell shoes, but also users could find out which stores sell the specific brand they are looking for.

Kiosk-based store directories provide much more than just a static floor plan. They can be an effective advertising tool as well as an indispensable customer aid.

Note

Kiosk-based store directories can be designed to display information in multiple languages. They can also be designed for handicapped users as well as users with below-average reading skills.

VI

The Edge of the Web

Tip
In designing your
kiosk, be sure to
make the best use
of its multimedia
capabilities—
video, music, and
hyperlinks.

The mall-based kiosk directory can go one step further. If these kiosks are all on the Web, imagine how simple it would be to allow anyone in the world to browse the shops of your mall. All you need to do is give the shops the capability to have their own pages within the directory.

Users at the physical mall can look at the directory, visit the pages, and find out about deals and specials. Onsite kiosks can be made to print coupons for even better discounts at selected stores.

Users at the virtual mall can also visit the stores, purchase from the shelves, and in general browse just as if they were actually there.

◄ See "The World
of Multimedia
Advertising,"
p. 235

Finally, if you owned a chain of malls, this scheme would work well for tying all your malls into a huge virtual and physical network.

Airports

Airports are traditionally places where kiosks have always had a home. From the early days when flight insurance could be purchased from a kiosk at the last moment, to today where unattended check-in and check-out kiosks give you fast car rental, kiosks have many uses in airports.

Kiosks are now beginning to appear not only in terminals, but also in airplanes themselves. Many flights now feature flat-screen monitors built into the back of every seat. Small remote control devices provide integrated keyboard, mouse (cursor), telephone, and credit card swipe.

These kiosks dispense to users free in-flight information, arrival time, and safety briefings. However, a swipe of your credit card unlocks hours of games, shopping, news, sports, and business services, as well as telephone and modem capabilities.

Also appearing in airports are new business kiosks that accept your credit card and then give you access to a private room with a couch, computer, fax, television, phone, and other business tools. These rooms are perfect for the quick lay-over nap, or a quiet place to take care of business between flights.

Imagine if both of these modern airport kiosks were also wired to the Web. Passengers could surf the Web, making content inexhaustible. Interactive WWW games could be created, pitting passengers against passengers in other flights around the world. In-flight airline home pages could direct users to pages specifically designed for their age group, directing them to URLs around the world with information of interest.

Frequent flyers could have stored profiles that would allow them to access frequently used business services, faxing services, e-mail, and NetNews.

The airport business kiosks could also benefit from the Web, again hooking up the lay-over travelers with needed business services, worldwide shopping, and communications as they wait for their next flight.

Hotels

Many hotels in large convention towns are already experimenting with kiosks as an efficient and cost-effective way to dispense information about current events, local restaurants and attractions, transportation, and more. These kiosks often are located in the lobby and use a touch screen. Many offer added services such as printing out maps and directions to desired locations.

Almost all hotels also feature another type of kiosk in every room. The in-room entertainment system, which allows users to dial in their favorite movies for a fee, can be considered a form of interactive kiosk.

In some bolder establishments, computer games and other diversions are allowed via the same entertainment system. Some games even allow hotel guests to play against each other.

Now, imagine piping the WWW to each and every room. Guests entering into the Web channel could start at the hotel's home page and have access to a wealth of information of the type delivered by the kiosk in the lobby. In the privacy of their own rooms, guests could make dinner reservations, find out about shows, book tickets, and explore the shops near the hotel.

Services that need to be conducted outside the hotel, such as making dinner reservations, could be handled automatically via the computer over the Web. Automated faxes could be sent if the restaurant wasn't hooked up to the Internet and it had a fax machine. The final option would allow hotel staff to make the reservations.

Likewise, this same in-room kiosk system can take care of the user's billing, check out, room service, business services, and much more.

Libraries

Many libraries, such as the Library of Congress, have provided terminal access to their online card catalogs and periodical and book searching capabilities for some time now.

VI

The Edge of the Web

These card catalog kiosks are limited in what they can provide, but nonetheless are still an improvement over the traditional card catalog.

The digital revolution now taking place is slowly but surely converting much of the actual content of libraries to digital format. After this digital conversion has been implemented on a significant part of the literature (a process that will take some time), you can expect to see integrated, networked library systems. In such a system, anyone anywhere could check out a digital copy of a book from any library within the network. This could happen from the convenience of your home or from a library kiosk system.

However, research kiosks are far more likely to appear in libraries. These terminals will enable users to surf the huge content of the Internet from the library. This ability to access the Internet will not only provide public access to the Internet—most likely for free—but it will also be a tremendous benefit to the libraries themselves, drawing more people back into a public institution.

Because the content of the Internet and WWW is virtually limitless, each library that hooks into the Internet will instantly expand its own informational content to that of the entire Web. Because libraries are concerned with learning, information, and knowledge, this marriage between the traditional and the modern is a match made in heaven.

Schools

The benefit of the Web to schools is unlimited. From the sheer access of information and culture to the capability to use this information internally for teaching and learning, kiosks in schools are a very important tool.

Because of the Web's natural capability to entertain and involve users, it makes an ideal teacher's aid. Each school-based, Web-based kiosk is capable of dispensing the entire world of Internet knowledge at rates set by the individual.

> **Note**
>
> Students who learn slower or faster than the rest of the class would be helped by Web access, because it lets them learn at their own speed.

With the Web's built-in demographic capabilities, teachers will be able to track an individual student's progress with ease.

Schools can be hooked up to other schools, enabling students to share in group projects. Likewise, clubs and extracurricular activities can be coordinated and supplemented through the use of the Web.

Kiosks sprinkled throughout the school would give ample opportunity for students to access information about school events, activities, special programs, tutoring help, and much more.

Learning at home via the same Web network would enable hospitalized and severely handicapped students to study and learn with their peers, as well as allow them to participate in any Web-based extracurricular activities.

Tip
Students can use the Web as an invaluable homework and special project aid.

Government Access

The U.S. government is pushing for the Internet and WWW in a big way. For example, a project we recently completed for the U.S. Postal Service involves a Citizen's Kiosk that enables citizens to access local and federal government information, all from a walk-up kiosk. The interesting thing to note about our implementation—and indeed, the task we were given—is that it was to work via the Web.

The following is the government press release issued late in 1994 after our completion of a pilot version of the Citizen's Kiosk, which explains the project from the government's perspective:

Service to the Citizen Kiosk Pilot Program

Designed by the Postal Service, the "information" kiosk is a key element in the Clinton Administration's re-inventing government initiative. This kiosk sets forth the vision of an increasingly effective government that employs state-of-the-art technology to deliver service to the public.

The White House asked the Postal Service to lead an interagency effort to define how to provide electronic access to government information and services using kiosks as a delivery vehicle. Since May 1994, the Postal Service has worked with representatives of more than 18 federal agencies and 50 state and local governments to shape a model for government-wide service delivery. The task force has concentrated on researching new technologies and applications while analyzing the underlying business case for making electronic service delivery a reality. The results of these findings will be published in November 1994.

(continues)

VI

The Edge of the Web

(continued)

The Postal Service: A Unique Institution

One of the central elements of the Postal Service's mission is to "bind the nation together." As electronic service delivery is used throughout the American economy, one of the most important tasks of the Postal Service is to guard against the risk of creating two societies: the electronic information "haves" and "have nots." The Postal Service, with its 40,000 locations, is the only federal agency that maintains day-to-day contact with the American public. The Postal Service, which has played an essential role in developing America's infrastructure by becoming an active participant in the evolution of the nation's railroad system, the telegraph, and the airplane, has a unique opportunity to contribute to building the Information Superhighway. For more than 200 years, America's postal system has been the trusted third party in the communications chain that binds the nation together. This public trust can now be extended to help the information revolution move forward.

The kiosk of tomorrow may offer one tool for extending the traditional postal mission by providing service to America. The kiosk delivering these services will be a completely new concept—networking government service information through the Internet and other value-added networks.

Government services that can be delivered through a kiosk:

- Expanded federal, state, and local agency office hours and locations

- Capacity to print forms for local, state, and federal agencies

- Access to job bank information

- Ease in filling out applications for local, state, and federal services

- Ability to pay fines, automobile registration renewals, etc.

- Capability to order local, state, and federal information and products for delivery by mail

- Help in solving real life situations such as loss of job, retirement, health problems, births/deaths

- Ability to obtain recreational information and reservations

- New access to Electronic Benefits Transfer systems

Postal kiosk services:

- Mailing information

- Stamps by mail

- Sale and display of commemorative stamps

- Expanded office locations, hours, and service

- Electronic Commerce Services (authentication, certification, electronic date and time stamp)

- USPS delivery of government service information ordered via kiosks

- ZIP code look-up

Pilot Testing

The Postal Service is working with kiosk providers to test market interactive software and to refine customer service concepts.

Initial test units will be used as a technology and operations pilot test in the Washington, D.C. area and participating agency locations and at highly visible sites within the city. Following the tests of these first interactive units, kiosks will be market tested in urban and rural areas throughout the country.

The public's reaction, software and hardware usability, kiosk operation and support, usage rates and identification of the most popular topics, and willingness to pay for convenience are all factors that will contribute to evaluating the success of the program.

As successful market tests guide design and appropriate interagency agreements are negotiated, nationwide delivery models may be considered. Working with federal agencies, state and local governments, and private sector providers, the kiosk partnerships of the future will pioneer new forms of service delivery to citizens.

VI

The Edge of the Web

You can see by the preceding description that the government stands committed to pursue global networks as an effective means for communicating with citizens. Not only can it help lower government costs and increase efficiency, but it also opens up much of government to citizens, allowing them to access information with unprecedented ease.

> **Note**
>
> The press release mentioned the worry of the "haves" and the "have-nots." In other words, government does not want a technological rift between its citizens, and therefore is trying to place these kiosks such that they provide open access and are usable by the majority of the population.

Benefits of Networked Information Kiosks

As already mentioned, networked information kiosks provide many benefits. The following sections reexamine these benefits in more detail.

Simple Architecture

WWW kiosks possess a fairly minimal architecture. At the simplest, they only require a 486 CPU with 8M of RAM, a minimum of 20M of disk, and a modem. Add to these requirements a WWW browser, adequate enclosure, and a telephone line, and your kiosk is ready to go!

A primary benefit of this simple architecture is that there are few components. In fact, the components are so generic that you can change configuration at any time, enabling you to take advantage of technology breakthroughs and price wars without having to reengineer your solution.

Also, as with any system, fewer parts mean fewer places it can break down.

Instant Demographics

WWW kiosks are brighter than traditional kiosks in their capability to collect demographics about their users. This capability makes the kiosk a market research firm in a box.

Keep in mind that the kiosk is always hooked to the Internet; it has the capability to instantly tell a central computer about each and every transaction. Every event is logged, including how long the user takes on each page he visits.

◀ See "The HTTPD Log," p. 342

This information is extremely valuable in providing real-time statistics of users' likes, dislikes, and buying habits. This information also enables you to fine-tune your pages for maximum effectiveness. And because this all happens in real time, you can implement changes on the fly with a minimal amount of problems.

You can increase the type of demographic information available if you make your kiosk system a login system. For instance, a mall-based kiosk system might require users to register at a counter where certain demographic information like age, sex, and address could be visually verified. Shoppers could be given a login name or a magnetic ID card.

You could offer coupons and discounts to shoppers as an enticement to enroll. What's the trade-off? You would receive much more detailed demographic information.

Remote Updating and Maintenance

As already mentioned, one benefit to WWW-integrated kiosks is that they can be updated remotely. Because the kiosk will be running TCP/IP to reach the Internet and Web, it is also accessible from the outside. If you want to update your machine from a remote location, you can simply ftp your files to the machine, which causes them to instantly update for the user standing in front of the kiosk.

This capability can drastically cut your field update calls by allowing you to update all your kiosks at one time from a remote location.

It makes sense that if you can update the machine remotely, you can also perform maintenance of the machine remotely. Remote maintenance includes being able to start remote diagnostics and testing as well as perform routine maintenance such as disk defragmenting and file cleanup.

Kiosks in remote areas can be designed with redundant subsections, which allow remote commands to switch the kiosk to use backup hardware in case of failure.

Tip

Remember that all facets of your machine can be updated. This includes not only any content stored locally on the kiosk, but also the kiosk software itself.

Planning a Kiosk System

This section concentrates on the actual design for a kiosk system. A generic design that will fit many uses is suggested, including design elements to enhance handicapped access.

Putting Together the Pieces

A key element to any kiosk is a unified design. This means that the bits and pieces of the kiosk must work together as a whole. In other words, if you want to use all the benefits that WWW kiosks have to offer, try to create a design in which each component strengthens the other. See figure 20.4,

VI

The Edge of the Web

which provides a good example of a unified design. Too often, companies choose inferior components to save a dollar or two now, when the extra dollar up front would have saved thousands of dollars later on in maintenance and support costs.

Fig. 20.4
American Touchscreen's page at **http:// www.hevanet. com/kiosk/ kiosks. htm** offers information and pictures of kiosk systems.

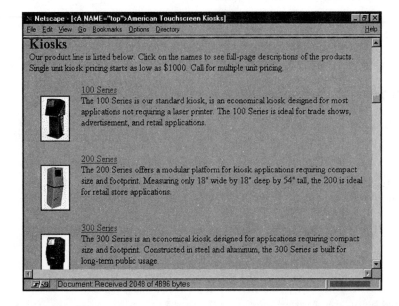

To begin the design, you want a device that is as easy to operate remotely as it is for the user standing in front of it. For this, choose a fast PC or RISC processor such as an SGI or Sun, running some flavor of UNIX. UNIX is a good choice because of the amount of preexisting software that supports its architecture, along with its multitasking capability.

> **Caution**
>
> Spending more money up front on superior components and software will reduce your long-term investment and support considerably. The old adage, "You get what you pay for," holds true for kiosk design. Picking cheap components to save a few dollars up front can easily kill a project with incompatibilities and costly failures in the field.

The machine should have a good amount of RAM for fast memory caching—at least 8M. It also needs a good amount of free, high-speed disk space. At least 20M of free space should be enough. It should also have a touch-screen monitor that duplicates as the keyboard and the mouse pointing device.

The Internet connection could be as slow as 28.8 baud, but placing an ISDN or other 56K line into the kiosk would be better. In some situations, a T1 line may be preferable. You will want the higher speed lines if you are going to be accessing movies and audio stored remotely from the kiosk. If the high band-width information, such as movies, is stored locally at the kiosk, then lower speed lines are feasible.

Your server will at least be running a WWW browser such as Netscape or Mosaic. You will want to modify the browser's controls to show only the forward and back buttons and the slider.

To summarize, the components for a Web-based kiosk are as follows:

- High-speed computer

- At least 8M of RAM

- At least 20M of free disk space

- High-speed data line, ISDN, 56K line, or a T1 line

- Modified version of a Web browser

> **Note**
>
> You might want to examine NCSA Mosaic's Kiosk mode. This browser can be launched with the command line flag **-kiosk**. This runs the browser in a mode in which the user is more restricted. Because you do not want users to access controls to shut down the browser or change URLs themselves, use this mode to restrict users' capabilities.

> **Note**
>
> The enclosure for your kiosk can be obtained from any of several professional kiosk housing manufacturers. Consulting a technical or industrial yellow pages directory or searching the WWW should return a list of kiosk manufacturers who would be more than happy to assist you in designing your enclosure.

VI

The Edge of the Web

▶ See "Adding
Images To Your
Pages," p. 534

Depending on what you want from your kiosk, you might also run a WWW server, such as CERN or NCSA, on the kiosk itself. Running your own server enables you to handle things like ISMAP (an image that is pickable) and cgi-bin programs without having to go to a remote machine. This also allows you to access any kiosk from any remote location just as if you were at the kiosk itself—in other words, anyone anywhere in the world can bring up a kiosk just by accessing the kiosk's own server.

Handicap Access

Designing your kiosk for handicapped access means more than just having an enclosure that is not too tall and not too short. Even slight handicaps can render a kiosk unusable if you are not careful in the design.

Most important is your use of color. Blind users aside, a significant portion of the population is color blind. For totally color-blind users, many words and icons may simply disappear. For example, a totally color-blind individual would have a hard time seeing green wording on a red background of the same intensity. Because both colors have the same intensity, the user sees only a bright solid area.

Likewise, embodying functionality in the color of one of your elements is a bad idea. In other words, a Stop icon should be shaped like a stop sign; it should be colored red; it should have the text "Stop" beneath or within it; and it should have Braille labels as well as audio prompting available for visually impaired users.

> **Note**
>
> Keep in mind that the term "handicapped" also includes socially and educationally disadvantaged persons as well. The sophistication of the kiosks should be kept to about an eighth-grade reading level and should avoid culturally specific language and references, such as jargon and slang.

Blind users can be accommodated with audio prompting as well as Braille labels attached to the area around the terminal. By placing these in an easy-to-find and consistent place, blind users can quickly become used to orientation and functionality.

New technology is also bringing about Braille screens. These screens consist of a flat ribbon with rows of pins flush to the surface. Micro-miniature solenoids activate the pins based on the text of the line being read. A text-to-Braille converter raises the pins to form the letters of the text, which users can sense by moving their hands over the surface.

This technology makes it possible for complete content to be delivered to fully blind users—one of the most difficult groups to make the primarily vision-oriented kiosks work properly for.

Physical Security

One important factor in creating your kiosk is keeping it physically secure. The kiosk itself contains computing hardware as well as telecommunications equipment.

Furthermore, your kiosk might use credit card handling and/or money receipt dispensing. Care must be taken not only in creating the design, but also in placing the kiosk.

Placing kiosks in frequented, well-lit areas not only provides security for the kiosk, but also for the user. Security cameras can also be used to view the kiosk within building and mall security systems. A camera can also be placed so that the kiosk naturally comes under the observance of a regular patrol or security. Kiosks with security cameras are already commonplace in banking ATM machines, where all transactions are recorded on film or video.

Of course, because the kiosk is attached to the Internet, attempts at vandalism can also be instantly relayed to the central computer, from where aid can be instantly dispatched.

One of the better designs for a kiosk is similar to an ATM, where servicing the kiosk is done via restricted access. These systems are often recessed flush with a wall and thus are not as portable as other kiosk designs. Security in these units is usually much better than with their portable cousins.

As opposed to placing cameras around the kiosk, the camera can easily be imbedded within the kiosk itself in a fashion similar to ATMs. If the kiosk is on a fast enough link, the image taken at regular intervals can even be relayed to the central computer location.

VI

The Edge of the Web

From Here...

This chapter covered exciting ways for businesses to use Web-based kiosks to sell products and services, and for advertising and other promotional uses. It also looked at the ways schools, libraries, and the government will be using such kiosks to provide basic services to citizens.

You may also want to refer to the following chapters:

- Chapter 5, "Choosing Hardware and Software," offers more information and suggestions for computer requirements and configurations.

- Chapter 9, "Information on the Net," provides key information on placing pictures, audio, and other sophisticated information on the Web.

- Chapter 10, "Advertising on the Net," discusses hints and tips on using the Web as an advertising medium.

- Chapter 16, "Your Presence on the Net," provides information to help you make sure that your Web-based kiosk puts its best foot forward.

- Chapter 22, "The Future of the Net," offers insights into what lies in store for the Web.

Chapter 21

Non-Traditional Groups That Can Benefit from the Web

So far this book has presented many ideas about how to make money on the Web. These sorts of ideas usually lend themselves to business people, but other groups may want to use the Web to reach the large and growing number of users on the Information Superhighway. For example, artists, musicians, and writers can use the Web to gain exposure to unprecedented numbers of people. Social and civic groups can use the Web to provide information to members or to the public in an easy and convenient manner. Government agencies, from the city to federal level, are finding the Web an economical method for disseminating mountains of information.

Sometimes these groups and individuals wouldn't think of venturing into this area of service and promotion due to costs related to the technology or to the lack of knowledge needed to manage the technology on their own. But you can use shortcuts and strategies to keep your costs to little or nothing. Since many computer programmers like to be on the cutting edge of technology, your artistic venture on the Web may be done gratis by some enterprising high-school or college students. Likewise, private clubs and civic groups may be able to find members or other individuals who will donate the time and skills needed to put your group on the Web.

But that doesn't mean that artists, writers, and musicians don't have the skill to launch themselves on the Web. Remember that creating simple HTML documents isn't much more difficult than using modern word processing programs. In fact, if you have a home computer and are competent at using it, you have the necessary skills to create your own home page.

This chapter explores

- How artists, musicians, and writers can use the Web

- Methods for keeping your costs down

- Interesting projects that have been done on the Net and ideas for new projects

- How local and regional government organizations can benefit from the Web

- Good uses for social and civic groups

- Tips for non-profit groups

Artists

Many art forms don't require artists to stay abreast of current technology and how it relates to art. But if you're a serious artist, you can't afford to miss out on the exposure, marketing, and promotional and sales potential of the Web. Through the WWW, any artist can reach a viewing audience that up until this point could be reached only through showings at big-city galleries, advertisements in expensive magazines and newspapers, or articles in those same publications. And any art form—not only those that are high-tech—can use the Web.

Many artists and art groups have been slow to embrace the computer as an artistic tool. Part of the delay can be chalked up to technophobia, part of it to snobbery, and part of it to plain fear. Some fine arts supporters question the originality of computer art, because sometimes computer art is categorized as photography.

In the end, it boils down to the fact that the computer can be just another tool for many artists. Whether the art is good depends on the artist, and whether the art that's created is original depends on what the artist is turning out. Most people would consider a hand-signed, numbered, limited-edition lithograph or wood print as original art. But similar considerations can be made when qualifying artwork that comes from a computer.

Innovative artists, galleries, and museums may want to explore using the Web to create art. Collaborative fine art and performance art are just two areas that are pushing the boundaries of the Web.

Note

There are questions about the copyright security of artwork placed on the Web. You should stay informed about copyright laws and the Internet. You'll also want to take appropriate steps to safeguard your work.

◀ See "A Word About Plagiarism," p. 244

The Net as an Artistic Sales Tool

While it's true that most artists create for the pleasure of it, even artists have to eat. And for that matter, what aspiring or veteran artist hasn't dreamed of making a living doing what they love best?

Artists can use the Web to do the following:

- Advertise or create gallery showings and openings

- Sell art directly online

- Advertise services such as portrait painting or painting lessons

- Promote themselves

A simple home page can feature almost any type of artwork, from traditional to avant garde. Any medium from clay to video tape can be expressed. You can easily scan photographs of even the most rugged art form into the computer.

You'll want to pick an name for your site, such as *Dave's Art Gallery* or something more trendy or high-tech. If possible, you should use your name to funnel viewers who are interested in your particular type of artwork. If you're trying to sell neon sculptures, you don't necessarily want to attract someone interested in folk art. Something like *The Plasma-Light Gallery* would attract clients who are interested in neon sculpture, whereas *Folk Art Village* might make a good name for the other site.

When you advertise your art site, make sure that the descriptions you use are to your best advantage. If you have one line to describe your site, don't say something like "high-quality art from a variety of artists." This really doesn't tell the reader very much. Instead, maybe a short two- or three-item list of what you feature would be better, such as "featuring landscape paintings, woodblock prints, and primitives," or "specializing in kinetic sculptures and holographic art."

The way you decide to sell your artwork is up to you. If you're on a big commercial provider, that provider may allow you (for a small fee) to run

Tip

When taking photographs of artwork that you'll later place into digital form, pay attention to the quality of the photograph. The lighting should be even to avoid unnecessary shadows.

VI

The Edge of the Web

credit card transactions through it. If not, you'll have to rely on your own credit card clearing capability or the post office to deliver the checks to your mailbox.

Tip

If you're an artist living in a college town, you may find public access sites to the Web, where you can advertise and promote yourself for little or no cost.

If your Web access and service is through an educational organization, you may encounter problems running a commercial enterprise from it. It's against the law to make money from free educational access. Although advertising your upcoming gallery opening will probably sneak by any regulations, open selling of your artwork won't.

> **Note**
>
> Usually educational providers do not allow commercial ventures on their servers. If you have your artwork on an educational provider, most likely you won't be able to sell it from that WWW server.

If you've started your endeavor as a simple home page and then decide to sell some work, check to see whether the educational system has a commercial portion of its system that you can switch to. If not, you'll have to find a commercial provider.

Using a commercial provider can be a major financial burden for an artist. As mentioned elsewhere in this book, art sites on the Web tend to be very popular. This means that the site will have a large amount of throughput, and since most commercial providers charge for their Web sites by storage and throughput, high throughput can mean high monthly bills. This is especially true because art tends to be rather large when converted to digital pictures.

One way to get around paying for a WWW site is to find a Web service provider that's new and is willing to put your pages up for free, perhaps as an experiment. Depending on the deal you negotiate, the new Web service provider may create your pages as well as assume your storage and throughput charges. There's a potential downside to this, though. New Web services, like any new business, may not be viable in the market and may not be there next year.

For this reason, you may decide to spend the money and go with an established provider. We firmly believe that if you're spending money to sell products on the Web, you should show some sort of financial return. For this reason, you may want to consider the following:

- Make sure that buyers feel they're getting a "work of art." Hand sign the work; if it's a one-of-a-kind, mention it; if it's a numbered limited series, make sure that buyers know that. Mention the medium the artwork is produced in.

- Consider offering a variety of types of artwork. For example, you might reprint your work on note cards and T-shirts.

Other marketing considerations might include the following:

- Offer to "lease space" to other artists for a fixed fee. This way, you can open a "gallery" and have other artists help support the fees.

- Create and offer clip art, which can be sold by the image or by the package.

> **Note**
>
> You can promote and sell any type of art through the WWW. Computer art is often found on the Web because its digital format is ready for the Internet. But sculptures, water colors, oil painting—you name it—can also be sold on the Web. Just photograph the artwork and scan it into the computer.

Regardless of whether or not you have to pay for your Web access, it's a good idea to create and organize your Web site in an economical fashion. Doing so is part of being a good Internet citizen and also helps if you ever have to move your site to a provider who charges for access.

Here are some organizational hints:

- Use links to minimize material that viewers may not be interested in.

- Use postage stamp-sized images linked to larger versions that viewers can request to see if they're interested. The throughput on small images is relatively minor.

Individual artists may find it convenient to band together and make their own galleries or cooperatives on the Web. An annual co-op fee could get the endeavor started. As the online gallery starts generating sales, the profits would be paid to co-op members.

◀ See "Looking for Existing Information," p. 206

Tip
Another good WWW searcher is Yahoo (**http://www.yahoo.com**), which has WWW listings under categories such as Computers, Art, Music, and Finances.

Already many online galleries are accepting shows from new or established computer and electronic artists. A cruise of the Web using a browser such as Lycos will provide you with a list of galleries that are looking for exhibitors.

Art Museums and the Net

While many museums are still exploring the feasibility of being on the Web, museums and art galleries of all sizes are incorporating at least some aspect of the Web into their program. The most widely recognized museum in the world, the Louvre in Paris, was among the Web's first art pages. Figure 21.1 shows a page from the Louvre's Web site.

Fig. 21.1
Even the Louvre in Paris, France, has a presence on the Web through the WebMuseum (**http://www.cnam.fr/louvre/**).

Mary Ann Kearns, director of the 911 Gallery in Indianapolis, Ind., likens online galleries and museums to artist Marcel DuChamp's *valise en boite*—portable works of arts that were meant to reach the common people.

Art is most powerful when it reaches and enriches the lives of many people. Online WWW pages have allowed museums and galleries in small out-of-the-way places to reach a worldwide audience. But it has also allowed anyone, anywhere, to view artwork from some of the world's best-known museums without having to travel to Paris or New York. Figure 21.2 shows a page from the electronic 911 Gallery.

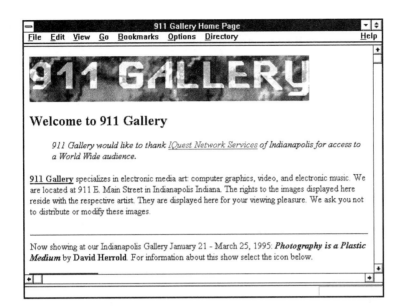

Fig. 21.2
The home page of 911 Electronic Gallery leads users to both current and past artists' showings (**http://www.iquest.net/911/iq_911.html**).

Museums and most galleries can fund online projects by the same means they now fund other traditional projects. The combination of art and technology is an area of arts funding that now enjoys popular support within the public as well as private sectors. A great number of the telecommunications and computer companies already have programs in place to fund such art projects. Hardware companies can donate equipment and the personnel to set up the Web. Programming the site may be done under auspices of a local college or university computer department.

If you run an art gallery at a college or university and don't already have an online gallery, you should make an appointment with someone in the computer department today. You may even find some undiscovered computer artists among the staff and students. The computer department can use the chance to train students in a real-life application, and you can benefit from their skills.

The Web as an Artistic Medium

Not only can you use the Web to show existing art, but on the Web you can participate in the creation of art as well. Computer artists all over the world have been able to collaborate on projects that wouldn't be feasible in other mediums.

VI

The Edge of the Web

Interactive video programs now in existence are pushing the current limits of what you can do on the Internet. However, artists have been slow to use the Web itself for the creation of art because of the Web's limited interactive nature. Remember, Web users must request information one step at a time. For example, you can't load a page and a sound file at the same time. One or the other must happen first, and then you must request the next event.

Current developments such as Netscape's PULL feature allow you periodically to pull an image, sound, or document from a server. This allows pages to be more interactive and lets you have non-movie animations, living poems, interactive conference rooms, and much more. As time goes on, the WWW will quickly become increasingly interactive and—finally—fully immersive.

Past events on the Internet provide clues as to what forms of interactive artwork could be created on the Web in the future. The IPI (Interactive Painting International) art piece that was created for the 1992 SIGGRAPH Art Show in Chicago is just such an example. Featuring a huge video wall and artists from the United States and 14 countries from all over the world, the system allowed the artists to paint together on a huge canvas in real time. The artists were connected to each other through the Internet, and as each one painted, the artwork-in-progress instantly appeared on the screens of the other artists. Artists could paint on top of each other's work, as well as send audio messages to other participants. The attendees at the SIGGRAPH '92 show could all see the art being created in real time on the video wall.

As the Web's power increases, artists who are now pushing the envelope with their ideas and innovative programming techniques could become the leaders of entirely new art fields.

> **Note**
>
> Again, if you have great ideas but lack the technical expertise to pull them off, we highly suggest that you find a collaborator to work with. Thousands of high-school and college programmers would love the chance to do something different and exciting with their talents. They can easily use these for special projects or thesis statements.
>
> Also, many large, high-tech companies are interested in donating personnel, equipment, or grants to help prompt novel uses of high technology. Even if the projects are art-oriented, they often push the envelope of bandwidth and technology, making them very useful as experiments to companies so they can predict the Internet's future growth and needs.

Musicians and Bands

Many popular rock and alternative groups are already online, usually due to the work of an adoring fan. But increasingly, bands—and the music industry in particular—are seeing the commercial benefits of an official presence on the Web.

The graphical nature of the Web makes it a natural medium to display photos of bands and musicians. You can also offer tour information, online merchandising, and fan club services on the Web. With the sound and video capabilities of HTML pages, you can use samples of actual songs and video clips from concerts to promote CDs and videos. Consider also the commercial possibilities for other areas in the music industry, including music archives and the selling of sound clip libraries.

If you want to get on the Web but aren't sure how, look around you. Maybe someone in your band is good with computers. Or you can get a fan who is good with computers to do the work for free or trade (such as admission to shows). In this way, you may be able to get your information to the Web community for very little cost, although you may still have to pay your monthly provider bill.

> **Note**
>
> As a musician, like with any other artistic group, you should take all necessary steps to protect yourself from unlicensed use of your material. Include copyright notices in visible locations in your Web sites. And when creating a Web site, remember to make sure that you have legal rights to use photos, songs, and other copyrighted material.

Recording Labels

If you're now thinking of signing with a manager or recording label, you might want to consider their marketing strategies for the Internet and the Web. This new marketing trend is one that most musicians won't want to miss.

As more and more bands and recording labels are learning about the merchandising potential of the Web, individuals, bands, and—more commonly— recording companies are establishing official Web sites to promote groups and to merchandise everything from CDs to T-shirts. One notable site is Warner Brothers Records, which maintains a presence for many of its popular bands and stars (see fig. 21.3).

Fig. 21.3

Warner Brothers Records is one of the larger record labels with an online presence. The Warner Brothers site can be found at **http://www. iuma.com/ Warner/**.

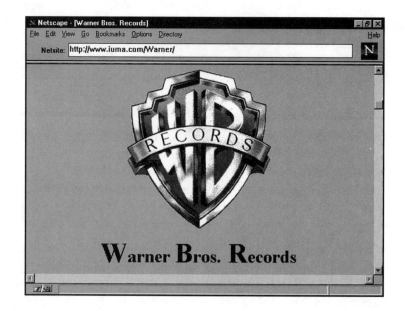

Recording label sites also help decrease the number of non-official sites, thus lowering the amount of plagiarism and copyright infringement.

> **Note**
>
> If there's already a bootleg site for your band, you might consider incorporating the work into your official site. Coming down hard on the creators of such sites can be detrimental to your Web image. Instead, bring the programmer on board, clean up the parts that create copyright violations, and add merchandising. The programmer can be compensated monetarily or with tickets.
>
> Remember that these high-school and college students don't realize they're violating copyright laws when they create these true labors of love. You want to avoid, at all costs, having a bad image on a medium with as much global impact as the Internet.

Tip

Even if you don't have a band, you can become an online music promoter. Your financial investment would be modest if you back it up with time and leg work.

Grouping bands in categories such as by recording label can be a very successful way to market bands. If potential buyers look for something by one band while they are there, you might be able to tempt them with something from one of the other bands on your label.

Even if your band doesn't record on a major label, you may decide it's worth it to advertise with bands that appeal to a similar crowd. For example, your Web page could list bands that specialize in parties and weddings, with music styles ranging from classical to alternative.

Or, as suggested earlier for fine artists, your band might form a cooperative venture on the Web with other bands. A site for grunge bands in the Seattle area might prove profitable. A country-western cooperative could be popular in many areas, especially if you include someone who could teach line dancing. A cool Web site could benefit your public image.

A Web page featuring various bands would probably be very useful for bands in towns that have universities with large computer science departments, such as Ann Arbor, Mich.; Las Vegas, Nev.; and Blacksburg, Va., to name just a few. Check around; if your town has a large Internet presence, it would probably do you good to get your name on the Internet also.

Merchandising

As anyone in the music industry today can tell you, spin-off merchandise for bands can generate substantial income. But because space is limited, record stores aren't likely to carry merchandise for every band whose CD they carry. If the band members could only get the information to the public, a band could merchandise many things, such as

- T-shirts and sweatshirts

- Baseball caps

- Bumper stickers

- Pins and jewelry

- Calendars

- Fan club memberships

- Photos

- Concert memorabilia and other collectibles

An enterprising entrepreneur in the musical field can undoubtedly think of many more possibilities for merchandising. The limits are placed by what's legal and what the fans will buy. If you like to doodle or do quick sketches, you might want to sell them; such work by the late John Lennon goes for big bucks. If you are a musician with a strong local or regional following, maybe your fans would like to have such a piece of memorabilia. You can find out with a minimum of investment on the Web.

Think of it. What would it cost to run a full-page, full-color ad in *Rolling Stone* magazine for a month? A strategically placed ad that was well advertised could reach 4 million people. The Web can reach that 4 million for a fraction of the cost of the traditional ad.

Music Stores on the Web

Not only do bands and recording labels sell music over the Web, but so do music stores.

If you currently have a catalog resale service, you may want to consider putting your catalog on the Web, as many of your competitors already have done. Since you're already doing a mail-order business, accepting orders from online customers shouldn't be a problem. The text is already written and just needs to be entered into the computer. Orders can come in via mail or phone as they do now, or you could create an online ordering system.

◄ See "Credit Card Transactions," p. 275

> **Note**
>
> If you want to sell music over the Web, remember that you'll be reaching an international audience. You may have orders from overseas. How will you deal with transactions from Europe or Japan? Keep this in mind as you design your Web site.

As with any Web site, you'll want to make sure that

- The name of your site attracts your intended audience

- You advertise the site in all appropriate lists and robots

- You organize your site so that it's easy to use and cuts down on wasted bandwidth

Keep in mind that sheet music over the Web is now very popular. Many people labor long hours to piece together popular music and provide ASCII versions of guitar tablature. A business providing this service would most likely be well-received.

Interactive Experiments

The same limitations of the current Web that affect interactive art projects also affect interactive musical collaborations and performances. The Rolling Stones was one of the first bands to do this when, in 1994, the group performed a concert (music only) through the Internet via the MBONE system.

Performance artists such as Laurie Anderson have incorporated the World Wide Web into part of their performances by having visuals and lyrics that were inspired and taken from the Web itself.

Although there's the potential for great things down the road, not many people seem to be pushing the frontier of the Web in its audio capabilities.

One reason, of course, is the size of audio files. Normally, unless the file is very small, there's some delay as the host machine downloads the huge file and then plays it back to you. Users at colleges and universities or at companies that get their Internet feed over dedicated high-speed lines have a quicker return than users going through their phone lines, but now even the fastest lines have some lag on the millions of bytes contained in even short audio files.

> **Note**
>
> This isn't meant to discourage musicians from using the Web, but is rather a call for a hurdle to be overcome. In the short time that it has taken to write this book, the functionality of the Web has grown considerably, giving less expensive alternatives to musicians and others who have large amounts of data to present.

Wouldn't it be fun to broadcast a concert and let viewers choose the camera angle they wanted? They might have the option to choose a close-up shot of the lead singer, a view of the whole band, or maybe a view of the audience.

Other innovative ideas would include letting the online audience have input on stage conditions, such as lighting or background graphics. Try to envision a video download screen with buttons on the bottom that might have choices such as

```
Click here to make the stage lighting more red, or
here to make it more blue.
```

The computer could tally votes and actually affect the stage lighting in real time. Or maybe online viewers could submit pictures to be shown on the video walls that many bands use.

Not all these ideas are now available, but all are doable. It just requires someone with a vision.

Writers

Of all the artistic groups, the Web is probably the most accessible to writers. You can present words in a very cost-effective way and reach a large audience in a stylish presentation that many writers ordinarily couldn't achieve on their own.

VI

The Edge of the Web

Also, you can use the graphic capabilities of the Web in a way to greatly enhance your written works. You can easily integrate photographs, pictures, and sketches into your Web site. Not only that, but you can also easily include audio or video tracks of you reading your works.

Whether you work alone or under the auspices of an online publication, you should be able to find some avenue of the Web that can promote your work. Many college-aged writers have examples of their work on their home pages. And many online publications are already on the Web.

If you're planning a Web site that features writing (yours or others'), make sure that you look at what other people are doing. This isn't an endorsement to rip off other people's designs, but just as writers should study the work of other writers, authors on the Web should study the work of other Web authors. See what makes an effective presentation. See what draws a reader in and what may turn them off or seem ostentatious or too far out.

Poetry, Fiction, and Interactive

As you can well imagine, the Internet has allowed many writers to explore the absolute boundaries of their craft. The Web is especially powerful in the field of interactive writing, where the reader can create as well as control the flow of the written word. All these factors push the limits of current notions of the written art form for both the traditionalist and the experimentalist.

You can choose various ways to present your material. You can use traditional methods, such as starting at the beginning and going to the end, or a non-traditional method, such as creating a table of contents and using links to access each chapter or heading.

A more experimental form would be poetry collections or short stories that are accessed by clicking a picture or using HTML's ISMAP capability to choose a portion of a picture. The online *Wimsey* site (**http://www.wimsey.com/**) has a magazine shop featuring the *NWHQ* magazine. The designers of the online shop made a poem of the titles of the short stories and poems that made up the issue. When you first enter the site, you're presented with poems and pictures (see fig. 21.4). There are no instructions; it's a bit of an adventure because you don't know what to expect. You notice words are linked, so you pick one and you're launched into a poem or short story.

Fig. 21.4
The opening page of the *NWHQ* online magazine site has links to the contents organized in a very artistic manner (**http://www. knosso.com/ NWHQ/ index.html**).

Within the Wimsey collection is a series of works that are accessed through a picture of a dog (see fig. 21.5).

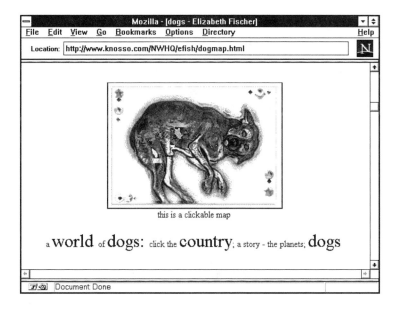

Fig. 21.5
This page within the *NWHQ* site contains a clickable picture of a dog that's linked to a series of interrelated stories (**http://www. knosso.com/ NWHQ/efish/ dogmap.html**).

VI

The Edge of the Web

Tip
Remember to create visual interest when designing your Web site. Layout considerations, font sizes, bullets, icons, and graphics will all add appeal to your written work.

▶ See "Basic HTML," p. 521

As you can see from figures 21.4 and 21.5, when using the Web as your medium, you have access to graphics that can add to your presentation. You might want to include a photograph of yourself, use other artists' artwork (if you can get their permission), or use inexpensive clip art.

Many font sizes are available within HTML, and browsers such as Netscape have special capabilities for sizing as well as centering and flowing text. When laying out your Web site, you'll want to use this feature for titles and to separate different areas of your pages.

If you want titles or text in something other than the normal typeface, you can use transparent GIFs. Figure 21.6 shows an example of a transparent GIF versus a non-transparent GIF. Notice that transparent GIF, rather than having square borders and boundaries, is free-form and appears to be sitting on the surface of the page. This calls visual attention to the image and serves to break up the page. The regular GIF maintains its background color and sits on top of the browser's background.

Fig. 21.6
A transparent GIF and a non-transparent GIF are compared. Note that the browser replaces the background of the transparent GIF with the browser's background.

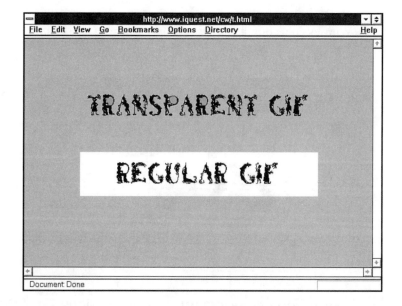

> **Note**
>
> Most graphical WWW browsers honor transparent GIF images; however, there are a few less popular ones that do not. You should always choose a pleasing background color for your images—even if they are transparent—in case the browser cannot display the image transparently.

Of course, you'll want to choose images and typefaces that are complimentary to your written work. You'll also need to choose a name from your site. It can simple and straightforward—*Short Stories By John Smith*—or it could something such as the title of a piece of work.

Just as when you put your written work into a printed form, you need to consider many things when publishing on the Web. The size of the work, the paper you'll use, what the cover will look like, and the typeface are all traditional considerations. You need to make similar decisions (such as the background of the image, the placement, and text sizes) when you create your online publication.

Traditional Publications Online

This is a field that will only continue to grow. Publishers of small press publications are beginning to discover that the Web is a cost-effective way for their traditionally high-quality (but low circulation) publications to find a larger audience.

A traditional journal or magazine doesn't have to go totally online to reap the benefits of the Web. Perhaps a magazine might decide just to give highlights from a recent issue, as well as subscription rates and information for submission of materials. A magazine with a system that's sophisticated enough might even take subscriptions over the Web with credit card information. Another possibility is to give only back issues of your magazine online. You could have a delay of three or four months, with highlights from the current months. This would give your readers value, serve to attract new readers, and still not cut down on your subscription rate.

> **Note**
>
> Find the available sites for online publications by doing a search via your favorite robot or searcher. Try to be specific in your request. A search for **magazines** will give you a lot of material you don't need to see if you're specifically looking for fiction magazines. Instead search for **fiction** or **short stories**. If you're looking for a specific genre, such as science fiction or horror, include that in your search request also.

Traditional print medium publications can use the Web to increase their subscriber base. For example, a poetry journal might feature a poem, changing it monthly or quarterly as new issues came out. You could offer subscription information for those who wanted to explore your publication in the future. To cover Web site costs, the journal could make the selection of the

Tip
With the simple additions of forms to your Web site, you can get feedback on your work (if you want it), or you can use forms for collaborative or interactive projects.

VI

The Edge of the Web

online poem open to a competition that costs a nominal fee. It isn't unusual for contests to charge a reading fee. Charging even a dollar can add up to considerable money when hundreds of poems come pouring in (but be sure to cover your costs). The journal gets more public exposure, which turns into more subscriptions. Poets get the chance to present their material in a forum that they might not otherwise have access to.

Online-Only Publications

With the advent of the Internet and the World Wide Web, many magazines are bypassing paper altogether and going straight to the electronic medium. If you're thinking about putting together a journal or publication, you might think about going online only. With the increasing cost of paper, printing, and postage, the amount of money it takes to produce a publication sometimes gets out of the reach of the small publications market.

The Web offers a great way to produce a quality product for an economical investment. But you may be wondering how to cover production costs if you don't have a product that readers can hold in their hands.

Tip

If you feel like going through the hassle of becoming a not-for-profit corporation, you might find that businesses may be even more likely to give you money or act as a sponsor to your publication.

Currently, charging for online publications isn't a very popular practice. There are too many good free ones, and in general, information is viewed as free. But you could derive the money you need to fund an online publication with contests and reading fees. Also, you can possibly try generating advertising and sponsor revenues. If you have a simple login system and generate information about the numbers and type of people coming into your site, you could possibly have companies sponsor your publication in return for advertising and promotional space. In keeping with the Net's atmosphere, such advertising shouldn't be too pushy, but a tag line with a small logo at the top or bottom of your page thanking the nice people at XYZ company for their generous financial support, and links to their site (if they have one) wouldn't be out of line.

Online Books

This is one area that has resisted being overtaken by the Internet and the Web. In fact, this is one area where the Web (with current technologies) will find it difficult to overcome printed technologies. There's something substantial about having a book between your hands that a computer won't have for a very long time. Nonetheless, this hasn't stopped several writers from serializing their books on the Web and, in some cases, releasing their work only on the Web.

As time goes on, however, more books are appearing in digital form. Several universities have active projects to convert literature into digital form. Part of the push is an attempt to catalog and preserve the historical content. However, much of the push is to also expand literature databases, which are extremely useful as research tools.

Local and Regional Governments

As life becomes more hectic and more filled with rules and regulations, individuals and businesses are finding it difficult to manage all the information. Large federal organizations often find themselves unable to keep up with the regulations, but so does city government. Most cities have hundreds of pages of local ordinances that need to be kept track of and updated as laws change, and residents need to have an easy way to check current laws and changes to laws.

The federal government is already largely on the Web. From the White House (**http://www.whitehouse.gov/**) to the Social Security Administration (**http://www.ssa.gov/**), most of the major agencies are represented. Additionally, current recommendations from Washington to every level of government suggest that legislation, laws, and notices be available to everyone in an easy and convenient way. These recommendations are causing even more agencies, in both federal and local government, to place their information on the Web for public access.

Access of Government Information To Citizens

Have you ever tried to get through to the IRS during tax season or reach someone at the Bureau of Naturalization and Immigration? It can be a headache. These agencies receive so many calls that they literally can't handle them all. Many of the calls simply request standard information. Now, automated phone voice systems handle dispensing such information. For many, such systems aren't a good method for two reasons:

■ Automated voice systems can run up phone bills—for either the callers, if a call is not toll free, or for the agencies, if it is toll free. Callers are forced to listen to a series of messages that many times don't even pertain to their question.

■ These systems don't provide printed information, so you aren't provided hard copy of the details for future reference.

The mountain of laws and regulations isn't only on the national level. Building codes and state laws concerning alcohol, weapons, and motor vehicles are just a few of the areas that add to the maze of regulations that some citizens may not even be aware of.

School systems will find the Web invaluable in disseminating information to parents about such things as vacation schedules, weekly lunch menus, dress codes, and special events. There are no flyers that can get lost on the way home or thrown out. The information is always there when parents or students need it.

You can present simple information or small amounts of it in standard Web pages, but for large amounts of information, a searchable database may be a more economical and effective way to disseminate the information. By using this type of technology, a city or state government can easily provide the thousands of pages of ordinances and regulations to the user in both category-style lookup and free-text searching. For example, if city residents want to know the rules regarding putting a pool behind the house, they could search **residential pool** or **fences** or a myriad of other choices. This would quickly bring them to the desired regulations.

Likewise, governments wanting to attract businesses into their states or cities might provide real-estate information, aerial photographs, and other related material.

◄ See "Examples of Good Uses for Kiosks," p. 452

Because you can easily package the Web in the form of kiosks, governments can provide open-access kiosks in malls, post offices, and libraries.

Efficient Citizen Feedback

► See "Adding Forms To Your Pages," p. 539

Using forms can also be valuable as a mechanism for citizen feedback. The Web can offer, for example, the Electronic Town Hall concept, similar to what candidate Ross Perot proposed during his 1992 presidential campaign. This type of feedback can be extremely successful because citizens can give instant feedback and have a readily accessible forum that's always there.

Many workers can't take the time to call government offices during business hours. And many times, lunch hours don't afford enough time to do all the things a person needs to do plus deal with local government. These same people are likely too tired to attend a local zoning meeting that might affect their lives. However, if they're allowed to contact these organizations at their own leisure, they just might become more active citizens.

The Net as a Mechanism for Lowering Overhead

Cutting government spending is on everyone's mind these days, and the Web can provide a way to help cut expenses. Not only can it cut cost between government and citizens, but the Web can also help cut costs internally.

Memos, multiple drafts of legislation, proposals, and calls for bids can consume many reams of paper. Often the material is repetitive, showing minor differences in the text for each new revision. If the material were made online over the Internet, it would decrease the amount of tax dollars that were spent on paper, printing, distribution, and then finally disposal of all that printed material.

Many browsers offer annotation capability, and shared Web project systems also exist. This way, committee members can perform markup interactively. With the advent of digital signature systems, secure transactions can be easily accomplished.

There's also a time-factor advantage in that material will be available sooner because recipients won't have to wait while the material is being printed, collated, and delivered.

Private Organizations

Groups and organizations as diverse as the Girls Scouts to the local AA chapter can benefit from a presence on the Web. You can easily make available information such as the time, date, and location of upcoming meetings over the Web instead of through countless phone calls.

When designing a Web site, private organizations should remember to use all the capabilities the WWW has to offer. If your main goal is disbursement of information, there's no reason not to use the graphics capabilities of the Web. Include photographs of members or club functions. You can also use clip art to create a pleasing presentation.

Allowing Members-Only Access

Often, private organizations may not want the public to have access to some or all of their information. In this case, you can institute a simple login system. You can design your own system, buy off-the-shelf solutions, or have one custom designed for you. The decision depends on your need for security, how much money you can spend on software, or your programming skills.

Tip

If you have a members-only access, you probably don't want to advertise your site on hotlists.

VI

The Edge of the Web

In some cases, an organization may want to have public and private areas. You may want the users to have access to background information, a statement of purpose, and contact information, but you may not want them to access the notes of the last meeting or the meeting schedule, something only your members should have access to. You could do this two ways:

- Have two separate systems: a free access site for the public and a second login site for members.

- Have one site with a section that is accessible only to those with valid logins.

In actual programming terms, the solution to problem is the same; the difference is how the material is presented to users. In the second case, casual users would be more aware of the area they couldn't access. You might consider this type of setup if you're interested in advertising the added benefits of membership in your group.

Also, in certain situations you may need separate logins and passwords for each individual, especially if you need to keep track of an individual's usage. However, if your security needs aren't great or you would like to keep track of usage by a group, you might assign logins to a particular group of people, perhaps based on geographic location or hierarchy in the group.

For instance, in a given organization the general membership might all log in with the same code word—something that's easy to remember. On the other hand, the president and other officials would have a different login that would give them access to a higher level of information.

Unlimited Capability for Services

For group members, a wide variety of services can be performed that aren't currently available or are available on other, sometimes less viable methods.

You can set up conference rooms so that members can leave messages in text as well as pictures to each other. This might be helpful if you have a committee that's planning a big fund-raising event. Rather than play phone tag with one another, committee members can leave messages and instructions, even sketches and pictures. Also, it leaves a permanent record that members can refer to later, if needed.

Many services need to respond to repetitive requests for information. You can make such information available through a Web site. Depending on the complexity of information provided, the site could range from a simple page listing addresses, names of officials, and the like, to a lot of information requiring a searchable database.

Non-Profit Organizations

Non-profit organizations can really profit from the World Wide Web. These groups can often get fantastic Web pages created, at little or no cost, just by providing the tax benefit to the designer and provider.

The benefit to non-profit organizations is fairly obvious. It boils down to exposure. The ability to present ideas and projects, or to solicit help, donations, time, equipment, or support is unprecedented. Not only does it offer the organization exposure, but it also offers extremely little overhead. Because there are no printing costs and minor distribution costs, the organization can put more of its money to the proper chartered use.

Tip

A non-profit institution on the Net has a domain name ending in .org, for organization.

Grant Opportunities and the Net

Because the Internet and Web are the latest in communication technology, many grants exist to help people explore the possibilities and future of the Net. Since the growth rate—in user population and in new technology—is so steep, there's much interest in how to exploit the capabilities of this medium.

Also, many new capabilities are needed, such as more secure systems, transaction handling, advanced capabilities such as 3-D and immersion, as well as much-needed improvements in bandwidth and machine speed.

As governments, institutions, and businesses rush to understand, comprehend, exploit, and predict the Net, all this wondering and needing will boil down to a great deal of experimentation and research. And this means that grants will be available for doing this type of research.

If you are using grants as a part of your work, you might look into integrating the Web and Internet as a part of your research. Doing this certainly won't hurt and might just be one of the factors that helps sway a grant in your direction.

VI

The Edge of the Web

From Here...

The Web is a fresh way for artists of all fields to reach a new audience. It also provides a cost-effective manner for social and civic groups—as well as local and regional governments—for disseminating information and providing good public relations.

From here, you may want to read the following chapters:

- Chapter 4, "Planning a Web Site," provides helpful tips to keep in mind as you're creating your Web site.

- Chapter 7, "Picking a Name for Yourself on the Net," offers tips on coming up with an effective Web site name.

- Chapter 10, "Advertising on the Net," shows you the best ways to advertise your Web site.

- Chapter 14, "Subscription Services, Virtual Malls, and Instant Products," offers information on login systems and products that artists can create and sell on the Web.

- Chapter 16, "Your Presence on the Net," teaches you tips on creating an effective Web presence.

- Chapter 17, "Security and the Net," gives you important information to safeguard your Web site.

Chapter 22

The Future of the Net

This chapter explores the possible futures of the Internet and World Wide Web. By understanding how and where the Net and Web are moving, you can better predict what will be available in the near and not so near future.

The Web's future poses many interesting questions. How will it affect television? Shopping? Will it turn people into computer-desk potatoes? As the Web appears in more and more families' homes, how will society deal with its adult content?

In this chapter you learn

- Throughput and bandwidth issues for the future

- Future enhancements that will make the Web even easier to use

- The future of full multimedia on the Web

- Cash transactions and the future

- Virtual reality and the Web

- The Web's influence on the future of culture, art, education, and business

What is Needed on the Net

As more people take advantage of the Internet and Web, different needs and uses will emerge. You can expect the Web to evolve and change, but it should also maintain certain constants, including the following:

- An adherence to the open and cooperative values of the Internet

- The continued use of existing methods for transmitting information

- Continued growth in the business sector and the new growth of an at-home Web clientele

This section contains a "wish list" of functionality and capabilities that are crucial for the Web's continued growth and success.

Higher Bandwidth and Throughput

As more people accomplish increasingly difficult tasks through the World Wide Web and Internet, the bandwidth of the Internet will have to grow accordingly. The problem is that the number of new users and capabilities is increasing faster than the physical growth of the communications lines.

The Internet and Web are the hottest new moneymakers, and companies are flocking to them at full speed to stake their claim and begin to reap the benefits. This influx of new businesses requires increasingly faster lines as users disperse more data through them.

For example, Internet telephone systems are already beginning to appear. These programs give users enough bandwidth to use the Net as a video phone. And as this book has previously mentioned, video signals require a lot of bandwidth.

It is one thing for a few thousand users around the world to experiment with real-time video over the Internet. It is quite another for millions of users to be video conferencing at the same time on the Internet. The telecommunications lines that formerly only had to support scientists trading information back and forth aren't quite yet ready for this enormous growth.

> **Note**
>
> Plan to make use of new telecommunications technology as it becomes available. For example, it may not currently be feasible for you to incorporate audio into your Web site. In a year or two, when the technology is faster, incorporating audio into a Web site may be considered routine.

Currently, the number of new, local Internet providers is growing rapidly. Often these providers consist of a couple of friends tying their Macs to the Internet with a 56 baud modem. Although some of these companies will be able to expand, most will fold under the onslaught of more capable providers.

Many large, commercial, traditionally non-Internet network providers are also running full tilt to get on the Internet. These companies realize that to keep their customers, they must provide access to the Web. The alternative is to lose all their customers to the Web.

If a major non-Internet provider with 2 million customers suddenly turns on the Web and Internet for their clients, you instantly have a million new users. This already occurred when Prodigy and America Online went to the Internet and the Web.

With all these new Web providers, the telecommunications lines could potentially start to jam up. Currently the Internet is taking the load very well. However, as more people, cities, and countries come online, a faster bandwidth will be necessary.

This problem transcends the United States borders. One problem facing many developing nations is that they have only a limited access to bandwidth coming in and an increasingly aware citizenship that wants access to the world that the Internet has to offer.

> **Note**
>
> Many countries are hooked to the Internet by a fractional T1 line (a 256K line or, in some cases, even a 56K line). Often these lines—which service universities, businesses, and government—are extremely strained with user load. Countries with small Internet feeds often charge by the byte, even for e-mail, to try to limit overuse of the network.

Throughput to the user is another issue that will be of increasing importance. Some businesses offer their employees high-speed access to the Internet, and students have similar access at universities. However, most home computer users and many small and middle-sized businesses are accessing the Internet at modem rates. Although 28.8 baud modems are fast and provide acceptable access to the Web, they are just at the threshold of what is bearable when it comes to such advanced features as video.

Much like old green-screen monitors in a world of full-color, high-resolution graphics, modem technology pales next to its high-bandwidth cousins of ISDN, T1, and T3 lines. Although offered by some phone companies for a reasonable rate, ISDN is still not widely used. (Also, many telephone companies are unable to install it correctly.) For most home computer users, T1 and T3 lines are still simply too expensive. However, as new telecommunications technology develops, the price of T1 and T3 lines should decrease. Remember this as you develop your WWW site.

VI

The Edge of the Web

Tip

When creating your site, remember that what you deem to be an acceptable length of time to wait for data over your T1 line may be unacceptable to those of your clients using 28.8 baud modems.

On the horizon are cable modems. This technology will enable you to download from a network quickly. Cable television already transmits multiple, selectable video programs to homes over a single wire, so it seems a natural extension to provide the Internet through the same mechanism.

Note

As you plan your Web site, consider developing trends on the WWW. For instance, you might decide not to include a video clip in your Web site because most of your targeted customers would have to wait for the video to be downloaded. However, you might plan to add video in a year or two, after the phone lines become faster.

Current systems display some flaws: the desired content and Internet traffic often impose a much larger load than cable can handle. For example, current video cable technology can provide each home a choice of about 100 channels. The feed of many-to-one requires only simple switching technology. However, on the Internet, the user can access millions of places. The server would have to be much larger to handle the connection load of an entire city.

To handle this connection load, channel modems are often designed to work off central hubs, where a server powers a neighborhood rather than an entire city. In this way, servers can be distributed to handle the load. These systems have worked in tests of a few cable modems. However, as soon as everyone in a neighborhood turns on his or her modem and starts surfing through video and audio, the system bogs down.

Telecommunications technology should rise to meet the demand. After all, this market is becoming extremely consumer-driven, which means that technological advances will be rapid and costs will quickly become affordable. Where virtual reality has failed to deliver enough quality in a short time, the Internet is at least delivering on its promise.

The Internet community already is laying the foundation for the needed technology. Many providers are switching to fiber optics, which provides cleaner and higher bandwidth. T1 installations are becoming more common, and some providers are even using one or more T3 lines. Selected areas are using newer protocols that are much faster than T3, and more backbone connections are being created.

Greater User Friendliness

One reason that the Internet seems so capable is that it had a long head start. Because it has been used in education and government for years, the Net has had time to get established and work out all the quirks. The Internet is attractive to new users partly because it is already a thriving community with millions of places to go. It's like going to a party: instead of being the first to arrive, you would rather show up when it's in full swing.

It took a long time for the Net to gain mass popularity, mainly because it used to be much more difficult to use. It required that you type in "computerese" commands, specifying devices and other things that the casual computer user simply didn't want to bother with. WWW browsers brought the complex world of the Internet into the point-and-click world of the home computer user, suddenly making the Net very attractive for even the most inexperienced user.

As time goes on, the Net will only become easier for both users and programmers. The current technology of image layout and other formatting features of Web browsers is still quite primitive. Still to come are more complex interfaces that provide total control over the way that text flows over images and the capability to overlap images with transparent backgrounds. These simple capabilities will enable you to integrate text and images more closely, and to create "rooms" in which moveable objects can sit on backgrounds that are not moveable.

Several companies already are beginning to buck the traditional standards of HTML. Netscape Communications is pushing the standards of HTML and providing new extensions (that is, new commands) almost monthly. Currently, Netscape browsers enable you to do the following:

◀ See "Clients and Browsers," p. 35

- Center text

- Change text color

- Specify background colors

- Display flashing text

- Create complex-textured backgrounds

- Control justification

- Control text layout

The HTML 3.0 standard proposes most of these capabilities. However, some of Netscape's extensions are not included in the proposed standard, although Netscape is working hard to have the standards committee adopt them.

VI

The Edge of the Web

> **Note**
>
> One problem facing future growth is that the standards committees move extremely slowly compared to the pace at which the industry is growing. Of course, the Web is growing so quickly that even under the best circumstances it would be difficult to keep up. Often new features are implemented a year or more earlier than the standards committees adopt them. However, because user demand is driving the Web's growth, that growth itself will continue to promote the standardization of an increasingly powerful and user-friendly system.

One way to research new HTML techniques while remaining completely compatible with the standards committee is to implement *gating software*. With gating software, developers can extend HTML and other networking paradigms so that they can research new possibilities and directions without violating standards. A new feature implemented using gating techniques works instantly and without difficulty for all Web browsers, even though those browsers never had the capability before.

Gating systems work by acting as a filter for converting advanced capabilities into the accepted standard. By using a gating system, you never violate the standard, but are free to develop new capabilities that the standards committee may eventually adopt.

For instance, our own gating system enables Web authors to use such advanced capabilities as inline calendars, user authorization, automatic form handling, page counting, and shopping, all without a server. The HTML does not define these capabilities, at least not without requiring that users have their own server. These gating techniques will help spawn many independent researchers while keeping their discoveries and products compatible with the rest of the world.

Full Multimedia

As more users demand full multimedia, the industry will develop the technology. If the medium's standards committee doesn't adopt the technology, innovative programmers will find ways to develop it on their own. Already, users who want to show video clips but can't afford the time and monetary costs associated with video on the Web have adapted the Macintosh QuickTime movie format. This format enables users to include small videos (about the size of a postage stamp). Often these videos run at reduced frames per second, which greatly reduces overhead compared to that of standard video.

The Web will never be truly multimedia until it allows businesses to initiate sound and video files without user input. Currently, for example, you cannot even automatically play your company jingle when the user brings up your page (although a proposed standard does allow this capability). The same general rule applies to video. You can provide a link for users to access such material, but they must first ask for it; you cannot have it play on its own.

Obviously, for many advertising and demonstration purposes, the following capability would be fantastic. When the user selects the link to your page, it presents a full-color video with music or voice-over, which then slowly fades into the first page of your company's home page. Of course, current bandwidth and usage charges for the video would price such a multimedia presentation beyond the reach of most businesses. But even if they wanted to spend the money, they still couldn't implement such a presentation because HTML does not yet make it physically possible.

Until these multimedia dilemmas are solved, the Web's potential will be limited. However, full multimedia is coming quickly due to increasing user demand. Not long ago, color and fancy-texture backgrounds, centered text, and other new capabilities introduced by Netscape weren't possible. Already Netscape has introduced the capability for a document to pull new data in fixed intervals. You can use this capability to load a page, play a sound, and then load graphics, all without the user requesting anything beyond the first page—although the effect is not as fluid as described in the last paragraph's example.

Security

As Chapters 17 through 19 explained, more built-in security measures are needed. In the future, you should see many such measures developed.

Current Web security is adequate for the average business user. But as more secure standards are implemented, the Internet and the Web will move into every aspect of the business and the home. If you doubt this, consider that about 15 years ago, many people had the same doubts about computers, which you can now find everywhere—in cars, homes, and offices, and as grocery store scanners, home appliances, vending machines, and toys.

◀ See "Crime and the Net," p. 385

Security measures will be very important as immersion technology related to virtual reality becomes more prevalent. Hackers messing around with people in cyberspace could introduce whole new dangers. For example, hackers could infect computers with programs that flicker the visual display at such a rate to induce trances or epileptic convulsions. Or in completely immersive

◀ See "Creating a Secure System," p. 438

VI

The Edge of the Web

technology, where tactile sensations are produced via gloves or body suits, pain or injury could be inflicted if safety features on the equipment were bypassed by hackers.

◄ See "Soliciting Help," p. 431

The new frontiers of the Web will also produce new security hazards that all companies will want to keep informed of. The sites mentioned in Chapters 17 through 19 most likely will continue to be the best places to find out about new threats to security on the Web and how to combat them.

Tip

The new advances in Web security technology should not encourage businesses or individuals to slacken their attention to security.

New advances are likely not only in encrypting techniques but also in ease of implementing such security measures. Also, as digital signature technology becomes more prevalent, using that technology will become increasingly natural. Not too long ago, only a small portion of society used credit cards, but today most adults carry several credit cards. Likewise, in a few years, digital signature should be everywhere and will probably replace current standard banking procedures.

Simple Cash Transactions

In the future, simple cash transactions on the Web should become as commonplace as the use of ATM machines. The Web should also become more immersive and virtual. This trend is likely to change the way that cash transactions are conducted.

For instance, on a virtual Web, instead of paying by typing your information into an on-screen form, you might instead hand the virtual clerk a virtual credit card. Such a card might be one of many that you keep in your virtual wallet. One day you might pay with your virtual Visa card, the next with your virtual Mastercard.

In reality, the clerk acts as the graphical interface for a cash transaction handler, and the virtual Visa card is a file that contains the credit card information for your Visa account. You would have a file for each credit card in your wallet protected by your digital signature.

When you hand your card to the virtual clerk, you are really just initiating the transfer of information from your system to the cash transaction handler's system. Making it look like you are handing the credit card to a person simply places the transaction in the comforting realm of everyday experience.

> **Note**
>
> The information file doesn't have to look like a credit card. For instance, if a customer is shopping in your company store, which issues its own online cash, perhaps the file that contains your credit information would look like currency issued by the company bank.

The next section discusses further how a virtual Web might look and how users will interact with it.

How the Future Net Will Look

As the last section indicates, the Web is heading in the direction of total immersion and virtuality. If you visit any new, first-rate arcade in a big city, you'll find virtual reality games that anyone (who is willing to pay the price) can play. Often, the lines for these games are quite long. Some businesses offer nothing but virtual reality gaming.

Unfortunately, these games fail to deliver an actual virtual reality environment, mainly because of the power required to achieve a believable virtual environment. However, the Web will help to change this by advancing real-time graphic capabilities. It will also set new standards for the telecommunications and computer infrastructure.

Likewise, as computers and telecommunications become faster and more sophisticated, and as virtual reality technology (such as headsets and body suits) becomes more usable, this technology will naturally filter down into every level of the Web, including the user interface.

That prediction may sound incredible. But note that people in large cities such as Tokyo and New York already pay big bucks to play video simulations of golf; in Tokyo, people can ski down a hill that is located inside a building. The next logical step is to cut down on the physical space it takes for these amusements and to make them virtual. After such technology is developed, its price will soon decrease, and every computer will have an optional virtual interface.

VI

The Edge of the Web

> **Note**
>
> Virtual reality and total immersion Web technology should be particularly appealing to those who live in overcrowded cities. Tokyo, for example, with millions of people living in close quarters, could benefit by releasing its citizens into cyberspace, where they can find privacy and space.

A Fully Graphic Internet

The Internet and Web are a long way from being fully immersive and virtual. In fact, they are a long way from being fully graphic. However, at their current rate of growth, you should begin to see more integrated and capable systems using the following:

- *Text*. Strides are necessary to control the color of backgrounds and text (Netscape already provides some of this control). Font types and special designed fonts will begin to appear, enabling users to create pages that have a much more personalized look. Text flow will be greatly improved, so that you can place pictures anywhere and have text flow evenly around them.

- *Overlapping elements*. These elements are needed to make more artistic use of the Web possible. Being able to place text or pictures over other pictures will help you present information in new and novel ways.

- *Interactive user input features*. More intelligence and options in the handling of interactive user input will begin to appear. Buttons that are animated when pushed and forms that are intelligent about content (for example, recognizing when input must be numeric or alphabetic only, or when a field must be filled out) will all enhance the environment's overall quality.

- *Real-time interaction*. The capability to interact in real time will become more prevalent. Pictures and text will change automatically, without the user's request (this is already beginning to happen). Interactive sessions such as chat and video conferencing will be possible within Web pages. Including inset video within a window should be easy after Web pages develop the capability to split their focus within a single page (that is, different parts of the same page will be capable of doing different things at the same time).

- *3-D capability*. The Web will become three-dimensional by enabling objects to turn and rotate, either automatically or by user control. This capability will be the final step toward a fully immersive Web.

Virtual Reality and the Internet

Anyone who has seen recent popular movies and television shows is familiar with the concept of virtual reality (VR). Movies like *Total Recall* and *Lawnmower Man* and television programs like *Star Trek*, *Wild Palms*, and *VR 5* all have introduced the concept of virtual reality to nearly every home in America and indeed around the world.

Currently, the hardware (such as helmets and input gloves) to implement VR is clumsy to wear and the images are less than real-world quality, but improvements are being made.

A total virtual-reality interface to the Web will certainly open up new business possibilities. Someone will have to supply virtual landscapes and buildings as well as the programs to produce virtual personalities that users will need to represent themselves in VR.

As people clamber to create their unique identity on the Internet, businesses will emerge to develop virtual products for customers to wear and use in virtual Web space. You will no longer surf pages with a mouse, but instead will be transported (virtually) to a business in which you can walk, talk, meet, touch, and purchase.

Home pages will cease to exist, as today's static, two-dimensional video brochures turns into true 3-D versions of the places they represent. Bars will look like bars, hotels will look like hotels, and offices will look like offices—all with more imagination because design options will be unlimited.

Instead of running to Lycos or the NCSA What's New list, you might slip on your VR helmet and hop into a phone booth on a busy VR street. Looking up the place where you want to go, you dial in the number and are then instantly transported to the neighborhood near your destination. You'll experience all this without leaving your easy chair.

This fantastic dream is really not at all impossible. The existing structure of the Web actually lends itself to this type of scenario rather well. Consider that each server on the Web represents a neighborhood. With the proper VR hardware and software at the server, users local to that server could access the Web. Users coming into the server from anywhere in the world will enter the neighborhood represented within the server. Businesses, schools, and homes would all exist within that server for that neighborhood. Users will "see" the buildings because the server will represent the scene as fully 3-D, not the static two-dimensional presentations that you are used to today.

VI

The Edge of the Web

How distant is the realization of this dream? The answer depends on many factors, but in fact such technology is almost possible today. Servers exist that are easily powerful enough to present at least rudimentary 3-D representations to multiple users. High-speed silicon graphic workstations—already proficient at virtual reality and fast 3-D—are approaching the price of a well-equipped PC, enabling home users to begin to tap the power of major graphic workstations (low-end SGI systems with full 3-D capability currently cost between $4,000 and $10,000). All you need is an HTML-like graphics language for 3-D objects that embodies the graphics as descriptions rather than raw data (making throughput fast). These standards are already being proposed.

Before the end of this century, you should begin to see immersive technology merging with the Web. Within 10 to 20 years, this technology should affect major changes in how you interact moment to moment and day to day.

In fact, two companies are already pushing the envelope of immersive Web technology. Both SUN and SGI (Silicon Graphics) have created state-of-the-art browsers that put the envelope of current Web technology. SUN's Hot Java product allows developers to easily extend the capabilities of the Web (see fig. 22.1).

Fig. 22.1
Hot Java, from SUN, allows you to extend the capabilities of the Web. Hot Java can be found at **http://java. sun.com/**.

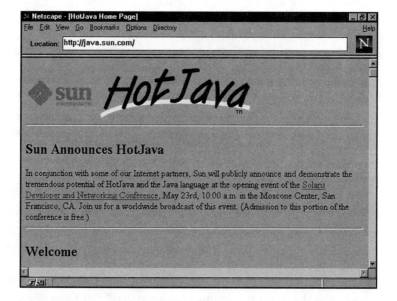

SGI's WebSpace product gives true 3-D capability (including immersive interfaces) to the Web (as shown in fig. 22.2).

Fig. 22.2
Silicon Graphics'
WebSpace gives
true 3-D capabili-
ties to the Web.
It can be found
within **http://
www.sgi.com**/.

Living and the Internet

As the Internet and Web evolve and begin to influence society, your lifestyle at home will change substantially.

Already the Web offers far more content than all the television and cable stations combined. How often have you checked the TV listings only to find that nothing is worth watching on any of your 140 or so channels? On the Web, something is *always* happening. With several new sites coming online each hour, you could never begin to see everything worthwhile that the Web has to offer.

Because of this variety, vastness of content, and the further integration of computers into society, soon we will all have the Web in our homes—if not by computer and telephone line, then by television and Internet-driven content. (Don't expect television stations simply to give up to this enhanced competition; they too will learn to use the Internet and Web to their advantage, as some are already doing.)

In the future, you will start your day by consulting your Web appointment schedule and looking up the weather reports and news for the day. With interactive video conferencing, your personal home page will act as a telephone, television, virtual secretary, fashion consultant, gopher, and all-around helpful servant.

You may begin to work at home, avoiding long commutes, rush hours, and pollution. The impact on the environment from this one single savings will be significant. Productivity will increase as people no longer waste time at the water cooler, in cars, or going out to lunch (walking to the kitchen is much easier than going out to a restaurant). Employee morale will also increase as people will naturally spend more time with their families each day. Businesses will save huge quantities of money as their overhead and insurance rates fall drastically (employees working at home require far less overhead than employees working in an office environment).

When you do venture outside, you take your portable telecommunications device, which enables you to stay attached and communicating at all times. This device will serve as your phone, television set, watch, and other everyday objects. Just as you don't think twice now to put on a digital wristwatch and slip your cellular phone into your pocket, in the future you won't think twice to slip your Web card into your pocket before you walk out the door.

Security companies will want to start now to investigate ways to enhance their systems with the Internet. Home security systems will provide a virtual representation of your home while you are out. With a properly designed system, you could see what is happening at your home from anywhere in the world. Interesting features in a virtual-reality home security system might include information on how many times a particular person came to your front door and video clips taken by a camera focused on your front door. With these and other features, you could answer your front door from anywhere in the world.

Shopping and the Internet

Immersive shopping systems are already in development. Some of the big computer shows have already presented such systems. In a virtual shopping system, you may enter the shopping site through a door, walk to different departments, and then browse or ask the clerk for something specific. By looking or pointing at a tag inside the collar of the garment, you can find manufacturing information, materials content information, and cleaning instructions.

You will be able to inspect products, ask manufacturers specific questions, or consult instant lists of comparison products, suggested uses, and Better Business Bureau reports. Armed with intelligent agents that sniff out information for you, you would simply tell your shopping cart what you need; the cart then fills the order, based on its stored profile of your likes, dislikes, and spending habits.

If you are considering purchasing an item of clothing, you can try it on your virtual self (assuming that your virtual representation is actually representative of your body), or a virtual model could show it to you.

Stores will deliver purchased goods much as they currently do for catalog orders. However, the demand for virtual products will also grow. What you wear when you take a stroll on Virtual Street will become important. With the capability to design your own persona, you will constantly try to outdo others in their virtual attire and grooming.

Individuals, artists, and companies will open virtual shops that meet the need for virtual clothes and other virtual products. Purchasing virtual clothing from a virtual shop could involve purchasing a limited license for the use of the "bits," which when applied to your virtual personality would dress it up in a stunning high-fashion outfit. You could purchase expensive, unique designer outfits on a timed account, stipulating that the clothing simply disappears when the time runs out.

Education and the Internet

As the virtual Web becomes commonplace in the business sector, it should also emerge in schools. In all facets of education, the Web of the future offers outstanding possibilities.

Imagine a class in New York City taking a virtual tour of Greece, hosted by a class in Athens. The class in Athens takes 3-D cameras into the streets and sites of the city and then beams the video in real time back to the students in New York City. In this way, the students in New York take a live, educational tour, while the students in Athens gain experience in effective presentation and planning. The next day, the New York students might present a tour of New York to the students in Athens.

Now imagine what this type of system can do for the entire educational system. Students no longer have to go to class in school buildings, but can attend classes at home. Bussing and school overcrowding would no longer be problems. No matter where a student lives, he or she can receive a quality education with one-on-one learning.

Furthermore, students can learn at their own pace without the extreme competition of traditional schools. National education centers could set standards for virtual classes, programs, and projects, to ensure the same level and quality of education to everybody, while offering a completely personalized curriculum.

Schools that in the past were too poor to provide proper funding for equipment will instead enable users to simulate their experiments and equipment needs. For example, computers could simulate chemical reactions calculated based on the substance and quantities of the chemicals that the students mixed. Writing students would have expert prompting systems at their disposal encouraging them to improve and experiment with their style. History departments could reenact famous political situations, enabling students to witness them from opposite viewpoints and to experiment with outcomes and scenarios.

And throughout all of this, all the information and learning is constantly recirculating in feedback, enabling all students to learn from each other as well as from the system.

The Net After Hours

Of course, people seeking to meet others in cyberspace will fall prey to the same problems that they currently have on the Internet and Web. Because you are meeting only "virtual people," you have no way to ensure that the people you meet actually look the way that they represent themselves. If you are a bald, 300-pound man with bad teeth, you are under no constraint to present yourself that way. In fact, you don't even have to represent yourself as a man or even as a human being. Your graphical cyberspace representation can be a cat, a dragon, or a troll. You could even be a cat-headed human with wheels for feet. Anything goes. This will be part of the fun of cyberspace on the Web.

Cyberclubs and bars will open. Big bands could play cyberconcerts. If you buy a ticket, you could sit in the audience or view the stage from any angle you want. Private clubs and communities will spring up, catering to anyone's virtual needs and desires.

Gaming rooms and huge virtual entertainment systems will also appear. Fantastic games with vast numbers of playing levels will emerge to capture the entertainment dollar.

Virtual vacations and getaways will enable users to transport themselves anywhere for a relaxing few minutes near a waterfall in Hawaii or a quiet stroll around a Tibetan monastery.

The Global Community

The Web and Internet are already creating huge social and political changes as people from different cultures begin to share ideas and concepts freely.

The Net's Impact on Culture

A virtual Web should increase communications among people of diverse backgrounds and geological locations that might not otherwise get to interact. Although the Web will definitely result in some cultural loss, the Net will greatly bolster other aspects of cultures.

> **Note**
>
> The de facto standard of the English language on the Internet is pointed out by some as a trend towards a loss of cultural identity by non-English speaking cultures.
>
> On the other hand, the ability for members of national, cultural, or religious groups that are separated (due to emigration or war) to keep in contact with one another via the Internet and WWW is one beneficial point for maintaining cultural continuity.

Users can already talk in real time to people from around the world, and many are beginning to discover what it's like to think in a foreign language and live in a foreign country. Internet Relay Chat is fun and educational for just this very reason. In IRC, users engage in simple conversations in which they learn more than they ever would in years of history and geography courses.

Instead of getting news from filtered media sources, users can now find out the real story from people who are actually there. This ability has already had tremendous impact on political developments in nations where media coverage is limited. The political, social, and economic impact of this sharing and understanding will make for many a future thesis project.

◀ See "IRC," p. 46

The Net's Impact on Science and Technology

The Net has already made a huge impact on science and technology. After all, that's why the Net was invented in the first place.

The Net has made it much easier to publish scientific works. Although getting published in prestigious journals is still difficult, anyone can publish on the Web. In the future, journals themselves will probably publish on the Web.

The interactive nature of the Web will enable more researchers from around the world to work together, and share data and information. With the sheer amount of information on the Web, knowledge systems will become commonplace, enabling researchers to solve problems that in the past might have

VI

The Edge of the Web

taken huge quantities of resources. Millions of scientific opinions, solutions, discoveries, and methods will be available at the touch of a button (and, in fact, already are).

Just as education will benefit from the virtual laboratory, so will science and technology. Researchers will be able to simulate and test complex and dangerous experiments in a virtual environment before ever attempting to perform them in a physical environment. Not only do virtual raw materials cost much less than physical materials, but virtual mistakes don't have nearly the same impact as real ones. With proper expert systems and simulations, preliminary product safety testing will take weeks rather than years.

From Here...

This chapter looked at current technical restrictions of the WWW and gave some options for how they might be dealt with. Problems such as the decreasing availability of bandwidth, the need for true multimedia capabilities, and arising security concerns will all need to solved in the very near future.

Social implications will also become a major concern, resulting from the increasing WWW interconnectivity of people from all over the world.

For more information, refer to the following chapters:

- Chapter 3, "Why the Net is Good for Business," discusses the factors that govern the Internet and business.

- Chapter 8, "Etiquette and the Net," describes key concepts governing behavior in cyberculture.

- Chapter 9, "Information on the Net," gives the best places to keep up with Web trends.

- Chapter 14, "Subscription Services, Virtual Malls, and Instant Products," presents ideas for possible Web businesses.

Chapter 23

A Few Last Words About Making It Big on the Internet

This book has covered a very broad base of information for a wide variety of businesses and organizations. While anyone who wants to put up a home page just for fun will find this book useful, the overall purpose of this book is to allow the reader to tap into the great moneymaking potential of the Web.

The Cost of Getting Involved

As you discovered, the cost to launch your business will hinge on several factors:

- How much material you want to present

- The amount of HTML coding that can be done by yourself or other people within your organization '

- Your use of specialized higher functions of the Web

- The provider charges required by your site

If the cost of your Web site is more than you expected, you might want to cut down on the amount of information you are presenting or how you present it. You may decide that you do not want to implement all your Web ideas at once, but start with a basic setup and plan for future growth. In this way, Web sales can pay for your future Web growth. You should, however, make the initial design interesting and "meaty" enough to make people want to visit the site.

▶ See "Basic HTML," p. 521

If you are at all capable with computers, we highly suggest you learn HTML programming. There are also many commercial programs available to help you create HTML documents. Familiarizing yourself with HTML can cut down on your costs associated with the Web. Even if your company can't handle creating forms or some of the higher functions, doing the HTML programming yourself and hiring experts to do the more sophisticated work can potentially save you hundreds or thousands of dollars, depending on the size of your site.

> **Note**
>
> Remember that a well-thought-out plan for your Web site and its future development will cut down on costly redesigns and reworkings of your Web site. This is especially true if you are planning a database or other custom software. Taking time before starting the actual work to determine how the information will be accessed, by whom, how often, and at what times can eliminate the need to go back and redo poorly planned sites.

Tip

Remember that it is entirely possible for you to create a site that not only pays its own way but also makes a profit for you (beyond product sales). By this we mean selling your Web space to your own sponsors.

The final word on the Web and your business is that it should pay for itself, either through sales, public relations, or the cutting of overhead expenses. A good Web site can benefit many areas of your business.

The Basic Benefits To Business

When you calculate the costs of the Web, remember to weigh them against the amount of value you receive from the Web. The WWW provides many services to business that are much more expensive in their traditional forms. The Web can be used for the following:

- Marketing

- Sales

- Promotion

- Advertising

- Communications

- Research

- Collecting user demographics

- Cutting overhead costs

Not only is the Web very capable of fulfilling these functions, but it does them in a way that minimizes the use of materials like paper, ink, gasoline, and personnel hours.

◀ See "The HTTPD Log," p. 342

You have seen how big companies and high-tech corporations can benefit from the Web. Smaller businesses and organizations such as the following are also using the Web:

- Flower shops
- Gift stores
- Antiques stores
- Hotels
- Bed and breakfasts
- Restaurants
- Jewelry stores
- Realtors
- Art galleries

- Fraternities
- Travel agents
- Newspapers and publications of all sizes
- Lawyers
- Accountants
- Engineers
- Rock groups
- Civic organizations
- Clothing shops

Figures 23.1 through 23.3 provide examples of different groups who have posted pages to the Web.

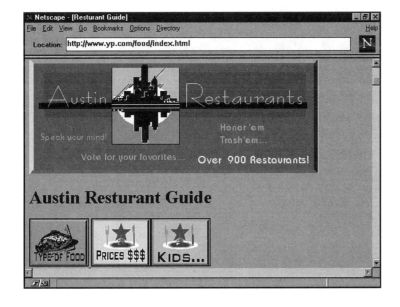

Fig. 23.1
The Austin Restaurant Guide allows users to look at local area restaurants and rank their favorites on food, service, and quality **(http://www.yp.com/food/index.html)**.

VI

The Edge of the Web

Fig. 23.2
Lonely Planet is a
real travel book
publisher with a
presence on the
World Wide Web
(**http://www.
lonelyplanet.
com.au/lp.htm**).

Fig. 23.3
Many antique
shops have found a
place on the Web
(**http://www.
ic.mankato.
mn.us/antiques/
AOronoco.html**).

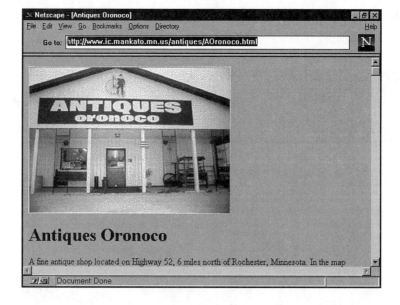

◀ See "Benefits
Common To
All Businesses
on the Net,"
p. 79

If this book hasn't already touched on an area that directly relates to your
business, with a little thought we are sure that you can think of some way
that it could benefit you.

There are very few businesses that can afford not to do some type of advertising or self-promotion, and the WWW is one method that will become an increasingly important way to reach potential clients, as well as being quite a bit cheaper than traditional media. Television and catalog shopping continue to be popular ways to make purchases. Web advertising, online catalogs, and virtual malls are the next step in this trend.

◀ See "Planning Your Net Business," p. 93

The current orientation of the Web is geared at the college-educated and professional user, who is an important market group for many businesses. But as the Internet and the WWW becomes increasingly available to the average citizen (through government public access and the trickle down of technology), an even wider audience will be available with even more benefits to businesses.

Etiquette

When corresponding on the Internet and the WWW, it's important to remember its origins as a collaborative, grass-roots effort among scientists to further the sharing of information and ideas. Businesses on the Web which only seek to take and not give anything in return may not be too welcome on the Internet.

Businesses should also remember that while the Internet itself is free for many people, the products consumers will consider spending their money on have to be a good value, unique, or offer convenience. Simply charging for general information will not work because that information will most likely be available elsewhere for free.

Whatever your involvement is in the Internet and the Web, to achieve the best results you must adhere to the loose, mostly unwritten laws of the Internet.

Here are just a few of the major rules as a refresher:

- Don't promise things you can't do.

- Don't abuse e-mail, no matter how tempting. Mass mailings are definitely a big mistake.

◀ See "Etiquette in Mass Mailings," p. 195

- Don't use computerese and hacker jargon that you aren't familiar with in an attempt to fit in or be cool. Jargon presented in this book is meant to inform and not necessarily give you instant understanding to the Internet culture. As you naturally become part of the Internet culture, you will begin to learn, use, and create jargons naturally.

- Avoid entering into flame wars in e-mail, NetNews, and IRC. Such wars can have negative effects in business dealings and can give you a bad reputation on the Net.

- Answer your e-mail. If you provide an e-mail address for people to contact you or if your have information from forms put into an e-mail address, remember to check them and send appropriate responses. Many users view e-mail as an almost instantaneous form of communication and expect messages back the same day.

- Remember who your audience is. If you are targeting senior citizens, they may not appreciate a confusing, hip-hop presentation. With appropriate use of graphics, almost any type of look can be achieved on the Internet. Make sure your image is the one you want to project.

- Demonstrate good behavior when in someone else's site. Being in someone's site is like being invited into their office or home. Looking at data that is not yours is not only impolite, it's illegal.

A good site where you can get a good feel for the Net and the Web is the online version of the Hacker's Jargon book currently located at

http://www.ccil.org/jargon/jargon.html

as well as many other sites.

> **Note**
>
> Ideas covered in this section are more fully covered in Chapter 8, "Etiquette and the Net."

Good Design and Organization

Even if you have a great product or service to offer, a poorly designed Web site will not reach its optimum impact. Web sites that are crowded, hard to understand, too weird, or too boring, may turn off potential clients. Most Web sites should make use of the common design theories used in print mediums:

- Don't crowd too much information into one space (we call this "leaving whitespace").

- Use graphics and texts that are appropriate to your subject.

- Choose graphics, texts, and other design elements that are of a similar nature and that compliment each other and not clash.

- Organize the material so that it leads the viewer through the material in an easy and logical manner.

Remember to make use of links in your Web sites to help organize your information into easily digestible portions and also to lead the viewer from one section of information to the next. The use of easily identifiable icon buttons can be used to draw the viewer's attention, prompting them for input.

Large amounts of information might best be organized by a searchable database. Databases will save viewers time in allowing them to simply type in information requests, bypassing more cumbersome menu selections. They will also help your business save money by cutting down on your throughput charges.

◀ See "Databases and Virtual Shopping Systems," p. 330

Make the best use of the visual nature of the WWW and include graphics in your presentation. Simple clip art, company logos, and photos of company personnel can be used to help create visual interest to your Web site. Make sure, however, that for any graphics you use, you have the rights to use it. If you don't have access through normal channels, you may find sites on the Web that offer graphics for public use. Do a Web search to find sites that offer free artwork.

◀ See "Your Home Page," p. 364

Security

Security is something that everyone on the Internet and Web need to keep in mind. Remembering that the Web is an outgrowth of a grass-roots efforts and is loosely policed and governed can mean that the potential for abuse can arise. Most Internet and Web veterans would like to see this unofficial regulation and open nature of the Web continue; however, flagrant abuses of the system mean that government and industry authorities will increasingly have to step in and regulate the Web and Internet.

The security of the Internet and the Web is everyone's business. Students and hackers should remember that what were considered annoying pranks in the past are now crimes which result in punishment, usually on a federal level.

◀ See "Crime and the Net," p. 385

As a user of the Web, you should make sure that your Web provider has included proper security measures, such as firewalls, properly secured mail and directory systems, secure password files, and possibly proxy servers, encryption, and other methods of data hiding.

◀ See "Working with Firewalls, Wrappers, and Proxies," p. 441

VI

The Edge of the Web

If you are directly hooked into the Internet for long periods of time, you want to make sure that your machine is also firewalled, because enterprising hackers and warez pirates will undoubtedly find your machine and try to make use of its resources.

Tip
Do not hesitate to notify your pro-vider of any illegal or suspicious activity you notice on the Web.

◀ See "Soliciting Help," p. 431

You can access CERT (Computer Emergency Response Team) at **http://cert.org/**. They have information online as well as via FTP covering what to do if a break-in occurs, as well as suggestions for making a more secure system.

You also want to keep an eye out for new releases of secure servers and servers which can handle credit card transactions and digital signatures. This new breed of servers and browsers will make many transactions appear more secure.

Stability

The overall stability of the Internet and Web is inherent in its non-central design. However, occasional problems within the telecommunications lines (which the Internet for the most part is dependent upon) can cause Internet communications to bog down. For instance, if phone service is down in Chicago or Los Angeles, you might have trouble accessing portions of the Net in a timely fashion.

◀ See "The World Wide Web," p. 19

Some users question the stability of the Web and the Internet, suggesting that it's only a fad which is likely to be replaced with some newer, more innovative form of technology. The history of the Internet has only shown growth and technologies that have been promised for years; on the contrary, broadcast and cable television stations or telecommunication corporations have not been forthcoming. The Internet and the Web today fulfill many of these promises (such as interactivity) and show great potential for filling those areas that haven't been filled yet.

Use of Demographics

◀ See "Demo-graphics and the Net," p. 56

Advertising and marketing is most successful when targeted toward an easily identifiable group. Using the methods outlined in the book, demographic information can be collected with varying degrees of validity. Such techniques for collecting demographic material include the following:

- HTTPD logs

- Page counters

- Forms

- Sticky pages

- E-mail addresses

HTTPD logs provide very accurate information if you have access to them. Page counters can be easily created. Even just a perusal of e-mail addresses of visitors to your site can provide useful insights into the makeup of your site's visitors.

◄ See "The HTTPD Log," p. 342

Demographic information about the users who come to your site can also be used in selling advertising space on your Web site.

◄ See "Other Methods for Collecting Demographics," p. 348

Careful Watch of Future Trends

There will undoubtedly be many fads and trends with the Web and the Internet. The nice thing about this medium is that businesses and individuals can experiment with them for a minimum financial involvement. The Web in many ways is still like the Wild West; for courageous and enterprising individuals and companies, you could say, "Thar's gold up in them thar hills." For many, the Web offers economic opportunities that some say will be bigger than the PC revolution.

◄ See "How the Future Will Look," p. 499

Closing Words of Encouragement

From here, if you don't already know how to program in HTML, we suggest you turn to the Appendix and see how easy it is to create HTML documents. If this is an avenue you want to explore, make sure to visit the appropriate Web sites to find the latest developments in HTML programming.

You might still be a new WWW user, finding yourself in a similar spot that we were in when we began to investigate the Web. We knew about the Internet and how cool the Web was, but we could just never figure out how to make money on a service that once was only available for free, non-commercial use. However, once we broke through the old notions of the Internet and started looking at the Web as an avenue for commercial ventures, we haven't been able to stop thinking of ways the Internet and the Web can be used.

We hope that this book has sparked your imagination for the profitable and creative ways the Web can be used. Happy cruising.

VI

The Edge of the Web

Appendix

An Introduction To HTML

Appendix

An Introduction To HTML

HTML programming is a procedure involving the creation of ASCII text files with HTML commands embedded within the text. Knowing the basics of HTML is useful if you want to create your own WWW pages. Familiarizing yourself with HTML is useful even if you are not creating your own page, allowing you to understand the basics so that you can better express what it is you want designed.

Basic HTML

This section outlines basic HTML commands. There are many commands which won't be discussed, because there are some commands which can be better implemented other ways or simply aren't all that useful. Instead, we will focus on the commands that will give you full control over your environment.

> **Note**
>
> We encourage you to find other HTML books and documents, both at your local bookstores and also on the Web, to find out more about the other HTML elements. In particular, you should refer to Que's Special Edition *Using HTML*, Special Edition *Using the Internet*, Special Edition *Using the World Wide Web and Mosaic* (which includes four chapters on how to set up Web pages and sites with HTML), and *Using Netscape* (which provides user-friendly instructions and tips on HTML basics).

Many people ask whether editors and filters exist which you can use to write HTML. The answer is yes, but we do not recommend any of them for the following reasons:

■ Editors and filters do not stay current with the latest releases of HTML quickly enough. This means that you are unable to take advantage of new features until your particular HTML editor or filter catches up.

■ In general, we find that HTML filters and editors create very inefficient HTML, and in some cases even HTML that is incorrect.

We prefer to write our HTML "by hand." This gives us far more control over our HTML and is really very simple indeed. Anyone who knows how to use a word processor can write HTML. Commands are easy to learn and remember.

The HTML Element

HTML documents are ASCII text files which have embedded HTML commands within them. An HTML command is known as an *element*, often called a *tag*.

The Web browser and server can differentiate an element from the rest of the document because elements *always* appear between < and > characters.

The following lines show you what appears to be an element and what isn't an element:

`<hello there>`	looks like an element
`<hello there`	not an element
`hello there>`	not an element
`<"hello there">`	looks like an element
`"<hello there>"`	looks like an element

The universal rule of browsers is that if the term is placed between < and >, it is an element. If it's an element that the browser does not recognize, it is ignored. In our example, `"hello there"` is not a real HTML command. However, because it appears between < and >, the browser recognizes it as an HTML command albeit an unknown one. Because it is unknown, the browser will ignore it.

The ability of HTML to ignore elements it doesn't understand is extremely useful because it allows the language of HTML to improve without making all the existing pages and browsers out there obsolete. If a new command is added to the language that browsers don't know about, they simply ignore it.

Even if the browsers are updated, users who are slow to upgrade their browser do not find themselves at a disadvantage.

There are two types of HTML elements:

1. The first type stands by itself as a command. The command is all that's needed. For example, if you want to place a picture in a document, you would use a single command to do so. The <P> and <BR> are examples of these types of elements.

2. The second type of HTML element comes in pairs. An element begins the command, and another element ends the command. For example, if you wanted to make a portion of text bold, you would need to indicate the start of the bold text and the end of the bold text. The <B> and </B> paired elements are an example of this type of command.

It is a universal law of HTML that the element which terminates the command starts with / and is followed by the character or characters that started the command. For example, in HTML to make something bold you use the <B> command at the start of what you want to be bold and a </B> command at the end of what you want bold, like this:

```
this is the original sentence

this is the <B>original</B> sentence
```

In the second sentence, the word "original" would appear in bold text. The first <B> command started the bold, and the </B> command terminated the bold. The / character always terminates.

Given a list of fictitious commands, what would the terminators be? For example, what are the terminators for the following commands?

```
<pour drink>

<open door>

<walk dog>

<start>

<stop>
```

If you said the following, you were right:

```
</pour drink>

</open door>
```

```
</walk dog>

</start>

</stop>
```

Another rule of HTML is that you never interleave commands which have /
terminators; instead, you always nest them. For example, this is wrong:

```
<A> <B> </A> </B>
```

This is right:

```
<A> <B> </B> </A>
```

Some commands have *parameters* attached to them. You place the parameters
to the right of the command name and to the left of >, for example:

```
<A put your parameters here>
```

Tip

The parameters
always go to the
right of the
command.

The command in this example is <A> (the anchor command, which is discussed later), and the parameter is put your parameters here.

Parameters may be either single words, which are used to turn modes on
and off, or words equated to a value. For example, in this fictitious HTML
element,

```
<close door=front window=south lock>
```

the command is close and it has three parameters: door, window, and lock.
Both door and window have values (front and south). The lock parameter has
no value.

Caution

Since the < and > characters are used to signify HTML commands, you cannot put
them in your document unless you are actually specifying a command.

> **Note**
>
> If you want to use < and > in your document without a command, you should use **&lt** for the < character and **&gt** for the > character.
>
> The & character by itself is also reserved as well and **&amp** produces the & character.
>
> You can use other & commands for all sorts of foreign and special characters. Consult HTML documentation on the WWW to find out the complete list.

That is pretty much all you need to know about how to put commands together. The next section discusses the actual commands you need.

HTML Document Structure

The HTML standard specifies that a well-structured HTML document should consist of a header and a body. The *header* serves to describe the document to the browser, and the *body* contains the actual text and commands of the document itself.

HTML is extremely forgiving, and all the browsers out there will accept documents without the header on it. However, you should write your documents with the proper headers, because there are certain advantages to doing so that we discuss further in this section.

HTML documents should be placed inside of an <HTML> and </HTML> element. In other words, the very first text in your document should be the <HTML> command, and the very last text in your document should be the </HTML> terminating command. This ensures that the browser and server will identify the document as an HTML document. Again, all browsers will figure it out if you don't have this element; it's just "well-spoken" HTML to include it.

Immediately beneath the <HTML> command should begin your header. The header is started with a <HEAD> command and is terminated with a </HEAD> command. Between the header commands you can place a <TITLE> command and </TITLE> terminator. Anything between the <TITLE> command and terminator will be used as the title to the browser page.

Most browser pages have a spot where they show the title of the document they are currently displaying. To set the document title, you should use the <TITLE> command.

Once you have started and ended your header, you should begin the main portion of your HTML document. To do this, you begin with a <BODY> command and then place your document, remembering to terminate it with a </BODY> command.

Tip

If you are going to offer HTML programming service, you definitely want to adhere to HTML programming standards, as some potential clients may view it as a clue to your professionalism.

Here is a basic structure that illustrates this setup. We have indented the commands to show you the structure, but you do not need to do this when you write HTML.

```
<HTML>
  <HEAD>
    <TITLE>
        The Intergalactic Web Emporium
    </TITLE>
  </HEAD>
  <BODY>
      Your main document information and HTML goes here.
  </BODY>
</HTML>
```

In general, when users write HTML, they compress all of this down to save room, like this:

```
<HTML>
<HEAD><TITLE>The Intergalactic Web Emporium</TITLE></HEAD>
<BODY>
    Put your main document and HTML here.
</BODY>
</HTML>
```

It's really no different except how many bytes are transmitted over the Internet. If you are paying for throughput, compressing the extra carriage returns and spaces really add up after thousands of users access your pages.

> **Note**
>
> The <TITLE> command must appear within the <HEADER> command or it will be ignored.

Remember, <HTML>, </HTML>, <BODY>, and </BODY> commands are not really needed in your document. All browsers will display it correctly without them. However, if you want to write good HTML, you should include them.

HTML Document Formatting and Document Formatting Commands

Each user accessing the Web is doing it from different platforms, hardware, and software. Because of this, screen sizes, color capabilities, available fonts, and hardware audio capabilities will vary. In order to be platform-independent, browsers have to adapt to the user's configuration. This means that many of the characteristics of your pages will be different depending on the user accessing it.

In order to make sure that your page looks the best for the most number of users, browsers automatically format your document for you. They do so using certain rules and protocols. They also offer you commands to override that formatting if you should desire.

One of the first things that HTML does is remove extra spaces from your text. There is no difference between

```
hello               world
```

and

```
hello world
```

The extra spaces in the second example are removed.

Similarly, HTML completely removes all carriage returns from your document. Instead of breaking lines where you specified in your actual ASCII file, the browser breaks the text at the edge of the user's screen, based on the size of screen the user has set. This ensures that the text does not go beyond the user's view.

The following shows examples of these rules:

```
This      is an

example             of some       text

which is formatted.
```

If this text appeared in the file like it appears here, it would be changed on the user's screen to appear as

```
This is an example of some text which is formatted.
```

> **Note**
>
> Some browsers do not replace the carriage return with a space. You should place a space at the end of all your lines to ensure that words do not get jammed together from two consecutive lines. For example,
>
> ```
> hello
> world
> ```
>
> can often appear as
>
> ```
> helloworld
> ```
>
> if there is no space after `hello`.

Appendix

The fact that HTML removes extra spaces and carriage returns is both a blessing and a curse. While it ensures that browsers will correctly display the text on various sized monitors, it completely relieves you from having to worry about where line breaks go and other formatting considerations. Luckily, HTML has a command which helps you force spacing to be where you want it to be.

The <PRE> and </PRE> commands may be used to specify that text is spaced exactly as you specify it. Any text which appears between the <PRE> and </PRE> elements are displayed as is, with extra spaces and all the carriage returns you specify. The following example is shown in figure A.1:

```
<PRE>

  Welcome to

          My      Home      Page!!!!

  I hope

          you

                enjoy

                      our

                            site

  </PRE>
```

Fig. A.1
This page shows an example of text without the <PRE> and </PRE> commands, and with the <PRE> and </PRE> commands.

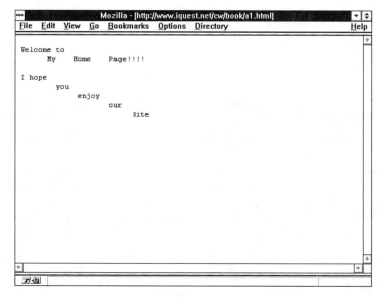

Notice that the <PRE> and </PRE> commands changed the look of the text. Text inside of PRE mode is displayed using non-proportional fonts, while text outside of PRE mode is displayed using proportional fonts.

What if you want the look and feel of the proportional fonts but still want control over the spacing? HTML does not allow you to have proportional fonts and maintain horizontal spacing, but it does allow vertical spacing controls. The <P> and <BR> commands are used for indicating paragraph and line breaks. These commands simply insert returns in your document; no terminating </P> or </BR> commands are necessary.

The <BR> command will merely move text to the start of the next line. The <P> command will do the same thing but also leave an extra carriage return. Here is an example of our use of <P> and <BR>; figure A.2 shows the results of this example:

```
This is<BR>an example<P>of the<P>line control<BR>commands.
```

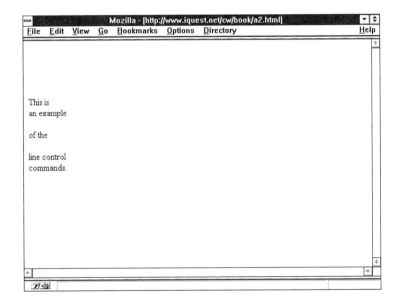

Fig. A.2

You can force line and paragraph breaks by using the <BR> and <P> commands.

Another useful command which breaks up text is the <HR> (horizontal ruling) element. By placing <HR> anywhere within your document, you will cause any text above and below <HR> to be separated by a line which stretches from left to right on the screen. Use <HR> to place logical breaks between sections of text within your pages.

HTML Character Formatting and Character Formatting Commands

HTML has a wealth of commands to help you format text to add emphasis to your documents.

One of the more useful features of HTML is that you can have text of various sizes. This allows you to have major and minor headings, as well as text which is smaller than normal, for things like footnotes. The commands that do this are <H1> through <H6>. The <H1> through <H6> terminating commands are </H1> through </H6>. <H1> is the largest text possible, and <H6> </H6> is the smallest text possible. For example, to make text as large as possible you would type:

```
<h1>This is very large text</h1>
```

To make text very small, you would type:

```
<h6>This is very small text</h6>
```

When you terminate an <H?> command with its terminator </H?> command, the text that follows resumes normal text size. Figure A.3 shows the various sizes available with the <H1> through <H6> commands, along with normal sized text.

Fig. A.3

This page shows an example of normal text and text viewed with <H1> through <H6>.

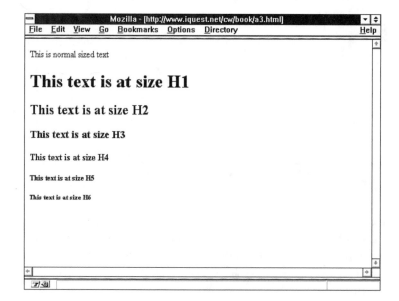

You should note that the these commands imply a return at the start and end of the commands; therefore, you cannot use these commands to change the size of text in the middle of a sentence. For example, the following string is handled as shown:

```
Normal Text<H1>Large Text</H1>Normal Text
```

and is actually interpreted as

```
Normal Text<P>

<H1>Large Text</H1><P>

Normal Text
```

HTML also gives commands which allow you to emphasize text by making it bold or italic. The <B> and </B> commands are used to make text look thicker and darker. Type **<B>** at the start of the text that you want to make bold and **</B>** at the end. You can imbed <B> and </B> inside of any other HTML (such as between <H1> and </H1> commands), though on some browsers, in certain configurations, it might be ignored.

The <I> and </I> commands work like the bold command, but make the text italic instead. Figure A.4 shows an example of text that has been bolded and italicized. The displayed text is as follows:

```
Use <B>bold text to emphasis</B> or <I>italic text to call
attention</I>
```

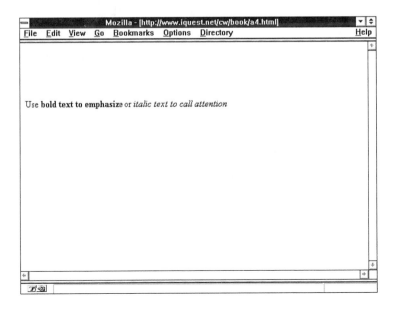

Fig. A.4
The use of <B>
bold and <I> italic
commands can
add emphasis to
a page.

Working with Indentation and Bullets

As we mentioned earlier, without the use of `<PRE>` and `</PRE>`, you cannot place consecutive spaces in text because the browser will remove them. However, indentation commands exist which let you move the left margin to the right. There are two types of indentation commands, and they work identically unless you also include bullets within your indented text. You can either use `<UL>` and `</UL>` or `<OL>` and `</OL>` as indentation commands. The indentation can be nested to indent even further. For example,

```
First<UL>Second<UL>Third<UL>Fourth</UL>Third</UL>Second</UL>First
```

will produce

```
First

        Second

            Third

                Fourth

            Third

        Second

First
```

> **Note**
>
> Each `<UL>` and `</UL>` implies a `<P>` (or carriage return) as well.

It doesn't matter whether you use `<UL>` and `</UL>` or `<OL>` and `</OL>`, as long as you are not creating bullets. However, you should always terminate `<UL>` with `</UL>` and never with `</OL>`, and likewise for the `<OL>` command.

Now, how do bullets relate to `<UL>` and `<OL>`? You can create a bullet at any time, even without `<UL>` and `<OL>`, by using the `<LI>` command. To place a bullet next to text, you would type

```
<LI> Line 1 <LI> Line 2 <LI> Line 3
```

This line would output as

```
    * Line 1

    * Line 2

    * Line 3
```

Note that <LI> implies a <BR> in front of it. If you place <LI> inside of a nested <UL>, you will get bullets that indent. This makes sense, but there is one addition. Each level you indent will give you a different shaped bullet.

Where <OL> differs from <UL> is that if you indent with <OL> and use <LI> instead of bullets, you get numbered lists. Each list starts at the number 1, and each bullet increments the number. If you indent again, the new indent starts at 1, and when you back up an indent with </OL>, it picks back up where that indent was. Figure A.5 shows the following text, to demonstrate the use of indentation and bullets:

```
<LI>This is our menu:
<UL>
LI> Choose from the following selections of fine wines. We
encourage you to try our California selections as they are having
an excellent year.
<OL>
<LI> California Wines
<UL>
<LI> Northern California
<LI> Southern California
</UL>
<LI> French Wines
<LI> Italian Wines
</OL>
</UL>
```

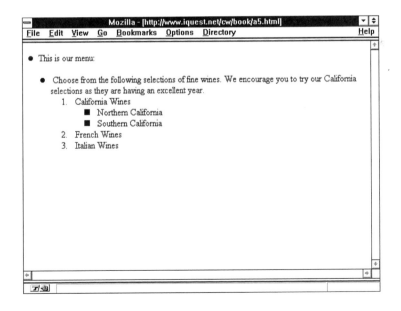

Fig. A.5

Indentation, bullets, and lists offer a good way to break up sections, making your page easier to read.

> **Note**
>
> Text flow on long lines is handled correctly by making the text line up to the edge of the indentation. Long text with bullets and numbers also line up correctly, flush with the text and not the number or bullet.

Adding Links, Images, Sounds, and External Files To Your Pages

HTML lets you point to other documents in a manner which allows you to move around documents and data with ease. HTML also allows you to integrate inline images, sounds and other files into your pages. This section shows you how to do this, and gives some tricks to use when designing your pages.

Adding Images To Your Pages

Inline images allow you to have stunning graphics stand right next to your text. This is useful for creating icons, buttons, custom bullets, logos, and nifty backgrounds. You can include GIF format images (CompuServe format) or JPEG (compressed) format directly into your documents.

The `<IMG>` command is the HTML element which inserts a picture into your document. This command uses parameters to tell the browser where the data for your picture is. The format of the command is as follows:

```
<IMG SRC="url" ALIGN=alignment>
```

The SRC parameter is required. The ALIGN parameter is optional. `<IMG>` will insert a picture directly into your document at the command's position.

SRC specifies the location of the picture. If the picture is in the same directory that the document containing the `<IMG>` statement is, only the image name is needed. If the image is in a subdirectory relative to the current document, only the subdirectory and file name are needed. If the image is in another directory system or on another server, a full URL is usually needed. The following shows examples of the `<IMG>` command used with different URLs:

```
<IMG SRC="image.gif">
```

`image.gif` is taken from the same directory as the document itself.

```
<IMG SRC="file/image.gif">
```

`image.gif` is taken from the directory `file`, which is in the same directory as the document itself.

```
<IMG SRC="http://www.site.com/images/cars/image.gif">
```

`image.gif` is retrieved from a remote machine named www.site.com, and is found in the WWW directory /images/cars within that machine.

Note

You should place data such as the URL for the SRC parameter within quotation marks. While many browsers understand it if the quotes are missing, some browsers won't display the page correctly without the quotes.

The optional ALIGN parameter tells how the image will be aligned with other images and text. ALIGN lets you specify how text flows around the image. You can specify the alignment you want to use as BOTTOM, MIDDLE, or TOP. If the ALIGN parameter is missing, it is assumed to be BOTTOM. This specifies that adjoining information should be justified at the bottom of the image, in the middle of the image, or at the top of the image. To help illustrate the different alignment options, figure A.6 shows the following HTML code:

```
<IMG SRC="image.gif" ALIGN=BOTTOM> This text is at the bottom<BR>
<IMG SRC="image.gif" ALIGN=MIDDLE> This text is in the middle<BR>
<IMG SRC="image.gif" ALIGN=TOP> This text is in the top<P>
Here are some tricks you can do:<P>
<IMG SRC="i1.gif" ALIGN=BOTTOM>
<IMG SRC="i1.gif" ALIGN=MIDDLE>
<IMG SRC="i1.gif" ALIGN=TOP>
<IMG SRC="i1.gif" ALIGN=MIDDLE> <p>
This is what happens with long lines:<p>
<IMG SRC="i1.gif" ALIGN=TOP> This line unfortunately is so long
that when it displays it wraps. Look what happens to the part that
wrapped around.
```

Note

If you want a large title aligned to the middle of a picture, you need to place the picture inside the commands which make the title large. The font size commands imply <P> in front and behind.

This line puts a picture next to the title text:

```
<H1><SRC IMG="i1.gif" ALIGN=MIDDLE> Welcome to my page</H1>
```

This line puts the picture above the text:

```
<SRC IMG="i1.gif" ALIGN=MIDDLE><H1> Welcome to my page</H1>
```

Fig. A.6
By using the ALIGN parameter, images can be displayed next to each other at different vertical levels.

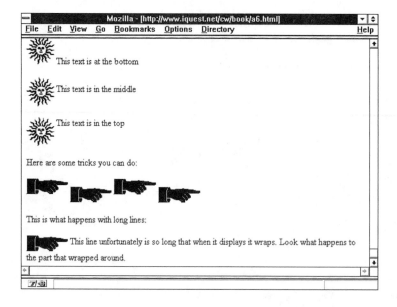

Remember, you can load both GIF and JPEG files using the <IMG> command. Just type the correct extension of the image for your file (either **.gif** or **.jpg**).

> **Note**
>
> On DOS machines where extension size is limited to three characters, some extensions are modified slightly. For example, ".html" is ".htm" on DOS. You want to be aware of this when you are moving documents between DOS and UNIX machines. You may need to rename your files.

Adding Hyperlinks To Your Pages

It is a rare site that only has one page of information. Most sites split their information into two, three, or even hundreds or thousands of pages of information and use hyperlinks to move between the pages. Hyperlinks can also point to pages on other sites anywhere in the world. The mechanism of moving between these pages and for moving to pages outside of your site is known as a *hyperlink*, often abbreviated to just *link*.

For example, suppose that the first document in your site has a reference to another document with your personal information, sort of a "welcome mat" page. In this case, you need some way to get to the second page. You could do this by putting a link around some words. When the page is displayed, the words are displayed in a different color, indicating it is a link, and users know that they can touch it to go to the indicated information.

To place a link to another document, you use what is called an *anchor*. This is another HTML element which looks like this:

```
<A HREF=url> place your description here </A>
```

The `<A>` command is the anchor command. Note that it has a terminating `</A>`. Any text between `<A>` and `</A>` will be part of the link. When it is displayed, it looks different than the surrounding text, which indicates to the user that it is a link.

For example, this line,

```
<A HREF="myinfo.html"> Go see my personal information </A>
```

would link immediately to a document named myinfo.html when the user points and clicks the text, `Go see my personal information`. The URL is relative to the directory that the current document is in, because it does not contain a domain name.

You can point to files in subdirectories within the current document's directory. You can organize your files neatly and make use of advantages of categories for demographics and billing simplicity, for example:

```
<A HREF="personal/myinfo.html"> Go see my personal information </A>
```

Selecting the text in this example would immediately lead the user to a document named myinfo.html, which is stored in the directory named `personal`, which is relative to the directory that the current document is in.

You can also point to documents not on your site. For example, you could type a link to the White House in your page by specifying the entire White House URL as shown:

```
<A HREF="http://www.whitehouse.gov/"> Go see the White House </A>
```

This line would go immediately to the White House home page if the user selected the text `Go see the White House`. The URL is the full URL to the White House itself.

You can link any type of object you want—images, sound files, buttons, words, letters, paragraphs. There is no limit. Simply put `<A>` and `</A>` around the item, and it instantly becomes a link.

Appendix

Adding Sounds and Other External Files To Your Pages

You can add sounds to your pages by simply specifying a sound file. Likewise, you can add movies to your page, or binaries, or any other type of computer data or document. You can also make images which pop up in a window instead of appearing inline with your graphics.

HTML's ability to do this turns it into a mechanism that can actually take data from a remote site and put it on your computer permanently (if you desire). This is extremely useful because it gives a mechanism to actually distribute products right over the Internet.

To make a sound or pop-up image, place a link to the desired file using the anchor capability instead of the <IMG> command.

Sounds, for example, are usually expressed in Sun AU format files. These are files ending with an .au extension. Files in .wav format are also beginning to appear, but are not yet universally understood by all browsers. To place the link to a sound, type your instructions using this example:

```
<A HREF="bell.au"> Pick here to listen to Big Ben </A>
```

When the user selects the link Pick here to listen to Big Ben, the sound file bell.au will be retrieved. Because the file is not an .html file, the browser will look for a viewer that can handle it. Most browsers have viewers for sound files, pop-up GIF and JPG files, and sometimes movies. Most browsers also allow you to add viewers to them for other file formats, and many viewers are available via the Internet (look at the NCSA, CERN, and Netscape sites) for a variety of platforms.

Likewise, to load a GIF file in a pop-up window, you could type your text using this format:

```
<A HREF="picture.gif"> Pick here for the big picture </A>
```

The image picture.gif would be loaded from your current document directory—not inline, but as a pop-up window—when the user selected Pick here for the big picture.

In an effort to save throughput charges, many people provide a small picture (known as a *thumbnail* or *proxy view*) which is linked to a larger picture. If the user likes the thumbnail picture, the user can click it to load the larger picture. Doing this saves bandwidth, because big pictures are only transmitted when the user specifically asks for them; for example,

```
<A HREF="big.gif"><IMG SRC="small.gif"></A>
```

This example places a link to a big picture named big.gif around a small picture named small.gif. The small picture appears inline, directly into the document; selecting it will cause the big picture to be loaded.

To create an MPEG movie you might write something like the following:

```
<A HREF="camp.mpg"> Click here to see my summer camp movies </A>
```

In fact, you can load any data you want using this method. If the browser does not have a viewer configured for the extension of the data, it will simply ask you if you want to save it to your hard drive. For example, if you wanted to give a downloadable product catalog in Word for Windows format, you might place a link that says:

```
<A HREF="catalog.doc"> Click here to download our catalog </A>
```

Selecting Click here to download our catalog would cause catalog.doc to be retrieved from the current document's directory. Since there is no viewer for .doc files, it would save it to your hard drive. If you configured a viewer to point to Microsoft's Word For Windows, clicking the text would load the document into the word processor, which would pop up in a window on your display. Neat, eh?

Likewise, if you wanted to distribute demo programs of a software product, you might place the following link into your page:

```
<A HREF="demo.exe"> Select here to download a demo of our new game </A>
```

Selecting the text would access demo.exe, which would be saved to your hard drive for later execution. Likewise, the executable could be compressed and transmitted in compressed form, for savings on throughput (in other words, demo.zip or demo.Z).

Adding Forms To Your Pages

One of the more useful functions of HTML is to accept interactive information from the user and route that information to you. The forms capabilities of HTML will allow you to retrieve orders, acquire user demographics, gather user profiles, play games, and much more.

How Forms Work: An Introduction To cgi-bin

In the following section, we show you how to add forms to your pages. However, first you should learn how the data that the user enters gets to you.

Just placing a form in your page does not ensure that you will receive the data. Part of the form definition, as the next section explains, is a pointer to the program or script that knows what to do with the data.

If you place a form in your page and do not have a place to send the data, your form will not work (in other words, you will never receive the data the user sends).

Caution

Currently, the form can only be pointed to software and not to an e-mail address (the mailto: capability is not universal among browsers and is not recommend for use until it is universal).

The forms must be received by a program on the server side that knows what to do with the data. This type of program is known as a *cgi-bin program* and can be used for forms and also standard anchor links (for example, you can put a reference to a cgi-bin program into the HREF of a <A> </A> link).

cgi-bin programs may be written in any language (we prefer C) or even in inefficient shell scripts. Another popular approach for creating cgi-bin programs is the interpretive language of Perl. Our personal recommendation is that you go with C over all others because it allows the design of efficient programs. This is important if you are creating cgi-bin programs on systems that are, or will be, very busy.

We won't show you how to write cgi-bin here, because it's beyond the intended scope of this book; however, it will be useful for you to know how it works.

When form data comes into the server, the server examines the URL and detects the request for cgi-bin. It finds the correct program as specified by the URL (the next section will show how to format URLs this way) and starts the program running. The data that the user filled out in the form is transmitted to the program as standard input (STDIN). The program munches on the information and then sends back a special header, describing the data that follows, and then the response. This data goes back to the server via standard output (STDOUT) where it is handed back to the user.

You do not need to know this information to design forms, but you need some form of this technology to be able to use forms. If you have your own server, many of these programs are available for you in the public domain.

Note

NCSA maintains an FTP archive of cgi-bin public domain programs. You can access this archive by pointing your browser to

ftp://ftp.ncsa.uiuc.edu/Web/httpd/Unix/ncsa_httpd/cgi/

Note

If you do not have your own server, companies stand ready to help you with automated form facilities such as our FORMS4U service at

http://www.iquest.net/cw/web/forms4u.html

or our GATE service at

http://www.iquest.net/cw/gate/extension.html

The cgi-bin program can do many things with the data. It can take the data, integrate it in a database, and send new information back to the user. It can also take the data and send it to you as e-mail. Anything is possible and is limited only by your resources, time, and imagination.

The FORM Element

To create a form in your HTML document, you should use the <FORM> element. This element is closed with the </FORM> element, and all the form data and information must appear between the two commands.

The following is an example of using the FORM command:

```
<FORM METHOD=POST ACTION=url>

your form data and other form commands go here

</FORM>
```

The METHOD parameter has a value of either GET or POST. The current standards recommend highly that you abandon GET, which is older technology, and only use POST. This parameter relates to how the information is sent to the cgi-bin program (GET means send it on the command line, POST means send it via standard input). So, basically, just type **METHOD=POST** in your form line and you will be ok.

The ACTION parameter specifies the URL of the cgi-bin program to send the form data to. This should be an absolute address (full URL); for example,

```
<FORM METHOD=POST ACTION="http://here.com/cgi-bin/doit?23">
```

In this line, the ACTION contains a URL to a cgi-bin program called *doit*. The ?23 after `doit` is optional and is a parameter which is passed to doit on the command line when it is called.

The ? separates `doit` from the parameter, which in our case is 23. You may have no parameters (in which case you don't need ?), one parameter, or as many as you want or need. Whether or not you have parameters for the cgi-bin program depends on the cgi-bin program. Refer to the documentation for your cgi-bin software to determine how to correctly interface to it.

When the server in the example gets the form, it will run to the cgi-bin directory and execute the doit program. It will pass doit the value 23 on the command line, and the contents of our form (whatever that may be) via STDIN.

After the doit program processes the information, it will send back to you, via the server, a response. If the response is formatted as HTML, it is displayed as HTML. If the response is audio or image data, it is displayed in your browser that way.

The following sections outline what can exist between the <FORM> and </FORM> commands. These elements let you accept the data from the user in a variety of formats.

Form Elements That Accept Typed Data from Users

The elements in this section all accept free format text from the user and must all appear between a <FORM> and </FORM> statement in your document. By free format text, we mean anything the user cares to type.

Text entry can be accepted in one of two ways:

- A single line at a time

- Multiple lines at a time

To accept a single line of text, use the <INPUT> form command; for example:

```
<INPUT TYPE=text NAME="users address" SIZE=20 MAXLENGTH=100
VALUE="please fill out">
```

The only parameter that is really necessary is the NAME parameter. If there is no TYPE parameter, it will default to text; likewise, there is a default SIZE and no default MAXLENGTH or VALUE.

The TYPE parameter identifies that this is a text input selection. As you will see in the discussions that follow, there are other values that can replace the text value.

The NAME parameter assigns a name to the data the user is going to type. You may choose anything you want for the name; if you choose a name with spaces in it, you should enclose it in quotation marks as shown in the example. The data is transmitted to the server like this:

```
"name"="value"
```

So, if the user typed an address into this example line, the server would see

```
"users address"="555 someplace road, somewhere USA 55555"
```

By transmitting both the name and the value, the server can equate the values entered by the user to specific names, so that it can figure out what data is what.

The SIZE parameter is optional. If included, it sets the size of the window the user can type into. This does not limit the amount of text the user can enter, but only the amount that is viewed while the text is being typed. If the user types information longer than the window, the information will scroll so that the user can see what's being typed. If SIZE is not present, the window is set to a default size based on the browser.

The MAXLENGTH parameter is also optional. If there is no MAXLENGTH parameter specified, no limit is placed on how much the user can type.

There may be a case where you want to accept text data from a user but you want to do so in a way that what the user types is not visible to others standing around the user. (This also means it's not visible to the person typing.) The TYPE parameter can be used to do this by setting it to the value **password**. In this case, whatever is typed by the user into the field will be hidden by replacing each character with a character such as an asterisk (*). The following shows such an input statement:

```
<INPUT TYPE=PASSWORD NAME="code">
```

Often you will want to accept more than one line at a time from a user. HTML covers this need with a <TEXTAREA> command. Unlike <INPUT>,

<TEXTAREA> has a terminating </TEXTAREA> command. The format for this command is

```
<TEXTAREA NAME="name" ROWS=n COLS=m> </TEXTAREA>
```

As with <INPUT>, the NAME parameter assigns the data entered by the user to the value of NAME. The ROWS and COLS parameters allow you to specify the number of rows (*n*) of the window and the number of columns (*m*) of the window. As with <INPUT>, the user is allowed to enter beyond the size of the window simply by scrolling.

You may ask yourself why <TEXTAREA> requires a terminating </TEXTAREA> and <INPUT> does not. <TEXTAREA> allows default text to be loaded into the text window by placing the desired text between the <TEXTAREA> and </TEXTAREA> commands; for example:

```
<TEXTAREA NAME=address ROWS=4 COLS=60> Please enter your address
here

</TEXTAREA>
```

Here, the text area will be created and will already have the default text Please enter your address here inside of it. The user may edit the text and change it to reflect the user's address.

> **Caution**
>
> Not all browsers honor the capability to have default text within the TEXTAREA. In some cases, the information you place as default text won't show up, and in other cases it will appear outside of the TEXTAREA. We do not recommend that you try to input default data to the <TEXTAREA> command.

The following example shows various uses of the <INPUT> and <TEXTAREA> commands:

```
<FORM METHOD=POST ACTION="http://here.com/cgi-bin/doit">
<PRE>
Please enter your name:     <INPUT NAME="name">
Please enter your phone:    <INPUT NAME="phone" SIZE=10>
</PRE>
Please enter your address:<p>
<TEXTAREA NAME="address" ROWS=4 COLS=40> </TEXTAREA>
</FORM>
```

Figure A.7 shows the results of this text. Note that the <PRE> and </PRE> commands were used to line up the input boxes.

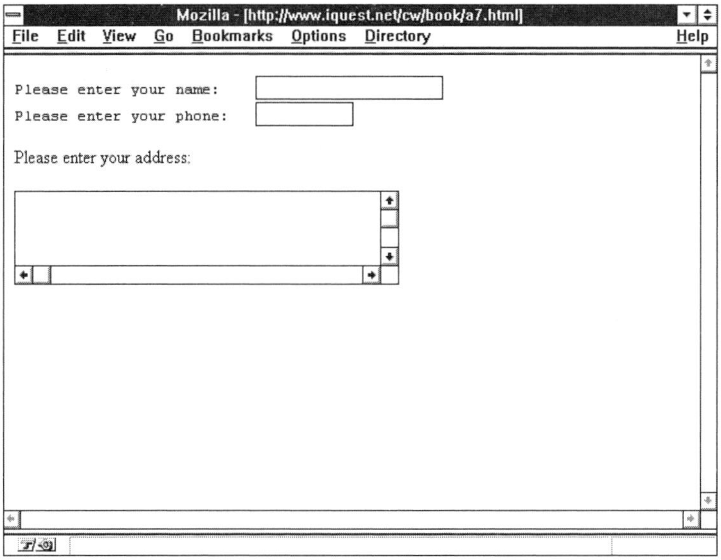

Fig. A.7
Using the
text input form
commands <INPUT
TYPE=text> and
<TEXTAREA> allows
you to accept
more than one
line of informa-
tion at once.

Form Elements That Simulate Buttons and Check Boxes

HTML allows the user to select choices from either radio buttons or check boxes. The difference between the two is that a radio button allows the user to pick only one of many choices, while check boxes allow the user to pick any number of selections offered.

The HTML for both a radio button and a check box uses the <INPUT> syntax, with TYPE set to either "radio" or "checkbox." For example:

```
<FORM METHOD=POST ACTION="http://here.com/cgi-bin/doit">
Please pick the color for your car:<p>
<INPUT TYPE=radio NAME="color" VALUE=1 CHECKED> Red
<INPUT TYPE=radio NAME="color" VALUE=2> Green
<INPUT TYPE=radio NAME="color" VALUE=3> Blue
<INPUT TYPE=radio NAME="color" VALUE=4> Grey
<INPUT TYPE=radio NAME="color" VALUE=Other> Custom designed<p>
</FORM>
```

The TYPE="radio" parameter specifies that this is a radio button. Note that NAME is the same for each of the buttons (color). Because NAME is the same, it identifies them as belonging to the same group. Remember that radio buttons can only have one button out of the group selected at any time.

The VALUE=*field* specifies what should be sent to the server if that button is selected. The value can be text or numeric, as shown in the example.

Note that the first button has the parameter CHECKED in it. This tells the browser that when these buttons are initially displayed, the red choice should already be selected by default (perhaps that is the most popular color chosen).

To create a check box set of buttons where you can pick as many as you want, format them as follows:

```
<FORM METHOD=POST ACTION="http://here.com/cgi-bin/doit">
Please pick the options for your car<p>
<INPUT TYPE=checkbox NAME="option" VALUE=1 CHECKED> Tinted Windows
<INPUT TYPE=checkbox NAME="option" VALUE=2> Sports Mirrors
<INPUT TYPE=checkbox NAME="option" VALUE=3 CHECKED> Detailing
<INPUT TYPE=checkbox NAME="option" VALUE=4> Turbo Charged Engine
</FORM>
```

These four buttons are very similar to the radio buttons. The TYPE is "checkbox" instead of "radio," but NAME operates similarly by creating a group of the buttons. VALUE also serves the same purpose as with radio buttons.

Note that one major difference between check boxes and radio buttons is that more than one can be CHECKED at a time as default. Figure A.8 shows both the radio button example and the checkbox example as they would appear (the <FORM> elements have been added).

Fig. A.8
The use of the radio button and checkbox type form commands allows the user to make easy selections.

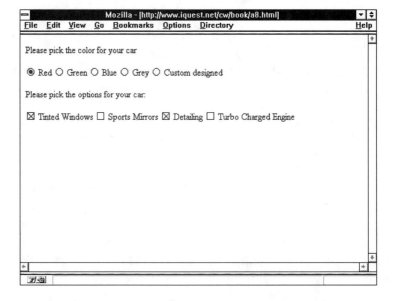

Form Elements That Let You Pick from a List

Forms have two mechanisms available which let you select one or more item from a list of items. The <SELECT> and </SELECT> and <OPTION> commands work together to create lists. For example, suppose you wanted to pick a list of items for a pizza. You might do the following:

```
<FORM METHOD=POST ACTION="http://here.com/cgi-bin/doit">
<SELECT NAME="pizza" MULTIPLE SIZE=4>
<OPTION>Bacon
<OPTION>Cheese
<OPTION>Ground Beef
<OPTION>Ham
<OPTION>Olives
<OPTION>Onions
<OPTION>Pepperoni
<OPTION>Tomato Sauce
</SELECT>
</FORM>
```

This text would create a window which contained a list. The SIZE=4 parameter would set the window to show four items at a time in it. The MULTIPLE parameter allows the user to pick more than one item.

The NAME parameter serves the same use as it does in the other form elements—in other words, to associate a name to the data. In this case, the name "pizza" is associated to the data the user picks.

The various <OPTION> commands specify the items which appear in the list. Because there are more items than the window size (SIZE=4), a scroll bar appears in the window that allows the user to see the other items in the list.

An alternative to this approach happens if you leave the SIZE and MULTIPLE parameters out. In this case, instead of showing the items in a window, the browser shows a single item in a pickable button. Selecting the button pops up a list of all the items from which the user can select a single item. The following example, along with figure A.9, illustrates this:

Tip

Remove the MULTIPLE parameter if you only want the user to pick a single item.

```
<FORM METHOD=POST ACTION="http://here.com/cgi-bin/doit">
<SELECT NAME="pizza">
<OPTION>Bacon
<OPTION>Cheese
<OPTION>Ground Beef
<OPTION>Ham
<OPTION>Olives
<OPTION>Onions
<OPTION>Pepperoni
<OPTION>Tomato Sauce
</SELECT>
</FORM>
```

Fig. A.9

The use of multiple and single pick boxes offers an alternative for making selections to check boxes and radio buttons. We have duplicated the single pick box a second time to show you what the list looks like when picked.

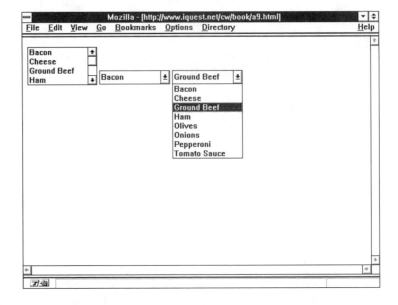

Submitting the Form and Our Full Example

When the user is finished filling out the form, the user needs some way to submit it. The <INPUT> command again comes to the rescue with the following syntax:

```
<INPUT TYPE=SUBMIT VALUE=" Select here to send this form ">
```

Wherever this element exists, a button appears with the text Select here to send this form inside the button. The TYPE=SUBMIT parameter specifies that if the user presses the button, the current form is sent to the server. The form is sent regardless of what the user has filled out.

> **Caution**
>
> Most browsers require you to have a TYPE=SUBMIT in your form if you want to be able to actually send the form somewhere.

One small note about resetting forms: you can also create an element with TYPE=RESET. When this button is pressed, it causes the form to reset to its default values. This element is not mandatory and is only sometimes used. Its format is

```
<INPUT TYPE=RESET VALUE=" Select here to reset this form ">
```

The following is an example that uses most of the form elements we have discussed. Figure A.10 shows how this form looks on-screen.

```
Use this form to fill out what you would like in a house:
<FORM METHOD=POST ACTION="http://here.com/cgi-bin/doit">
<PRE>
Your Complete Name:   <INPUT TYPE=TEXT NAME="name">
Your Phone Number:    <INPUT TYPE=TEXT NAME="phone">
</PRE>
Your Current Address:<P>
<TEXTAREA NAME="address" ROWS=4 COLS=60></TEXTAREA><P>
Please select your income level:<P>
<INPUT TYPE=RADIO NAME="income" VALUE=1> &lt 50,000
<INPUT TYPE=RADIO NAME="income" VALUE=2> 50,000 to 75,000
<INPUT TYPE=RADIO NAME="income" VALUE=3> 75,000 to 100,000
<INPUT TYPE=RADIO NAME="income" VALUE=4> &gt 100,000<P>
Please select the items that you require in your house:<P>
<INPUT TYPE=CHECKBOX NAME="outside" VALUE=1> City Water
<INPUT TYPE=CHECKBOX NAME="outside" VALUE=2> Pool
<INPUT TYPE=CHECKBOX NAME="outside" VALUE=3> Garage
<INPUT TYPE=CHECKBOX NAME="outside" VALUE=4> Security
<INPUT TYPE=CHECKBOX NAME="outside" VALUE=5> Fence<P>Select the
type of houses you are interested in from the following list<P>
<SELECT NAME="house" SIZE=4>
<OPTION>2 bedroom 2 bathroom
<OPTION>3 bedroom 2 bathroom
<OPTION>2 bedroom 2 bathroom 1 office
<OPTION>2 bedroom 2 bathroom 2 offices
<OPTION>3 bedroom 2 bathroom basement
</SELECT><p>
Select <INPUT TYPE=SUBMIT VALUE=" here "> to submit this form!
</FORM>
```

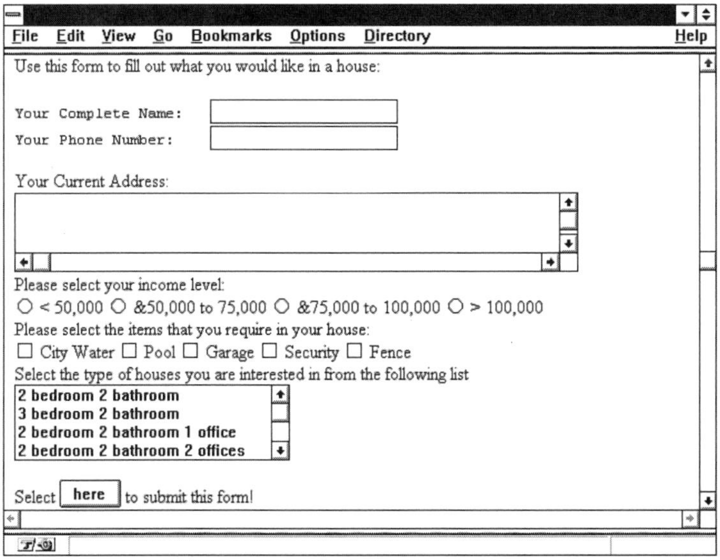

Fig. A.10
This page shows the complete form with check boxes, input areas, radio buttons, and submit buttons.

From Here...

Creating your own Web pages with HTML is fun, easy, and can save you lots of money. As you surf the Web, you will come across numerous sites that offer tips and insight into programming HTML (as mentioned earlier, CERN, NCSA, and Netscape sites all offer much in the way of HTML programming information). If you are interested in mastering HTML, visit these sites for the latest and greatest the Web has to offer.

Remember that you can use the VIEW SOURCE option of your browser to view the source code of any Web page that you visit. This can be an invaluable tool in figuring out new and innovative HTML techniques.

After reading this section, your best bet is to experiment with the examples we have given. Start to modify them with data relative to your business, add your own personal data, and before you know it, you'll have a great-looking Web page. The main thing to do is to experiment with this new tool and see what it can do for you. If you don't like what you see on-screen, tweak the parameters and the code until you get what you want.

Following this strategy, you should soon be able to create Web pages that will promote your business, sell products or services, supply customer support, and much more.

So what are you waiting for? Go turn on your computer!

Glossary

Archie A UNIX program for finding files on the Internet.

ARPANET Advanced Research Projects Agency's Network; the network created by the Department of Defense Advance Research Project Agency (DARPA); the network from which the Internet arose.

ASCII A protocol for pure text.

bandwidth The amount of information that can be transmitted at one time through a communications channel.

baud The number of bits per second of communications over phone lines.

bps Bits per second; the rate at which modems and other computing devices transmit data.

browser A program that lets you access the World Wide Web.

bulletin board BBS; an older system that allows users to call and interact with each other. Similar to the Internet, but on a much smaller scale.

cache The act of storing a remote document locally to increase access speed on repeated requests.

CERN The European Particle Physics Laboratory in Geneva, Switzerland; the group that invented the World Wide Web.

CERT Computer Emergency Response Team; whom you should report security breaches to.

cgi-bin Custom programs that may be used to extend the Web and make it interactive.

client Sometimes used as a browser; other times this means a computer contacting a host.

clip art Ready-made artwork useful in creating Web pages.

CPU Central Processing Unit; the brains of any computer.

cracker Someone who breaks into computer systems.

crawler A program that moves along the Web looking for URLs or other information; a type of intelligent agent.

cyberspace A term for immersive virtual reality, sometimes used to denote the Internet.

database A collection of organized, searchable data.

decryption The act of making a secure file readable.

digital signature A secure mechanism to verify the identity of an individual.

DNS Domain Name Server; a system that can resolve an IP address to a name.

domain name The name of a system on the Internet. Each system has a unique domain name. The domain name is used as part of an Internet address.

element A basic HTML command, such as <P>, indicating a new paragraph.

e-mail Electronic mail; personal messages sent between users on the Internet.

encryption The act of making a readable file secure.

FAQ Frequently Asked Questions; a list of helpful suggestions on various topics.

Finger A program that identifies a user. See *WHOIS*.

firewall A security measure that helps to limit pirate attacks.

flame, **flaming** Expressing displeasure with another user.

FTP File Transfer Protocol; software that transfers files to and from remote computers.

GIF Graphic Interchange Format; a file format for images developed by CompuServe.

Gopher A menu-oriented, FTP-type program that does not allow the use of pictures, links, or other advanced WWW features.

GUI Graphical User Interface; a graphical screen that lets the user interact with the computer.

hacker Someone who is good at computers; a computer guru; sometimes mistakenly used for the term "cracker."

home page The first page of any site on the Web.

host A computer system that may be contacted by other computer systems.

hotlist A list of a user's favorite sites on the Web.

HTML Hypertext Markup Language; the language of the WWW, which formats documents to look presentable.

HTTP Hypertext Transport Protocol; the protocol of the WWW, which allows text, images, audio, and video to be combined into a single document. HTTP also allows the linking of documents and document components.

HTTPD The server software for the World Wide Web responsible for handling WWW requests.

hyperlink An HTML element that, when clicked, allows people to move to other documents, images, sounds, or movies.

icon A small image representing a function or action. For example, a small picture of a stop sign might indicate the way to stop a program from running.

inline image An image appearing to be part of the document it is with.

intelligent agent A program that searches the network looking for items that match criteria you specify.

interactive Allowing users to change the course of events based on their own decisions with regard to the rules of whatever they are interacting with.

Internet The term for the worldwide network of computers and users.

IP address A numeric address composed of four elements that uniquely identify a computer on a network.

IRC Internet Relay Chat; a real-time talk forum.

JPEG File format used for compressed images.

kiosk A small stand-alone structure used to disseminate products and/or information.

lag The amount of time between making a request or sending a message and actually receiving a response.

lamer Someone who doesn't know what he or she is talking about; always used as an insult.

listserver. A program that automatically dispatches outgoing e-mail based on incoming e-mail.

login The act of accessing a remote computer.

MILNET The part of the original ARPANET currently used by the military. It was renamed when ARPANET split.

Mosaic The name of a popular browser from NCSA for accessing the Web; the first browser invented for the World Wide Web.

mouse An input device used by one hand, with choices entered by pushing a button.

MPEG File format used for compressed movies.

NCSA National Center for Supercomputing Applications; the developers of Mosaic.

netiquette The etiquette of the Internet.

NetNews A forum for interest groups.

Netscape A popular WWW browser that currently offers many cutting-edge HTML features.

newbie Someone who is new to the Internet; sometimes used as an insult.

phrack Someone who breaks into computers and phone systems (originating from the terms "cracker" and "phreak").

phreak Someone who breaks into phone systems.

pirate A software pirate; a warez pirate; someone who steals computer programs. Usually pirates will sell or give away the programs they steal. See *warez* and *warez site*.

proxy A method of hiding data by rerouting requests.

public domain Software which is free.

robot An automated program that will go out and search or retrieve information for the user.

server A software program or hardware device that serves data.

shareware Software which is openly available, but not free.

SLIP/PPP Serial Line Interface Protocol or Point to Point Protocol; currently the quickest and most powerful method to access the Internet with a modem.

subscription service A Web system that requires users to log in.

surf To use the Internet or World Wide Web.

SYSOP The system operator of a computer system responsible for the day-to-day operations of a computer.

TCP/IP Transmission Control Protocol/Internet Protocol; the standard of communications on the Internet.

Telnet A software program that lets you log into remote computers.

throughput The amount of data transmitted through the Internet for a given request.

UNIX A popular operating system for Internet servers.

URL Universal Resource Locator; the means of identifying a home page on the Web.

viewer An adjunct program that handles non-standard data.

virtual Something that exists only in an electronic medium, such as a computer.

virus A program that infects other programs and computers, resulting in some sort of misfunction.

WAIS Wide Area Information Server; a distributed informational retrieval system.

warez Stolen or "hot" software.

warez site A place on a computer where stolen software can be found; quite often placed surreptitiously on legitimate computer systems by pirates.

WAV Popular file format used for audio files.

WHOIS A program that polls the domain name database; allows the user to determine who owns and administrates a domain name.

World Wide Web An organization of files on the Internet.

wrapper A program that helps improve security by watching users access systems.

WWW The World Wide Web. Other popular abbreviations include the Web and W3.

Index

Symbols

#www, 47, 91, 222
* (asterisk), 189
> (greater than sign) tag character, 525
@ (at sign) special character, 39
24/7 acronym, 49
3-D capability in future on Net, 500
911 Gallery (art gallery) home page, 64, 472-473

A

<A> tag, 537
abbreviations, 50
accepting text with <FORM> tag, 542-544
accesses, 342
accessing
    government information, 485-486
    internationally, 395-396
    Internet, 34-35, 133-137, 152
    private organizations for members only, 487-488
    remote computers, 41-42
account names (e-mail), 38
acknowledgments in home pages, 369
acronyms, 49
ACTION parameter, 542
addicted to IRC (Internet Relay Chat), 192-193
addresses, 61
    e-mail, editing, 249-250

including in traditional advertisements, 234-235
IP addresses (Internet Protocol), 159-161, 553
see also URL (Uniform Resource Locators)
administrators, *see* system administrators
Advanced Research Projects Agency (ARPA), 12
Advanced Research Projects Agency's Network (ARPANET), 551
advertising, 70-71
    art sites, 469-472
    borders on pages, 238-240
    bullets on pages, 238-240
    e-mail messages, 231
    entertaining users, 379
    combining with traditional advertising, 234-235
    companies, 71
    cost of, 243-244
    errors in postings, 248-252
    hyperlinks in, 242-243
    locations, 228-231
    malls, 246
    multimedia 235-241, 497
    multiple entrance points, 174-176
    multiple presences, 169-174
    musicians/bands, 476-478
    netiquette, mass e-mailings, 195-197
    NetNews, 231
    order taking services, 254-258
    plagiarism/stealing, 244
    posting errors, 247-248
    prices for, 144
    products, 70-71

promotional devices, 231-234
publications, online-only, 484
services (professional), 72
subscription systems, 315-317
sites (unique), 378-379
virtual communities, 246
advisory sites, 432
airports/airplanes, kiosks in, 454-455
ALIGN parameter, 535
America Online, 30
American Touchscreen's (kiosk) home page, 462
Ameritech home page, 62
amusement park home pages
    Busch Theme Park, 3
    Sea World, 3
anchors (HTML), 537
Anderson, Laurie (performance artist), 478
Andreessen, Marc, 20
Andy Warhol Museum, The (home page), 64
Annotate menu, 211-224
annotation capability, 487
announcing pages, 108-109
anonymous access, 41
antique shops home page, 512
Apple Computers
    domain name, 159
    home page, 61
approving credit cards, 278-279
Archie, 42-43, 127, 551
archive software, 17
ARPA (Advanced Research Project Agency), 12

X-Y-Z